W9-APW-713

DOUBLE LIVES

DOUBLE LIVES

Spies and Writers in the Secret Soviet War of Ideas Against the West

STEPHEN KOCH

THE FREE PRESS
A Division of Macmillan, Inc.
NEW YORK
Maxwell Macmillan Canada
TORONTO
Maxwell Macmillan International
NEW YORK OXFORD SINGAPORE SYDNEY

The Free Press
A Division of Macmillan, Inc.
866 Third Avenue, New York, N.Y. 10022

Maxwell Macmillan Canada, Inc.
1200 Eglinton Avenue East
Suite 200
Don Mills, Ontario M3C 3N1

Macmillan, Inc. is part of the Maxwell Communication Group of Companies.

Printed in the United States of America

printing number

1 2 3 4 5 6 7 8 9 10

Library of Congress Cataloging-in-Publication Data

Koch, Stephen.
Double lives: spies and writers in the secret Soviet war of ideas against the West / Stephen Koch.
p. cm.
Includes bibliographical references (p.).
ISBN 0-02-918730-3
1. Communist strategy—History—20th century. 2. Communism—History—20th century. 3. Espionage, Communist—History—20th century. 4. Propaganda, Communist—History—20th century. 5. Münzenberg, Willi. I. Title.
HX518.S8K62 1993
324.1′75′0904—dc20 93-11523
CIP

To the memory of my father

ROBERT FULTON KOCH

1907–1951

Again, ye have heard that it hath been said by them of old time, Thou shalt not forswear thyself, but shalt perform unto the Lord thine oaths:

But I say unto you, Swear not at all; neither by heaven, for it is God's throne:

Nor by the earth; for it is his footstool: Neither by Jerusalem; for it is the city of the great King.

Neither shall thou swear by thine head, because thou canst not make one hair white or black.

But let your communication be, Yea, Yea; Nay, nay: for whatsoever is more than these cometh of evil.

—MATTHEW 5:33–37

As cited by Arthur Koestler at the opening session of the Congress for Cultural Freedom, June 25, 1950

Contents

Acknowledgments

To write a book is to explore a world, and the world I have explored in *Double Lives* has been, until now, largely hidden. I owe gratitude first to those many people who visited the place before me and consented to show me its covered paths. But the roster of those people, and the many others who shared what they know, would overwhelm this page; a genuinely descriptive account of my obligations to them all would soon look like a new book, a kind of shadow, or double, of this one. In the bibliography, the reader will find a necessarily undescriptive list of these many helpful people.

Yet here I must pay particularly grateful tribute to the memory of Babette Gross, the widow of Willi Münzenberg, who in Munich during the summer of 1989 granted me a week of indispensable interviews. Those memorable exchanges were made possible only through the good offices of Dr. Peter Lübbe, who persuaded a skeptical Babette to speak with me, and made the contact possible. But this is only the most significant of many kindnesses. Dr. Lübbe, with his encyclopedic erudition about the history of German communism, has assisted me more than once.

For me, conversation is an arena of creation. It was during a talk with Michael Scammell over lunch in London that I quite suddenly glimpsed the whole shape of this book, like a night landscape made white by lightning. His friendly attention as I then and there took my first lurching steps toward what I'd seen must have seemed to him a small enough thing: chat over the salad. It was more helpful than he can know.

In Moscow, my research was accomplished through Dr. Roman Sheinen and S. Todd Weinberg. Without them entry into the archival labyrinth would not have been possible. I should add that indispensable information from the archives of the former Soviet Union has also most generously been shared by Professor Harvey Klehr, to whose collegial help, more generally, I owe much.

My publisher and editor Erwin A. Glikes grasped the potential value of this project from the moment it was proposed to him and he has remained steadily faithful to it in the long time since. His incisive editorial intelligence and his many conversations with me have been indispensable to shaping the book. I am grateful too to all those many at The Free Press who have been so helpful, with a particular note of thanks to John Urda.

My connection to Diana Trilling began with a simple interview, conducted at a very early stage of my work. In retrospect, that meeting must be called momentous. Mrs. Trilling has been witness and counsel to this project in its every phase. As the book deepened and developed, so too has our bond.

Now for the final paragraph. It is a good and proper part of writerly decorum at this place on the page to recognize the role of one's spouse. That is what I want to do. Yet as I try to formulate this most important acknowledgment of all, the acknowledgment to Franny, I find myself, for a change, without words. Nothing can say it. Nothing. Rather than say it badly, I will end with a kind of silent nod over what is known to ourselves alone.

PART ONE

Lying for the Truth

Chapter 1

Lying for the Truth

On October 22, 1940, not far from a tiny French hamlet near Grenoble called Montagne, two hunters out with their dogs stumbled across something gruesome hidden in a small stand of woods. At the foot of a fine old oak sat, upright, the decomposing body of a man. The man had been dead for a long time, and he appeared to have been hanged.

What the hunters found that day would become more than a legend of their town; it would take its place among the enduring mysteries of modern politics. For this was the body of a man named Willi Münzenberg, and Willi Münzenberg had lived and died as one of the unseen powers of twentieth-century Europe. When the hunters found it, his corpse was almost entirely covered with fallen leaves. Only the vile face and the popped stare of strangulation were visible—that and the noose. The reek was awful; the body had plainly been there for months. The knotted cord around its neck seemed to have snapped, probably quite soon after he had been hanged, and when it broke, the body had apparently dropped to the base of the tree. There it had stayed, knees up, all through that summer of the French defeat, sitting oddly undetected until October began to cover it with the drift of autumn and the hunters' dogs, yelping and whining, discovered the thing.

The French villagers knew nothing about Willi Münzenberg. Münzenberg was and is not a famous name, though this man's power had given him a potent grip on the workings of fame. Since his radical youth in

1917, Münzenberg had been a largely covert but major actor in the politics of the twentieth century. As a founding organizer of the Communist International and a leader in the structure of Marxist-Leninist power outside Russia, Münzenberg had played an especially influential part in the conspiracies, the maneuvers, the propaganda, the secret policies and actions that had led to this very spot: here to the fall of France; here to Hitler's war on the West; here to these woods, and this death.

October 1940 came in the bitter first autumn following the French debacle at the hands of the Nazi *Wehrmacht*. France was huddled in the morose stillness of defeat. The nation's downfall seemed complete; for the moment, the war had finished its vicious business in France and moved on.

For the dictators, all was going well. Stalin had consolidated his alliance with Hitler. The secret services of the two totalitarians were now working in a sinister collaboration that was defined by their gangster enmity, bound tight in a brotherhood of loathing. Poland had been successfully partitioned between the two; Finland was in Stalin's hands. The Nazis were driving west, and the war with its horror was focussed on England.

For this was also the autumn of the Battle of Britain. All through the months since France had fallen, the *Luftwaffe* had been carpet-bombing the cities of England. Every night the London sky was lit with tracers and fire; the air was filled with the shattering scream of bombs and the pounding of anti-aircraft defense. The prospect of an English defeat was imminent and real.

But in that French valley of the Isère River, the only gunfire being heard was the occasional muted crack of a hunter's shotgun kicking its echo across the lovely wooded countryside. And through that countryside the two men from Montagne now rushed back into town, along with their dogs, to alert the gendarmerie to what they had found.

Almost certainly, Willi Münzenberg had died in those woods five months before, on June 21, 1940. Whether he died by suicide or murder is not clear. June 21, 1940, however, was the day that the French government fell to the Nazis, and as we shall see, much rests on this exact coincidence of one man's death with a nation's fall. In those days of the French collapse, the countryside around Montagne had been filled with exiles and refugees streaming southward. Everyone was in flight. Yet Willi Münzenberg's flight differed from most. For one thing, it was being tracked by the secret services of at least three nations. It seems that even in those worst of times, certain important players were exceptionally interested in whether this one man, running, left France alive.[1]

Why, in a collapsing world, would several governments have been so interested in this middle-aged man from Germany? Who was Willi Münzenberg?

He was a major German communist, but he was more. Since around 1921, Lenin had empowered Münzenberg in a series of tasks, some very public, some very secret, that left this dynamic man the *de facto* director of the Soviet Union's covertly directed propaganda operations in the West.

The field of covertly directed propaganda operations is an area in the world of secret services which until now has rarely been mapped. As a result, the role of such operations in both the cultural politics of this century and its power politics has rarely been understood. Yet if we follow Münzenberg from Lenin's side to the forest where he died, his path will serve as an Ariadne's thread through much in twentieth-century politics. The byways of his career link the most secret operations of revolutionary politics to central cultural events of the century. We will see the Kremlin tied to Bloomsbury; we will watch the effects of his operations move from the Elysée to Hollywood and back to the Left Bank; from the life of Ernest Hemingway in Spain to André Gide speaking at the state funeral of Maxim Gorky. It is a thread that snakes through many mysteries, and across many encounters with betrayal, terror, and murder, not least of which is the possible murder of Münzenberg himself. It leads to the Second World War. It leads to the founding events of the Cold War.

Münzenberg was a companion of Lenin during their pre-revolutionary days in Switzerland, and he was an important personality in the original Bolshevik circle. In 1915, Lenin was cooling his heels in Bern, fretful and furious as he waited for War to become Revolution. Münzenberg was then a young German radical, unaffiliated except through his talents and his rage. In 1914 he had met Leon Trotsky, and Trotsky, taking his measure, decided to bring him to Lenin himself.

What Trotsky had spotted in the cocky 26-year-old German hothead was a talent for secret work. Münzenberg was presented to the future dictator as a wunderkind, a kid with a knack, like a computer whiz of a later age. Beginning in his teens, Willi had been promiscuously supplying all kinds of revolutionary groups with freelance clandestine networks:

undercover systems for transmitting information, laundering money, forging passports, and beaming people across heavily guarded borders as if by magic. It seemed the boy could spin a network out of nothing. When Lenin met him, Willi's information was already speeding around Europe totally undetected: Conspiracies travelled in jam jars and cigar boxes; forged papers arrived in food parcels; plans for covert action stayed concealed, but moved. Münzenberg even had managed, quite on his own, to place an operative inside the Vatican. Trotsky understood that here was a young radical Lenin could *use*.[2]

Lenin was duly impressed and introduced his discovery to Karl Radek, whereupon Münzenberg and Radek became a kind of team. Karl Radek was an exceptionally talkative and calculating Polish radical and literary intellectual. He was destined to become the Revolution's rationalizer. He was brilliant and glib, the cynically amused protégé of another Pole, Count Felix Dzerzhinsky, that man without humor whom infamy will forever remember as the inventor of the police state.[3]

Among Lenin's men, the bond that held Dzerzhinsky, Radek, and Stalin together is an affiliation of the very greatest interest. Taken in their ensemble, they represent three of the essential strands that bind the knot of the terror state. Dzerzhinsky was the true believer, the sanctified fanatic of absolute state power. Stalin on the other hand was its ultimate politician, its grand tactician and bureaucrat. Radek was the new state's propagandist and apologist, the creator of its intellectual rationale, the man who fabricated its "human face," and much of its lie.

Dzerzhinsky was the founder of the Cheka, later to be renamed the OGPU, then the NKVD, then the KGB, the man who made the secret police the prime instrument of revolutionary justice.* It is therefore especially fitting that in the great days of August 1991, the liberation from Marxism-Leninism in Russia should have been celebrated by the crowd tearing down the monumental statue to this monster of sanctimony where it stood in front of KGB headquarters.

Count Felix was the great ideologist of hatred and as such he is easy to hate. The difficult thing, and the more troubling thing, is to imagine how he was able to marshal so very much commitment and love. For Dzerzhinsky was far from being a mere brute; he was not an empty monster. He was a man whose passion, self-sacrifice, and faith won to the

* In most cases here, I will refer to this organization by whichever name was contemporary with the event under discussion. More generally, I will frequently use the German word *apparat* in a sense familiar to many communists of the period, referring to the several arms of Soviet secret services considered as a single co-ordinated ensemble.

Revolution the allegiance of people driven by what were surely among the highest moral aspirations of their time. For the young Whittaker Chambers, as for the young Isaac Babel, Felix Dzerzhinsky was a visionary, a being who was bringing real justice to the real world, empowering life's highest ideals.[4] In the glory days of the Revolution, when Dzerzhinsky and Lenin were laying the foundations of the totalitarian police state, life in the Cheka seemed invested with the prestige of a righteous elect, both at home and abroad. Abroad, what was "secret work" but the business of the ultimate liberation of humanity? And at home, who were agents of the Cheka but the Revolution's avenging angels? Indeed, in the days of its innocence, before it became so very obviously the province of murderers and thugs, the revolutionary secret police looked like the natural habitat of the new clerisy, a puritan high-priesthood, devout in its atheism. Here were the avengers of all the ancient evils; here were the enforcers of new heaven, new earth. Isaac Babel, the gentle ironist who himself perished in the Terror, began his career as a revolutionary by serving in the Cheka. One of the NKVD agents most useful in running the Cambridge spies was a lapsed priest, a man with a tortured but plainly superior moral nature: Theodore Maly. We will hear a great deal more about Maly.[5] Diana Trilling reports that she and Lionel Trilling were married by a rabbi for whom Felix Dzerzhinsky represented (with only a touch of irony) a heroic paragon.[6] No leader of the Revolution, not even Lenin himself, was more perfumed with the odor of sanctity than this sardonic and self-exalted Polish aristocrat, a Savonarola who reached his apotheosis in that totalitarian power of which he was a prime inventor.[7] Ascetic, ravaged by revolution, bleak in his unforgiving certainties, radiant with hatred, Dzerzhinsky was Saint Terror.

Dzerzhinsky's protégé Radek, on the other hand, was the jeering cynic of the revolution's rationale. Just as Dzerzhinsky thought any death was justified if it served the Revolution, so Radek thought that any lie was vindicated in the glow of its truth. The union between them is only apparently improbable. Dzerzhinsky's sanctity and Radek's cynicism combined in a fusion of belief and disbelief, faith and scorn, bound together from their earliest days in Warsaw. It is one of the exemplary moral alliances of our era. Meanwhile, outside Russia, in the West, the jovial dynamo who organized that alliance and made it into a new system of power, lying for the truth, was Willi Münzenberg.

Münzenberg was unusual within the senior ranks of German communism in having actually sprung from the working class. Very few of the true leading lights of German communism were the tough proletarians of the Berlin slums who made up the Party's mass base. Most of the real leaders were intellectuals, daughters and sons of the upper-middle class. But Willi was the real thing: the son of an alcoholic tavern-keeper in Thuringia, who while the boy was still young had killed himself one day cleaning his gun while drunk. In his teens, Willi survived as a barber's apprentice. It is possible that the genuine deprivations of his youth partly explain why Willi, unlike his more privileged peers, never affected the look of poverty once real power came his way. On the contrary: He swept up and down the Kurfürstendamm in an enormous chauffeur-driven Lincoln limousine; he moved through the halls of power protected by a bodyguard. Like a captain of industry or a Chicago gangster, his own barber shaved and manicured him every day. He lived in an upper-class neighborhood of Berlin. His apartment was filled with Biedermeier; his entire manner of life was undimmed by the usual dour communist style.

Yet despite his elegant surroundings, he was a real communist, and a tough one at that. Willi's youthful photographs show a hard but well-dressed young German with a tight compact body about to spring, light on his feet, solid with energy. His head is large for his small body, and squarish; his forehead is high and impressive, crested with short tousled hair. His eyes, though warm, are shrewd. They assess the camera with a sly lethal glint. The line of his mouth could easily turn cruel; his smile seems granted only very conditionally. There is more than a little of the German tough guy about him. Safely behind closed doors, he moved with all the abrupt habits of command, rapping out his orders like a drill sergeant, foul-mouthed and ungrateful, striking the table with stubby strong workman's hands. Commanding, he was obeyed. He was simultaneously a born executive and a born agitator, and he remained both even after Lenin had made him the "red tycoon," wearing tailored suits and riding in that limousine. Arthur Koestler, who knew him well, called him "a fiery, demagogical, and irresistible public speaker." His voice rang to the rafters of the meeting halls of the Weimar Republic. He brought crowds shouting to their feet. He had the incendiary gift. Koestler reports that "he gave the impression that bumping against him would be like colliding with a steam roller. . . . Willi sauntered into a room with the casualness of a tank bursting through a wall. . . . His person emanated such authority that I have seen socialist cabinet members, hard-boiled bankers, and Austrian Dukes behave like schoolboys in his presence."[8]

Münzenberg was "married," although in the Bohemian style of radicals between the wars, there never had been a wedding ceremony. His wife was a beautiful woman named Babette Gross, fine-boned, very tall, willowy. She was an intensely intelligent aristocratic Prussian; her father had been a rich brewer in Potsdam. She was highly educated; easily and fluently multilingual, as was her sister, Margarete Buber-Neumann who, after a first marriage to a son of the philosopher Martin Buber, was married a second time to a prominent German communist: Heinz Neumann, a revolutionary intellectual in the upper reaches of the German Party.

Though a fierce radical and committed communist, Babette was very much an upper-class girl. In youth as in age, the habits of her class must have merged with her politics and her style. To Willi, she must have looked not only beautiful, but like the key to a world. Even when I knew Babette Gross, in her great age, the marks of that Prussian father were still stamped on her. She assumed authority in a way that was surely parallel to the way Willi had seized it. They were a pair as man and woman; they must also have been a pair in their feeling for power.

In fact, much in German communism during its grand epoch between the two wars can be traced to a few intensely intellectual, often academic, families of the upper-middle class, people who belonged more to the world of Thomas Mann and his famous brood than Brecht's back streets. One thinks not only of Babette and her distinguished sister, but of two brilliant academic clans, the Eislers and the Kuczynskis, both family friends of the Manns, both filled with radical intellectuals who became spies, agents of influence, and covert operators in both the Second World War and the Cold War: Hanns and Gerhart Eisler, and their sister Ruth Fischer; Jürgen and Ruth Kuczynski, guided by their father, Robert René Kuczynski.[9] Robert René was closely associated with Willi all through the Weimar years and remained a virtual "Münzenberg man" even after Hitler scattered the German left, and Robert René became an influential refugee teaching at the London School of Economics, serving the Revolution covered by the duplicities of Münzenberg's more-or-less legal wing. Kuczynski's children Jürgen and Ruth walked deeper into the shadow zone around Willi; both took the step into true espionage. During the war Jürgen served as a penetration agent inside the O.S.S., betraying the Americans. Ruth was trained as a spy in Russia, at a school for covert action founded hand in glove with Willi by the Comintern secret service. She worked in espionage first in China, under cover of Willi's illegal operations there, and later, during the war, in England, later famous under her code name "Sonia," spying against the British, hovering around Bletchley Park.[10] Here were people who instinctively understood the war of ideas in that adversary culture to which Münzenberg came as a stranger, but which he learned to manage and master as few people ever have.

. . .

When I met her in 1989, Babette Gross was 91 years old and still willowy. Like her sister, she had long since become a lucid and committed anti-communist. As with her sister, her intelligence was still held in the grip of the tremendous events she had lived through. That July, after long consideration, Gross decided to grant me a full week of interviews in her small apartment on the Einsteinstrasse of Munich. I would arrive every day with my tape-recorder, and she would guide me through the history of the century as seen from the perspective of her place beside Münzenberg. It was strange to hear her speak of Lenin as a living man: "Münzenberg was always very impressed with Lenin's *political* skill. You know, Lenin never forgot a name." Of Trotsky, whom I gather she'd known in Mexico: "He always behaved exactly like a classical French man-of-letters." Though always very direct and plain, she would sometimes brush near the grand manner: for example, she twice spoke of "my sister, Buber-Neumann."[11]

With Willi, she had known not only most of the senior people in the German Party, but also many of the founding personalities in its secret service apparatus. Among these were Ignace Reiss, the great espionage master who in certain ways founded Soviet secret work in Europe. I asked her about Richard Sorge, the no less extraordinary German spy who, under cover as a Nazi, penetrated the Japanese high command until his betrayal in the last days of the war. Babette gave me a long look, then a smile. "I knew him," she said, "when he was young and beautiful."

She spoke relaxed, idiomatic, excellent English, remarkable in a woman who (at least so far as I can determine) had never lived in an English-speaking country. She was utterly alert, and her self-possession was at once aristocratic and easy. In her many hours of talk with me, her conversation was always exact and searching; her style of political analysis, whether about events unfolding that July in Germany or conspiracies half a century old, was relentless and incisive. No detail escaped her interest. She tolerated no nonsense, and no deviation from the exact truth as she saw it. Listening to Gross talk about current European politics reminded me that this woman had shared a life with a man whose own political briefings, after he broke with Stalin in 1937, used to be held in a private dining room in Paris while senior agents of the intelligence services of several countries gathered round to listen like so many sophomores.[12]

When I knew her in July of 1989, Babette did not have long to live. In the fall and winter of 1989, she was watching the collapse of German communism as it accelerated and burst past every effort to hold it back.

In her phone calls with me during this period, she retained her customary comprehensive attention to the inner workings of the scene. Her entire life had been lived either with or against the events now coming to their tremendous conclusion; she had lived at or near the center of the greatest political drama of her century. Now that drama was moving toward its end. As was her life. She became ill, and ill she went to Berlin for treatment. And so she was in the city of her youth as everything came full circle. Babette Gross was in Berlin as the Wall came down, and having seen the last fall, there she died in January 1990.

Karl Radek seems to have been Münzenberg's patron in Lenin's inner circle and was the means of his rise, though at the ripe age of 30 Radek wasn't all that much Münzenberg's senior. Before the Revolution, Radek's position among Lenin's men was rather like that of a press agent. The Bolsheviks were newspaper addicts, every one of them. It was one of their most characteristic obsessions. The sealed train that carried Lenin to the Finland Station was stacked to the ceiling with every paper in every language. The revolutionary passengers behind the drawn curtains of the cars passed the rocking hours reading every report. Radek's skill at this stage consisted of inventing the right news angle; planting the right story at the right time; heading off this or that opponent with this or that burst of bad publicity. Chewing on his pipe-stem, sneering at the journalists he conned and flattered, the youth was already an adept in the uses of information and disinformation. Radek and Münzenberg together escorted Lenin to the crowded platform in Zurich and the train into which the Bolsheviks were sealed ("like a bacillus in a tube," Churchill said) for their trip north through Germany, en route to their revolution. Radek was placed in the compartment beside the future dictator, while Münzenberg stayed behind, apparently because of a problem over his German nationality. Just before the train pulled out, it was to Münzenberg that either Radek or Lenin himself turned and shrugged off the famous line: "Six months from now we either will be in power or hanging from the gallows."[13] So it was. After Lenin captured the Revolution, he was able to make his protégés two of the most powerful people in the world.

Münzenberg found himself in power. He was a man of action who was deprived of life when deprived of the resources of command. Unlike his allies Radek, Bukharin, and of course Lenin himself, he was in no way an intellectual. He had none of an intellectual's feeling for how to mine isolation, how to make even powerlessness a kind of opportunity. He was also a provincial. Though he orchestrated the voice of the International, he never spoke anything but his native German, and it was rather rough German at that, thick with a country accent from Thuringia. He had no particular literary skills. Hundreds of books were written to order for him, some memorable, and some even of lasting importance. He himself could barely bang together a more or less four-square paragraph. Virtually everything published under his own name was ghost-written.[14]

The type of personality required to organize life in the shadowland of secret services is less that of the buccaneer than the executive. So it was with William Donovan of the OSS; so it was with Sir William Stephenson, Churchill's "Intrepid." So it was with Münzenberg. The Central Party Archives show conclusively that Willi's front organizations and networks of fellow travellers and propagandists were thoroughly intertwined with the secret services of the Comintern, and with the Soviet's other covert agencies as well.[15] But Willi was not the man in the trenchcoat; that he left to others, people who reported to him, or to his men. Still less was he some shuffling bureaucrat from le Carré. He thought like a tycoon. Had he not been a revolutionary, he would have made a brilliant self-made millionaire. His saluting staff, his Biedermeier, his hovering barber and his limousine, all make one think less of le Carré's Karla than of Henry Luce.

Here is Gustav Regler's picture of Willi once he had fled from Nazi Germany and taken charge of the Soviet propaganda response to Hitler's seizure of power: "He now passed his days in a small room at the back of a house on the Boulevard Montparnasse, seated at a desk piled high with papers. . . . The telephone was scarcely more than a token of his isolation. When it rang his secretary would dash in and answer it while Münzenberg waited impatiently and finally solved the problem with a single sentence. He had the calm and intensity of a chess master walking from board to board, playing twenty games at once."[16]

Both before Hitler and after, Münzenberg's true role in the world was a closely guarded secret, though in keeping with his particular talent, it was concealed in conspicuousness. His talent was for propaganda, albeit of a special kind. For Willi Münzenberg was the first grand master of two quite new kinds of secret service work, essential to this century, and to the Soviets: the covertly controlled propaganda front, and the secretly manipulated fellow traveller. His goal was to create for the right-thinking non-communist West the dominating political prejudice of the era: the belief that any opinion that happened to serve the foreign policy of the Soviet Union was derived from the most essential elements of human decency. He wanted to instill the feeling, like a truth of nature, that seriously to criticize or challenge Soviet policy was the unfailing mark of a bad, bigoted, and probably stupid person, while support was equally infallible proof of a forward-looking mind committed to all that was best for humanity and marked by an uplifting refinement of sensibility.

To create his networks of fronts and fellow travellers Münzenberg used every resource of propaganda, from highbrow cultural opinion to funny hats and balloons. He organized the media: newspapers, film, radio, books, magazines, the theater. Every kind of "opinion maker" was involved: writers, artists, actors, commentators, priests, ministers, professors, "business leaders," scientists, psychologists, anyone at all whose opinion the public was likely to respect.

Münzenberg's own public life was very visible. Before his flight from Germany after the Reichstag Fire in 1933, he was a German publisher, and in fact a big-time publisher, controlling an impressive network of left-wing publications. He was also a politician. As a Leninist he naturally despised representative democracy and intended to destroy it. But he found it useful to serve in the Reichstag, holding down an exceptionally safe seat provided by the Party. The gloomy Sessions Chamber of the Reichstag, the hall where German democracy gathered, was a stuffy place, lined with dry wood panelling and hung with musty brocaded curtains. On February 27, 1933, that wood and brocade would kindle into a bonfire momentous enough to grant Hitler totalitarian power and give shape to the ideological clash that led to the Second World War. But until then, the Reichstag regularly rang with the voice of Münzenberg's radical anger. He flourished there, striding past his rival and secret admirer Goebbels, whitened by glaring flashbulbs, ready to tangle yet again in the checkmated politics of a Weimar Republic that it seemed nobody important had the smallest wish to save. Certainly not Goebbels. And certainly not Münzenberg.

Lastly, Münzenberg was nominally in charge of a communist relief organization known as Workers International Relief, or the WIR. To invoke only a few of the organizations that were its clones, it was also known by its Russian acronym, MRP, and Münzenberg had great influence in closely affiliated organizations such as MOPR, the Red Aid, and (in America) the International Labor Defense, or ILD. WIR was not taken very seriously by the grandees of power in Europe. It appeared to be a merely idealistic, or at least unexceptionable, institution, a sort of Red Cross for the Revolution, sponsoring good deeds for the hard left: cultural events to awaken the world's conscience; fundraisers for the persecuted; mobile soup kitchens for strikers in bleak factory yards.

Soup kitchens were the least of it.

Willi Münzenberg's true, and secret, job in the political world, the job insiders *did* take seriously, was to manage the unseen ties between this propaganda and great power.

His heyday lasted for a little less than fifteen years, from the Volga Famine in Russia and the Sacco-Vanzetti case in America to the Spanish Civil War. During that time, he was amazingly successful at mobilizing the intelligentsia of the West on behalf of a moralistic set of political attitudes responsive to Soviet needs. In the process, he organized and defined the ''enlightened'' moral agenda of his era. In a sense, Münzenberg's apparatus was as instrumental as any other single factor in giving direction to the political attitudes we now call The Thirties. Hundreds of groups and committees and publications operated under his auspices, or those of his agents. The writers, artists, journalists, scientists, educators, clerics, columnists, film-makers, and publishers, either under his influence or regularly manipulated by his ''Münzenberg men,'' present a startling list of notables from that era, from Ernest Hemingway to John Dos Passos to Lillian Hellman to Georg Grosz to Erwin Piscator to André Malraux to André Gide to Bertolt Brecht to Dorothy Parker . . . to Kim Philby, Guy Burgess, and Anthony Blunt. Indeed, the entire cultural and intellectual apparatus of ''idealistic'' Stalinism outside Russia, and much of its secret *apparat,* operated within a system Münzenberg had guided into place.

Of course most of the fellow travellers who were run by these agents, and certainly most of the people who poured their idealism into the Münzenberg fronts, had no idea that their consciences were being orchestrated by operatives of Stalin's government. Most were true believers, people with dreams about a radical new Soviet-led, socialist ''humanism.'' With a light sneer, Münzenberg dubbed this vast soft horde of the radical devout ''innocents.'' His own phrase for the fronts he created to guide and direct their morally committed but politically naive commitments was ''Innocents' Clubs.''[17] The phrase is revealing. On the one hand, it points to all those thousands who were not, in the jargon of the secret trades, ''witting.'' This was virtually everyone. In any covertly run front organization the number of people who know, *really* know, the agenda, and the true identity of its shapers, must be very, very few. The fewer the better.

But the word ''innocence'' also suggests a motive. I refer to the need for righteousness, righteousness in the Biblical sense. The thirst for moral justification for one's life in the world is one of the deepest needs, one of our most powerful and essentially human drives, ignored at our cost and peril. In his ''Innocents' Clubs,'' Münzenberg provided two generations of people on the left with what we might call the forum of righteousness. More perhaps than any other person of his era, he developed what may well be the leading moral illusion of the twentieth century: the notion that in the modern age the principal arena of the moral life, the true realm of good and evil, is politics. He was the unseen organizer of that variety of politics, indispensable to the adversary culture, which we might call Righteousness Politics. "Innocents' Clubs": The very phrase suggests how the political issues Münzenberg manipulated came for many to serve as a substitute for religious belief. He offered everyone, anyone, a role in the search for justice in our century. By defining guilt, he offered his followers innocence, and they seized upon it by the millions.

Except that in this forum, high, serious, honorable moral commitments found themselves joined, covertly, to profoundly sinister events. Münzenberg served Stalinism with every resource of propaganda and invented more, from the protest march to the mock-trial to the politicized writers' congress to the politicized arts festival to the celebrity letterhead to the ad hoc committee for causes numberless. As Koestler said, Münzenberg "produced Committees as a conjurer produces rabbits out of his hat."[18] And his models for molding progressive opinion endured, outlasting him, running on their own moral momentum. Plainly, a phenomenon such as the Bertrand Russell War Crimes Tribunal, held in Stockholm during the Vietnam War, was set up in conscious or unconscious emulation of Münzenberg's paradigm. In fact, much of the Peace Movement of the Vietnam Era, with its marches and interlocking committees, worked in the same way. Early in this century, Willi had uncovered the tremendous power available to those who know how to set the agenda of the Good. But he also knew, as his fate demonstrates, that this is a form of power that can be used for evil ends.

The instrument through which Münzenberg organized this cultural power was the Communist International, or as it was almost always known, the Comintern. The Comintern was in many ways the quintessential Leninist institution, shaped from its inception by the two leading passions of Lenin's political personality: his obsession with secrecy, and his preoccupation with absolute power. Its aims were never even remotely democratic, never even remotely meliorist, and never were intended to provide any real assistance, however minute, to any branch of the left not entirely under Soviet control.[19]

Lenin created the Comintern in 1919 as a means of spreading the Russian Revolution and of consolidating Marxism-Leninism's dominance over the worldwide left. The new dictator's purpose was to gather the world's radicals into one grand network of communist parties under the control of *the* Revolution, *his* Revolution. In his fantasy, Lenin saw the Comintern laying a kind of long fuse that would snake from Russia into Europe, and above all to that grand, glorious, but unexploded bomb that weighed most on his mind: Germany. *The powder keg of Europe:* It was one of Lenin's favorite clichés. *Iskra,* so one of the most important early revolutionary journals was named: "The Spark." Lenin proposed to make the keg blow with a spark set by him and sent sizzling through the Comintern's invisible incendiary network, a vitalizing fire that would burn from his office straight in to the great German ammunition dump. Luckily for the Europe of the twenties, the fuse fizzled. Even so, the Comintern's network had been well and truly laid down, and by the time Stalin came along it was still in place, ready for the new dictator to use. Europe, meanwhile, had run out of luck.

So the "First Congress" of the Comintern in 1919 was a meeting supposed to initiate the transformation of the world. Despite this ambitious aim, it was not a very impressive convocation. It was neither representative nor particularly international. Lenin slouched on the podium of a crowded little hall near the Moscow Courts of Justice and presided over thirty-five scrappy "delegates"—mainly foreign socialists who happened to be in town. Few had any real connection to their national politics. One English "delegate" was merely Cicherin's secretary, a Russian emigré who'd once been a tailor in England. The Japanese were "represented" by a man with the un-Nipponese name of Rutgers, who'd chanced once to spend some months in Japan. At one point Lenin slipped a note to Angelica Balabanoff ordering her to take the platform and "announce the affiliation of the Italian Socialist Party." She stared back. There was no such group in the room, nor had she been in contact with them. "There was," wrote one English witness "a make-believe side to the whole affair."[20]

The Congress was make-believe because Lenin did not want it otherwise. On the contrary. The last thing he wanted would have been some dreary posse of international socialists weakening his grip with the babble of their little ideas, their niggling opinions, their trifling—a favorite word, "trifling"—reservations. The "congress" was a facade, held to give the look of a broad base for what Lenin always intended to be a compact, secret, strictly obedient weapon under the control of his government. Once the brow-beaten delegates dispersed, he simply dashed off an article in *Pravda* blandly announcing that "the Soviets have conquered throughout the whole world."[21]

. . .

That was the imaginary Comintern. The real Comintern was a corps of disciplined professional revolutionaries, put in place to enforce Leninist hegemony throughout the socialist movement world-wide. To this end it ran its own propaganda network and had its own secret service, with both branches intimately linked to one another and to the other Soviet secret services. Their work was at once legal and illegal, and in Münzenberg's case, the two often mingled in special ingenuity. The Comintern's secret service was known as the OMS, and Münzenberg worked in steady collaboration with it; the Central Party Archives show Münzenberg's enterprises intermingled and surrounded by elaborate secret service work. Münzenberg worked in close collaboration with the director of the OMS, Mirov-Abramov. In addition, substantial evidence strongly indicates that his principal lieutenants were covertly linked to branches of the Soviet services outside the Comintern.[22] One of Münzenberg's tasks was to invent ways to blur the distinction between legal and illegal work and, trailing clouds of deniability, install his men in the resulting never-never land.

While the cultural network had a very public face, it worked in tandem with deep-cover espionage networks. The evidence is strong that two of Münzenberg's principal lieutenants, Louis Gibarti and Otto Katz, were not only "Münzenberg-men," and so agents of the Comintern, but (probably without Willi knowing for sure) agents of the NKVD as well.[23] Gibarti and Katz: an extraordinary team. They *did* know something about trenchcoats, and careful tracking of their artful dodging through the first half of the twentieth century will turn up surprise after surprise. Gibarti was an elegant but slightly seedy Hungarian, affable, multi-lingual, and outspoken. He looked, said Babette, like "an opera cavalier." Gibarti ranks as a founding father of the modern mingling of propaganda with espionage and covert action. Though his modus operandi made him seem like a "legal"—in contrast to illegal—Comintern agent, Gibarti's "perfectly legal" organizations were pioneers in the art of doing secret service business in the open. It was Gibarti, for example, who in 1934 guided a young recruit named Kim Philby through a "perfectly legal" front in Paris and on to Vienna, where Philby took up his first real job as a secret agent.[24]

"Legal" operations, meanwhile, might pursue their propaganda ends while supplying illegal operations with cover. Consider, for example, those honey-hives of the intellectuals, bookstores. In the early days, the Comintern often used bookstores simultaneously as propaganda outlets *and* as fronts for transmitting information for the espionage *apparat*. In Shanghai, Richard Sorge made use of such an establishment within the network; its wonderful name, the "Zeitgeist Bookshop." In New York during the thirties, a then communist bookseller named Walter Goldwater was approached by Whittaker Chambers, using the name "Hugh Jones," and asked to establish a bookstore near Columbia University, the back room of which was to be used for the apparatus of espionage. Similarly, Münzenberg was a pioneer in the creation of a "Press Agency" which on the one hand might place perfectly legitimate journalism from independent writers and sources in legitimate journals, *and* at the same time place fabricated stories which the *apparat* wanted placed for propaganda, *and* serve as cover for working agents, *and* serve as cover for the flow of information obtained in espionage. Münzenberg's man Gibarti seems to have helped invent this sort of front.[25]

But Münzenberg's information network controlled newspapers and radio stations, ran film companies, created book clubs, ran magazines, sponsored publicity tours, dispatched journalists, and commissioned books. It planted articles and created organizations to give direction to the "innocent." To use the jargon of a different age, it was a media combine. Yet it differed in a number of ways from the BBC, Time, Inc., or even from an explicit instrument of political propaganda like Radio Liberty. For example, many people working for it did not publicly acknowledge the connection. Many operated under aliases. Many led classic double lives, sometimes totally changing their identities, concealing their true mission from their friends, even their spouses, and certainly from employers, who often included unsuspecting editors, publishers, and producers whose ideas were very remote from the real agenda.[26] They were, in short, secret agents, people who lived and worked, however publicly, in a place I shall be calling the secret world: the realm of intelligence gathering, covert action, undercover penetration, clandestine influence, quiet sabotage, discreet blackmail—what the American counter-spy, James Jesus Angleton, quoting T. S. Eliot, called "a wilderness of mirrors." Nor did the work stop with the media. Münzenberg also courted business people who could be used in industrial espionage, both in Europe and the United States. Given Lenin's obsession with electrification, for example, an early target was General Electric.[27] And back when the revolution was still young, it was Münzenberg's task to create for much of this vast unseen enterprise a persuasive public face.

Münzenberg clearly understood that the Revolution required something more than winning over "the masses." Speaking to a Comintern packed with intellectuals, he pounded at his point: ''*We must organize the intellectuals.*'' The revolution *needed* middle-class opinion makers—artists, journalists, ''people of good will,'' novelists, actors, playwrights . . . *humanists,* people whose innocent sensitivities weren't yet cauterized to nervelessness by the genuine white-hot radical steel. Lenin himself recoiled at this idea. Here were the people he loathed most—he who loathed so many people. Middle-class do-gooders? Bourgeois intellectuals clutching their precious ''freedom of conscience''? Lenin would kill and imprison them by the thousands. It took him a while—until 1921—to consent to use them, too. ''We must avoid being a purely communist organization,'' Münzenberg explained to his men. ''We must bring in other names, other groups, to make persecution more difficult.'' Middle-class opinion makers, liberal sympathizers, however much *echt* Bolsheviks despised them, must be used. Co-option may have struck hard-line Leninists as soft, but as Münzenberg pointed out, the powder keg was not blowing despite all kinds of sparks. Münzenberg dismissed these impatient purists and the fanaticism of absolutes with sardonic weariness. ''I too,'' he drawled, ''prefer the red hundreds.''[28]

Finally, there was the pursuit and organization of that special category of influential opinion maker, the fellow traveller. Little though he liked bourgeois humanists, or indeed any kind of humanist, Lenin came to see what Stalin never doubted: that to achieve its end, the Revolution outside Russia would need to exploit non-communist sympathizers, especially leaders in culture, sympathizers capable of setting the agenda of the Good. Western opinion could never be marshalled strictly from a Bolshevik platform. The world's idealists would never trust a leadership so obviously defined by fanaticism, so plainly committed to pure post-legal *force majeure,* so manifestly bound to hatred. The image of the ''human face'' needed to be created by ''spokesmen'' who attracted sympathy, not fear; famous, prestigious, and ''independent'' spokesmen, the more so the better, who would reassure the non-communist world that despite appearances all was well, Utopia really was a-building; that they had been over to see the future, and the socialist future was sweet and good.[29]

These spokesmen would have to be organized, promoted, and made reliable. It was essential that closely controlled fellow travellers such as Romain Rolland and Henri Barbusse, Lincoln Steffens and Heinrich Mann, be made to believe in their own independence, an independence they would of course rarely exercise. Every resource of manipulation, from rudimentary group psychology to plain bribery, was used to keep these ranks of the famous and influential left safely Stalinist in everything *except* name. As for the name, *that* had to be avoided at all costs. That would destroy the most useful thing about them, which was the deceptive but indispensable look of their "independence."

Managing these "independent spokesmen," keeping them saying the right things to support the cumbersome Big Lie they served—all this could be a very tricky business, and Münzenberg devoted all his ingenuity to it. "[Münzenberg] left nothing to chance," Babette Gross writes, "particularly not the manipulation of fellow travellers."[30] From the tightly interlocked sets of fellow travellers in Hollywood to the systems of Parisian left-wing cultural chic, he arranged the celebrities into guided and controlled networks, assigning agents to their management, focussing on given communities in the arts, in journalism, in the academy. Here again, non-paranoiac Westerners may have some difficulty grasping that an elaborate secret service network was set up to keep this large number of celebrity sympathizers appearing in the right places and reading the right lines. It is quite true that once a fashionable opinion was properly launched, it would quite spontaneously develop and grow among the ranks of enlightened people. Gibarti is said to have called this ripple effect in cultural politics "rabbit breeding."[31] But the original instigation of that fashion, its placement among the leaders of cultural politics—this was the province of professionals.

All this of course had to be secret and denied. Besides the public charade, there was the deeper matter of managing what we might call the denial within. Every device of vanity and venality, misused trust and intellectual obfuscation was employed. But there was something more. The fellow travellers needed to believe too that their Stalinism was an indispensable part of their own integrity, a key to the working of their intelligence, and to the practice of their arts. They needed to *believe*. In order for this to happen, the apparatus had to seize on the most salient moral claims of the adversary culture from which almost all these people emerged, and make it theirs. If Americans in the adversary culture understood that the oppression of blacks was the society's great institutionalized crime, Stalinism would take the highest of high ground on the "Negro question." No matter that Stalin ruled a country where a significant part of the population languished in slave labor camps. If the English adversary culture saw philistinism and middle-class repression as the enemy, Stalinism would embrace iconoclastic taste and sexual liberty as nobody else did; the Bohemianism and flamboyant homosexuality of Guy Burgess were an indispensable part of his slick Stalinism and central to his place in Bloomsbury. No matter that Soviet sexual policy and taste were intolerant to a degree that made Colonel Blimp look liberated.

The net effect of these facades was to bind Stalinism to the self-evident truths of a given adversary culture, and make that Stalinism feel indispensable to an enlightened life. The role of this in the ''denial within'' could be very potent. It could be addictive.

But direct management was also required. Agents were often specifically trained to enter the life of this or that ''independent thinker''—assuming the independent thinker was famous or influential enough. The idea was to influence and monitor the fellow traveller's life, and, if possible, run it. With the more important cultural grandees, intimate friends, sexual partners, and even wives could be assigned: political operatives put in place to manipulate the great man in question, while remaining in regular contact with Münzenberg's people.[32]

The Russian writer and historian Nina Berberova writes with astringent authority about a cohort of agents or near-agents, the women whom she calls the ''Ladies of the Kremlin.''[33] These were women who became influential figures in European and American intellectual life partly on their own, but above all through the men in their lives. The men, most often, were famous writers, ''spokesmen for the West.'' Meanwhile, the consorts whom they most trusted were guided by the Soviet services.

Leading this list were two members of the minor Russian aristocracy: the Baroness Moura Budberg, who was mistress to both Maxim Gorky and H. G. Wells, and the Princess Maria Pavlova Koudachova. Exactly what the Baroness Budberg's connection to the Soviets may have been remains mysterious, though its importance cannot be doubted. We have more certain knowledge about the Princess Koudachova, who first became secretary, later mistress, wife, and at last widow to the once enormously celebrated pacifist novelist Romain Rolland.

Maria Pavlova Koudachova was an agent directly under Soviet secret service control. There is some questionable evidence to suggest that she was trained and assigned to Rolland's life even before she left Russia after the Revolution. In any case, after Koudachova was permitted to leave Soviet Russia, she sought out the novelist in Switzerland and there began what was her entire life's work: insinuating herself into every corner of his existence and managing it for the *apparat*. It was a remarkably successful effort. The Central Party Archives in Moscow contain innumerable files documenting activities in which Rolland's prominence and wishful principles were exploited, used, and reused, while he danced the dance of ''innocence.''[34] By the time she married Rolland, the Princess had come to dominate the author's every public move, and she continued to do so until the day he died, whereupon she became the manager of his legend and archives. Throughout, Koudachova worked in close and regular collaboration with, among others, Münzenberg's agents.[35]

Romain Rolland's vanity required that he see himself as possessed of an almost uniquely self-directed and courageous mind. In truth, he was a quite self-infatuated person, easily led and easily frightened. As Koudachova steadily pulled him more and more deeply into his life as a Stalinist apologist, she was in turn supervised by Gibarti, and no doubt many other agents as well. Through all the years of manipulation, Rolland kept himself complacent with half-ignorance, the deniability within. True, by 1932, he clearly understood that Gibarti was a Comintern operative: There exists a letter to Henri Barbusse from Rolland, expressing sudden panic that his own reputation might be sullied by exposure of Gibarti's real role.[36] But could he ever let himself grasp the real role of his own wife? After meeting Maxim Gorky in 1934, Rolland confided to Koudachova how shocked and saddened he was to see Gorky surrounded by political spies in his own household. What the Princess replied is not on record.

That she was a secret service operative, however, and one expressly planted in Rolland's life, cannot be doubted. Babette Gross put it to me plainly in the summer of 1989. "She was an apparatchik," she said flatly. "And she ran him."

Mme. Berberova proposes a number of other candidates for inclusion among the "Kremlin Ladies": The wives of both Paul Eluard and Ferdinand Leger were among them. Perhaps. Certainly one of the most important was Elsa Triolet, sister of Mayakovsky's great love Lily Brik, who in Louis Aragon found her very own "great poet." With Aragon, Triolet presided over the high chic of European Stalinism for thirty years, knave to Aragon's fool, intimate with the most repellant figures in the Stalinist apparatus.[37] In America one might add Ella Winter to the list, who began her career in politics being introduced by Felix Frankfurter to Lincoln Steffens in the midst of the Versailles Conference. Steffens fell in love with her, and their relation lasted the rest of his life. Throughout the twenties Winter moved more and more obviously into the role of a classic fellow traveller, resolutely guiding the famous muckraker into the paths of her Stalinism as she did so. By the time of his death, it must be said that Lincoln Steffens had become a creature, an intellectual abject.[38]

After Steffens's death, Winter proceeded to another marriage that was exceptionally useful from the *apparat's* point of view. This one put her in a leading position managing the networks of Stalinist fellow travellers in Hollywood, a long-standing special concern of the apparatus, with much attention from Gibarti, Katz, and many others. Winter met and married a very successful Hollywood screenwriter, Donald Ogden Stewart—a companion of Ernest Hemingway and John Dos Passos; a runner with the bulls at Pamplona in the company of the circle immortalized in *The Sun Also Rises*.[39] Stalinism and Hemingway aside, Stewart was an attractive but malleable guilt-ridden lightweight. And at his side, Ella Winter was ideally placed for an active life among networks of Stalinist opinion in the film colony.

Like Koudachova, Ella Winter worked closely with Münzenberg's men, especially those who were active in Hollywood. She knew Otto Katz well, and Gibarti referred to Ella Winter as "one of the most trusted party agents for the West Coast."[40] Gibarti had every reason to know.

So Münzenberg had been among the most potent organizers of the apparatus of the Comintern.[41] He was so successful, in fact, that by 1921 the Comintern's head, Gregori Zinoviev, was beginning to feel threatened and at the 1921 Congress, Zinoviev momentarily maneuvered Münzenberg out of his main Party position of the time, running the Young Communist League. It turned out to be a fortunate fall: It left Willi free for his new and great political role.[42]

He found that role in catastrophe.

One event above all others at last forced Lenin to assign Münzenberg the task of manipulating opinion in the bourgeois West: famine.

In 1921, a combination of drought, the aftermath of the civil war, and the disasters of agricultural collectivization brought down upon the Soviet Union a famine horrific beyond anything previously known in modern European history. Before the Revolution, Russia had been, time out of mind, one of the principal agricultural exporters on the planet. Under the Soviets, it would never be so again.[43] With 1921, famine descended; around the Volga and in the Tatar Republic, mass starvation proceeded to kill, according to the surely underestimated official toll, not less than two million people. In hordes, the starving lined the banks of the Volga, vast numbers of them infected with the typhus that had been all but pandemic in Russia since 1919. They moved toward the river, bowed with Russian patience, or perhaps it was the numb inertia of agony, clustering on the banks by the tens of thousands, "singing and dying," huddled in their masses, waiting for the boats they fondly imagined must *surely* be being sent to feed them, save them. As people within the crowd died, the corpses were passed, hand over hand, out to the rim of the throng, and piled by the hundreds in the spring grass along the muddy banks. It was not uncommon to break into peasant houses and find an entire family seated around a table, the Bible open before them, dead in their chairs.[44]

Lenin's attitude toward the famine was "curiously remote, cold and disinterested. He seemed to regard the famine as only one more of the obstacles that blocked his path."[45] He was also afraid. The Kronstadt Rebellion had just been crushed with particularly merciless violence. With it was crushed the last plausible claim to a "democratic" Soviet. Though the civil war had been won, hopeless little rebellions kept cropping up everywhere. And now—famine, disastrous famine, gaping at the whole world. In private, Lenin conceded: "We are barely holding on."[46]

At this moment Radek intervened with Lenin, insisting that some international propaganda response was needed and promoting Münzenberg for the job.[47] Willi was summoned to Lenin's study in the Kremlin. He sat in one of the leather armchairs across from his leader's desk. It was a room remote from the old Tsarist apartments, and without regal pretensions. The only hint of omnipotence was technological: an array of telephones, the best in Russia, over which the dictator of the proletariat governed, shouting.

The dictator pointed his beard at him, outlined the situation, and analyzed the options with systematic inaccuracy. No help whatever, he told Münzenberg, could be expected from the West. Only the "international proletariat" could conceivably be expected to give aid. "His plan," Münzenberg said, "was to organize an extensive international relief action, and charge me with its organization."[48]

Lenin was wrong about the response of the West. When (perhaps at Münzenberg's behest) Maxim Gorky was permitted to make a public appeal for help, relief was committed in vast amounts within ten days.[49] The success of Gorky's appeal left Lenin angry and chagrined. For years afterward, its existence was officially denied. Two weeks later, Münzenberg's new enterprise had been established.

By far the major share came from the American Relief Administration run by the future President of the United States, Herbert Hoover. The U.S. Congress promptly appropriated twenty million dollars. Millions more were contributed by individuals. By August 20, supplies had started rolling into Russia. At the peak of the disaster, the ARA was feeding more than ten million Russians every day.[50] The Europeans likewise responded, with a program run by the Norwegian explorer and humanitarian Fridtjof Nansen. In terms of material aid, the relief Münzenberg organized through the Comintern trailed far behind. Had Lenin's analysis been correct, the Volga catastrophe would have been almost unmitigated.

An appeal for relief was also set up within Russia. An "All Russian Famine Relief Committee" was assembled in Gorky's name, including fifty or so non-Bolshevik intellectuals summoned back from oblivion and insult to help rescue the country. The committee launched its appeals; response swelled and became so successful that Lenin and Kamenev thought it menaced Bolshevik hegemony. Non-Bolsheviks mobilizing opinion? The men in the Kremlin panicked and immediately moved to destroy what they had created. When the committee assembled for its third meeting, Kamenev made sure that his own plants within its ranks, and Gorky himself, were absent; he then surrounded the building with black marias and ordered the Cheka to charge the committee room, weapons drawn. Every non-Bolshevik in the place was arrested and taken to the Lubyanka. Some were released; many others, among them the novelist Bulgakov and Tolstoy's daughter Alexandra, were summarily sentenced to death. Of course, even by Bolshevik standards, these people had committed no crime. Lenin himself conceded the point. "We know perfectly well the loyalty of the committee," he said. "It was necessary for us—for political reasons—to destroy it."

When Gorky presumed to ask why all his non-communist literary friends were in prison awaiting death, Kamenev answered with an interesting image. The committee resembled, he said, a willow twig in water. The twig had begun to sprout. "It had become a center of attention for the so-called Russian 'public.' This we could not permit." The sprouting willow twig had to be smashed. Gorky reeled on Kamenev in humiliation and rage: "You have made me into an *agent provocateur!*"[51]

Exactly.

One of Münzenberg's prime tasks was to counteract the "bad impression" created by the success of this foreign relief.

The bourgeoisie could not be seen to be accomplishing what the Bolsheviks were failing to accomplish. So they must be thwarted. Lenin ordered Litvinov to hamstring foreign agencies with every possible bureaucratic obstacle. When the famine was past, about half the Russians who'd worked alongside the foreign relief people—as many as 100,000 Soviet citizens—came to their reward: summary arrest by the Cheka and the gulag, an institution already entrenched. It was assumed that any Russian who'd worked with these do-gooding bourgeois Americans and Norwegians must be tainted with "counter-revolution." Lenin even ordered that adults, though they were starving, be forbidden access to the ideologically incorrect foreign food. Only children were "immune to capitalist contagion." This insane regulation stood on the books for a full year, though of course the Americans and Scandinavians quietly disobeyed it wherever possible. At last Lenin came to see that feeding children while starving their parents to death was not, after all, an ideologically sound device for cementing socialist loyalty.[52]

Yet the WIR did produce real help, and Münzenberg brought all his managerial brilliance to the task. Tumultuous rallies and heart-rending compassionate appeals were organized around the world. Shiploads of grain pulled toward Petrograd. Fisheries were spawned in the Caspian Sea. Fleets were launched. Münzenberg's entrepreneurial genius transformed relief and propaganda into a kind of communist multinational, with himself as its clandestine CEO. In a sense, the MRP—the Russian acronym for WIR—became the Comintern's stake in the "New Economic Policy," or NEP, with which Lenin briefly permitted some marginal entrepreneurialism to help break the crisis.[53]

The leading concern, however, was always for propaganda. I asked Babette Gross when propaganda, rather than relief, became the prime interest of the WIR. "At the first moment," she replied, with her typical simplicity.

But with the famine under control, the new propaganda combine did begin to expand in new directions. Münzenberg's fisheries and farms soon gave way to newspapers, magazines, and film production companies, as well as press agencies. The combine had offices around the world, with branches in Moscow (staffed mainly by Germans), and its headquarters in Berlin. What had begun as a network for relief became a network for molding opinion and (not least), for secret political action. Münzenberg had assembled what amounted to a huge, secretly co-ordinated media consortium. It came to be known, with cheerless Bolshevik irony, as "The Münzenberg Trust."

The story of the Münzenberg Trust has rarely been told. Arthur Koestler only hints at its complexity in his autobiographical book, *The Invisible Writing:*

> Out of the pamphlets issued in support of the relief campaign grew the Trust's own publishing firms, its book clubs, its multitudes of magazines and newspapers. By 1926, Willi owned two daily newspapers in Germany with mass circulations, *Berlin am Morgen* and *Welt am Abend;* the *Arbeiter Illustrierte Zeitung,* a weekly with a circulation of one million, the communist counterpart of *Life;* a series of other magazines including technical magazines for photographers, radio amateurs, etc., all with an indirect communist slant. In Japan, to quote a remote country as an example, the Trust directly or indirectly controlled nineteen magazines and newspapers.

> It also financed communist avant-garde plays which were in great vogue at the time.''[54]

In the United States, the *Nation* magazine was for many years edited or greatly influenced by people, ranging from Louis Fischer to Julio Alvárez del Vayo, whose careers were shaped in close collaboration with Münzenberg and his men.[55] It was a propaganda combine extending from Moscow to Berlin to Paris to London to New York to Hollywood to Shanghai to Delhi.

Nor did Willi limit himself to print. Münzenberg's impact was no less powerful in the theater and the graphic arts. From Georg Grosz to Erwin Piscator, much of vanguard Weimar culture was funded by Münzenberg. Then there was his impact upon the emergent cinema of the left. At a very early stage of its existence Münzenberg used one of his many dummy corporations—Aufbau, Industrie & Handels, A.G.—quietly to buy up distribution rights in the USSR to almost all German films then on the market.[56] The revenues from this shrewd investment soon engendered the capital needed for a German-based distribution company called Prometheus Films, the instrument through which Soviet cinema of the grand epoch was released and promoted in the West. Prometheus's first release was Eisenstein's *Battleship Potemkin,* with a score commissioned by Münzenberg's in-house composer, Edmund Meisel. Eisenstein's great prestige in the democracies was very much a creation of the Münzenberg machine. Prometheus soon became a production company for German film as well, and in 1927 Münzenberg added yet another subsidiary, *Welt Film,* for the equivalent of 16 millimeter non-theatrical distribution. Through this company the Trust encouraged the creation of college film societies in England and America, all featuring Soviet cinema, the gathering places for a new left-wing university elite, where *Potemkim* and *October* were screened in basements against bedsheets. In the United States, a parallel organization used many names and passed through many forms, until it ended, rather innocuously, as a company called Brandon Films.

Then in 1924 Willi moved even more dramatically. A complete production company was established in Moscow, capitalized, staffed, and controlled by Münzenberg; that is, by the Comintern. Following the Russian acronym for WIR, which was MRP, the company was Mezhropohmfilm Russ and it became the prime production house of Soviet cinema in its grand epoch, the studio for Vertov, Dovzhenko, Pudovkin. Mezhropohmfilm made real movies, including a number of very great ones, for real audiences. Meanwhile its networks provided legal cover for many secret agents with quite different missions, and with the addition of this third pillar to his tripod, Münzenberg's hegemony over Soviet cinema became close to complete, and firmly located on the Berlin-Moscow axis.

Though he was a master at manipulating the innocents, Münzenberg was certainly no innocent himself. It was his regular task consciously to deceive the world about the horrors being perpetrated by the regime. Willi may have honestly believed that he was lying for the truth, but he did clearly know he was lying. Consider Münzenberg's public relations work for the White Sea Canal. In June 1933, Münzenberg was taken north of Leningrad and given a guided tour of two of Stalin's pet projects: the construction of the White Sea Canal and its successor project, the Moscow-Volga Canal, both enormous adventures in incompetent engineering which had turned into what were then the largest and most brutally run concentration camps on earth. It would be many years before Hitler had anything that could approach the nightmare reality of these awful places. The White Sea Canal crawled with 300,000 slave laborers rounded up by the OGPU. Solzhenitzyn estimates that during the winter of 1931–32 alone, some 100,000 of these forced laborers perished in that horrific ravine, frozen to death, worked to death. If true, this would mean that almost a thousand people died there every day.

This organized human catastrophe was too large to be kept entirely secret, and in time word began to leak to the West. The result was bad press, and Münzenberg was ordered to counter it. It was time for the fellow travellers to extol the achievements of the White Sea Canal and the Moscow-Volga Canal. To this end, it was decided to take Münzenberg to the Moscow-Volga Canal and give him a first-hand look.

It was summer now. The dying had abated. Münzenberg was led to the edge and there he stood and stared down into that vast murderous ditch. The pit below was filled with new slaves in their ragged thousands. He stared down and was genuinely shaken. He is said to have whispered under his breath that it was like watching slaves crawling on the pyramids of ancient Egypt.[57]

Did this stop him? Not at all. Münzenberg had his assignment and he performed it. By summer's end Russia's leading literati, with Maxim Gorky at their head, were busy writing articles about these shining triumphs of socialist engineering, the White Sea Canal and the Moscow-Volga Canal, while in the West Münzenberg saw to it that the White Sea Canal shone near the peak of Europe's idealistic goals. Detractors were vilified as enemies of the working man. As the campaign developed, the fellow travellers pulled out the stops: Sidney and Beatrice Webb, and Amabel Williams-Ellis (sister of John Strachey, one of Münzenberg's best men in England) gushed at length about this uniquely uplifting example of socialist compassion. Of course the poor fools didn't know what they were talking about; they merely mouthed information the apparatus put before them. We must blame Münzenberg and not merely the egregious Ms. Williams-Ellis and people like her for the claim that the White Sea Canal, filled though it was with prisoners, was an inspiring example of what a really creative and humane police force could accomplish.[58]

The Comintern was the apple of Lenin's eye. Stalin, on the other hand, despised the institution, as he despised so many things, and so deeply. To be sure, he used the Comintern apparatus with ruthless virtuosity and raised it to previously unknown heights of activity. Even so he had contempt for its furtive intriguing intellectuals, its internationalist palaver, its big dreams. He took control of it early, and finding its obedience insufficiently abject, he penetrated it from top to bottom with his other services. Eventually he dissolved it. He used to call its Moscow headquarters, in passing, *lavotchka:* the "grocer's hut," "the gyp-joint."[59] Yet he also made it one of the most efficient and pervasive secret institutions in history.

Münzenberg was Stalin's tool. This must be said. A certain kind of revolutionary sentimentality might wish to preserve Münzenberg's memory—first smeared, then all but obliterated by Stalin—for the Leninist paradise lost of the Zimmerwald left and the glory days in Zurich. And much in Münzenberg is very sympathetic. Even after they had become passionate anti-communists, Koestler and Regler retained a certain affection for their days with Willi. And it is true that toward the end of his life Münzenberg did, slowly, with the caution of a man dismantling a bomb, disengage himself step by meticulous step from the apparatus. He had seen that apparatus turn upon his closest associates and murder them, and he knew perfectly well that eventually it would destroy him too, unless he did something, something very shrewd, to save himself. In Paris during the phony war, he guarded himself using all his skill. Stalin's band of elite assassins, the Bureau of Special Tasks, watched him. The Gestapo watched him. British intelligence, riddled with Soviet agents, watched him. Willi watched them watch, protecting himself until June 1940, when things fell apart, and he was fleeing south through France, toward the valley of the Isère, and his last day.

Like Lenin, like Stalin, Münzenberg was almost laughably ignorant about the United States. He visited it only once in his life, in 1934, and was surprised to discover how agreeable, how free and open a place it was, compared to what he had known.[60] Yet even at remote control, Willi managed to insinuate his plans and people into the moral life of America with durable results. Around 1925, the Comintern entrusted Münzenberg and his propaganda machine with a little-known but large role in giving shape and political function to the Communist party of the United States as it was to be under Stalin. At that time, the American Party, that congregation of the militant naive, home and battleground for John Reed and Louise Bryant, needed to be re-assembled. It had been left in a shattered state by its late-Leninist internal struggles combined with devastating police action inflicted on it by what later became the FBI.[61]

The course adopted then is revealing. No effort was made to create a mass-based movement appropriate to the seizure of power in America. It is plain that Stalin had no serious interest or belief in an American "revolution." He never attempted to create an American Party or communist movement capable of even remotely challenging the constitutional power, as he would do in Germany, Italy, France, Greece, and the Balkans. That was not to be the American Party's job. The apparatus of American communism would be directed instead toward discrediting American politics and culture and assisting the growth of Soviet power elsewhere. It sought not revolutionary power inside America, but moral authority developed through the propaganda of righteousness politics. It sought not the outright destruction of the American democracy, however much that might be desired, but practical influence on its culture, the placement of agents who would over the long term seek to smooth and promote the advance of Soviet influence and assist the apparatus in its work of espionage. The American right may have given itself nightmares about the red flag flying over the Capitol and commissars storming the East Room, but I know of no evidence showing that such a thing was ever really part of Stalin's dream; his 1927 remark, made to gullible visitors, that the Sacco-Vanzetti scandal showed America in pre-revolutionary turmoil, was surely a matter of atmospherics. Lenin's mind was centered upon Germany; Stalin's was on Russia and its vast sphere of power. America lay beyond a very distant albeit important place, an irritating mystery. An irritating *myth.* And it was in the arena of myth, not that of the seizure of power, that America had the Soviets' full and frightened attention.

For the world proletariat of 1925, the leading counter-myth to the myth of revolution was, by far, the *idea* of America. That vision—the notion of the melting pot, the Golden Door, the Land of Opportunity—this is what held the real political attention of the International. To the Bolsheviks, this was the true American menace. And in 1925, the task of the American Party was to counteract it.

So Münzenberg's first idea was to create and sustain a world-wide anti-American campaign that would focus its appeal upon the mythology of its immigration. The purpose of such a campaign would be to instill a reflexive loathing of the United States and its people as a prime tropism of left-wing enlightenment. To undermine the myth of the Land of Opportunity, the United States would be shown as an almost insanely xenophobic place, murderously hostile to foreigners.

To this end, Münzenberg surveyed his options, in search of a cause that would disgrace America in the eyes of the proletarian foreign-born. He found it in the obscure, dying case of two anarchist immigrants who'd got themselves into some very bad trouble: Niccola Sacco and Bartolomeo Vanzetti.

Every so often, talking with me in Munich, Babette Gross would drop a remark that made the foundations of the world seem to shift a little. One of these was over Sacco and Vanzetti. The Sacco-Vanzetti case? "It was," she said with a dry shrug, "Münzenberg's idea."[62]

Münzenberg's idea! Is that *possible*? With the Dreyfus case, this is perhaps the most famous legal struggle in the whole history of modern propaganda and injustice. It seemed at first incredible to me that this epochal case could have been manipulated at such distance, and so cynically.

And indeed the origins of the Sacco-Vanzetti case are far more complex than that. Yet in one sense the Sacco-Vanzetti campaign does turn out to have been "Münzenberg's idea." It was indeed at Münzenberg's instigation that communist propaganda networks world-wide took up the plight of the two Boston immigrants and made it the centerpiece of a vast new anti-American operation—just as a little later it was Willi's executive decision to turn the Scottsboro Boys into prime martyrs for the International. The Comintern and Willi's organization were the ones who transformed a case of troubled local injustice into a world-wide *cause célèbre*.

In that effort, however, the communists latched onto the Sacco-Vanzetti case as latecomers and opportunists. Sacco and Vanzetti were not themselves communists, and theirs was not, at first, a communist struggle. The two Italians were anarchists, and so their political myth was shaped during the early 1920s, by anarchists, guided especially by that doyen of Italo-American radicalism, Carlo Tresca.

By the mid-1920s, however, the political sponsorship of the case decisively changed. In 1926, the American Communist party stood directionless and in disarray, very much in need of a new motivating spirit and a new task. At the same time, the International was demanding its anti-American cause. The Soviet propagandists decided to satisfy both these needs at once. In 1926, speaking to his colleagues in the WIR, Münzenberg announced it was their task, as propagandists, to rescue the American Party and supply its new direction. And so it was: the first task of a revived American Party was to seize and hold the Sacco-Vanzetti case for its own, while around the world the Comintern turned it into *the* preoccupying moral issue of the era. By 1928, Willi was cooly and quite correctly claiming credit for the Sacco-Vanzetti campaign, understood as a world-wide political moral mania, and among the highest triumphs of his *apparatus*.[63]

Here is how it worked. Way back in 1920, two Italian immigrants, both militant anarchists, were arrested and charged with stealing the payroll of a Braintree, Massachusetts, shoe factory and murdering its paymaster and his guard. In 1921, they were tried, convicted, and sentenced to death.

At first, the plight of these two ill-fated men seemed to interest nobody. A socialist newsman sent up from New York reported back to his editor, "there's no story in it. . . . Just a couple of wops in a jam."[64]

The two men belonged to a small anarchist cell of Italian immigrants like themselves. When the pair was arrested, this group immediately formed a defense committee. Naively convinced that the two would probably get off, they proposed creating "great publicity for the anarchist movement."[65]

But Sacco and Vanzetti did not get off. Nor did their case advance the anarchist cause; its later co-option by the communists was used to betray and undermine American anarchism. The Defense Committee was right about one thing: These two men's condemnation offered the basis for a political vision.

That vision in its anarchist incarnation was the creation of one man above all: an eccentric Westerner, one of the grand lawyers of the American left, a brilliant but more flaky Clarence Darrow named Fred Moore, recommended to the Defense Committee by Carlo Tresca. Moore was, in the words of his assistant, Eugene Lyons, an "artist handicapped by a genius for non-conformity."[66] He was a heavy-using cocaine addict (the Defense Committee more than once used their less idealistic Italian connections to keep him supplied), a drawling Westerner with his revolver often slung in his back pocket, given to affronting judicial dignity by padding around courtrooms in his stocking feet.

Moore invented the case. He set out to rescue his clients with any and every maneuver a fertile legal mind could conceive, convinced they were lost without the pressure of outraged world opinion. To this end, long before Münzenberg knew anything about the case, he single-handedly created the *political* argument of Sacco and Vanzetti: that they were powerless, despised, radical immigrants being subjected to judicial murder by a smug, chauvinist, puritanical, nativist, red-scared New England establishment.[67] In promoting this defense, Moore was unscrupulous, ingenious, indefatigable, driven. Of his passion and sincerity there can be no doubt. He was a man obsessed. And his belief in his clients' innocence was quite genuine. At first.

Except unfortunately their innocence *wasn't* quite genuine. Best evidence shows beyond all reasonable doubt that Sacco was in fact one of the Braintree gunmen and the murderer of the guard, whom he shot to death after the man had fallen to his hands and knees, begging for his life while struggling to reach his own revolver. Vanzetti may have been innocent of the Braintree holdup, though he probably knew or guessed Sacco's guilt. He certainly had guilty knowledge of Sacco's participation in an earlier robbery where no blood had been spilled.

In a way, the facts make the two men's political solidarity all the more compelling. One word of the truth from either man—Sacco in ordinary decency; Vanzetti in ordinary self-protection—would have saved Vanzetti's life. But it also would have demolished their cause in *disgrazia*. Bartolomeo Vanzetti laid down his life on the bloody altar not of justice but of propaganda. He died lying for the truth.

The murky integrity of this self-sacrifice gives Vanzetti—he was in every way the more interesting of the pair—a tremendously affecting dignity. It also sustained his stumbling, broken, justly famous eloquence. "If it had not been for this thing, I might have live out my life talking on street corners to scorning men. I might have die unknown, unmarked, a failure. Now we are not a failure. This is our career and our triumph."[68]

The little coterie of anarchists on the Defense Committee also knew the truth, and they too maintained the vow of silence for *la causa*. The last survivor, a man named Ideale Gambera, wrote a full account of the affair for disclosure by his son after his death. Gambera died in 1982, and his son released the documents to Francis Russell, a principal scholar of the case. It was the last word.

Somewhere along the way, Fred Moore seems to have stumbled onto the truth as well. There is no evidence that this in any way modified Moore's passion for his clients' defense, but in 1923, in the midst of a paranoid psychotic episode (he'd attempted suicide and was hospitalized) Sacco dismissed Moore in a violent incoherent rage.[69] Taking his dismissal with dignity, Moore packed up, got into his car, and drove back west, selling knickknacks as he went to pay for his gasoline.

The case now began to die. The appeals dragged on, but the headline makers of the world had dropped the Massachusetts fishmonger and shoemaker. Then, in 1925, on orders of Münzenberg and the Comintern, an American branch of the Red Aid called the International Labor Defense, created in Chicago with James Cannon as its director, was set up to be the focus of organization for the new American communism. Its first mission was to make the Sacco-Vanzetti case into a world-wide myth.[70]

The campaign became a juggernaut, tenaciously co-ordinated from Berlin, vast and unrelenting. Now, once again, protest meetings gathered to shout and sob in the great squares. From all its outlets, organs of the Trust produced an unstanchable stream of attacks on the assassin viciousness of American justice, defending the innocence and holiness of the immigrant martyrs in Braintree. Around the world, heart-rending appeals for cash were staged to provide for Sacco and Vanzetti's defense and "protection." Children gave their pennies, workers donated wages, philanthropists opened their checkbooks.

The *apparat's* fund-raising was, incidently, an almost complete fraud. Sacco and Vanzetti and their Defense Committee saw next to none of the money raised in their names. Of the approximately half-million dollars raised in the United States, the Defense Committee received something like $6,000. Of large sums collected in mass protest meetings around the world, the Defense Committee saw precisely nothing.[71]

Cannon seems to have understood that Sacco was guilty, and so Münzenberg very possibly also knew the truth.[72] Not that anybody cared. The communist goal was never to save the lives of Sacco and Vanzetti. Acquittal would have dissolved the whole political point. Katherine Anne Porter, like hundreds of writers and artists of the time, participated in the Boston deathwatch. She reports an exchange with the Comintern agent who was her group leader, Rosa Baron, "a dry, fanatical little woman who wore thick-lensed spectacles over her accusing eyes, a born whip-hand, who talked an almost impenetrable jargon of party dogma. . . . I remarked . . . that even then, at that late time, I still hoped the lives of

Sacco and Vanzetti could be saved. . . . 'Saved' she said, ringing a change on her favorite answer to political illiteracy, 'who wants them saved? What earthly good would they do us alive?' "[73]

Russell described the European demonstrations:

> Demonstrations took place that autumn in France and Italy, with lesser demonstrations in Switzerland, Belgium, Spain, Portugal, Scandinavia, and South America. A bomb exploded in the American embassy in Paris. Another was intercepted in the Lisbon consulate. Reds in Brest stoned the consulate there. American consuls in Mexico were threatened with death if Sacco and Vanzetti were executed. In Rome, thousands of workers marched on the American embassy demanding justice for their compatriots.
>
> Some of this agitation was anarchist inspired, some actually spontaneous, but most of it was directed by communist leaders in Paris.[74]

Best evidence suggests that one of the witting Münzenberg men on the scene in Boston was a rather appealing personality of the American left, named Gardner Jackson. Jackson was another charmer, a hard-drinking sandy-haired journalist in the Will Rogers vein, who loved cowboy boots and old tweeds, a radical who had spent his life claiming to be just a guy on the left, nothing but a rich boy from Wyoming who liked his bourbon and wanted to see the little guy get an even break. In truth Jackson was intimate with Münzenberg's most senior operatives in America, and though he was probably a much-manipulated fellow traveller rather than a fully witting operative, by 1939 Gardner was fronting for Gibarti in the Roosevelt administration.[75] He was almost certainly a front man in the Sacco-Vanzetti campaign as well.

With his lanky manner and sinning smile, Jackson was very successful with women. Dorothy Parker, for example, became quite infatuated with him during the Sacco-Vanzetti protest, and it may well have been he who guided Parker toward what seems to have been her secret membership in the Communist party.[76] It was a link of real importance to the apparatus six or seven years later when, along with Lillian Hellman, Parker became a leading celebrity front figure in Hollywood fellow-travelling networks. Looking back on *la causa* from the Hollywood Hills, Parker seems to have found some essential element of her identity in this kind of politics. It may seem bizarre today to see communist politics shaping and giving direction to the smart-cracking bittersweet comedy of such a woman, with her curious comic blend of self-righteousness and self-contempt. But in its time, Parker's union of style and Stalinist attitudes was a natural fit. Through the chic of her hard-left commitments, Parker could both validate her love of glamour, and mask it with an appropriate look of disdain for all the vanities.[77]

Right around the same time, Gardner Jackson was developing his influence over another woman in Boston. This was Marion Frankfurter, the wife of Felix Frankfurter, then a leading professor of law at Harvard, and later one of this century's great justices of the United States Supreme Court. Frankfurter was drawn into the affair by the dual force of his passion for justice and his concern for his wife. Marion Frankfurter had a frightening history of mental instability. Her delicate psychiatric state preoccupied her husband and of course tangled his otherwise steadfast loyalty and courage with inevitable emotions of guilt, fear, and the wish to escape.

During the Sacco-Vanzetti campaign, Gardner Jackson placed the cultivation of a thoroughly ingratiating relationship with the Frankfurters high among his prime concerns. His point of focus was Marion. Jackson was a famously seductive man; though his attentions to Marion Frankfurter were surely platonic, they were also incessant. He lucidly saw and exploited her insecurity, her need to anchor herself in a cause, her problem balancing her own sense of inadequacy against the brilliance of her incandescent and intensely ambitious husband.

Marion Frankfurter became preoccupied with Gardner, and through him, with the case. Gardner in turn flattered Marion continually. He arranged to have her join him as co-editor of Sacco and Vanzetti's letters. He involved her at every public level.[78]

It seems plain that the real purpose of this tactic was to reach Felix. Gardner seems to have guessed that Frankfurter's wish to support his wife's cause would lead him into the fold as well. He was correct. The couple became mutually obsessed, egged on at every step by Jackson, who became their constant companion, a daily intimate of the house. When the condemned men's last appeal was denied, the outraged Felix proceeded to write one of the most powerful polemics of his career, a denunciation of the case's legal history, a brilliant exercise in controlled vituperation. The piece appeared in the *Atlantic*. It was more influential than any other factor in marshalling American non-radical opinion behind the pair, and it was even more influential in Europe. Münzenberg's Berlin office arranged for it to be reprinted throughout the world, while in London H. G. Wells produced a flamboyant summary which promptly became the received British view.[79]

What followed was orchestrated multinational mass hysteria.

. . .

August 22 was the night of the executions, and around them the *apparat,* poising itself for the outpouring of international grief, organized a vast international deathwatch. Francis Russell describes the event:

> After the news flashed from Charleston that Sacco and Vanzetti had at last been executed, the reverberations were international. Demonstrations in American cities were duplicated and in many places exceeded all over Europe. In Paris the Communist daily *Humanité* printed an extra sheet on which was splashed the single block word "*Assassinés!*" Crowds surged down the Boulevard Sebastopol, ripping up lampposts and tossing them through plate glass windows. Protective tanks ringed the American embassy, and sixty policemen were injured when a mob tried to set up barricades there. Five thousand militants roamed the streets of Geneva the evening before the executions, overturning American cars, sacking shops selling American goods, gutting theaters showing American films. One of the greatest demonstrations in the history of the Weimar republic took place in Berlin; there were tumultuous demonstrations in Bremen and Wilhelmshaven and Hamburg, and a two hour torchlight parade in Stuttgart. During that turbulent week, half a dozen German demonstrators were killed. No one was killed in England, but on the night of the executions, a crowd gathered in front of Buckingham Palace and sang "The Red Flag."[80]

The night of the executions was marked by a vigil at Charleston Prison. Before this dour building an enormous crowd gathered in the dark. "I was never in that place before," Porter wrote, "but I seem to remember that it was a great open space with the crowd massed back from a center the police worked constantly to keep clear. They were all mounted on fine horses and loaded with pistols and hand grenades and tear gas bombs." The law in its generosity provides that the condemned are entitled to every minute of their last day. After having been granted this largess, Sacco and Vanzetti were led to the death chamber at midnight exactly. Sacco entered it first, at 12:11. Vanzetti followed at 12:20. By 12:27 both had been pronounced dead. Both men met their end with indescribable dignity.

And so the American Communist party was revived, in part, to function as a local instrument in a world-wide and remarkably successful effort to create a new anti-American myth, the support and development of which persisted for decades to come. But there were many other aspects to this apparatus for orchestrating the mythology of progressive thought. Between 1928 and 1932, for example, an international movement on behalf of ''Peace'' was mounted by the fronts and fellow-travelling networks.[81]

Stalin was, after all, a Marxist-Leninist, and his thinking in all its cynical paranoiac brutality was guided by Marxist-Leninist assumptions. Just as he understood himself as the absolute and ultimate enemy of the liberal democracies and their bourgeois order, so he assumed that the rulers of those democracies cherished equally lethal intentions toward the great Revolution over which he presided. The Marxist-Leninist political culture, for such obvious though often ignored reasons as this, is typically a playground for paranoiacs—that is one reason why a man like Stalin flourished within it. The dictator feared above all a vengeful counter-revolutionary invasion from the West; to him it seemed certain to come. How could it not, given capitalism? And because of a broad constellation of reasons, Stalin was not at all sure he either wanted or could make the Red Army into a force capable of deterring such an invasion. It was in this anxiety that we can locate his response to a plan presented to him by his Western propagandists, calling for a great, broadly based campaign endorsing pacifism in the democracies.

Insiders came to call this plan the ''Peace Conspiracy'' and it seems to have been set before the dictator sometime in 1928, right after the triumph of Sacco-Vanzetti. It is said that the prime author of the peace plan was a French Münzenberg-man named Guy Jerram. Wherever the idea originated, the peace conspiracy found favor in the Kremlin. By the middle of 1928, the propaganda apparatus on all its fronts had seized upon pacifism as the principal issue of the hour, and it continued to promote ''peace'' with all its sententious fervor for the next four years. Louis Gibarti's various fronts, especially an organization active on college campuses called the League Against Imperialism, took up the cry. College campuses were in fact a prime locus for the whole campaign: The ''Oxford Oath,'' adopted in 1934 by the Oxford Union, categorically resolving ''under no circumstances to fight for King and Country,'' is a belated echo of all this agitation. At the League Against Imperialism's first Congress in Brussels in late 1928, the touchstone of talk about the colonial struggle was for this reason not ''armed struggle'' as one might expect to hear among those seeking to throw off the imperialist yoke. No: ''Peace.''

The campaign for ''peace'' culminated in 1932 at a huge congress, also organized under the covert direction of Münzenberg and Gibarti, known as the Amsterdam Congress Against War. It must be said that the kaleidoscope sentiment endorsed by these successive congresses really all came from the same operation. Precisely the same secretariat and cast of characters were behind the Amsterdam Congress as the Brussels Anti-War Congress, and the Archives of the Central Party in Moscow likewise show that these, in turn, were central to the founding events of the anti-fascist movement after the Reichstag Fire.[82] Gibarti was the legman running them all, and under his direction the support system continued to grow. Because the Congress later held its Paris meetings in the Salle Pleyel, Amsterdam later became known as the Amsterdam-Pleyel World Congress Against War, and when the Nazis assumed power its secretariat was moved to a suburb of Paris—Aumont. It finally reached its last incarnation under a new name, the largest and most broadly based of all Münzenberg's organizations: the League Against War and Fascism.

There was of course something inherently contradictory in the spectacle of a set of revolutionaries espousing "pacifism"—even an elaborately disguised set of crypto-revolutionaries hiding behind the mask of humanist sentiment. Revolution *is* war, one of the most important varieties of war. It is class war; it is "armed struggle." And though the truth was not necessarily plain even to the insightful in 1930, it certainly became plain after 1937 that any organization whose chieftain was Joseph Stalin was unlikely to embrace the non-violent cause with anything like sincerity. Yet the contradiction between pacifism and revolution proved, in practice, remarkably easy to elide. "War" in this Soviet-sponsored rhetoric of righteousness, and in fact generally on the left thereafter, was never taken to mean *class* war. Meanwhile, because the pacifist propaganda was linked to the League Against Imperialism, the inherent ideological incongruity would be played out in events to come, especially in India, where non-violence (to the considerable albeit concealed irritation of the communists) really did come to the fore as a meaningful tactic of political action. But the interplay between pacifism and anti-imperialism was part of a long process. Nehru himself (like the Nicaraguan insurrectionary Sandino, a Gibarti discovery) was a delegate to the Brussels congress in 1932, and when it was over Nehru was spirited across the German border and taken to Berlin to meet with Münzenberg personally. Münzenberg had a profound effect on Nehru. Many years later, in his keynote address to the Bandung Conference of 1955, the Indian leader paid tribute to Willi. It was one of the few times Münzenberg's actual place in modern politics has ever been publicly acknowledged.[83]

But of course neither Willi nor Gibarti had any genuine interest in pacifism as a means of anti-imperialist struggle; the apparatus's sole interest in pacifism, like its sole interest in any other subject, was Soviet power. The degree of Gibarti's indifference to real non-violence may be measured by the non-existent role pacifism played in the Comintern's propaganda policies in China in the period just before Brussels, and just before Stalin endorsed Jerram's plan. Gibarti had begun his anti-imperialist activities working in Berlin on the Comintern propaganda over China.

Whatever the purpose, the language of pacifist righteousness was being used to solidify a network, and that network could change its priorities as the needs of the time and the regime shifted. If it is properly run, an organization devoted to promoting peace can as easily promote war. It is simply a question of finding the right line. And this organization was guided by people who, when it came to finding the right line, were the best in the business.

Here we confront yet another major mystery in the history of communist thought. How could it be that while Münzenberg and his propagandists could have been wasting their energies on a campaign against a largely imaginary threat from the liberal democracies, Stalin remained almost systematically perverse in his response to gathering Nazi power? The year 1932, with its many frantic electoral campaigns in Germany, its banning and then legalization of the SA, its interminable demonstrations and wild provocations and street violence, made it plain to most informed observers that events were leading to Hitler's seizure of power. It was equally plain that that result was not inevitable. During the course of the year, the Nazis repeatedly swung from exulting confidence to despair. Clearly, Hitler's rise might have been stopped by a resolute but flexibly united center and left. Such a course, however, would have required communist participation and even leadership, and so required Stalin's consent. That consent he would not give. At a number of junctures Stalin might easily have ordered the German communists to enter a political alliance with the Social Democrats which might have put a permanent cap on the National Socialists' hopes. The Russian dictator understood the stakes; he did not fail to grasp the forces at work. It did not matter. He refused to act.

The explanation is only partly ideological. To the communists, the Social Democrats were not a left-wing party at all. They were the arch-enemy; the "true" fascists. In the cant of the day, they were "social fascists." Alliance with them was forbidden from Moscow. Meanwhile, the claim was spread through the apparatus that "Hitler was only a puppet whose installation in power was only bringing the victory of communism closer."[84] Today this view seems perverse to the point of insanity; yet there was a sense in which Stalin possibly was right. For the communists actually to have joined a real anti-Nazi coalition in this moment of moments might well have meant a surrender to bourgeois democratic forces, and the creation of a stabilized democratic regime such as the German Party, in its revolutionary form, could not have survived.

It is plain that the people closest to it accepted the "social fascist" line in the hope of real revolution: *their* revolution. Yet they were also torn between its promise and its manifest untruth. So it was with Münzenberg, whose specialty was after all that of creating the illusion of unity with precisely the adversaries the policy condemned. As the year progressed, Willi grew more and more agitated, torn, insomniac: At night he paced the rooms of his apartment, feeling anxiety and panic he otherwise could never let show, hoping for revolution, fearing the worst. Few understood better than he the interpenetration of Nazi and communist constituencies. "Brown on the outside," he would say of the unemployed urban tough guys in the SA, "red on the inside." Münzenberg had moreover significant links, most of them secret, with the left wing of the SA, especially as run by Gregor and Otto Strasser.[85] At least to this degree, and probably deeper, his apparatus reached into the Nazi party. Add to this the handicap of his oldest and deepest intellectual habit: revolutionary thought. Guided by "revolutionary" logic, everything in him despised the compromises of parliamentary peace. "I too prefer the red hundreds," he had said: And it was so. Willi really did hope, really did believe, that a true German revolution might, just really might, come out of these events. Babette Gross would recall standing with Münzenberg and other German leaders on a street corner just weeks before the Amsterdam Congress. It was the day of the internal quasi-legal shake-up of the German conservatives known as the "Papen coup." The situation was so fluid that revolutionary outbreaks were expected at any moment: Münzenberg and his people stood with Babette as if in a metaphoric flinch waiting for the explosion they expected the Papen coup to provoke. Instead, the Nazis, assisted by communist restraint, rolled on toward their victory unhindered by a united left. I recall a remark about this made to me by Babette, and remember especially her cold tone, controlling its bitterness: "*We wanted a revolution,*" she said. "*And we got one.*"

All this is the more striking when we consider that through 1932, as Nazi power was gathering force, Münzenberg was organizing in Amsterdam the largest assembly of the world-wide right-thinking left ever brought together in one place: the Amsterdam World Congress Against War. It took place in August 1932; yet the theme of this great Congress—note well—was not opposition to Nazism at all. It remained, and remained inexplicably, pacifism.

Pacifism? The Amsterdam World Congress Against War represented the triumph of Münzenberg and Gibarti's kind of political organizing: It was a pre-war high point in Münzenberg's capacity to draw the left in general into the Soviets' gravitational field. The Central Party Archives make it very clear: What happened in Holland was certainly a communist-controlled congress, but it was anything but a congress of communists—one of several reasons why its true sponsorship was mainly concealed.[86] The congress was genuinely diverse. While Stalin kept the German left fragmented, his propagandists gathered under one banner every branch of enlightened progressive opinion from around the world. Here, on the level of propaganda, was precisely the coalition Stalin had prohibited in practical fact. Enjoying their semblance of unity, the delegates gave themselves over to the gratifications of spectacle. It is said that Goebbels adopted much of Amsterdam's *son et lumière* for his own later totalitarian liturgies in Potsdam and Nuremberg. There were well over 2,000 delegates. They represented every stripe of left-wing opinion, from real pacifists to trade unionists; every political progressivism imaginable. The whole was covertly financed and run by the International; the cash flow, along with its secret accounts, was managed through couriers from Moscow meeting regularly with Münzenberg's confidential secretary.[87] But the congress generated the illusion of a vast diffuse goodwill, a wide united front.[88]

It was nothing of the kind. The essential and always neglected truth about this astonishing and delusive gathering is not its size or its extravagance but its almost breathtaking insistence upon addressing and attacking anything, *anything* except the prime political menace of the hour. On the contrary, a skeptical witness might plausibly claim that the goings-on in Amsterdam functioned more to distract the delegates from the Nazi threat than to confront it. Amsterdam took place during the very same days and hours, literally, that the National Socialists were most noxiously consolidating their strength. And yet much, *much* more time at Amsterdam was devoted to condemning the United States, to martyrizing Sacco and Vanzetti and the Scottsboro Boys, than was wasted on any undue attack upon the ''brown'' threat, even though that threat was right at their backs. There exists a German newsreel, made a mere two days after the Amsterdam Congress concluded, showing Willi striding into the Reichstag just steps away from Goebbels, ready to confront a new and even more desperate parliamentary round in the Nazi's ''legal'' advance. The disaster was taking place. Yet what was the Congress's response?

The truth is that while the sleepless Münzenberg may have agonized over Stalin's policy toward the Nazi rise, the Amsterdam congress was for all its fine sentiments and display of ''unity'' a propaganda shield designed to cover, precisely, Stalin's decision to let Hitler divide and conquer Germany. It was *part* of that policy; its was the face of that policy for the alarmed right-thinking world. In the weeks that the Nazi menace was gathering all its forces against a systematically divided German left, Münzenberg, working on orders from the regime, was busy distracting people with a grandiose illusion of *seeming* unanimity and strength.

Not for the first time, and certainly not for the last, Stalin was sponsoring the appearance of anti-fascism in such a way as to have the curious result of *not* hampering Hitler in any practical terms. Amsterdam was an assembly of what was potentially fierce anti-fascist opinion, the largest ever held. Yet it barely addressed the question of the Nazi rise. Never once was Amsterdam's spirit of unity taken up as something to be repeated by the left in Germany, unified to stop Hitler. *Amsterdam was not directed against the Nazis.* In August 1932! Even now the absurdity of it takes one's breath away.

But as we shall see, the absurdity was part of a larger illusion. From the days of Hitler's "legal" rise to power until the moment when the Nazi-Soviet Pact precipitated the Second World War, the Communist International's "anti-fascist" enterprise, of which Münzenberg was the European man-in-charge, never once presented a meaningful threat or even serious inconvenience to Nazi power. It is impossible to avoid the conclusion that it was, moreover, sometimes made innocuous by conscious political design. Comintern "anti-fascism" made a great deal of noise about the Nazis of course, but time and again the International managed to focus its perfectly real powers of disruption anywhere except on the Germans. The party fomented action all right, but there was not really much of it in Germany either before or after Hitler became Chancellor. It happened in Austria, in Spain, in countries where as it turned out even Hitler himself sometimes had mixed feelings about the "fascists" the communists were really attacking. When it came really to confronting the true Nazi menace head-on, from first to last, the Comintern's "anti-fascist" operation resorted to sound and fury, and refrained.

There is therefore, beneath the sinister bravura of these events, a deep and poignant political tragedy. Around the world, the will to resist on the part of enlightened people everywhere was significantly misled. The people whom Münzenberg had assembled in Amsterdam were the very people who, above all others, might have stopped Hitler's advance. These were the people who knew why it had to be stopped, and who might really have stopped it if the organization mobilizing and guiding them had chosen to do so. These were the most enlightened figures in the worldwide political left: from trade unionists, pacifists, and plain old socialists to anarchists, idealists, and agitators. The place was overflowing with right-thinking journalists and idealistic opinion-makers. Here was the cream of the political constituency that might have joined in a genuinely effective coalition of opposition, an international version of that indispensable coalition of the German center and left which the desperate hour so obviously required. Here was a group which might have played some real role arresting the horrors about to be unleashed upon Europe.

But no. Münzenberg's apparatus was resolute in guiding these delegates into opposing any evil *except* the Nazi evil. Amsterdam was a Congress of the right people; God knows it gathered at the right moment. But did it name and meet the right enemy? The crisis of legality in Weimar was unfolding hour by hour. The Soviet invisible hand held the weapon of enlightened opinion in the West firmly in its grip. And it waved that weapon in the face of any adversary it could think of *except* the nightmare one so obviously before it.

Of course, such a thing could not last. Pacifism and anti-Imperialism and anti-Americanism, however lavishly Amsterdam featured them all—these were varieties of righteousness which for the moment had run their course. They were about to vanish, for at least the next ten years, from the vocabulary of the Soviet-sponsored left. Münzenberg's apparatus was about to be totally transformed by precisely what it had contrived to permit.

It was about to be transformed by Hitler.

Chapter 2

Fire and Fraud

Berlin: February 27, 1933. The night was moonlit and freezing, and Adolf Hitler had been Chancellor of Germany for exactly one month. The streets of the central city were almost deserted. At 9:40 a theological student, hurrying home hunched against the cold, was crossing the empty plaza in front of the somber granite pile of the Reichstag—a monument to Kaiser Wilhelm's taste in architecture—when he glanced up and caught inside the glass and steel dome the small, soundless orange flicker of what looked oddly like fire. And fire it was. Within a short time the orange flicker was filling the entire dome with what were obviously roiling flames, and not long after that the inferno pent within burst up through the melting and shattering glass and roared high into the night sky, while whatever was left of Weimar democracy sank into its final and fatal convulsion.[1]

In the weeks before, Münzenberg had been carefully prepared for Hitler's assumption of power, which seems to have been quite clearly foreseen by the Soviets. Three months after the Amsterdam Congress, in early January 1933, several weeks before Hitler became the Chancellor on January 30, Münzenberg was summoned to Moscow for consultations on the German situation. There plans were laid for him to move his headquarters to Paris in the event the situation "deteriorated further."[2]

And when the situation did precisely that, Münzenberg, for one, knew perfectly well that he was in grave danger and appropriate precautions had been taken. The night Hitler took office, not long after his return from the Moscow consultations, Münzenberg left his lavish apartment on the Tiergarten, never to return. Berlin on that night of January 30, 1933, was streaming with the SA's celebratory torchlight parades, and though he was still a public man, still a member of the Reichstag, it was obvious that Münzenberg should no longer be spending his nights in a place where he could easily be found. A safe apartment had been prepared for him in an obscure new building in a worker's quarter of West Berlin, and there he was driven, crawling through the fascist celebrations.[3] Legality was unravelling fast; the impending terror storm must have been palpable. The chanting of the mindless minions as they waved their torches was only the ceremonial manifestation of the organized SA sadism which now riddled German life, and which was about to become a new state.

Münzenberg's chauffeur and bodyguard was a young man named Emil, a tough young son of the Berlin working class. That night Emil drove the boss in the Lincoln, and as they crept west through the besotted city they would have passed near the Chancellory. There, lit by the blazing windows, bobbing and prancing in delight, Hitler looked down as his followers filed past in fascist ecstasy. In a separate window, von Hindenburg stood near, stolidly thumping his cane to the beat of the rising martial chants.

And then, a month later, came the Reichstag Fire, and with it the actual execution of the death sentence on Weimar that had been passed when Hitler took power. The fire took Münzenberg by surprise; for that matter it seems to have taken Hitler by surprise as well. The burning of the German legislature took place on the second-to-last night of February 1933, thirty days after Reichspresident von Hindenburg had appointed Adolf Hitler the Republic's last legal Chancellor. Who set the Reichstag Fire, and why, remains one of the enduring mysteries in the history of totalitarianism. Its circumstances are wrapped, perhaps permanently in multiple clouds of disinformation and lies. Yet the Reichstag Fire blazons a very clear mark on the landscape of modern history; it was one of those occasional moments after which the whole of political life is unmistakably changed.

This spectacular catastrophe was the pretext by which German totalitarianism was brought into being. In response to the arson, the newly and legally elected Chancellor Hitler seized the police powers which he knew were essential to his plan to strangle Weimar democracy and establish absolute Nazi power in Germany. With it, Hitler embarked upon his war of state-sponsored terror against his "enemies": the Jews and the democratic Allies who had imposed the Versailles treaty.

But his first target was the German communists, and it was on the communists that Hitler blamed the fire. Georgi Dimitrov, a Bulgarian Stalinist and leading figure in the Comintern, along with two of his lieutenants and Ernst Torgler, an important politician in the German Party, were seized and charged with organizing the conspiracy to set the fire. With German communism thus under attack, the Soviet Union naturally responded, returning assault for assault, or at least propaganda for propaganda, and for the first time, the Soviets moved into what seemed a genuinely confrontational collision course with the emerging Nazi government. Hitler ordered a great show trial to be held in Leipzig, condemning the communists he had rounded up and accused of the fire, showing how the German Communist party had to be wiped out of the Reich. Münzenberg's apparatus, in turn, was ordered to transform the "Peace" movement and use it to mount a new, world-wide anti-fascist campaign pinning the fire on the Nazis themselves, and assailing the new regime. It was to be the first great confrontation between the two totalitarian states, and in the obviously gathering crisis, the Soviet state under Stalin was assuming the moral high ground.

Or so it seemed.

Based on the flamboyant evidence of this confrontation and the reflexive loathing that so obviously animated it, a new myth for the enlightened began to take shape. That myth would, in turn, shape many of the essential assumptions of the political thirties. It held that the Marxist-Leninist state, whatever troubling failings it might manifest as it struggled to reach socialism, had at least the virtue of being inherently, genuinely, almost involuntarily opposed to Nazism. As such, communism seemed to represent the only *real* resistance to the new horror so obviously taking shape. The democracies, through their real and supposed inaction, were depicted as bound by capitalism either to the ineffectiveness of liberalism—or worse, to a secret sympathy for the Nazis, fascist brothers under the skin. This myth therefore assigned moralized roles, casting the struggle between the two states as the definitive struggle between good and evil in the century. In it, the Stalinist line became good, or at least necessary to the good, by virtue of its supposed opposition to Hitler's evil.

It was a tremendously persuasive argument. Several generations of the most enlightened people in the West accepted it, or came close to accepting it. By 1935, the logic of this approach was extended to a new world-wide effort to capture the loyalties of the enlightened West in the great propaganda fraud known as the Popular Front, which used the claims of "anti-fascism" to keep enlightened sympathizers in line as the Great Terror ran its course. The Popular Front was if possible more far-reaching, more chic, more completely conformist even than Stalinist fellow-travelling in Paris during Sartre's heyday. While the slaughter rolled on, the Front captured the allegiance of uncountable numbers among the most intelligent people of their generation—people who, we cannot doubt, really did wish to serve intellectual freedom and human liberty, incited by the fascist menace and the addictive sensation of feeling right, *being* right, irresistibly right against the bourgeois wrong, right above all against a wrong so obvious as the wrong in Germany. What made them right? In a classic error, they were certain that the wrong made them right. By the thousands they joined. Stalin's logic was simple: Let the well-intentioned wring their hands over the slaughters in Moscow. No matter. Decent people would never dare turn their backs on "anti-fascism." *Any attack on Stalin is an endorsement of Hitler.*

The tremendous moral credit inuring to this new myth, which was added to (and was much greater than) the already existing moral credit of Revolution itself, came flowing toward the Soviets at exactly the moment that Stalin's government was moving toward its own most sinister and brutal phase. Paradox? It was not a paradox born in coincidence. It was a deception, and it was planned. For this first great confrontation between the totalitarian powers was itself a deception, and in every way a very different thing from what it appeared to be.

All this began with Hitler's seizure of power, and the Reichstag Fire. The actual Reichstag arson seems to have taken Hitler himself completely off guard. Almost no student of the event believes the dictator himself ordered the fire, and—note well—neither did Münzenberg's men at any point stress Hitler's personal role. Hitler had been dining that evening with Goebbels and his family. Word of the fire came by telephone as the group sat listening to records after dinner. Goebbels at first took the call as a practical joke and slammed down the phone. Only after a second call did the party break up as the Chancellor grasped the truth. "*Now I have them!*" he shouted in astonished delight, and left at once to be rushed to the fire.[4]

Whether he had foreknowledge or not, once on the scene Hitler instantly grasped its rich possibilities for demagogy and just as quickly seized on them in something like a caricature of the Hitlerian frenzy. Led to a balcony overlooking the Sessions Chamber, by then brimful with waves of flame, ''Hitler was leaning over the stone parapet, gazing into the red ocean of fire.'' Suddenly, he swung round. ''His face had turned quite scarlet, both from the excitement and also from the heat . . . and he suddenly started screaming at the top of his voice: 'Now we'll show them! Anyone who stands in our way will be mown down. The German people have been soft too long. Every Communist official must be shot. All Communist deputies must be hanged this very night. All the friends of the Communists must be locked up. And that goes for the Social Democrats and the *Reichsbanner* as well.' ''[5]

Thus was the Nazi line promulgated on the spot. Hitler decreed that this attack on German political life was a Communist outrage, a signal for leftist insurrection. The Reds were trying to storm the Berlin citadel with this bonfire; it had been set to rouse every subversive in the country against the re-emergent Reich. They were scared of the fascist power galvanizing around them; they were trying to grab the new Germany for themselves. But they weren't going to get away with it.

The Nazis had been looking for a pretext to strike and now they had one. The next day, Hitler promulgated the infamous Emergency Decree of February 28, the juridical cornerstone of Nazi totalitarianism. The idea girding its hysterical rhetoric was simple: The German police were no longer responsible to the judiciary. Thus empowered, the police worked through the night, and before the freezing break of day, the arrest squads were tramping through the streets of Berlin and the other major cities, legally completely unrestrained. Nor were they unprepared. Warrants by the thousands had already been stockpiled in the principal stations, signed and sealed in advance, with the names left blank, ready to be filled in with any Communist, or indeed anyone at all, that Göring and his minions wanted to haul in. They were the blank checks of state terror. The Gestapo-to-be scooped them up in piles.

None of this should have surprised any knowing observer. Hitler had steadily promised to destroy German communism, and now exactly fulfilling his promise, he struck.

Incredibly, most German communists, even many of the senior ones, at least appeared to be almost totally unprepared for that violence, and for most of them, this lack of preparation was quite real. Münzenberg himself, though he had been through the best briefings in Moscow, was only half-prepared for the threat. From the start, the Comintern had seemed systematically to underestimate the Hitlerian menace. The Amsterdam Congress itself ideally illustrates that policy; so does the ''erroneous'' doctrine of ''social fascism.'' Even as late as the Popular Front, and later, all the way to the end of communism, the lie was pushed: There is an unseen brotherhood between democrats and fascists which only the radical mind can expose.

Much about Hitler was underestimated in 1933, chief among them his uncanny *speed*. Nobody suspected that he could destroy the Weimar Republic in a single month or that by the middle of the next year von Hindenburg, that Teutonic grandee who had once deprecated Hitler as the "little corporal," would be on his deathbed addressing his Chancellor in a moribund senile babble as "your Majesty."[6] Among those minimizing the threat were the German communists.[7] After a last meeting with the editors of his daily papers, Münzenberg remarked that the German Party's leadership reminded him of "dancers who had failed to notice that the curtain had come down."[8] Yet ten days before Hitler's accession, Moscow had forbidden any forcible resistance to a huge SA demonstration outside Party headquarters. Ten days before the Reichstag Fire, the cream of the German left gathered for one last divided display of impotence. The Communist left assembled in one hall, the Social Democrats in another. Then came the fire, and the dictator struck.

Willi seems to have escaped arrest himself because of a flukish stroke of good fortune. Münzenberg was certainly among the most senior members of the International on the Nazi hit list, and that morning at first light, an arrest squad was at the door of the Tiergarten apartment. Of course Münzenberg was not there, nor had he been there for over a month. But he was not even in Berlin. Several hundred communist officials had already been arrested in the night, but Münzenberg was away, delivering a speech near Frankfurt-am-Main. He'd spent the night with WIR operatives there. When the police came knocking in Berlin, the door was answered by Münzenberg's indispensable confidential secretary, a young man named Hans Schulz. If only they had known! Schulz, with his plain, pale, deferential looks and gimpy leg carried in his photographic memory, famous throughout the *apparat,* untold and untellable amounts of secret information about covert operations in Germany and around the world. Schulz was Willi Münzenberg's personal contact with the deep-cover apparatus, carefully trained to be the keeper of Willi's secrets. It was Hans's memory that stored the information no one would dream of entrusting to paper. Hans simply *was* the right (or is it left?) hand of Münzenberg's secrecy; he was, in a sense, the unseen Willi. Long ago sent to Moscow for his education in secret work, Hans carried in that head more politically sensitive information than any twenty of the other communists rounded up that night. To the police, Hans Schulz looked like a rather washed-out little clerk, who very deferentially showed them from room to room. And of course they did not find their man.[9]

From Berlin the disappointed arrest squad flashed word to Frankfurt. There Münzenberg's haunts were well enough known for a second squad to be instantly dispatched to his favorite café. They were right: At that very moment, the Comintern's propaganda chief was strolling toward his breakfast, carrying a handful of his own newspapers, ready to catch up on the sensational news about last night's fire.

He never reached the café door.

I say the police failed to understand who Hans Schulz was. Yet it may be that some in the squad knew more than they admitted. Hitler's move to crush the German Communist party was made possible only by a simultaneous move from partial to absolute control over the German police, and at that moment, contrary to the common myth, the Berlin police were generally leftish.[10] That is one thing that gave Ernst Röhm's brownshirts their menacing importance; the need for a more fully obedient corps would also require Hitler completely to remake the German police by inventing the Gestapo. The last morning of February 1933 was the precise moment at which Germany was being transformed from a state with police into a police state, and it is notable that for Münzenberg's flight, the decisive move came from a cop. Just as the squad gathered to leave, a tiny event of revelatory interest took place in the foyer. One of the officers, who happened to recognize Hans Schulz's wife, the daughter of a prominent Social Democratic police official, took her aside and whispered: *Run. Warn your friends and run.* He was telling her what he knew and they did not. Overnight, the world had changed.[11]

This transgression in the direction of decency may well have saved Münzenberg.

Only a few minutes after the police had left the Berlin apartment, Babette Gross telephoned from Frankfurt, desperate for news. The cop's warning was repeated. Without it, she, her husband, all of them might have been rounded up with the other German communist leaders. Babette acted immediately. Münzenberg was to meet Emil in the café of the Frankfurt train station. The task now was to prevent that rendezvous. She and Emil rushed to the square in front of the station and posted themselves at each entrance. When he hoved into sight, he was springy, full of nerve even in danger, carrying his papers, looking forward to his coffee. Emil ran forward, took his startled boss by the arm, and gently but firmly led him to the car, as Babette jumped in and Emil began to drive.

The old life was over. Emil drove blindly, on the first road out of Frankfurt. It happened to be heading south. Münzenberg was running without a visa or passport; his driver didn't know where he was driving. Suddenly Babette Gross remembered that she had a relation in the neighborhood. Her sister Margarete had been previously married to a son of Martin Buber, and Martin Buber lived nearby, in Darmstadt. To Darmstadt they drove. It was far too dangerous for the Bubers to attempt to hide Willi there, but Emil took the car to within a couple of miles from the house, and Babette walked, alone, to her sometime relations' door. The Bubers were aghast seeing the terrified woman on their step and immediately grasped the danger. Buber had one useful suggestion. The Saar was perhaps seventy miles away. Though German, it was—as the result of a bitterly resented provision of the Versailles Treaty—not under German control. It was beyond the reach of the German police. It could be entered without a visa, and Buber had a colleague there, a professor whom he mistakenly believed could be trusted. Entering the Saar *did* require a passport however, and at this moment Münzenberg's passport was as good as an arrest warrant. In any case, he did not have it with him.

A new passport could be found only in Frankfurt. Armed with Buber's letter of introduction, Babette and Emil drove back north and, leaving Münzenberg on a promenade beside the Rhine in the suburb of Mainz, returned to the city. On this day when German totalitarianism was officially born, it was also carnival, and carnival was in full swing. Every office was closed; the streets were filled not only with police, but drunks and revellers. Leaving Emil below, Babette proceeded to the offices of a Trust publishing house, which she found deserted except for one young comrade, who was fourteen years younger than Münzenberg, and looked nothing like him. But some sort of passport was essential, now. The youth promptly turned over his. Below, the streets were delirious. The carnival processions swirled around her, but Babette could not find Emil. She ran to a nearby café they both knew. A waiter turned her back at the door with the news that the arrest squad had already been there, looking for her husband.

When she found Emil again it had begun to snow, and as they drove back to Mainz night was falling. They found Münzenberg wandering alone by the river.

It was time to move. The Lincoln crawled through the blowing dark, looking for the most deserted country byways heading west.

They felt their way to the border. The Saar would be only a way-station on their escape: Visas for entry into France still had to be finagled; Babette Gross would still have to return to Berlin for an essential supply of secret cash deposited with the Soviet ambassador. Nor was the Saar without its own dangers: Buber's colleague, possibly a crypto-Nazi, proved less reliable than supposed. But unless he got out of Germany proper, and quickly, Münzenberg was lost. He had to have an incognito; he had to cross the border; he had to disappear. For this, only the Saar would do.

It was deep in the small hours when the Lincoln pulled into the tiny customs station on the border. The snow was still flying across the almost deserted road. A guard walked out, leaned into the dark car, and waved his flashlight from face to face. Then he paused. Without asking for passports, the guard gave Emil a weary wave-through.

We can only imagine what must have been singing through the young driver's mind as he hit the accelerator and made that long heavy limousine move on out.[12]

All at once, an era was coming together.

Hitler had seized totalitarian power. Within a matter of days after the events in Germany, workmen in distant Washington would hammer together the platform on the steps of the United States Capitol Building where Franklin Roosevelt would take the presidential oath for the first time and then tell Americans that the only thing they had to fear was fear itself.

As for Münzenberg, once he had crossed the German border on that snowy first *Walpurgisnacht* of the Nazi terror, his path to Paris was reasonably direct. He remained hidden in the Saarland for perhaps a week, waiting for the apparatus to finagle the papers necessary for his entry into France. While he was still there, the Comintern in Moscow was undoubtedly informed of his whereabouts and the Party in France alerted to his imminent arrival. Then in early March, Emil drove the boss across the French border and directly to the City of Light.[13]

The great crisis in the history of German communism—in the history of Germany—had come. It was at this same time, in early March 1933, that Stalin ordered his apparatus to begin its campaign of counter-propaganda to Hitler's moves, a campaign in which Willi's apparatus, shifted to Paris, would play a major role. It was likewise at this time, and quite possibly earlier, that the Russian tyrant began in the deepest possible secrecy, to shape his real, rather than proclaimed, policy toward the new German government. Even among the most senior Bolsheviks, the number of officials privy to Stalin's true approach to the new menace were minuscule. Significantly, the chiefs of the Red Army and other armed forces were not among them, though key figures within the secret services most emphatically were.

Despite the outward appearance of hostility and confrontation emanating from such operations as Münzenberg's new ''anti-fascist'' campaign in Paris, the true policy of the Soviet government to Hitler's seizure of totalitarian power was in fact one of placation and appeasement. In the secret development of this policy, the most important insider of all was Münzenberg's old cohort Karl Radek. Radek the propagandist had been entrusted with the crucial task of shaping the ''anti-fascist'' movement, both in diplomacy and propaganda—a task in which his indispensable European right hand would be his old comrade Münzenberg.[14] The Central Party Archives in Moscow contain the originals of letters, personally signed by Radek himself and probably dispatched in code, giving specific instructions to agents in Berlin on the management of the Dimitrov trial.[15] But Radek played a more sinister role than that. For many years, among all the senior Bolsheviks, he was the most knowing on the subject of Germany, and from the days of the Revolution he had played a large role, both open and under cover, in Soviet-German relations. Even with the advent of Hitler, and despite the fact that he himself was a Jew, Radek was never really in favor of a genuinely anti-German policy. Neither was Stalin. ''Only fools can imagine we would ever break with Germany,'' Radek confided to his friend and fellow Pole, the intelligence officer Walter Krivitsky, at the height of the time Radek was in charge of guiding the ''anti-fascism.'' ''What I am writing here is one thing. The realities are something else. No one can give us what Germany has given us. For us to break with Germany is simply impossible.'' At the same time that Münzenberg was establishing himself in Paris, Radek was sent by Stalin into top-secret contacts with the German ambassador in Moscow, acting as the Soviet dictator's direct, confidential emissary. These discussions took place without the knowledge of the Soviet diplomatic service or the army. And the contents of these talks were . . . negotiations over matters directed toward mutual benefit.[16]

Simultaneously, a very high-level secret agent, a man who was very well known to Willi, was dispatched from Moscow to Paris, acting as the liaison between the Kremlin chieftains and the Europeans, and bearing precise instructions for Münzenberg on how to direct the new anti-fascist movement world-wide. This covert operative was also a protégé of Radek, very much within Radek's confidence. And he came to the West with specific instructions from Radek.[17]

This secret agent would play one of the most sinister and extraordinary roles in the era. A vast campaign, having as its first point of focus the Reichstag Fire, was organized in Paris, closely co-ordinated both with the vigilant operative from Moscow, and with the European and American *apparat*.[18] It would be the founding event of the anti-fascist campaign, and in that sense the first direct confrontation of the Second World War.

The propaganda campaign which Münzenberg would direct from Paris was designed both to facilitate and to cover this actual, and secret, relation between the German and Soviet governments. Stalin needed to appear entirely hostile to Hitler and Hitlerism; Münzenberg would help him create that appearance, as a cover for the actual appeasement going on and providing it with deniability. It would be, as we shall see, and as has not been understood before, a method whereby the actual acts of collaboration between the two dictators could be carried out.

The new anti-fascist campaign which Willi created with Radek raged. It filled the world press. Everything about it had the look of complete hostility and total confrontation. Meanwhile the Nazis in their arrests of German communists and with the show trial over the Reichstag Fire which Hitler now set out to mount, were no less directed to fierce confrontation. Among enlightened and educated Westerners, the communist campaign was of course by far the more plausible of the two; in fact it was persuasive—above all to anyone who needed little persuading about the Nazis. It hit the Nazis hard, especially the SA, and hit them again and again. To be sure, it promoted a number of falsehoods of its own, but they were all very plausible falsehoods, and besides, here at last was something like true anti-fascism. It seemed in essence right, and obviously so. How could it not be?

So it seemed. Except that nothing was as it seemed.

The focus of the Nazi campaign was Hitler's trial of the people he claimed were responsible for setting the fire and seeking to create a communist insurrection against the National Socialist State. While the Sessions Chamber of the German legislature was still a maelstrom of flames, the Berlin police had rushed into the smoking corridors and nabbed, red-handed, a singed, shirtless, and hysterical young man named Marinus van der Lubbe, who was immediately arrested and led away shouting "Protest! Protest!" in a thick Dutch accent.[19]

Marinus van der Lubbe was plainly one of the arsonists, and the only one ever caught. He claimed from the beginning that he had acted alone, and he persisted in saying so until he was beheaded a year later under the Leipzig guillotine.

Van der Lubbe's plain, simple, numb claim to sole responsibility was inconvenient. Nobody on either side wanted an incendiary who really had acted alone. Once Hitler had proclaimed the fire a communist conspiracy, the Nazis needed communist conspirators, not this solitary shirtless nit-wit. Nonetheless, instead of merely shooting their captive, the Nazis decided to exploit the fact that his seizure in the ruins had instantly made him world-famous. At least, he was incontestably guilty. So the Nazis would prop van der Lubbe in the dock surrounded by sundry Communist big-wigs whom they hoped, by hook or crook, to link to the Dutchman in a show trial justifying the anti-Communist terror.

Large-scale arrests of German Communists had been going on since that night. Yet some ten days after the conflagration, by what seemed peculiarly good luck, the Berlin police netted three particularly sensational communist fish. One of the arrested men turned out to be no less than Georgi Dimitrov, a senior Comintern officer and leading Bulgarian associate of Stalin; a famous and practiced conspirator. Dimitrov was accompanied by two fellow Bulgarians, Simon Popov and Vassili Tanev, who were quite obviously his lieutenants.

The three men were arrested on a tip-off from a waiter in a restaurant where they had gone to dine. It was a very odd restaurant for three foreign undercover operatives from the Comintern to choose; they had gone to dinner, at the height of an anti-communist police campaign, in a restaurant that was a favorite Nazi hangout, packed with people for whom arresting communists was a prime concern. The three Bulgarians entered this establishment as ostentatiously as possible and ordered their meal. With their alien looks and foreign accents, they attracted attention. When asked for their papers, the papers they produced were so crudely forged they were proved to be false within hours—though they were being carried by a senior official of a Comintern world-famous for its flawless forgeries.[20] They were arrested, and in no time indicted, along with a Communist deputy of the Reichstag Ernst Torgler, and van der Lubbe, as the masterminds of the arson.

Dimitrov's arrest and even his presence in Germany at the time of the fire remain highly mysterious. Dimitrov was a senior conspirator, not ordinarily assigned to Germany. His mere presence in the country at that moment requires explanation. It seems clear that Dimitrov was arrested while on some clandestine mission commissioned by Stalin himself. Precisely what this mission may have been has never been discovered.[21] Important members of the *apparat* have asserted that Stalin himself intentionally set up Dimitrov for the arrest. If so, why? If Dimitrov had been in any real danger from the Nazis, the explanation might have been that

Stalin was trying to rid himself of this complex Bulgarian operative by handing him over to the fascists. Radek's communications with agents in Berlin express concern that Dimitrov and his lieutenants might be "in direct danger." But this may have been tactical, either a claim made *pro forma* to an agent not in the loop, or a legitimate expression of anxiety felt before the deal was made. But as we shall see, it has become increasingly clear that despite appearances Dimitrov was never in any real danger while in Berlin. Indeed, this major Stalinist had rarely been safer. It would appear that Dimitrov's true assignment may well have been simply to enter Germany as conspicuously as possible and be arrested, arrested quite intentionally, in the days after the Reichstag Fire. In any case he was arrested.

Dimitrov's fellow Bulgarians, Simon Popov and Vassili Tanev, were both Comintern lieutenants. They look like the Rosencrantz and Guildenstern of the piece. After the Leipzig trial, when Dimitrov and the Bulgarians were acquitted and released—for they were, all three, acquitted and released—they were flown "home" to Moscow, where they were greeted with every possible sign of victory and rejoicing. There all three sat for heroic statues.[22] In due course, Stalin rewarded the new anti-fascist celebrity Dimitrov with promotion to the increasingly hollow position of director of the Comintern.

Popov and Tanev, however, did not fare so well. After their moment in the sun both were dispatched to the gulag, perhaps because they understood that moment too well. Tanev was never heard of again. Popov managed to crawl through all those endless days and endless years in the hell of cold—twenty years in all—until a thaw in 1955 led to his release.

But as we follow the unfolding of these events, it will become plain that this famous founding confrontation between the Marxist-Leninist state and the National Socialists was in reality largely a facade concocted between their two secret services for ends very different from anything then visible. The Communist campaign against the Leipzig trial was not in the least the straightforward attack on Nazi power which it appeared to be. Nor did the Nazi action in Leipzig have anything like this mere attack on the communists as its genuine end. The show was in fact almost certainly a covertly controlled collaboration between the two dictators. Six years before the Nazi-Soviet Pact, on the very first day of Hitler's power, the dictators were already secretly waltzing together, in full collaboration. It was a collaboration developed in deep mutual hatred, to be sure, but even so it was a collaboration; it served common ends, ends which did not challenge, but consolidated, the power of each. All this was happening under the cover—the ideal cover—of the anti-fascist campaign

Münzenberg was now creating. The outrage of battle took shape as an ideal mask, and half a century later, that mask is still firmly in place, even though it is a mask on the face of a corpse.

Many people, for obvious reasons, have for a long time had their reservations about the myth of a heroic communist resistance to Hitler before the war. But most have assumed that for all its faults, Stalin's anti-fascism was at least genuinely anti-fascist.

In truth, it both was and was not. We should consider a little more closely the motives of both dictators in this epochal charade.

Why were the communists prepared to co-operate in any way with the Nazis, who were so manifestly intent upon the destruction of communism? From the days of *Mein Kampf,* a book Stalin first read right about this time, Hitler had promised that his first order of business upon taking power would be to strike down the German Communist party, and in March 1933, he had neither the inclination nor the option to renege on this central pledge. Even so, Hitler did not want to antagonize Stalin unduly or prematurely. The Red Army *was* the Red Army. Above all, he did not want to provoke Stalin (or for that matter the Versailles signatories) into anything like military action before he was ready. Therefore the anti-Communist terror must take place. Everything demanded it. But it also must not threaten Stalin too dangerously. Hitler would have to act on his anti-Communist pledge while simultaneously placating Stalin through some special, mutually beneficial, and unpublished arrangement.

Remember we are still six years from the Nazi-Soviet Pact. That it was Stalin who most eagerly sought the Soviet alliance with Hitler in 1939 has long been well known. It is less well known that from the beginning, Stalin was secretly trying to engage Hitler in conciliation, appeasement, and alliance under the cover of confrontational "anti-fascist" talk.[23] Münzenberg's response to the Reichstag Fire was merely the first round.

It is not that Stalin failed to see Hitler as a threat: He saw everyone as a threat. But Stalin also believed in coming quickly to terms with a strong opponent. He did not pick fights with people who were even close to his own size. He therefore responded to Hitler with the classic combination of the carrot and stick. It was not a very serious stick; it was a stick mainly of words and diversionary covert action. But he swung it in a very distracting way.

Meanwhile, if Germany was going to re-arm, Stalin wanted it to re-arm for war in the West. Until the day that Nazi troops streamed across his own borders, it seems to have been a linchpin of Stalin's planning that

Hitler would never, *never,* embark upon a two-front European war. Not that Stalin necessarily opposed a European war as such. Like many Marxist-Leninists, Stalin probably saw the gathering storm as an inevitable and even desirable phase in the demolition of the bourgeoisie. But Stalin also understood history as ordaining that the new war be fought between the bourgeois powers. He wanted France, Britain, and the United States to menace Hitler. If there was to be a war, he wanted war in Western Europe, not Russia, and between what he viewed as the bourgeois powers, which would, preferably, destroy each other in the process. He did very little saber-rattling of his own.

In the meantime, the world's foremost communist was perfectly prepared to let large numbers of his beloved German comrades be trapped in the Nazi round-ups—especially if his secret service could have the proper input into which of them were arrested, and when.[24] Stalin was never, after all, notably protective of his own comrades, be they foreign or domestic. On the contrary: Nazi liquidation might well spare him troublesome actions he otherwise would have to undertake on his own.[25]

A further unseen purpose of the anti-fascist campaign was moral cooption. The communists were by no means the only people reacting with fear and loathing to German events. As the senior Bolshevik generally in charge of the anti-fascist response, and a practiced specialist in German politics, Radek was instructed to craft a new line lavishly admiring the Versailles treaty, which until then had been the object of incessant Communist invective.[26] In fact the Versailles signatories were very alarmed.[27] That the Versailles powers, including the United States, were not sufficiently alarmed to act with preemptive force to remove the Nazis from power in Germany in 1933 or 1934 is of course one of the greatest tragedies in all of human history. Nonetheless, Stalin saw that for the foreseeable future, a fully justified fear of fascism would dominate left-wing and even most centrist political morality in the democracies. He wanted the apparatus on the moral high ground. When the going got tough, the USSR would be needing anti-fascism's ethical authority.

Yet another purpose of the anti-fascist movement was intimately bound to the moral logic of the dual policy. This was espionage. Thousands of bright and idealistic young people in the liberal democracies would be recruited to Stalin's sphere of influence through the moral fervor of their response to the Hitlerian menace. Stalin could use the moral cover of anti-fascism to proceed to infiltrate Western governments. From these ranks came many of the great journalistic scandals of years to come: Burgess and Maclean, Hiss and Chambers.

Both the "anti-fascism" of 1933 and the Popular Front covered secret service recruitment. In 1939, Walter Krivitsky laid out the general map of this part of the Front with succinct clarity in his best-selling book. Under the Popular Front, he pointed out that: (1) The British establishment was targeted for espionage recruitment. Here is where we discover phenomena like the Cambridge group of spies. (2) The Washington bureaucracy of the New Deal was penetrated. Here is the circle around Münzenberg's American men, the circle of agents that included such people as Noel Field and, it is said, Alger Hiss. (3) The French government of the Popular Front was shot through with Soviet agents. The facts were published, and the facts were ignored.

Here is what Krivitsky wrote. In Great Britain, "anti-fascist slogans captured a substantial number of students, writers and trade union leaders. During the Spanish tragedy and in the Munich days, many scions of the British aristocracy enlisted both in the International Brigade (the army of the Comintern in Spain) *and in our intelligence services*" (my emphasis).[28] Thus the basis of the Cambridge recruitment casually dropped twelve full years before Burgess and Maclean had to run. Then came America: Bright young people from the Ivy League were the obvious targets. "With the thousands of recruits enlisted under the banner of democracy, the Communist Party OGPU espionage ring in the United States grew much larger and penetrated previously untouched territory. *By carefully concealing their identity, Communists found their way into hundreds of key positions*" (my italics). Finally, there was France, in many ways the most thoroughly penetrated of all:

> The *Front Populaire* was so intimately tied up with the Franco-Soviet alliance that it all but captured the government structure. True, there were those like Leon Blum who tried to keep the military situation from affecting internal politics, but to a large extent such efforts failed. Most of France, from General Gamelin and conservative deputy De Kerillis to trade union leader Jouhaux were so obsessed with the idea that France's security was linked to Moscow that the *Front Populaire* became the dominant fact of French life. On the surface, the Comintern operated through its sugar-coated organizations. Newspapers like *Ce Soir,* book clubs, publicity houses, theaters, motion picture companies—all became instruments of Stalin's "anti-Hitler front."Behind the scenes, the OGPU and the Soviet Military Intelligence were working feverishly for a stranglehold on the state institutions of France.[29]

The dimensions in espionage ran deep. Recruitment reached a very high level of sophistication; schools for training these recruits were created in Russia. If idealists could be made to believe that alone among the world's senior politicians, only Stalin *really* opposed Hitler, all kinds of people in or near the Western governments—right-thinking youths fresh from Cambridge, star *normaliens,* progressive young Ivy Leaguers at State—could be recruited into that battle and meticulously led into the secret work which had been the point from the start.

Meanwhile, when the nightmares of the Great Terror were unleashed, sympathizers all around the world could be induced to avert their eyes from the obvious truth—that Stalin was a murdering tyrant and the Revolution over which he presided a murdering tyranny—because who else was standing up to Hitler?

Who indeed?

In truth, both dictators were ideologically dependent on their mutual hatred. Each needed a monster to hate, and each found that need consummated in the other. The monster fascism, born of the Counter-Enlightenment, fulfilled the rationale of its loathing by directing itself against communism, *its* necessary monster, born of the Enlightenment.

Of course both fully intended to destroy the other—but each feared any premature military confrontation. This fear was the grounds for their collaboration.[30] Hitler was not entirely unafraid of an attack by Russia; and he was actively fearful of a preemptive strike by the Allies. Hence the illusion of confrontation and the secret fact of collaboration. To this, Stalinists added moral co-option of Western anti-fascism to their new myth; a myth given depth by the work of espionage and the simultaneous establishment of the networks and cadres in Germany and Eastern Europe essential to establishing Soviet power and eliminating all non-Stalinist rivals once the time for seizing real power came, after 1945.

Finally, there is the perverse logic of revolution itself. The notion that fascism was a necessary rite of passage toward revolution was widely held by Marxist-Leninists of the time. So was the recognition of a close proximity between the two ideologies. Fascism—the "icebreaker of the Revolution." It was a favorite Marxist cliché. Münzenberg himself used to speak of how the urban underclass that filled the Nazi ranks was composed of exactly the same people who provided the communists with their mass base.

"Brown on the outside," as he said. "Red on the inside."[31]

"*We wanted a revolution. And we got one.*"

Of course, most of the people who worked in Münzenberg's anti-fascist campaigns knew nothing whatever of all this. They believed in the anti-fascist cause and believed in it passionately. They served it passionately. Many gave their lives for it. Cynicism rarely generates loyalty and sacrifice of the kind that came into play during those extraordinary days. Real cognizance, meanwhile, was for the very few. How the fully witting agents of this lie rationalized, or failed to rationalize, their double lives must be left to the dark side of the study of souls. But almost everyone fighting in Münzenberg's anti-fascist campaigns was being used. Moreover they *were* fighting, often with wonderful bravery, and against the right enemy. Stalin wanted to take the moral high ground for evil reasons. But it *was* the moral high ground. Their heroism may have been compromised, but it was not diminished, by the way in which they were used.

If the name of Willi Münzenberg still retains the glow of some heroic light, however faint, it is because he organized and led the first systematic, full-scale campaign against the Hitlerian nightmare. Whatever the nature of Willi's cynicism and that of his men as they shaped the anti-fascist campaigns, whatever sins were committed under its cover, whatever sinister manipulations it masked, the passions that anti-fascism mobilized were genuine and justified. That is what makes this story not merely the account of some squalid gangster deal, but a tragedy.

Münzenberg was slow to surface publicly in Paris, but within days of his arrival, the city's cultural life and with it the cultural life of the West, had entered a new phase.

On March 23, 1933, days after Münzenberg's arrival, the new dispensation had its debut at an enormously glamorous protest meeting over the Reichstag Fire in which all Paris was present.[32] André Gide, Elsa Triolet, and Louis Aragon, all were there. André and Clara Malraux, sleek, superb, and newly famous, were carefully placed in the very front row. This sort of thing was the basis of a new cultural-political chic, and it would remain so until the end of the Spanish Civil War, the first of hundreds, perhaps thousands of such meetings held around the West. Causes were adopted, celebrities were enlisted. In public and in secret, both legally and illegally, all Münzenberg's skills seemed turned toward a single driven, absolute object: opposition. Opposition and nothing else.

In Paris Münzenberg settled into his refuge on the Left Bank, and with the help of the Comintern apparatus he was soon installed in a dingy set of offices at the end of a dark, almost unnoticeable alley on the Boulevard Montparnasse.[33] To rally and exploit the rising world sentiment against the Nazis, Münzenberg summoned up a new and refurbished array of fronts. Within weeks the Comintern had procured a publishing house for his use, likewise in the Latin Quarter: Editions du Carrefour on the Boulevard Saint-Germain, a publisher which, before the apparatus bought it, had produced elegant anthologies of poetry and luxurious monographs on modernist painting. One of the people most instrumental in the transfer of Editions du Carrefour to Comintern control was a dandyish young French writer whose two best friends were Raymond Aron and Jean-Paul Sartre. He was Paul Nizan, and the three friends together (naturally) called themselves the three musketeers.[34]

An anti-fascist underground was also established, designed to send agents into Germany both to maintain contact with the German communists left behind—and to perform other secret work within the Reich. The man who'd been introduced to Lenin as the wunderkind of the underground network was now assigned the task of penetrating Hitler's world. Münzenberg's ingenuity flowered. Once Dimitrov was arrested, for example, it was plain that Münzenberg agents had been placed throughout the prison where the Comintern official was being held. The Münzenberg men in Paris knew that Willi and Dimitrov were in regular and easy contact, right under the Nazis' noses! It was seen as a crowning tribute to their master's skill.[35] But it appears the communication between Dimitrov and Münzenberg was less a matter of deceiving the Nazis than it seemed.

Still, new networks were strung together all through Germany. Sympathetic countesses were dispatched to Germany with documents sewn into their clothes. They "rested" in clinics run by doctors who were also in the undergound, linked in turn to inconspicuous ladies in shabby coats, who were contacts for foul-mouthed street-fighters from Berlin's back streets, who in turn took their cue from some nonchalant fellow carrying a violin case. The penniless and the powerful were secretly joined in clandestine action. People who would never even have seen themselves as on the left found themselves joined with hard-core revolutionaries.[36] Journalists were given crash courses in undercover technique and sent into Nazi territory both to prepare their stories and to accomplish various less public tasks.[37] Münzenberg's new networks could spirit people in danger across the border, speed false papers into the right hands. They also maintained a flow of news about the mass arrests of communists, about Nazi rearmament, about the first government persecution of the Jews—and about the construction of a new, large political internment camp located in a little south German town called Dachau.

Inside Paris itself, there was already a fairly well-developed political apparatus waiting for Willi's command, geared both to propaganda and covert action. Willi was able to make use of the French Communist party, which was given a *mandat* by the Comintern—that is, a plenipotentiary command from the Moscow Center—requiring every possible assistance in his operations. Not long after, a similar *mandat,* written incidently on a piece of silk so it could be sewn into the courier's clothes, was signed by Münzenberg and delivered by Gibarti to Earl Browder, the head of the American Communist party in New York.[38] Münzenberg's prime contact within the French Party was its cultural commissar, with editor-in-chief of *Humanité,* Paul Vaillant-Couturier, over whom Münzenberg would have had authority in matters of management of the anti-fascist movement.[39] As a result, up through 1935, wherever one sees Vaillant performing some action linked to that campaign, anything from the courtship of André Gide to dispatching Malraux to Germany, it is a reasonable guess that the French propaganda officer had co-ordinated his actions with Münzenberg.[40]

But the machinery of Amsterdam-Pleyel was already installed in the French capital, bypassing the French Party and directly under Comintern command. Amsterdam-Pleyel had been alerted to the new tactics at Münzenberg's Moscow meeting in early January 1933. The Moscow Archives show a seamless transition between the enterprises of ''pacifism'' to the new search for remilitarization.[41] Working from headquarters in the small suburban town of Aumont, Münzenberg's man Louis Gibarti was in charge.

A word about Gibarti.[42] He seems to have joined the Soviet Services at the time of Bela Kun's regime in Hungary, serving at various times in Vienna, Moscow, and Berlin. The Far East was one of his earliest propaganda interests, where he must have been an early ally of Borodin. Certainly Gibarti was deep in the Comintern's work in East Asia. In this capacity, Gibarti developed important and long contacts with M. N. Roy, Nehru, and Ho Chi Minh. In a certain sense, Gibarti might be called one of the founders of the Third World movement. His interest in China lingered. During a secret mission to America in the thirties, one of the ''innocents'' Gibarti first contacted was the famous American China hand Owen Lattimore, who, he claimed, had been presented to him as an American fellow traveller, eager to give assistance to communist needs.[43] It should be added that the League Against Imperialism was always used as an instrument for propaganda, sabotage, and espionage.[44]

Comintern propaganda and covert operations in East Asia had inspired André Malraux's novels *The Conquerors* and *Man's Fate*. They were the kind of things Gibarti and his cohorts had lived through. It would be interesting to know how the young Malraux became so persuasively informed about this kind of thing, especially since (despite his own claims to the contrary) the author of *Man's Fate* had spent next to no time in China before he wrote his wonderful book.[45]

Dropping peace was easy. Overnight the World Committee Against War was renamed the World Committee Against War *and* Fascism. Thus was brought into being the largest, if not the most important, of Münzenberg's many contributions to manipulated political innocence.[46]

Paris meanwhile became the Mecca for all the many exiles in flight from the new Reich. They filled Montparnasse, crowded into the cafés. Mingling among them were spies. Ragged and terrified Comintern agents, riding out of the nightmare in third-class railroad cars, would stumble across Münzenberg's threshold, in from the fascist cold.[47] Nothing is more easily understood than how the German exile community, rightly afraid, rightly angry, and apparently without resources, was irresistibly drawn into Münzenberg's Paris ambit. There was hardly a German refugee in Europe whose life was not brushed by Münzenberg's work, and much in the subsequent political history of both Europe and America was founded in the flow of loyalties that came together here. Both Manes Sperber and Arthur Koestler have written with wonderful vividness about those days, working for Willi in the center of the hive. Half the intelligentsia of a great country had been thrown into a grotesque new diaspora. The consequences have rung down the decades.

A quieter and more concentrated instrument of the new policy was an organization called the World Committee for the Relief of the Victims of German Fascism. The World Committee was a smaller and far more fine-tuned front for propaganda and secret work than the League Against War and Fascism. Specific instructions for its creation were brought by courier from Moscow in early March.[48] Once again, Louis Gibarti was put in charge.

The World Committee did not court thousands of members. That was left to the big soft organizations. Instead, the World Committee sought politically important contacts, and it performed very particular secret tasks. For example, agents of the World Committee for the Relief of the Victims of German Fascism were involved in feeding disinformation to Winston Churchill.[49]

The nominal head and front man for the World Committee for the Relief of the Victims of German Fascism was a politically very respectable leftist who despite his independent look was a fully collaborating Münzenberg-man. This was Count Michael Karolyi, a leading politician of the high Hungarian aristocracy, who in the chaos of 1918 had been the first socialist president of Hungary. Because Count Karolyi's government has been overthrown in the Bolshevik uprising of Bela Kun in 1919, most observers assumed that Count Karolyi must be anti-Stalinist. This was a great mistake. Though they invariably retained grounds for insisting upon their independence, the Count and Countess Karolyi were in virtually all things enthusiastic admirers of and acolytes to the Soviet government throughout the late 1920s and 1930s. They continued to be until the crisis of 1948–52 in Eastern Europe, which culminated in the execution of many of their friends. There can be no doubt that Count Karolyi was witting in his role as head of the World Committee and as a general front man and advisor to Münzenberg. Meanwhile, the Countess showed great courage and ingenuity running covert missions for Willi inside the Reich.[50]

From the moment Stalin created it, almost certainly at Radek's suggestion, it was assumed that the World Committee, like the League Against War and Fascism, would serve as a cover and focus for secret work, a contact point for agents of influence and covert action. In America, Elizabeth Bentley took her first steps into the NKVD through the League Against War and Fascism.[51] In England, Maurice Dobb, the Cambridge advisor to the League Against Imperialism and an open communist, guided the youthful Kim Philby to Paris, there also to contact the World Committee.[52] From the World Committee Philby was sent on to Vienna, and the start of a momentous career. A curious detail: Both Gibarti and Gibarti's Comintern control in Paris, Gyula Alpari, were Hungarian. They were members of what I have come to call "the Hungarian Mafia," a group of cosmopolitan non-Russians, with Hungarians the most remarkable. The Hungarian Mafia: They constituted the founding core of the Soviet secret services. Kim Philby spent his last days at Cambridge, right before he was sent on for his momentous contact with Gibarti, dutifully struggling over a primer—in Hungarian.[53]

Then of course there was the question of Willi's own contact with the unseen world. Once a week, as dusk was gathering over Paris, Willi would leave his offices on the Boulevard Montparnasse for what looked like a stroll around the *quartier*. He would take off in some fresh direction each time, following his whim through the ancient maze of the Latin Quarter. As he walked he would invariably bump into a succession of German exiles, and since he knew them all he would stop and chat. One such little chat took place every week at exactly the same time on the rue de Montparnasse, a small street jutting off the great Boulevard of the same name. Münzenberg would stop and talk to a man who according to Babette looked "like a Jewish doctor." The two would talk, never for long, but without fail. Now and then the personnel would change, and Willi would meet with a taller, considerably younger man. Sometimes it was Willi's secretary Hans Schulz who made the rendezvous: Hans of the phenomenal memory, the one-man, secret service secretariat. The big city relaxed. The vesper sparrows circled over the famous rooftops.

This street-corner encounter was a weekly meeting of the Comintern's director of propaganda and his Comintern case officer. It lasted for only a few minutes, rarely more. The chat was concentrated. To the wise, three or four words could define policy and shape high politics. A question. A judgment. A decision. A command. They didn't take long. Even Willi was impressed by the terse economy of the transaction and the instant speed with which his questions and directives moved in absolute secrecy back and forth to Moscow. Ask, and it was answered. But *immediately*. The efficiency of the *apparat*'s web for transmission of information, above all via the so-called "red orchestra" of secret radio operations, had come a very long way since Willi was sending messages to Lenin in jam jars.[54]

These controls also met regularly with Louis Gibarti as well.[55] Meanwhile, the famous NKVD resident Ignace Reiss was active in Paris. Babette Gross had been good friends with Reiss's wife Elisabeth in Berlin before Hitler took power. In Paris, however, she was told by Münzenberg that she must feign absolute non-recognition of Reiss or Elisabeth Poretsky whenever their paths crossed.[56]

After 1935, Münzenberg's Paris contact was yet another figure in that Hungarian Mafia of agents to which Gibarti belonged. His real name—at least I know of no other—was Gyula Alpari, a name sometimes impossibly Anglicized as "Jlius," or as I shall call him here, "Julius."[57]

According to Babette, Julius was very much a family man, who regularly complained that his job kept him forever on the road. He and Willi Münzenberg went back a long way together, to the Volga Famine at least, and Julius must have known Gibarti for a long time as well, probably since their days together with Bela Kun in 1919. Despite his wish for a sedentary life, Julius had always been near the hot center. In Berlin during the early twenties, he had been editor of *Inprecorr,* a kind of *Congressional Record* for Comintern and the Revolution, and an invaluable document in the history of communism. But he had also been in the major European countries, and in America.

Here I might speculate that Julius, or at least some other Hungarian who bore a very marked resemblance to Julius (one candidate is a fellow Hungarian mafioso named Bèla Szantil), served as the Comintern's senior representative in New York during the Sacco-Vanzetti campaign. Certain it is that a figure almost exactly fitting his description was covertly in New York during this time, living in a tiny slum room in the West Thirties of

Manhattan, and serving as *the* Comintern representative in New York, quietly watching, recruiting, commanding.

It is through Whittaker Chambers that we know of the man's presence, since it was this agent who guided Chambers in his first steps toward espionage. If this New York Comintern rep was (as I think probable) Alpari, it would suggest that both Whittaker Chambers and Kim Philby had been enlisted with the assistance of the same member of the "Hungarian Mafia."

Chambers's encounter with the Mystery Man began in the main reading room of the New York Public Library. The bright kid from Columbia had been sent to the New York Public by his New York Party recruiters. There he was supposed to prepare himself for life as what they called, in their illiterate way, a "literate." A "literate," in the Party jargon, was a recruit who was being prepared for work as a writer and propagandist.

One evening, hunched over an important tome in the main reading room, Chambers became conscious of a foreign-looking man watching him rather intently, taking him in, glancing now and then at his book's spine. The man was intentionally letting himself be noticed. Chambers's book, incidently, was about the Hungarian revolution of Bela Kun. They made eye contact; the man began to talk in German about the book, about the Hungarian Soviet. The stranger discussed its leading figures "as if they were familiar friends."[58]

Chambers and the stranger met many times more in the main reading room, talking politics, until at last one night the older man deepened the moment with a simple straight question.

"*Sie sind ein Kommunist, natürlich?*" (You're a communist of course?)

"*Natürlich,*" Chambers replied.

"*Ja.*"

At this point the unnamed man suggested they leave the library and continue their conversation more privately. As they walked down the library steps the visitor turned to Chambers and in a relaxed but decisive way gave his warning: "You must not tell anyone that you know me or where I live."

He lived in a bare, furnished slum room in the West Thirties. When they reached it, the visitor proceeded to instruct Chambers in the discipline and duties of a professional revolutionist. Chambers was profoundly impressed. He knew that he had been carefully selected for this encounter. This was not just kid's talk, a bunch of smart Columbia boys hanging around John Jay Hall. This man was the Real Thing, one of the Elect, someone who had ministered to the Saints of Terror.

Their meetings in the furnished room continued, until at length the stranger told Chambers that it was time for them to end. As they parted, the boy at last dared ask his mentor's identity.

The answer was forthright: "I am the representative of the Western European Section of the Communist International."

It was that simple: the highest-level communist then in the United States. Whereupon, they parted. Chambers never saw him again and never learned his identity. Yet while certainty is not possible, it should be noted that Chambers's New York Public Library visitor of 1927 answers to the description of Julius, exactly.[59]

In any case, Julius was among the most senior figures in the Comintern secret service in Paris in 1935. His fate was suggestive and terrible. As the Nazis moved in on Paris in 1940, the secret agent did not seem to feel that his own situation in the French capital was necessarily in any particular jeopardy. After all, the USSR was deep in its alliance with Hitler. Yet surely there would be danger to the secret captain of the "anti-fascist" movement?

Apparently not. This man who had been at the heart of secret service activities against the Reich through the heyday of the thirties seemed peculiarly confident, even complacent. Babette Gross took note of this troubling calm. "He must have thought that his papers were exceptionally reliable," she remarked to me. Her voice was cold. It declined to disclose any inflection.

If he thought he was safe, Julius was wrong. By the end of 1940 Gyula Alpari was arrested by the Gestapo in Paris, surely with Stalin's complaisant knowledge, and in 1944 he was put to death in the Nazi prison camp of Sachsenhausen.[60]

But Julius and his "contacts" were all unseen. Münzenberg and his operation also required high conspicuousness. An essential part in Parisian influence is chic, and one of Münzenberg's earliest protectors in France was a brilliant and memorable figure in the history of chic named Lucien Vogel.[61] First in Berlin, and later in France, later still in the United States, Lucien Vogel was one of the influential and inventive magazine publishers and tastemakers of this century. Münzenberg had known him since the twenties. As early as 1926, Vogel worked at advancing the avant-garde of post-revolutionary Soviet art and taste. He was among the first to see its possibilities for European high style. He was curator of the Soviet Pavilion of the 1926 International Exposition of Decorative Arts, a dazzling showcase of Soviet constructivism and non-figurative art, the purpose of which was to fuse bolshevism in the mind of the European intelligentsia with the look of everything modern. And of course that was a very welcome project to Willi.

From publishing in Berlin, Vogel proceeded to Paris, where he proceeded to create what became a great glossy magazine of French high style: *Vu,* along with its literary companion publication, *Lu.* Both were vehicles for the Münzenberg Trust; both showcases for Stalinism under its guise of imaginary glamour. Meanwhile, Vogel performed many a service for Willi in exile. For example, almost all offers from the apparatus made to André Gide concerning possible trips to the Soviet Union or a possible film deal with Mezhropohmfilm Russ were conveyed through Vogel.[62] And it was Vogel's daughter, Marie-Claude, who served as Willi's handmaiden as he entered the French world.

In the second week of March, Emil drove Münzenberg in the Lincoln limousine down the budding *allé des arbres* that led to Lucien Vogel's country residence, an irresistibly luxurious retreat and house of spies located a little to the northwest of Paris in the Forêt de Saint-Germain. It was known as La Faisanderie. Built in the sixteenth century, La Faisanderie was a former shooting box of Louis XIV. It was a long, low, inviting house at the end of an impressively extended tree-lined drive, set in the middle of a park. In it, Vogel ran a continuous open house for the very fashionable left, the great good place for the Stalinist upper crust. Vogel knew Everybody. He was among the best-placed fellow travellers in Europe, an arbiter of taste, and a host to the manner born. He dressed, according to Count Karolyi, "like a grand *seigneur* of the '90's, with his inseparable pipe, bright checked suits, tight trousers and old-fashioned choker."

There was usually nothing clandestine about a weekend at La Faisanderie. It was merely select—a chaos of political and sexual crossing paths. Guests sometimes complained that it took a week to recover from the fun. The cool stone house was filled with "white Russians, Armenians and Georgians, dark-haired women with jet-black eyes who, lying on cushion-covered low couches would talk Russian loudly to each other, a language neither the host nor his wife nor any of the other guests could understand." Vogel lived "surrounded by Soviet Russians, journalists and officials." There were "smart American women, German spies, and agents and adventurers from all countries."[63]

Another habitué was Pierre Bertaux, a bright young man from a very proper French academic family that was close to André Gide and the Mann family. Pierre Bertaux started haunting La Faisanderie because he was in love with Marie-Claude Vogel, Lucien's daughter. And for a while this love seemed to be reciprocated, though eventually Marie-Claude unceremoniously dropped Pierre in favor of the doomed and dynamic young Vaillant-Couturier. The personal decision rang with politics. With Willi's arrival in Paris, Vaillant came into his political own, thrust in a way onto the world stage. His photographs of the period show a large, sensual face, sad with the distant gaze of a saturnine romantic. Vaillant seems almost to be considering his own early death. In truth, Vaillant was a brilliant organizer with a profound understanding of his country's cultural habits. The apparatus could not have chosen a better man. And Marie-Claude chose Vaillant.[64]

The rejected Pierre would himself move deep into the secret world, a democrat and anti-communist as well as a leading force in the resistance. Bertaux's father Félix had been the leading French Germanist of his era: The standard French-German dictionary of the period bore his name. Pierre was raised perfectly bi-lingual; he was completely at ease in unaccented Berlin *Deutsch.* This made him useful. The French government put him in charge of anti-Nazi broadcasts into the Reich and he also became an undercover operative. One of his earliest missions as a secret agent was to go to Germany, pry Thomas Mann's personal fortune loose from German hands, and get it to Switzerland. The mission succeeded.[65]

In an interview with me shortly before he died, Bertaux recalled La Faisanderie as if he'd walked into a magic forest. "It was a world apart," says Bertaux. "There were people everywhere in little informal groups, chatting, lots of canapés, lots of going to the bar, nobody got up when you were introduced, and among those who stayed you never knew who was sleeping with whom. It was all very discreet, and very sympathetic—but a little bizarre." By the time Bertaux first entered the social wonderland, Münzenberg had surfaced. The young man looked across the lounging room and there, he says, was the Red Eminence himself—"a fish in water."[66]

In addition to its delicious food, drink, and those lounging dark-eyed women, La Faisanderie was wall-to-wall spies. Its habitués included many in Münzenberg's entourage, including the ubiquitous novelist Egon Erwin Kisch. There was a sort of pseudo-writer and Comintern agent named Alfred Kantorowicz who during the Spanish War became a culture commissar in Spain and whom Münzenberg installed as the man "running the show"—the phrase is Arthur Koestler's—in yet another front organization, the Association of German Writers in Exile.

Also lining up at La Faisanderie's bar was the amazing and ingratiating

Mikhail Koltsov, a major figure in the NKVD, and a confidant of Stalin in a way Willi would and could never be. A man of surpassing intelligence and charm. Koltsov's access to Stalin may have made him—as he would remain during the Spanish Civil War—*de facto* the most powerful Soviet agent in Europe. Koltsov's close friend was Ilya Ehrenberg, Stalin's literary front man among Western writers. In his old age Ehrenberg used to wonder aloud why, why, Koltsov, so highly placed, so important, so obedient, had died in the gulag, while he himself somehow survived. Why? Feebly, Ehrenberg wondered why.[67]

There was also the question of the French government's connection to Münzenberg, as well as the response of the French Communist party. Münzenberg's presence in Paris created complications to both the upper hierarchy of the French Communist party and the French government itself. The ambivalence of the French government was especially interesting. One might assume the French center and right would have viewed Münzenberg as a dangerous subversive, and indeed this was so in many cases. But it was not altogether so.

The approach to the French government was arranged through a famous writer, Henri Barbusse, whose life, as the Moscow Archives clearly show, was as thoroughly managed by the apparatus as that of Rolland.[68] They were joined by the always well-connected Vogel.[69] It would be necessary to placate the nervous establishment and the nervous communists with a single stroke. To accomplish this act of mediation, Vogel and Barbusse brought in a new and remarkably arcane player, a lawyer and diplomat named Gaston Bergery.

Bergery was an intensely ambitious politician, and an especially shrewd and independent fellow traveller crucially placed between communist and non-communist worlds. He was married to the daughter of none other than Leonid Krassin, Lenin's principal business negotiator in the non-communist world, the object of the famous "Zinoviev Letter," of an earlier Somerset Maugham-like era. Bergery represented an unimportant splinter part in the Assemblée Nationale. Though lack of money and the right party connections doomed his hopes for elective power, Bergery had followed in his father-in-law's path and become a player in the realm of East-West big business. His connections were the best there were. Intimately though discreetly linked to the Soviets, he was also the French legal advisor to General Motors, a broker between two worlds, usable but not controlled by either. He was, according to Bertaux, "one of the most intelligent Frenchmen of his generation."

Bergery had ideal access to the Elysée and the then prime minister of the French republic, Camille Chautemps. Chautemps was a very insightful centrist politician who clearly saw the coming crisis with Germany. Bergery saw what Chautemps saw, and so they cut a deal. They had instantly grasped the desirability of integrating the Münzenberg operations into the French structure. Münzenberg might enjoy French protection so long as he directed his notorious capacities for subversion, disinformation, and trouble against the Germans, not the French. Who knew, they might even from time to time share in the fruits of espionage.[70] In a single stroke, the French would acquire a damaging instrument against the Nazis and co-opt the communists. A secret meeting of the cabinet was convened, and to the astonishment of the uninitiated, Bergery prevailed. Münzenberg *and* members of his apparatus would be supplied with *cartes d'identité* as *refugiés provenant d'Allemagne*. The condition was that they not interfere in French political affairs. The deal was of course unpublicized, and enforced by the collaborating watchfulness of the Communist party and the French intelligence service. But it was a deal, and a triumph. Münzenberg would be more than tolerated in France. He would be protected. From that point onward, one of the surest ways for a German in flight to find the French government's favor was Münzenberg's potent nod.

The *cartes d'identité* were issued. There was nothing to be done about it. The French police, along with the rest of the French right, looked on in impotent rage.

The willingness of the Chautemps government to engage in anti-fascist activity was very vital. At a quite early stage, Pierre Bertaux went to Chautemps with a suggestion that he set up an anti-fascist German-language radio station to be beamed into the Reich and covertly funded by the French government. Chautemps immediately accepted the idea and Bertaux duly put it into operation, delivering his last broadcast virtually the day the Germans marched into Paris.* According to Bertaux, Chautemps did not even need to reflect on this proposal. The moment the young man had finished his presentation, Chautemps simply said, "Fine. Go ahead."[71]

---

* The story of the history of various anti-fascist radio stations, some of them so small they operated from the backs of trucks or in the trunks of cars, is in itself a remarkable episode in the history of intelligence. Münzenberg and Katz were active in this area, as was Bertaux. One of the areas where it is known that Guy Burgess worked with the Münzenberg people is in providing English-language material for the communist stations. It is worth mentioning that all graduates of the Comintern's espionage school at Podlipki outside Moscow were trained in radio technique, and that transmitters usable for broadcasting might also be used for other sorts of intelligence work. (See Costello, *The Mask of Treachery*.)

Such was the ambience, secret and public, when Münzenberg arrived in Paris in March 1933. Everything was in place, except for one central detail: He would be needing a manager for the anti-fascist campaign, a right hand, a lieutenant.

This lieutenant was selected in Moscow in consultation with the two essential people: Münzenberg and Radek. Just as Stalin adopted his new policy with uncharacteristic speed, so the choice of Münzenberg's secret service shadow was made with uncanny swiftness. Fully primed by Radek himself, the chosen shadow boarded the train in Moscow. He carried most secret instructions for Münzenberg with him, and he was empowered in such a way as to be potentially menacing to Willi's power. He came to Paris by the long way, the *apparat*'s alternate route to the West—that is, not through Germany but north to Leningrad, through Scandinavia, and then south across the Low Countries into France, and on to the Gare du Nord.

This man was the secret agent of whom I have already spoken. He was the contact man with Radek, and he had been chosen to act as the liaison between Moscow and Paris. From this point on, he would look like Willi's right hand; and he would be as well, and in every sense, his spy. However the choice of this secret agent was made, it was a brilliant and daring one. The man who stepped off the Moscow train at the Gare du Nord was perfection composed of every improbability, the highest improbability of all being that with his ravaged face and tender smile, this sometime dilettante, this consort of Dietrich and friend of Kafka, this playboy of the Berlin theater was destined to become one of the most extraordinary figures in the history of espionage.

His name—his real name—was Otto Katz.

Chapter 3

The Lieutenant

Otto Katz, that master of the secret life, was at heart a man of the theater. The secret agent who became Münzenberg's right hand in creating the Soviet's great anti-fascist campaign of the 1930s loved the world of the stage and film, and he spent much of his life in its precincts. Its people were his friends. From Bertolt Brecht to Lillian Hellman, from Serge Eisenstein to Fritz Lang, Katz spent his days among the stars, a companion to theater folk, and in the ambience of the international cinema. He claimed, and it is conceivably true, that Marlene Dietrich had been his first great love. It fits perfectly that as he stood in the dock, about to be condemned to death, Otto invoked the name of Noel Coward.[1]

Katz was introduced to both his life in the theater and to his life in the secret world by Münzenberg, who in 1924 had discovered the very young Otto Katz, already a covert communist, already a man with developed feeling for high culture and duplicity, working as a publicist for a liberal magazine, *Das Tagebuch.*[2] By birth Katz was a Sudeten German from Prague, raised in the same Czech-Jewish upper-middle class and generation into which Franz Kafka had been born. It was his lifelong boast that in his youth he had belonged to Kafka's circle, and the claim seems not only plausible but even probable. It is certain that Katz was close to two of Kafka's close friends, Max Brod and (another Münzenberg-man) Egon Erwin Kisch. Kisch was a novelist; his name was one which the Viennese critic and satirist Karl Kraus used to conjure together with Kafka's in varying puns on *Kisch und Kafka*.[3] Kisch was also a committed communist and deep in Comintern affairs. He had come into Willi's sphere of influence quite early. Münzenberg had assigned Kisch as a "cultural worker" engaged in quietly advancing Soviet interests in Berlin literary politics. Otto Katz, in contrast, would find his natural habitat in the theater. Yet like the CIA's James Jesus Angleton after him, Otto began life as a poet, and like Angleton, he (apparently) founded a short-lived, highbrow literary magazine when he was a very young man. Nonetheless, Willi soon spotted Otto's possibilities in the more practical area of politics, and began to groom this smooth young dilettante for life as a Münzenberg-man, preparing him to be a guardian of the Comintern's interests on the cultural scene in Berlin, with a special focus on the theater. Otto's companionship with Kisch was thus cemented by a common task. In performing that task, Katz came to play a genuine and constructive role within the avant-garde theater of Berlin during its great epoch in the 1920s. During the twenties, he was a classic young radical shaping his identity, finding his path through advanced thought, well on his way toward becoming a typical but superior member of the vanguard intelligentsia of his era. From psychoanalysis to Dada to Constructivism, from Dziga Vertov to the Piscatorbühne, from Gropius to Walter Benjamin to Kafka, Otto was the very type of Weimar.[4] And it was precisely in sensing the strengths of that type, that Münzenberg also sensed Otto's possibilities as a spy.

And it was as a budding Münzenberg-man that Katz met his lifelong friend and political contact Bertolt Brecht, that anti-poet of Weimar's ending. In the same capacity, Katz insinuated himself into the theatrical career of the director Erwin Piscator. Brecht and Piscator: It was not bad company for an ambitious young man, and in it, always under Willi's watchful eye, Otto began to emerge as a rather stylish somebody. As a young man he was slender, and he would be slight in middle age; not tall; fineboned; with a high intellectual head and a hairline that began to recede early; along with huge, sad, knowing eyes that made you think, quite mistakenly, that you could see straight into his sad thoughts. He had a winning smile; lots of gentle appeal. From the beginning, Otto was possessed of almost legendary charm; he had a great theatrical gift for spinning at will the illusions of unearned intimacy. Yet in fairness it must be added that when it came to friendship he also possessed a gift for the real thing: His bond to Kisch seems to have been genuinely loyal, and it ran through his whole life.

Katz's connection to Bertolt Brecht, which was formed in the early days in Berlin and lasted all the way through Brecht's exile in Hollywood, had its emblematic side. Both figuratively and literally, Katz might be viewed as something like the secret face of Bertolt Brecht, a Brecht of the shadows. In any case, several of the most distasteful aspects of the playwright's personality find a dark reflection in the secret agent. I am thinking especially of their shared response to the grosser cruelties of Stalinism. Both men, whenever they confronted the plain, brutal, and publicly established horrors which their Great Leader regularly perpetrated, tended to respond not with anything so trite as mere denial or distress, but with something closer to a kind of sadistic and mildly titillated admiration. It was as though they viewed these crimes as a deep, yet somehow delicious, mystery, and yet a little laughable too. A kind of ultimate joke spun from the ultimate cynic's mind. Cynicism was indeed for both men a kind of common faith. They seemed to share a commitment to cynicism as the purest form of belief, convinced that the sharp cutting edge of their contempt and their habit of casting discredit had sundered the veil of the bourgeois fraud, unmasked the hoax of "humanism."

This contempt put them almost without effort in an invulnerable intellectual position, and nothing could dislodge them from it. Disabused of the bourgeois fraud in all its spiritual *kitsch,* Katz and Brecht could welcome "the measures taken" by their Leader as he so roundly rebuked those fatuous others who still clutched the humanist lie, the twaddle of decency and justice.[5] It is this shared faith in cynicism, this curious belief in disbelief, that makes it only too possible to imagine Katz joining in the saturnine joke of Brecht's post-Nietzschean wisecrack about the first victims of the Great Terror: "The more innocent they are," Brecht sighed, "the more they deserve to be shot."[6]

But what may well be a corollary to this, both Brecht and Katz likewise shared a common fascination with, and talent for, lying as such. They also shared a common fascination with the Lie. Both must rank high in the crowded company of this century's great liars, one in art, one in politics; they seemed to feel a common pleasure (shared with Radek, incidentally) in the Lie considered as a kind of higher, even the highest, Truth: the Lie vindicated.

But their deepest bond of all, fittingly, was cash, especially cash covertly conveyed. The FOIA dossier on Katz makes it plain that he was one of the Soviet case officers, probably the principal one, supplying Brecht with his covert subsidy during his exiled years after 1933, especially in Hollywood. Brecht's conscience was never purchased cheaply, and it was Katz who acted as Brecht's contact, mentor, guide, and bag-man for the regime.[7]

. . .

Thus Otto Katz became something of a player in the world of Berlin Theater, and from there the step into the world of the cinema was short. It is not surprising that when the time came for Otto to proceed to Moscow and enter his really serious training as a secret agent, the cover job assigned to him was as an officer of Münzenberg's Moscow film company, Mezhropohmfilm Russ.[8] Otto's link to the world of film persisted almost until the end. Its most important manifestation was probably in Hollywood, where the apparatus sent Katz incognito in 1935 to reorganize the film colony's networks of Stalinist fellow travellers and prepare them for the new tasks of the Popular Front.

For Otto Katz was to become, as well, a prime operative in the *apparat*'s penetration of Hollywood. How proud he was of his secret service achievements in Tinseltown! "Columbus discovered America," Katz used to boast, "and I discovered Hollywood."[9] Of course, Otto's work in the theater and in Soviet film, companion of Brecht and Dietrich, Eisenstein and Vertov, had prepared him for the scene, and as we shall see, Hollywood's Stalinist networks were well established by the time Otto arrived in March 1935, assigned with the task of preparing them for the Popular Front.[10] He appeared incognito, claiming the identity of a fictitious anti-fascist fighter named "Breda," and it was at this time, using this alias, that Katz personally supervised the establishment of the Hollywood Anti-Fascist League, placing Lillian Hellman's intimate friend Dorothy Parker, along with Donald Ogden Stewart, "in charge," acting as its celebrity window-dressing.[11] The Hollywood Anti-Fascist League became the key communist front around which the work of Stalinist politics was accomplished in Hollywood during the Popular Front.

But Otto's work in Hollywood spread in many directions. From the early days in Berlin, Katz had been associated with Gerhart Eisler, a senior *apparatchik* and one of the more important Soviet agents in America. Both in 1935 and in later years, Katz's work in America was often done in collaboration with Eisler.[12] Meanwhile, Gerhart Eisler's brother Hanns, a musician and communist *apparatchik* active in Hollywood, worked very closely there with Otto as well. Through Hanns Eisler, Otto proceeded to develop relations with the chic German emigré community in Los Angeles, especially affluent innocents, people at the level of the director Fritz Lang.[13] Katz always made it a point to develop connections with any considerable celebrity he could seduce, but especially to deepen his grip on committed Stalinist celebrities like Hellman, Hammett, and Parker. Lillian Hellman for example, who likewise knew and worked with Gerhart Eisler (though she later denied it),[14] was able both in Hollywood and New York to provide Otto with his open sesame to many an influential place.

Beginning with the Hollywood Anti-Fascist League, the networks and fronts Katz helped organize remained active through the Spanish Civil War and until the pact. Katz himself visited the film colony repeatedly, usually incognito, until well after the war had begun. The precise role and nature of the Stalinist fellow-travelling networks in Hollywood during the 1930s are still awaiting definitive scholarship although the Central Party Archives in Moscow have begun to dislodge considerable information about them, with Katz playing a prominent role. Much more digging remains to be done, but it will surely expand and transform our understanding of Stalinist power in the American entertainment industry.[15] But that such Soviet-sponsored networks did exist and were a matter of the most particular concern to those in the American Party entrusted with developing them is no longer a matter open to doubt. Otto Katz, like Gibarti before him, had a considerable role in the way this was done.

The intention of the Hollywood networks was never, incidently, particularly to influence the *content* of films. The real purpose was to find lucrative berths for favored people in the German communist diaspora, to generate publicity for the Popular Front, to Stalinize the glamour culture, and to tap Hollywood's great guilty wealth as a cash cow for the apparatus, an abundant provider of untraceable dollars. There are unconfirmed reports that Katz visited Hollywood even after Pearl Harbor, though by then he had been expelled from the United States on perfectly well-founded suspicion of espionage—espionage then being performed during the Nazi-Soviet Pact, on behalf of Hitler's most important ally.[16] Up until the Czech coup in 1947, after Katz had returned to Prague to help set up the Stalinist regime there, quite large amounts of dollars from Hollywood were still being brought, under cover, to the apparatus in Czechoslovakia, through people he knew in Los Angeles.[17]

Though Otto did not remain a poet, he was nonetheless a man of no mean literary skill. He was fluent—he was glib—in five languages: Czech, German, English, French, and Russian, and he wrote with verve, style and enviable speed in every one.[18] Under an array of false names, he wrote or edited a number of books, working most often under the name "André Simone."* On other occasions he used the name "O.K. Simon"—it was

* A detail of literary history: When Paul Nizan wrote his novel about young men brushing near the apparatus, *The Conspiracy*, he gave the real spy in the center of the boy's games Katz's pseudonym "André Simon." This is surely some sort of in-joke. Nizan knew Katz well, and was very

his pseudonym for the Left Book Club in England. Some of these books were quite successful; all are important as documents in this or that propaganda strategy. They are forgotten now, but if one reconstructs the composition of any one of them, useful insights into the covert needs of the Stalinist apparatus at a given moment will invariably emerge.

Lillian Hellman includes an affectionate and typically mendacious portrait of Katz in her memoirs, recalling the man who "persuaded me that I must go to Spain" as "slight" and "weary-looking," as well as "brave," and "kind."[19] Spinning the myth, Hellman idealizes the man. She traces a path for him through his times which, as no student of Hellman's life will be surprised to learn, the facts do not support. First she reports that Katz "stayed in Spain until the very last days of the Franco victory, when, in New York, a few of us found the bail to buy him out and to send him on to Mexico." It must be said that every clause in this summary is a new falsehood. In fact, Katz was not in Spain at all at the time of the Republican capitulation. Moreover, Otto was never at any time under arrest, or even in jeopardy of arrest, in Spain or anywhere else—not until his last, cruel incarceration in Prague, that is. Hellman's claim to have raised "bail" for his release from a Spanish prison is therefore necessarily a fabrication. To the fantasy that Otto had (by her goodness) been liberated from Franco's clutches, she next adds that he proceeded from Madrid to safety in Mexico. In fact, Katz spent much of 1939 and all of 1940 in New York, working quite closely with a number of people, notable among them Lillian Hellman herself, on various political and literary projects. This took place at the very same time that she and Hammett were the instigating spirits in the founding of the Stalinoid New York daily paper *P.M.*, exactly the kind of Münzenbergian publishing venture in which Otto specialized. In fact, from the Hollywood Anti-Nazi League, to the Spanish Civil War, to the founding of *P.M.*, Katz was surely Hellman's senior contact in the cultural politics of Stalinism. It is perhaps in consequence of that intimacy that every word she writes about Katz, apart from the words "slight" and "weary-looking," is a lie.[20]

Like Hellman, Arthur Koestler knew Katz well—far too well to perpetuate claims about his bravery and kindness. Koestler contrasted Katz with Münzenberg himself: Otto was, he wrote, Willi's "perfect complement. . . . [While] Willi was a rugged leader, Otto was a smooth and slick operator . . . dark and handsome, with a somewhat seedy charm. He was

---

likely introduced to Comintern work by him. (See Gross, *Münzenberg*, pp. 242–243.) Nizan worked on Katz's project *The Brown Book of the Hitler Terror* (see Pascal Ory's biography of Nizan for passages on Nizan's work on the French edition of *Le Livre brun*).

the type of person who, after lighting a cigarette, always closed one eye, and this habit became so fixed with him that he often closed his eye while thinking out a problem, even when he was not smoking."[21]

Otto's calculating squint was no less familiar to Claud Cockburn, the Stalinist journalist, British Münzenberg-man, and father to the Cockburn brothers, familiar figures in the left-wing journalism of New York in the seventies and eighties. Cockburn used to invent Soviet disinformation under Otto's supervision, and knew the secret agent perhaps the best of all.[22] There are several mysteries in Katz's relation to Claud, and most, no doubt, are sinister. Cockburn was an active Comintern propagandist, then as always a devoted and very sophisticated apologist for the regime, who seems to have been guided through the more delicate aspects of his work by Otto. While Cockburn's portrait of Katz in his memoir surely leaves much unsaid, much in it rings true. "He was a middle-sized man with a large, slightly cadaverous head in which the skullbones were unusually prominent. He had large, melancholy eyes, a smile of singular sweetness, and an air of mystery—a mystery into which he was prepared to induct you, you alone, because he esteemed you so highly."[23]

Here Cockburn puts his finger on a key to what was by all reports Otto's quite potent charm. Otto used his air of being an insider, his look of a smokey worldliness beyond worldliness, as a means of flattery and seduction. It was an indispensable reflex of his being. He could create the illusion of intimacy with whomever he liked, and using that skill he melted doubtful strangers such as Irving Thalberg and Norma Shearer in the palm of his hand. Katz's seductive power was tremendously enhanced by the allure of conspiracy itself. He *looked* like a spy, and he knew it. He used the glamour of the trench-coat to seduce. He had and wore a conspiratorial air; it was not something he played down; it was quite obviously part of his gift for making visibility the best disguise.

But charm is the most superficial form of intimacy. To know Otto really well was often to hate him with lasting venom. The widow of the German novelist Gustav Regler, who had worked with Otto daily during the anti-fascist days in Paris but was later, after his break, persecuted and put at risk by Otto and the communist establishment during his wartime Mexican exile, reports that her husband broke into a dance of joy when he heard the news that Katz had been hanged.[24] For hanged he was, in the last wave of Stalin's show trials in 1952, executed in the classic manner of the regime's gangster justice, in final recompense for all the faithful services he had performed, and consigned to that definitive silence which guards forever all those many things that Otto came to know too well.

Not surprisingly, Otto's seductive power was sexual as well as political. Take the Dietrich story: He insisted that he had been the Blue Angel's first husband, a union joined in their remote youth, when he had been a ticket-taker in a theater in Teplitz, and Dietrich was singing and dancing as a kid in the chorus line. He told the tale of their love to everybody. Cockburn claims that "whereas in every other connection you could call him a liar, hypocrite, and ruffian of every description without his turning a hair, if you appeared to doubt his assertion about Marlene he would fly into a passion, white with rage."[25] We know the spy was at least friendly with Dietrich. During the war, Paul Willert, who was by then a British intelligence and propaganda agent, remembers bumping into Katz and Dietrich together on a Hollywood lot, along with Fritz Lang. (Lang was then and later a complete innocent, incidently: He was a true anti-fascist, and all the documents I have seen indicate that Lang admirably and without any second agenda gave his money and energy to fight the Nazi enemy.) It was plain to Willert that Katz and Dietrich were good and old friends.[26] In *An Unfinished Woman,* Lillian Hellman reports (unreliably, of course) that while she was dining with Katz in Paris in 1937, a "famous and beautiful German movie star"—obviously Dietrich—appeared at their table, pausing to kiss him and mutter a confidence. "Please forget what you heard," Hellman quotes Katz as saying after Dietrich left. "We were in love with each other when she was young and I was not so *triste*."[27]

Otto was married to a pretty German wife named Ilse—his Ilschen. (One report in the FOIA dossiers claims that for reasons unknown he briefly divorced, then remarried Ilschen.) Koestler remembers from the Paris days running into Katz at the crack of dawn in the open market on the rue de la Convention, "an unshaven and tieless Otto, the collar of his jacket turned up, with a net shopping bag in his hand, bargaining with a fishwife, his left eye shrewdly closed, displaying the same earnest charm I have seen directed on other occasions at Miss Ellen Wilkinson, M.P., or Mlle. Geneviève Tabouis."[28]

Shopping aside, Otto Katz was not a dutiful husband. His affairs were numberless. I remember a moment early in my research, when the wife of a distinguished American academic emeritus, wrapped in an elegant Spanish shawl, leaned toward me and confided: "Young man, you've got to talk to us old ladies. We're the ones who slept with all those spies."[29]

Still, the playboy was serious. The roving eye, the charm, the aliases, the deceptions within deceptions, all served a single-minded focus on the political task. And there was more to him than conspiracy and seduction. The late Czech economist Eugen Löbl, who joined Katz in Prague as a fellow defendant in the Slansky Trials in 1952, knew Katz well in Prague after the war and never, so he told me, guessed that his friend was more than an exceptionally influential journalist. He remembered long exalting evenings of talk with Otto. "He was more than intelligent," Löbl gently recalled. "He was wise."[30]

He was also almost certainly a double agent within the Soviet system, spying on the Comintern he served for higher and hostile powers, closer to Stalin himself, an embodiment of all the intra-agency treachery that must have been at work among Stalin's services by, let's say, 1937. The issue remains controversial for a number of reasons. To begin with, there are many people who still imagine that the Comintern of the 1930s represented a less "Stalinistic" branch of the Soviet government than the NKVD, and that because it was a prime vehicle of Lenin's fantasies, the Comintern has been viewed as somehow more internationalist, more idealistically revolutionary, less bound to the secret police, than the NKVD. A Guy Burgess or Anthony Blunt, recruiting newcomers to the ring, invariably claimed their work was for "the Comintern," though their controls, Theodore Maly and Alexander Orlov, were both high-level agents of the NKVD, or what Babette Gross delicately called in my presence "the other service."[31] It was easier to entice a neophyte to commit himself to serving the International than a secret police.

This moralized distinction between the NKVD and the Comintern is still maintained by a number of students of the subject. It is for example almost universal among apologists for the Popular Front.[32] In reality the supposed difference is close to complete illusion. It is quite true that following 1935 all the Soviet services became more emphatically Russian and anti-intellectual than they had been under Lenin, and that this was part of a shift of secret service power away from the foreign intellectuals of the Comintern and toward the Russian policemen of the NKVD. It is also quite true that Stalin despised the Comintern and that the NKVD was the very instrument of his mind. But was the Comintern not Stalinist? It is true that some in the organization may well have silently harbored this or that private criticism of the Kremlin's policy or methods, but the notion that senior leaders of the Comintern after 1928 were ever in any politically concrete way even mildly menacing or hostile to Stalin's power is simply not demonstrable. Most were abject in their devoted obedience to the regime and they gladly performed its work without protest. Nor is there any reason to suppose the Comintern served as a haven for some sort of good "Leninism" that was morally more elevated than the bad "Stalinism" of the NKVD. Many of Lenin's most important appointments had of course been to the Cheka, and many of those Leninists survived and flourished in Stalin's NKVD and Soviet Military Intelligence, the GRU. In fact, when Stalin ordered the NKVD to penetrate, take over, and in effect liquidate the Comintern leadership, it was a Chekist from the earliest days, Mikhail Trilliser, an intimate of Dzerzhinsky and Lenin himself, to whom Stalin entrusted the job. Trilliser was in many ways the complete Leninist. Finally, during the Terror, Stalin freely slaughtered senior officials of both services.

Nonetheless, it is quite true that Stalin's policy was to penetrate the Comintern with the NKVD and GRU, and not the reverse. By 1935 the senior management of the International was entirely in the hands of the other services.[33] It ceased to have any meaningful separate existence. There is every reason to suppose that Otto Katz played some quite real role in this transformation, enacting the charade of a Comintern agent while in fact serving the more powerful agency. The fall of the Comintern was also what brought down Willi Münzenberg. But when Willi fell, Otto Katz, a Comintern ''type'' if ever there was one, did not fall with him. On the contrary. Katz's emergence as a major figure within the apparatus dates precisely from the moment of Willi's descent from the monster's grace.

The more interesting question concerns Katz's patronage. The senior Bolshevik closest to Katz's career was Karl Radek. This is only natural; as we have seen, Radek was likewise Münzenberg's best friend among the senior Bolsheviks, and any significant Münzenberg-man in Moscow was likely to seek him out.[34] But as we shall see, Radek was also the senior Bolshevik most involved in the real and deepest secrets of Stalin's German policy after Hitler took power. In particular, Radek was among the very, very few fully apprised of Stalin's policy of appeasement and collaboration with Hitler. In fact, he served as Stalin's highest, and most secret, emissary in the discussions that led to these arrangements.[35] This detail is crucial. It was to cover and give coherence to these secret actions that Radek was put in charge of the very same ''anti-fascist'' campaign of which Katz and Münzenberg were the European organizers. With Katz as his protégé, it is easy to understand why Katz was given the Paris assignment and the crucial new job as the secret agent in place for the anti-fascist agitation of 1933.

Since Katz would necessarily be working with a number of the most delicate and important secrets of the era, it is plain that Radek and Stalin both would have to repose the utmost confidence in their man. The job required a unique combination of talents. The secret agent most entrusted with the covert dimension of the anti-fascist campaign would need to have a great talent for publicity and the public life, joined to a no less powerful talent for secret action. He would need to inspire idealism and stir moral commitment of a very profound kind, while being involved daily in actions so cynical and duplicitous that the truth is almost ungraspable. He would need to inspire people to make the most profound sacrifices for one of the most momentous and urgent causes of the century, while he would also need to use them in the service of one of its greatest lies. Such an emissary would have to be a combination of contradictions, contradictions bound in a dark linkage of imagination and hardness of heart. That was what they found in Otto, and that was the man who arrived in Paris, bearing the secret agenda for the new movement, in March 1933.

It all began idealistically enough. Münzenberg's first job for Otto, back in 1927, had been to assist him in managing the theatrical career of the director Erwin Piscator, much of whose work was at this time overtly funded by Workers' International Relief.[36] Katz was installed as Piscator's administrative director, and in this capacity Otto found himself managing the egos and fortunes of Bela Belasz and Alfred Döblin, Bertolt Brecht and Walter Mehring, Toller, Tucholsky, and even Marcel Breuer and Walter Gropius. One of his big assignments at this time was to supervise Gropius's preparation of the blueprints for the "Total Theater" to house Piscator's enterprise.[37]

All aspiring warriors of ideas must become expert in the art of provocation. That is, they must learn how to create situations which will force their enemies into self-damaging actions. Katz became a master of this kind of manipulation, and his initiation into its art took place over the Piscatorbühne.

Here is how it worked. By 1927, Erwin Piscator had formed a flourishing reputation as director for the *Volksbühne,* the Berlin National Theater, an institution funded by the Weimar government, and exactly the kind of liberal, altruistic operation the *apparat* wished to discredit and destroy. In 1928, Piscator grew tired of being a mere director among directors in this too-anonymous but high-minded place. He longed to make a bigger splash in a theater he could call his own.

His problem was leaving the *Volksbühne*. It had always treated Piscator in an exceptionally supportive way. He was at perfect liberty to leave it whenever he chose to do so. If and when he came across some preferable outlet for his talents, he only needed to tender his resignation and move on. There were, however, no points in righteousness politics to be gained from so simple and unvictimized a course of action. Piscator needed some way to make his career move look like a saintly act, make his big break seem a rebellion against oppression. Righteousness required that some injustice drive him to the main chance, some social evil was needed to *force* him to make his step up. And if that injustice could simultaneously expose the meaningless sham of German democracy, Piscator's success could serve his friends and sources of funding in the Soviet regime as well.

Unfortunately no appropriate injustice was on hand. So one had to be concocted. This gave Otto his debut in provocation. He enlisted the playwright Ernst Toller, who was also very close to Willi, and together they cooked up a play which Toller was to write, a work intended to pose political and practical problems serious enough to assure that the National Theater would decline to produce it. It was written expressly in order to be turned down in this way. Thus, when the inevitable rejection came, Katz had only to whip up a hue and cry over this unconscionable act of oppression and "censorship." The Berlin intelligentsia assembled to protest. The press viewed with alarm. Everybody wrung their hands and signed petitions about the highest values of German culture betrayed—those values which Münzenberg, when dictating rhetoric to his staff, used to call "the tradition of Goethe, etcetera, etcetera." Piscator's departure no longer looked like the mere self-interested career move it was, but shone with the saintly glow of victimization. Piscator was not benefitting; he was suffering, and deserved the support of every decent German.

In fact, Piscator's plans to leave the *Volksbühne* were fully formulated long before Toller's play was written and before the "scandal" was invented.[38] Otto had done it all. It was a brilliant debut.

Yet the Piscatorbühne did not flourish. Within a year there was financial trouble and the enraged director blamed Otto, against whom in later years he would rail as "that nymphomaniacal [*sic*] playboy."[39] Münzenberg discreetly removed Katz and installed him instead in one of the Trust's book clubs, *Universum Bücherei*—which later became a model for Britain's Left Book Club. At *Universum Bücherei,* Otto's arrogance and obsession with fame and glamour drove the drab staff half out of their minds.[40]

Then in 1930, disaster descended. The government found gross tax irregularities in the Piscatorbühne's books, and held Katz personally responsible. One hundred thousand marks had to be produced, and produced soon, or the foundering agent faced jail. Katz of course turned to Münzenberg. Confronting the boss, all his smooth urbanity was blown aside. Katz staged a weeping, shouting tantrum of despair. He absolutely had to, had to, *had* to have 100,000 marks, or he would kill himself.[41]

Münzenberg knew an opportunity when he saw one. In a small stroke of administrative genius, he decided to save 100,000 marks—*and* introduce his man to another kind of debt. He would remove Katz from the reach of the German government and, at this most vulnerable of moments, promote him. Katz was dispatched to Moscow, there to become a manager in the Trust's Soviet film production house, Mezhropohmfilm Russ, a very big new job, and a new life. Note the psychology: To promote a man at the very moment he has crumbled into abjection, wailing about suicide, shows an unusually subtle instinct for power. "Willi," writes Arthur Koestler, "needed Otto, but he barely bothered to disguise his contempt for him. Once when I asked Willi when he first had met Otto, he said in his cozy Thuringian drawl, 'I fished him out of the Landswehr Canal.' The Landswehr Canal in Berlin is a narrow waterway conveniently located for the dumping of corpses and for committing suicide."[42]

And so Otto took up residence at Mezhropohmfilm in Moscow, head of its German section, at the heart of Soviet cinema in its grand epoch. He brought all his Weimar knowingness to the new job at a moment of German ascendancy throughout the film world. While such German transplants as Lubitsch and F. W. Murnau were sweeping down Sunset Boulevard, Piscator and Lotte Lenya were crossing Red Square.

Yet those who worked at Mezhropohmfilm while Katz was a senior executive say that although Katz's name was on the letterhead, he was rarely around. The real leadership came from another Münzenberg employee, Francesco Misiano, who was at least a genuine film-maker, something Katz never was—although the Archives show Misiano, like Katz, involved in Münzenberg's more strictly political enterprises as well.[43] Simultaneously Katz became a regular in the community of journalists and writers in Moscow, as always the man who knew everybody in the worlds of journalism, film, literature. As it happened, his old Czech friend Egon Erwin Kisch—Kafka's companion—was also in Moscow around this time. Kisch and Katz, close since Prague, now further solidified an enduring master-sidekick friendship which lasted to the end of their lives. Where Egon Erwin was, Otto was likely to be, Lone Ranger to Kisch's Tonto. And Egon Erwin, a genuinely likable man, was everybody's friend.

When he arrived in Moscow, Katz was little better than a dilettante's dilettante, both in culture and the secret life. He obviously overflowed with talent—with his languages, his speed at the typewriter keyboard, his brilliant connections, his charm, his zest for deception. But he lacked discipline; he needed a firm hand. He had the gift; now it was time to shape the playboy for his destiny as one of the "Great Illegals." The Soviet services now set out to prepare him for the genuine conspiratorial work of the *apparat,* trained in secret technique, and connected to the networks that really mattered. On the outside, Otto would look very much the same, but his gifts would now be anchored to something deep and unseen. He was almost never in his office at Mezhropohmfilm Russ. His work there was obviously a cover.[44] He was elsewhere, in training for his true lifework.

He was doing so at the highest level, almost certainly under the guidance of Karl Radek. In 1927, Radek had made a misstep, supported Trotsky at the wrong moment, and spent some time in banishment while Stalin consolidated his power. But by 1930 Radek had somehow found a way to restore himself to high influence. Stalin reposed special confidence in his views on cultural matters—and on Germany. And it was at this time that Otto Katz, following in the pattern of his mentor in Berlin, became intimate with Radek, his protégé in the new generation.

Otto's personality meanwhile was hardening, changing. "Only in Moscow did I really come to understand the mission and principles of the Communist party," he wrote in a letter to Klement Gottwald just before he was hanged. "As I look back on that period, now, during the last hours of my life, I can truthfully state that in Moscow, in the Soviet environment, I changed."[45]

It was so. In these years, Otto seems to have gone through that rare passage, a genuine transformation of personality. It is not that he became a different man, of course, but some playful, free, and human part of Otto's personality, something that once had rather naturally placed him in the company of Piscator, Kisch *and* Kafka, receded and became subordinate to another less attractive part,which had been so strengthened that it took permanent command of his being. Visiting Moscow in the early thirties, Münzenberg and Babette were deeply struck by the change. Babette found the playboy of Weimar "serious, determined and reserved. Whatever he thought about the hardships of daily life in Moscow, about the incipient Byzantinism of the Kremlin, he kept to himself. The current slogans came readily to his lips; he had become a loyal officer of the regime."[46]

By the time he was ready to be sent back to Europe in 1933, Otto Katz was a highly trained secret agent operating at a very high level of awareness. Over the next twenty years, Otto would play out many adventures close to the heart of conspiratorial events. In Paris he would be Stalin's unheroic insider in the anti-fascist movement, calculating its propaganda, calibrating its networks in Germany, giving his special orders to its couriers in the Reich. In London, Katz would touch the life of politics at all sorts of secret points, from the founding of the Left Book Club to the feeding of disinformation to British Conservatives. In Hollywood, it was Otto who under an alias set up and supervised much in the networking of Stalinist fellow travellers, while back in New York he assisted his friend and comrade Gerhart Eisler in espionage and other secret work. During the Spanish Civil War, Otto would help to import the NKVD terror onto the Iberian peninsula. During the Second World War, while Stalin was in his alliance with Hitler, Otto was busy in New York, until a recalcitrant and almost complacent State Department terminated his visa, something it did only after being repeatedly (and correctly) warned that Otto was a dangerous Soviet agent, and (arrestingly, arguably) "probably a Nazi agent" as well. When this trouble disrupted his New York work, Katz beat a tactical retreat to Mexico City, then a major center of NKVD activity in the Western Hemisphere. He is known to have worked closely there with the long-time NKVD chieftain Umansky, who was almost certainly assassinated by his own people. Katz spent the war much involved in Soviet operations within the United States and in the Caribbean, working among other things with Fidel Castro's predecessor, Fulgencio Batista. Batista was at this time much admired and promoted by the left, and Katz was empowered to make Batista grand offers on behalf of the Soviets if Batista would enter Stalin's realm of influence.[47]

At the end of World War II, Katz was summoned from Mexico City back to Prague, accompanied as always by Kisch. Katz became a high-level journalist and government official, and was present at the start of the coup and the creation of the Czech Stalinist state. By 1949, Otto was forthrightly in authority at last. Apparently he became just as forthrightly insufferable in the arrogance of power.[48]

At least for a little while. As the Cold War began, the spy was once again in Prague, empowered in the city of his youth; there where he had begun as a bright young man among Kafka's friends. If this was Katz's fulfillment, it was short-lived. I am tempted to paraphrase the opening sentence of his old friend's novel, *The Trial*.

Somebody must have been telling tales about Otto K., because he was arrested one fine morning

---

Stalin's gratitude was lethal. Only his indifference let people live. Otto Katz was arrested and put to death in Prague as one of the victims of the Rajk-Slansky purges, the set of show trials that swept in succession through all the states of Eastern Europe between 1948 and 1952, part of a vast, mad, but meaningful operation through which Stalin consolidated his paranoid power in his newly acquired territories. The Rajk-Slansky purges were an initiating event in the Cold War. In 1948 many people like Otto Katz, leading figures in the old cadres, people who in Europe had laid the groundwork for the expansion of communist power through the thirties and the war, were stepping forward, expecting their rewards in power. The Autocrat saw them as superannuated compromised servants, and the moment had come to be rid of them. By the hundreds, even thousands, they were rounded up, charged, and put to death. The politically unusable or invisible were simply executed. More conspicuous figures were disposed of in show trials, charged usually with a list of crimes contrived to advance current propaganda and turn their onetime double lives inside out, transposing decades of secret service into lives with the look of treason, socialist-style. In all the capitals of Eastern Europe, a grotesque theater of confession and death began a five-year run, political terror's travelling road show. Many of the "confessions" produced from city to city were bizarre contortions of precisely the history we will be exploring here; in fact an essential part of the point was the systematic effort to rewrite that history from the dock. Otto Katz had been a principal actor in that theater. Now, in Prague, a defendant in the Slansky trials, he stepped forward for his last long hour in the limelight.

It is seldom pointed out that a central character in this all-but-final wave of Stalin's terror was an American mole, and moreover an American mole who will become well known to us. His name is as obscure as that of his friend and (as I believe) fellow mole Alger Hiss is well known. Exactly why Hiss is so famous while Field remains obscure is a question well worth exploring. Field was in his way at least as important a secret agent as Anthony Blunt or Hiss, and one way of measuring his importance is the Stalinist response to the threat of his exposure. It became an initiating event, or at the very least an incident exactly coincidental with the commencement of the Rajk-Slansky purges.

In the summer of 1948, exposure of Noel Field's secret work seemed imminent. The place was Washington; the means the testimony of Elizabeth Bentley and Whittaker Chambers, testimony which exposed Jay Peters as what the Central Party Archives in Moscow now make very plain Jay Peters really was: the Hungarian *mafioso* in charge of sundry espionage networks in Washington—not least among them, a network that included Otto Katz's old colleague in secret work, Field. In other words, exactly the obedient old "anti-fascist" cadres Stalin was now preparing to discredit and destroy. And Noel Field, emerging from the heart of what was to become the Hiss case, became the instrument, the finger-man through whose charges all those deaths could be assigned. One of his targets was Otto.

At the time Chambers made his charges, the alarm running through the apparatus resulted in Noel Field's being summoned to Budapest, where he hoped to be given protection from the deepening secret service cold. But the shelter Field found in the East became the basis for a new deception. Field was arrested. So were his wife, his brother, and other members of his family. His previous relationship with Allen Dulles, through whom Field had served the Russians and worked against the Americans in the OSS, was now advertised as proof that he was in reality an "American master-spy." The "American master spy" next proceeded to "confess," and through his accusations the old networks could be brought forward and destroyed. Field was not an "American master-spy," of course; he was a devoted communist and *apparatchik*, and would remain so until his death many years later. His true role in 1948 was that of collaborator with the people running the Terror trials. Partly coerced, partly the good soldier, Field played his assigned role as accuser. Through his indictment large numbers of people were condemned to death. But not Noel Field. Field was not shot, not hanged—even though if what he claimed about himself was true, he could have been executed fifty times over. Neither were any of his relatives. Instead he and his wife were imprisoned and released a few years later, on the day—the precise day—Alger Hiss was released from Lewisberg penitentiary. They were "rehabilitated." It had all been, the apparatus explained, a misunderstanding.

Herta and Noel Field never revisited the West. Field became an executive in the Hungarian State Publishing House, and he and Herta remained devout Stalinists of the most chilling kind until the end of their lives.*

---

* As of my writing, information seems to have been uncovered in the Archives of the Hungarian secret police, now housed in the Ministry of Information in Budapest which—if the dossiers are in fact what is claimed for them—would confirm my view of the Fields' enterprise and greatly add to it as well. The dossiers in question have been read by Mrs. Maria Schmidt, a Hungarian scholar of the subject. She has recorded their file numbers and made copious notes. The dossiers are said to contain extensive transcripts of Noel Field's debriefing, made at the time of his "rehabilitation." In them it is said that Field describes in meticulous detail, during open and even cordial talks with his fellow agents, the whole range of his life-work in the Soviet secret services. According to Mrs. Schmidt, Field's membership in the espionage rings run in Washington by Jay Peters is documented, as is the work in espionage of Priscilla and Alger Hiss.

In the chapters to come, the reader will see that, in my view, a key to the Hiss Case is to be found

And so in the hysteria of a classic communist witch-hunt, Otto Katz was arrested. Of course Otto knew with whom he was dealing; he instantly made it clear to the secret police that he would gladly confess at once to anything they wanted him to say: anything, anything at all. This effort to sidestep the thugs in the basement failed. It was not enough simply to agree to what was wanted: It was necessary to be tortured anyway. And so Otto was tortured for months while the fabrications of his "confession" were developed.[49] This "confession," is an exercise in disinformation. It may be viewed as Katz's final service to the regime. It is filled with lies of course, but they are revealing lies, and since in their mendacity they almost always seek to cover something important, they repay study.

The man on trial made his confession then, from the dock, speaking painfully through dentures that didn't fit, and which had been given him only that day. His own had been smashed during his "interrogation." Who would have imagined, back in the old days of smooth talking in Paris and New York and Hollywood, that Otto Katz wore dentures! He stood in the dock struggling to shape his words. Still he managed to get the whole thing out, exactly what he had been ordered to say. At one high point he invoked the name of Noel Coward, whom Otto said had recruited him as a British agent during the war, all to further his treacherous Trotskyite work. He himself, he told the court, was scum, vermin. He was a writer, and yet what kind of engineer of the soul had he turned out to be? A traitor. What kind of model was he to others? A man who did not understand the people. A man who had betrayed everything worth living for. Along the way he smeared a great many other people, both communist and non-communist. Above all he smeared his own life, confessing in special abjection to being a Jew, and a bourgeois; a contemptible human being.

So it ended: the "trial" of Otto Katz. It was only in the last phrases of his speech, the part where he turned to the court and began to beg for death, saying that he was not fit to live even another day, that Otto's voice sank, subsided into a kind of gasping, and he could no longer be heard.

---

in Noel Field's historical role. If these dossiers are indeed what is claimed for them, they would be the most important piece of archival information known to me about the secret service work of an American involved in the enterprises that are our subject. Unfortunately, the papers in question have not as of this writing been declassified by the Hungarian government, and I am not aware of any scholar outside Hungary who has seen them. We can only hope that the Hungarian government will recognize what a service to history would be performed by granting open access, and act accordingly. Until that happens, however, it seems to me the attitude of the scholarly community toward this potentially momentous but still untested source must be confined to one of attentive curiosity.

A final word, about murder.

Since the disappearance of Otto Katz from the scene, there have been a series of claims made by people bearing varying degrees of authority asserting that during his days of training in Moscow, Katz may have been prepared as an assassin and executioner.

In many years of looking, I have found no proof of these accusations.

"Otto Katz? He killed Willi Münzenberg!"

In 1985, I interviewed for the first time Mr. Paul Willert, who had been a Münzenberg-man in Paris, Berlin, and New York before the Second World War, when he worked for British intelligence. And that was his exclamation when I raised Otto's name. Willert later told me that he merely suspected Katz's involvement, but he is far from the only person to have done so. Many people have believed, and claimed, that Katz was part of the *apparat*'s final accounting with Willi.

This is a doubtful business. That Katz was an accomplice at a distance—this is not only very plausible but likely. Katz said as much in his final letter to Gottwald, and rumors to that effect surrounded him, even among the *apparatchiki* at the time of the Slansky Trials.[50] Katz was unquestionably active in the *apparat*'s effort to discredit and defame Münzenberg once Willi made his break with Stalin, and after his death as well. Nonetheless, Katz was *almost* certainly in New York when Willi was murdered in June 1940.[51] So at least, Katz was not personally on the scene. Katz has also been accused, by "reliable" writers, of having been on the scene in Prague during the staged suicide of Jan Masaryk. This too is either disinformation or confusion. In fact the senior agent present in Masaryk's apartment on the night of his death was not Otto Katz but Bedrich Reicin, a quite different operative who, to be sure, Stalin likewise eliminated, along with Katz, in the Slansky Trials.[52]

Katz has also been accused of other involvements in the Czech coup. Nothing is more likely than that Katz was deep in various secret aspects of that black event, and it is no less likely that he bears some measure of responsibility for the many sinister killings that took place at that time. Still, his exact role remains, so far as I am aware, pure conjecture.

Finally, Katz's American Freedom of Information dossier from the FBI raises unconfirmed reports of his responsibility for a number of murders in Europe during the "anti-fascist" phase of his career, and Katz is plainly designated as a "trigger man" in State Department documents now on file in the National Archives, documents which in most of their other claims are quite reliably informed. I have been unable to prove or disprove them.

By far the strongest case against Katz concerns his role in Spain. That Katz was directly involved in designating victims for the NKVD Terror in Spain during the Civil War is a charge made with great confidence by very well-informed observers. Here the evidence for his involvement is close to conclusive.[53]

So the mystery of Katz's implication in these murders must persist in ambiguity. Nonetheless, one aspect of these charges is especially suggestive, since it carries with it the subtle odor of disinformation.

During the war, many knowledgeable people, caught up in the welter of secret service gossip, came to claim that Katz had a role in Willi's death. It became a kind of insiders' shibboleth.[54]

In 1955 a book appeared called *The Net That Covers the World,* written by an Austrian-born spy-writer named Edward Spiro, who used the pen name "E. H. Cookridge." E. H. Cookridge was a writer whose fiercely anti-communist books were written in a hyped-up, now-it-can-be-revealed style that hovers just millimeters above popular trash. Still, Spiro made his charges with great authority, and in their time his dubious studies were very influential.[55] Cookridge's book contains many inflammatory pages exposing the secret service activities of Otto Katz. The passages in question are sensationally written and totally unsourced, though they have a certain surface plausibility. It is only on examination that they prove to be either false or grossly misleading half-truths.

Most of Spiro's more sensational claims typically appear without the citation of any source. One reason for this silence is that Spiro was being fed much of his information, probably including his information about Katz, by a senior official in the counter-intelligence arm of British intelligence who insisted upon anonymity. This official may well have been none other than Guy Liddell, the man whom, as we shall see, the British writer Goronwy Rees was so convinced was a central figure in Blunt's ring.[56]

One of the false claims in Spiro's report is the claim that it was Otto Katz (and not Reicin) who was present in Masaryk's apartment on the night of Masaryk's "suicide." Some kind of blunder in research? The second large falsehood in Spiro's account is not so easily shrugged off. Spiro asserts that Katz was present in the South of France when Münzenberg was murdered, and goes on to quote what purports to be a statement made by Babette Gross, made presumably to British intelligence or to someone who passed it on to them, flatly asserting that to her certain knowledge Katz had been on the scene of Willi's death and had paid out large sums to the men she believed to be his actual assassins.[57]

This statement, apparently supplied to Cookridge by British Intelligence and purporting to be a direct quotation from Babette Gross, is almost certainly totally bogus, a forgery. When I showed it to Babette Gross herself, she had never seen it before and instantly pronounced it a fabrication. She claimed never to have made such a statement to anyone, anywhere, and certainly not to anyone in British intelligence. She told me that she had never even briefly been under the impression that Katz was in France when Willi died. She had listened with incredulity to the very slender evidence that he might have been. Reconstruction of Katz's movements at this time shows that he almost certainly was in New York. Babette Gross did not then, or at any other point, believe that Katz had been Münzenberg's assassin.

It should not be supposed, however, that because Babette Gross dismissed false claims about Katz she held any brief on behalf of her old acquaintance. Near the end of our many conversations, I at last asked her the most explosive question of all about this famous "anti-fascist."

It was very plain, I said, that Katz was an important Soviet agent. My question went further. Many well-informed documents in the existing historical record assert that Katz was also a Nazi agent. Did she herself believe this might be true?

Hearing this question, Babette expressed no surprise whatever. Instead she grew quiet, and rather solemn. When she responded, she merely pointed out that Otto Katz was close to Hubert Ripka at the appropriate time.

It was an oddly indirect answer to a straight question, an answer that could have meaning only to someone who knew its political context. *Otto Katz was close to Hubert Ripka at the appropriate time.*

Hubert Ripka? And who was Hubert Ripka? Ripka had been Czech President Edvard Beneš's foreign minister in the 1930s. It was a curious way to respond to a question about Nazis, but Babette would not say one syllable more.

Chapter 4

Trial, Counter-Trial, and the Dimitrov Conspiracy

The Soviet-sponsored anti-fascist movement, the response mobilized by Münzenberg and his people following Hitler's seizure of power after the Reichstag Fire, was a confrontation which at least seemed to be the first great battle in a new and genuine propaganda war between the Soviet apparatus and the Nazis. Hitler had set out to validate his seizure of totalitarian power with a protracted and highly publicized show trial, blaming the communists for the fire and for an endless array of other crimes against the German people as well. The staging of this judicial charade would be among Hitler's relatively few experiments with the show trial as a form. He soon settled into pure, plain, post-judicial murder to mete out the vengeance of a pure, plain, post-judicial terror state. There would not be many more Nazi "trials"; here Hitler would throw himself into a propaganda play of the sort more usually associated with Stalinist terror. A gaudy tribunal was set up in Leipzig, with its apparent purpose to arraign and condemn Marinus van der Lubbe as the arsonist, while condemning the communist celebrities who'd been put in the dock with Lubbe as the masterminds behind the fire.

With the Leipzig Trial, Stalin seemed at last ready to have the Comintern and Münzenberg really fight back against the gathering Nazi power. How could they not? The star prisoner in the Leipzig dock was Georgi Dimitrov, who was not a German at all but a Bulgarian and one of the most famous leaders of the entire Communist International; a man known to be one of Stalin's closest advisors, and therefore among the most important communists in the world. Not fight back when Dimitrov's life was at stake?

Well, fight back they did. Münzenberg, Katz, and the Comintern now seemed to turn their full powers against the Nazi regime; the Fire, and the Leipzig Trial, were the focus of a derisive fury without precedent.[1]

In June 1933 Münzenberg left Paris in deep secrecy for Moscow, where he prepared for the event. Münzenberg travelled by a circuitous northern route—not through Germany but Scandinavia—and on to Moscow for meetings with the Comintern and its secret service, mapping the final strategy of the response to the trial in Leipzig. These Moscow meetings happened in a welter of acrimony and new visions. Most of the time, however, Münzenberg was at Comintern headquarters in extended consultation with the Comintern director, Piatnitsky, and above all in meetings on the building's top floor with a man named Mirov-Abramov, who was director of the International's secret service. But Willi did find time for other activity that June. For example, he was taken to see the Comintern's brand new school for training in espionage, set up by Mirov-Abramov to prepare foreign communists for work under the auspices of the new "anti-fascism," as spies and covert operatives. This dour institution had been set up in the Moscow suburb of Podlipki. The place was patrolled by military guards armed with attack dogs, and was ringed with a double wall. Its "students" had quietly been singled out from the ranks of innocence and its many clubs, talent-spotted by the local parties, and evaluated by among others Hungarian mafiosi like Gibarti, Alpari, and Bela Szantil, amphibians between the worlds of legality and illegality. Despite its seeming raison d'être in "anti-fascism," the focus of training was *not* particularly on Germany. The students were expected to change their names and commit themselves to lifelong secrecy, and the apparatus made it clear that any breach of that secrecy, whenever and wherever in the world it might happen, would be punished by death. Its cover name, behind the barbed wire, was the "Eighth International Sports Base," and it gave training to candidates from Korea to Paraguay. There were many candidates from the United States and Great Britain. Babette Gross names three Germans trained at Podlipki, all of whom, after having been parachuted with radio equipment into the Reich, were found by the Gestapo and shot. One of the German recruits at Podlipki, though not one named by Babette Gross, was Ruth Kuczynski, daughter of Robert René, who later in England, during the War, became the spy connected to events around Bletchley Park and later celebrated under her code name: "Sonia."[2] So far as I am aware, the names of the American and British trainees have never been revealed. The discovery of their identities would surely open some fascinating leads.*

It is also important for our story to know that once Karl Radek had been arrested and condemned in the Terror, and Bukharin was being prepared as the next victim, Mirov-Abramov and a number of the Podlipki alumni who happened then to be in the USSR were rounded up and put to death. All were charged with espionage *against* the Soviet Union. This surely was an effort to cover some tracks. Close examination of the lives and fates of these doomed spies would probably have many lessons to teach about the *apparat*'s real work in the West under the guise of "anti-fascism."[3]

But while Münzenberg's order of anti-fascist battle was being drawn up in Moscow that June, hard new events were unfolding within the single-party structures of both the Soviet and the Hitlerian totalitarianisms. It was during that Russian June that Münzenberg was taken to inspect the slave labor camp building the Moscow-Volga Canal; this was the occasion when he gazed down into the pit and muttered under his breath about the slaves of ancient Egypt. That same month, at the funeral of an old revolutionary friend, Clara Zetkin, Münzenberg spotted Lenin's comrade Zinoviev wandering on the margins of the ceremony; in all innocence, Willi beckoned Zinoviev, urging him to come forward and join the rest in the dignitaries' box. Beside Münzenberg, Zinoviev broke down and confessed that he was in disgrace, forced to live outside Moscow, and that in the town to which Stalin had banished him he was having difficulty finding enough to eat. Zinoviev was only at the beginning of his fall from the Bolshevik Olympus; his descent would end years later, in another show trial leading to his execution, the initiation of the Great Terror. In contrast to Hitler, Stalin would be devoted to the show trial as a political form, a virtuoso, taking it to unimagined limits.

But during these same weeks Hitler himself, no less than Stalin, was confronting complications among his old comrades. There were, for ex-

---

* To the end of his life, Whittaker Chambers denied ever having visited the Soviet Union. This was a falsehood. He was demonstrably in the USSR beginning at least in April 1933 and ending in late June 1933. It is also true that he returned with the pseudonym "Hugh Jones" which for the rest of his life he steadfastly denied having used. That Chambers kept his Russian sojourn secret is surely connected to his training for the *apparat*. Meanwhile, the dates of his visit coincide with the creation of the Podlipki base, though he was back in the United States a little early to have taken its full course. The coincidental timing is at least curious. See Weinstein, *Perjury*, pp. 115–117. See also Walter Goldwater, interview with Diana Trilling, in the archives of Diana Trilling and used with her permission.

ample, problems with the brownshirts in the SA. Should Hitler make the SA more powerful? Less? In those weeks and months of 1933, the anti-bourgeois rhetoric of Revolution, so dear to the brownshirts' propaganda, was frequently heard on Hitler's lips. Sometimes in his speeches Hitler would sigh out loud about how much he yearned to unleash the fury of the fine fellows in the SA against the corrupt bourgeoisie that had oppressed them for so long. Yet he would refrain. He promised the thugs who ran the corps that they would soon find fulfillment in a transforming violence "comparable to the Russian Revolution." Yet at the same time he was also secretly telling Anthony Eden and diplomats from the other democracies that he thought it best to demilitarize and reduce the ranks of his private army. He blew hot and cold. Oddly so.

The Leipzig show trial opened in Leipzig on September 20, 1933. The star communist in the dock was of course Dimitrov, but bringing up the rear was the hapless German communist Ernst Torgler. Torgler was a rather popular communist politician so out of the insiders' loop that after the fire, he'd turned himself in to the police in a disoriented search for campaign publicity. To put it mildly, the move backfired. Torgler may have been a powerless front man, but he was a very visible politician. Every newspaper reader knew his name.[4]

The trial was understood by everyone as the first battle in the great war of disinformation waged between the right and left wings of the totalitarian age. In it, both the Communist and the Nazi propaganda apparatuses seemed locked in what appeared to be a pitched battle, giving no quarter, sparing no weapon in their absolute confrontation. Of course, ever since the Reichstag Fire itself and the arrival in Paris of Willi and Otto Katz, the propaganda apparatus had been at work organizing the anti-fascist forces. But now, with Leipzig, it seemed for the first time Willi and Otto had permission to hit the Nazis hard, hit them like they meant it, with no holds barred; their task was to humiliate the Nazis, to make them the laughing stock of civilization, to cover them with guilt and shame. At last the Communist International would confront the new totalitarianism of the right and spare nothing in the new, absolute confrontation.

Not altogether so.

It now seems clear that the appearance of absolute confrontation at this time was yet another illusion. It is close to certain that the actual exchange between the Nazis and the Soviets over Leipzig, even in those earliest stages of Hitler's regime, contained a very large element of secret collusion. The evidence makes it highly probable, close to certain, that the

Leipzig Trial was rigged between the two apparent adversaries and that it was not a confrontation at all, but—six years before the Nazi-Soviet Pact—a collaboration, an arrangement which I shall be calling here the Dimitrov Conspiracy.

We will be examining this extraordinary covert operation in some detail, but before we address the secrets of the Leipzig Trial, we should look at the public tactics of Münzenberg's great propaganda triumph.

They have been described many times.[5] Münzenberg instinctively understood that his task as a propagandist was to turn the attack on the communists around, to transform Hitler's effort to blame the fire on the communists into just another proof of Nazi criminality. Willi asked, as everybody asked, Who profited from the fire? *Cui bono*? The obvious answer made his method simple: Pin the fire on the Nazis themselves. Accuse the accusers.[6]

This was the response the world was waiting for. Münzenberg was acting on assumptions shared by most alert observers everywhere. The Nazis *looked* guilty. Because the fire was so dazzlingly—blindingly—convenient to their seizure of power, the only question was how they might *not* be the real arsonists. That impression was clinched by the transparent opportunism, violence, haste, and mendacity of the anti-Communist terror of March 1933. Münzenberg did not have to invent these suspicions; everyone shared them. Most people assumed the fire was exactly what it looked like: a Nazi-sponsored conspiracy to destroy the Weimar Republic and the German left.

Though Münzenberg never found any real proof that the fascists had set the fire, his assumption of Nazi culpability, at least at first, may well have been sincere. After all, he *knew* the Communists hadn't done it.[7]

Didn't he?

So who else? This buffoon van der Lubbe?

The simple question—who really torched the Reichstag?—remains open to this day. I am strongly inclined to agree with the preponderance of present-day scholarship,* which holds that Marinus van der Lubbe did

---

* That van der Lubbe acted alone is the case argued powerfully, though not unassailably, in *The Reichstag Fire,* by Fritz Tobias. This book has come to be viewed by many as the last word on this subject. While I, too, am inclined to view Tobias's conclusions as generally correct, I do not regard *The Reichstag Fire* as the last word. It finesses or does not even address a number of the most important questions raised by the trial, the foremost of which is how it happened that the verdict of the court was for the *acquittal* of four of the five defendants.

There is also the question of the book's tone: It is that of a raucous, rhetorical anti-communism combined with frequently unsubstantiated dismissals of this or that hypothesis as ''ridiculous,'' ''preposterous,'' and the like. These leave me anything but serene in my tentative agreement with its

indeed act alone. Yet there does remain some possibility that the Nazis, or some Nazi faction, set the fire. And in 1989, Babette Gross, ordinarily so scrupulously exact and unspeculative, astounded me by saying that she thought it at least conceivable that the fire really had been set by the Communist *apparat,* after all.[8] If this supposition were to be confirmed, it would raise most arresting and searching possible questions about the origins of the Second World War.

But the most likely fact is that van der Lubbe acted alone and was exactly what he seemed: a confused insignificant man, desperate for a place, *any* place, in a politics, indeed a world, from which he felt himself forever excluded. He was neurotic, hopeless, placeless, powerless; an early prototype for this century's long, ragged line of lonely fanatics and solitary assassins. He was a creature created by the new politics; he was one of its invisible men, seeking to validate and immolate his life of unseen desperation against the new demagogic visibility of the masses. The type has since become familiar, but in 1933, van der Lubbe was a fresh kind of freak for an emergent age. Nothing is easier than to imagine his wishful, bewildered little mind finding its place in the saluting seas of uniforms; he seemed born to sway with the totalitarian throng. He could easily have been a Brown Shirt, except that something, everything, in his make-up was irremediably humiliated, out of it, fatally lonely. "Protest! Protest!" he moaned as they dragged him out of the building he had burned. Protest indeed! In his assassin solitude, poor Marinus van der Lubbe was that new kind of lost soul: the other side of mass man.

The whole case for a larger conspiracy responsible for torching the Reichstag rests on one dubious assumption: That it was a physical impossibility for one person alone to have set so many small fires so quickly in such a very large building. This assumption dominated the claims of both Goebbels and Münzenberg. Tobias refutes it decisively. The boy had stuffed his pockets with cheap phosphorus and paraffin fuses, very easily

---

conclusions. Tobias deals much too airily with crucial witnesses who challenge his views: Hans Gisevius, for instance. He challenges too many people's motives. Most peculiarly, he entirely ignores the commentaries of Ruth Fischer and Franz Borkenau discussed below. Yet these are surely essential witnesses.

Many reliable witnesses were completely convinced of Nazi guilt. As we shall see, there was Gisevius. Arthur Koestler, a no-less-committed anti-communist than Tobias, and a Münzenberg-man who worked in the campaign, was fully convinced by Katz's main line. American intelligence people close to the case, likewise impeccably anti-communist (Mary Bancroft, for example), remained steadfastly convinced of Nazi guilt, though Mary Bancroft and Allen Dulles were greatly influenced by Gisevius and German conservatives close to him, who had their own reasons for insisting upon Nazi guilt.

Yet Tobias is probably right in his major point. Van der Lubbe probably acted alone.

lit and long-lasting—the kind used every morning by Berlin housewives to start the coal in their kitchen stoves. He had dashed through the empty building tossing one after another of these at anything that looked like it would burn. Much would burn. The vast Sessions Chamber was lined with tinder-dry wood and dusty curtains, and the snaking fire took only minutes to suck them up into an inferno.

It is *possible.* Van der Lubbe could have set the Reichstag Fire, as he seems to have done everything, all by himself.

But Goebbels needed a conspiracy, and so conspirators were produced. The four celebrity communists were herded into the dock. These were Dimitrov, the popular but generally powerless Ernst Torgler, and Dimitrov's two Bulgarian lieutenants Popov and Tanev. Not one of these men could be shown to have a provable or even plausible connection to the crime. But then the Nazis seemed to mismanage the Leipzig proceedings in all kinds of ways. One would assume that van der Lubbe could at least have been forced to "confess" to the right "conspiracy." But no: Van der Lubbe drooled and laughed; his great head lolled and rolled in bewilderment. Yet he never "confessed" to anything except his simple claim of having set his fire. As for the judges, it is true that by December 1933 Hitler had not yet entirely demolished an autonomous German judiciary. Yet the behavior of the judges was, if not utterly craven, nonetheless disgracefully partial by any standard. The thoroughly propagandistic nature of the whole event was perfectly evident to everyone. Above all, the ludicrous shakiness of the case is important; Goebbels didn't even *try* to make his frame-up look air-tight. He acted as if the credibility of the case were almost unimportant, and its carelessness only makes the eventual acquittal of all parties except van der Lubbe the more suspicious.

Münzenberg and Katz's strategy for the trial, later refined in the headquarters of the Comintern secret service in Moscow, seems to have begun taking shape almost from the day Willi arrived in Paris. Ten days after the fire, a young novelist and literary activist named Gustav Regler called from Germany and presented Münzenberg with a distant memory and an exceptionally useful bright idea. Until then, Regler had been a talented but marginal left literatus who looked like the young Siegfried and, as a good literary communist, was loosely tangled in Münzenberg's networks. Though everyone assumed that it had required many men to set all those fires in that vast building, no witness had actually *seen* anyone enter the building except the lone, loony Marinus as he teetered in through a broken restaurant window. The newspapers were wondering how all accused conspirators could have got in and out without being seen. For Regler, this speculation brought back a distant memory. From his days as a kid on the barricades of the 1918 revolution, Regler clearly recalled that one path into the Reichstag ran underground, through a tunnel. The tunnel housed steam pipes, and it ran from a separate power plant to the building's basement. Here was an obvious and plausible explanation: All those many arsonists must have come tearing in and out through the tunnel. Awakened by this inspired guess, the novelist took it upon himself to locate blueprints of the capital complex in a Stuttgart archive, whereupon he called Münzenberg with the information that for the right bribe he could have the blueprints photographed.

Willi instantly grasped the point. Regler was told at that moment, over the phone, that a book pinning the arson on the Nazis was being planned and he could consider himself hired as a collaborator. "Don't worry about the money," Münzenberg shouted. "Bring me those photographs!"[9]

The bribe was produced and the pictures made. It was only after Regler was safely on the train to Paris that he dared look at what he had. He locked himself in a lavatory. He slipped the pictures from their envelopes. There was the tunnel all right, just where he remembered it. It led straight from the power station to the Reichstag building. But Regler noticed something more. There was a *second* tunnel, branching off the main one, and running to the basement of another, adjacent building. That building was the official residence of the Reichspresident. And who was the Reichspresident? The man who lived in that house was none other than Hermann Göring. Which meant that there was a direct unseen pathway from Göring's residence into the Reichstag itself.[10]

Regler sank back against the rocking lavatory wall.

Eureka.

Münzenberg set out to prove that through this tunnel a pack of seditious Nazis, mainly from the SA, had streamed into the Reichstag that February night and, after seeing Germany onto the path to state terror, charged out again, back to the safety of Göring's residence.

As their first step, Münzenberg and Otto slapped together and published a sensational "exposé," the book for which Willi had hired Regler over the telephone. This was *The Brown Book of the Hitler Terror,* anonymously orchestrated and partly written by Katz, with the help of many a passionate intellectual drawn into what soon amounted to a Münzenberg propaganda collective in Paris.[11] *The Brown Book* published a few weeks before the Leipzig Trial began, was instantly translated into many languages, and was on display in bookstores everywhere as the event unrolled.

Then a second propaganda stroke was designed for the mass media—radio, newspapers, and the newsreels. This was a Counter-Trial, a "judicial inquiry" staged to "prove" Nazi culpability and held in London in early September 1933. The London Counter-Trial handed down its "verdict" the day before the Leipzig Trial began. Simultaneously, the Münzenberg-men set up various investigatory commissions and committees of inquiry to keep alive the flow of information and propaganda surrounding the event, while maintaining cover and control over the covert actions that ran alongside it.

There were, in fact, two *Brown Books: The Brown Book of the Hitler Terror,* and a much amplified and corrected companion volume, *The Second Brown Book of the Hitler Terror*. Both make hectic and troubling reading. They are obviously propaganda, but they nonetheless retain some of the honor appropriate to the first systematic effort made anywhere to expose German fascism. They document the rapidly growing catalogue of Nazi crimes, often accurately. The eighth chapter of the *Second Brown Book* deals with anti-Semitic persecutions, and although the entire discussion is discreetly anti-Zionist and canted toward a Marxist reading of anti-Semitism, the exposure and attack are there. *The Brown Books* are a collection of inspired guesses, lies, disinformation, and occasionally rock-solid evidence about the emergent Nazi horrors. Where did this information come from? From any place it could be found. From the new underground. From the *apparat*. From refugees. From a number of very shadowy conspiratorial figures, especially in Berlin. And from the empty air.

The fervor and relentlessness of *The Brown Books*' anti-fascism, the novelty and nerve of their exposures, made them two of the most important political tracts of the era. It is quite true that they are trashy, hasty, and dishonest in many ways, including a number of very sinister ways. Yet one need not slip into endorsing Stalinist propaganda to note that their anti-fascist harangue was, in essence, right. The books had considerable success all over Europe and America. It was impossible to be a politically serious person in the fall of 1933 and not have heard of *The Brown Book*. Here, a mere six months after Hitler's accession, stands a work filled with potent evidence that the Nazis were radically degrading and brutalizing the heart of German politics.

While he was secretly conferring in Moscow during the early summer of 1933, the notion of staging a Counter-Trial suddenly jumped into Münzenberg's mind as a memory from secret revolutionary tribunals conducted in Russia before the Revolution.[12] Since the device was a means for co-opting the Nazis' own propaganda show, it could not of course appear to be controlled by Communists. The London Counter Trial was an "impartial inquiry" conducted before an assembly of famous lawyers, jurists, and political and literary celebrities, ranging from Stafford Cripps to H. G. Wells, people whose views would be sought by any widely based anti-fascist movement, and who had been carefully culled for their fame and their appearance of independence. This independence was sometimes even real, though of course everyone was guided with exquisite meticulousness behind the scenes. As usual, there were also "fully witting collaborators." The French bar, for example, was represented by the very same Gaston Bergery who had arranged for Münzenberg's protection and collaboration with the Chautemps government. We may presume Bergery was still a silent partner for his friends in the Elysée and the *Deuxième Bureau*. Others, like the brilliant American civil rights lawyer Arthur Garfield Hays, were imported for their celebrity value and put through their paces as dupes.

This seems to have been the time of Otto Katz's first long sojourn in London, and in it he set out to deepen his contacts with all sorts of noteworthy figures on the left, ranging from Ellen Wilkinson to Victor Gollancz.[13] That aspect of his work was relatively public, and some of it was even publicized. He assumed a role; that of the anti-fascist idealist, fighting the Nazi juggernaut against all the odds, just one man in a small, fated band of a few decent men and women, who would fight for what they believed, and who might not live long. He began to cultivate the saturnine expression of an almost tragic courage. He began to tell stories of his "missions," going into Germany to save just one life, salvage just one ideal. His listeners were understandably moved.[14] These "missions," however, were almost certainly fictitious. I have found no evidence that Katz was ever in Germany while Hitler was in power.

Otto lost no time making English contacts of quite another kind, part of that clandestine work which was an essential aim of the entire anti-fascist enterprise. At the time Otto was working in London, the recruitment of the Cambridge spies was being clinched by his colleagues Blunt and Maly, and one of the Cambridge spies, Guy Burgess, would work quite closely with Katz in the years to come.[15]

But the great public event was Münzenberg and Katz's Counter-Trial in London, set up to ridicule the Nazi proceedings, and convened with great fanfare just before the Leipzig Trial commenced. It was generally a great success, though it was not flawlessly run. Blunders and haste let the mask slip more than once, and it made independents like Arthur Garfield Hays and H. G. Wells mighty uncomfortable from time to time. Hays's account in his memoirs of all that happened is quite damning.[16] Still, across the world, *it* was the news. The press was filled not with a Communist conspiracy but a Nazi conspiracy, or more exactly an SA, or "Brown" conspiracy. Goebbels and the Leipzig judges were thrown entirely on the defensive. This extravaganza made headlines, and lots of them, through two expeditious, showman-like, and devastating weeks. During those weeks, some strange manipulations and conspiracies took place, but no matter; before the civilized world reading the press, the Nazis had been humiliated and shown up, and the civilized world properly rejoiced. In Leipzig, Goebbels's trial mauled the judicial process month after yawning month. The world press sank into the muck of its boredom, with the tedium relieved only occasionally, as in the courtroom appearances of Goebbels and Göring themselves. These were buffoonish. Trussed out in one of his most ostentatious get-ups, Göring careened through his appearance ranting about the insults he'd endured in Münzenberg's campaign. He stomped his heels over *The Brown Book*. "It says that I am a senile idiot, that I have escaped from a lunatic asylum, and that my skull is collapsed in several places!" He wheeled on Dimitrov, hollering "wait till I lay my hands on you outside the sanctuary of this court!"[17]

The world snickered. Van der Lubbe hunched in his seat, numb and almost certainly drugged. His raw gawky arms and legs dangled miles out of his striped prison clothes. Sometimes he would moan, sometimes giggle. Torgler on the other hand was presentably dressed, even elegant. He enjoyed the services of an excellent lawyer who mounted a perfectly creditable defense of his client, which was after all "successful." But Torgler's mind seemed elsewhere. Behind his German composure, it seemed to meander in anxiety. There was fright in his eyes.

Meanwhile, Dimitrov was fearless. He exuded a confidence noted in every news report, visible in every newsreel. The Bulgarians turned downright jaunty as the days wore on. In the dock, the three of them cracked jokes with their guards; the ruddy-cheeked young German cops in their kepis and Teutonic boots were frequently heard suppressing guffaws. Dimitrov was radiant with confidence and contempt. It seemed nothing could shut him up. Everyone noticed his cocky boldness. Dimitrov baited the court. He hectored the tribunal, jeered at its pompous deliberations. In the final days he outraged it by transforming his own defense into an extremely stirring piece of Communist oratory which electrified the room and was ended only when the guards, laughing no longer, dragged him away.

Dimitrov's bravery on this occasion, which came to be the basis for his world-wide celebrity as a communist hero, was however deceptive, and it brings us to the true, and secret, agenda of the Leipzig Trial. Half a century later, it is almost entirely clear that Dimitrov was so very brave as he hectored the Nazis from that Leipzig dock for the simple reason that he was in no danger and knew perfectly well that there was nothing for him to fear. As Dimitrov deployed his rhetorical fire, denouncing the proceedings as rigged, he had his own private, deep-cover secret: It was that the proceedings were rigged, all right—but in his favor. Say what he might, he was safe; he was delivering his ''anti-fascist'' tirades under Hitler's unseen protection; he was the beneficiary of an agreement already reached between the Soviet secret services and the highest-level Nazis, through which he was assured of acquittal and a triumphant return to Russia at the end of what was a propaganda charade played out as a whole high drama of defiance.

Because the Leipzig show trial ended in acquittal. Then and since, in all the propaganda and counter-propaganda about the event, this astounding final turn, perhaps the central fact of the entire affair, is invariably shunted aside and forgotten.

Acquittal? Acquittal in a Nazi show trial this important? How was such a thing even imaginable? Though the point seemed missed at the time, the results totally vitiate the propaganda point of both sides. Of course, it disposes of Hitler's claim that the fire had been a conspiracy led by Dimitrov.* But it also undermines the counter-claim that the Nazis had staged the Leipzig Trial merely to smear the communists and cover their own tracks. Instead of coming to grips with this essential fact, virtually all discussion then and since has been absorbed in the question of who was smearing whom.

This, it would seem, is to miss the point. And to miss the point was the whole idea. For the truth is that this acquittal had been arranged between the two secret services from the beginning.

This is what I am calling here the Dimitrov Conspiracy. Its agenda makes plain that the secret service collaboration between the two great twentieth-century tyrannies did not begin, as many even now still might wish to believe, with the arrangements consequent upon the Nazi-Soviet Pact of 1939. Their collaboration began virtually at the first moment, in the opening weeks of Nazi power. Moreover, this treacherous and unseen af-

* In the politics of the matter, bear in mind that Dimitrov and his lieutenants were not German communists at all but foreigners, and plainly agents of Moscow and the Comintern. To select them as the defendants and fall guys would seem an international matter, a provocation directed at the USSR. Yet the trial rather downplayed Dimitrov's links to Moscow, just as Münzenberg downplayed Hitler's link to the fire.

filiation was consummated not despite, but *through* the Soviet-sponsored "anti-fascist movement," which came to play such a large role in the moral life of this century.

In this latter capacity, as a grand deception in the war of ideas, the Dimitrov Conspiracy assumes a troubling importance, far beyond that merely of being one more seamy secret deal consolidating the new gangster power of German fascism. Both as a practical matter and as a metaphor, the Dimitrov Conspiracy reflects an unseen spiritual bond between the two totalitarianisms of the century. It seems to me likely that it took many enlightened people in the West so long to recognize that communism is monstrous because communism is a monster born from the ideals of the Enlightenment, and the Enlightenment is necessary, indeed indispensable, to the hope of civilization in our era. For that reason, many people whose humanism is grounded in that Enlightenment have from the beginning found it difficult to discern the evils of the Marxist-Leninist State, even long after those evils were forthrightly manifest to any observer without the need to deny them. We are looking here directly at one link between civilization's best and its worst. Protecting the progressive ideal seemed to rest on denying or evading the manifest horrors that had sprung from their radical application. And within the needs of such a denial, Münzenberg and his heirs moved and found their element.

On the other hand, such people encountered no difficulty seeing the evils of Nazism. What was difficult? Those evils were blatant, evident on its face. In the progressive West, it was promptly very clear that Nazism would and could bring nothing but evil to humanity. That much moral perception was easy. Unfortunately, the totalitarian age gave the world two monsters, and they accompanied one another. In retrospect, they seem almost necessary to one another. If the evil of fascism was obvious, the evil of communism presented tremendous obstacles to lucid recognition. The Dimitrov Conspiracy provides an early insight into how these evils worked together, how indeed one served as the other's mask. To a degree that could never have been guessed at the time, the secret arrangement at Leipzig suggests that these two monsters, one visible, the other obscure, were twins.

Here is how it worked. Speculation that the Leipzig Trial was run according to a secret pre-arrangement between the collaborating secret services of the Nazis and the communists is far from new. Rumors of some deal between Hitler and Stalin over the Reichstag Fire Trial were rife at the fringes of the *apparat* almost from the beginning. Franz Borkenau gives an early account of those rumors in his book *European Commu-*

nism. But those are only rumors. Likewise, in the upper circles of the Bulgarian Communist party, which Dimitrov dominated until his death, the story was often heard, told with assurance.[18]

In 1952, these rumors were solidified through the research of Ruth Fischer and disclosed in her book *Stalin and German Communism*. Ruth Fischer, a member of the Eisler family, a major figure in the early German Communist party, a founding personality in the Czech Party, and later a major and passionate anti-Stalinist, explored the matter in considerable depth in her book. Fischer's archives in the Houghton Library at Harvard contain a large amount of unpublished material and correspondence gathered in her exploration of the question.

Here is what Ruth Fischer wrote:

> While the [Leipzig] trial was running its course, I met two important witnesses in Paris—Wilhelm Pieck, who at this time was eager to speak to Maslow and me [Maslow was Fischer's lover and fellow defector from the KPD], and Maria Reese, a Communist Reichstag deputy and the intimate friend of Torgler. (Later she returned to Germany and became a Nazi sympathizer, but this fact does not impinge on her creditability; she was getting the full details from Torgler's lawyer, with whom she was in almost daily contact.) Independently, both of them told me the same story, that before Dimitrov stood up in the courtroom to make his courageous peroration, he knew of the secret arrangement between the GPU and the Gestapo that he would leave it a free man. The other two Bulgarians were included in the arrangement, but Torgler and van der Lubbe were not. Pieck and Reese were both much concerned with this fact, but from different points of view. Pieck, knowing that Torgler had been abandoned by the Politburo, was fearful that he might see through the combination and made a statement in the courtroom baring the secret deal between the two state police forces. When I saw him, therefore, Pieck was busy arranging for a refugee from underground Germany to arrive in London [that is, at the ''Counter-Trial'' then being staged in London under the supervision of Otto Katz] with the startling message that Torgler was a traitor to the anti-fascist cause. Maria Reese's reaction, of course, was quite different; she later wrote a pamphlet breaking with communism, but with only vague allusions to the deal, since she hoped to save Torgler's life and did not want to antagonize the Gestapo. Pieck's courier did go to London and delivered a message in a loud stage whisper, but since Torgler never revealed the arrangement by which Dimitrov was saved, the charge against Torgler was allowed to peter out.[19]

It seems the truth began to slip out through Ernst Torgler, and what seems to have been his girlfriend's alarm at the decision not to include him in the secret deal. The effort to discredit Torgler at the London

Counter-Trial strongly suggests that Otto Katz, as the stage-manager in London, was also party to the conspiracy. But there is more. Arthur Koestler, who had worked with Münzenberg at this time and was an intimate friend of Otto Katz, likewise asserted his dark suspicion that some such collaboration had taken place,[20] while André Malraux, another writer intimate with Katz and Münzenberg's Paris operation, also pointed out his belief that covert collaboration between Hitler and Stalin began at this time, though Malraux did not provide any details beyond his dark thoughts.[21]

Then in 1980, Peter Semerdjiev, a defecting communist, once a member of the Bulgarian Communist party's Central Committee, and an intimate of Dimitrov during the post-war years when Dimitrov was communist director of Bulgaria, published in Paris the memoirs of Dimitrov's lieutenant, Blagoj Simon Popov. In the preface, Semerdjiev re-asserted Fischer's claim, and greatly elaborated upon it, adding information he had learned while working as Dimitrov's subordinate on the Central Committee in Sofia. According to Semerdjiev, the Dimitrov Conspiracy was quite well known among senior communists around the Great Bulgarian Leader.

"In this parody [the Leipzig Trial]," Semerdjiev wrote,

> the main characters are the two dictators, Hitler and Stalin. . . . The script of the trial was prepared by the two dictatorial regimes. On the one hand Moscow, through the Comintern, attempts to raise public opinion and to facilitate Soviet infiltration into the political life of Western Europe. On the other hand Hitler[,] who had just come to power, desperately needed to attract around him the extreme chauvinistic factions in his country. The trial itself is preceded by a secret agreement between the diplomatic services of Hitler and Stalin in the capital of Denmark. According to this agreement, the three Bulgarian "indicted" will be acquitted and immediately exchanged against "German spies" caught on Soviet territory. This diplomatic act is brought to the knowledge of the Bulgarian "accused" before the trial. This is why[,] contrary to what happens to the Germans in the same trial, they have the necessary privileges in food, lawyer's defense visits to the family, correspondence, newspapers and a special room where they receive foreign correspondents.[22]

Semerdjiev admits that he does not have documentary confirmation of the information he learned while on the Central Committee; in his opinion that material was of such sensitivity that it had all been removed to Moscow. Nonetheless, he was able to add many details. As he understands it, Stalin's strategy went through some profound modification sometime between March 1, when Hitler issued his emergency decree, and the time of Dimitrov's arrest on March 9. It was a shift toward greatly raising the political and propaganda stakes invested in the trial, and greatly deepening the Soviets' own involvement.

When Dimitrov was seized in that oddly vulnerable arrest in the Berlin café (though Semerdjiev believes the arrest was probably not planned; that it really did come as a surprise), Stalin promptly responded by arresting some twenty German technicians and specialists who happened to be in his capital, and holding them as hostages to Dimitrov's release. According to Semerdjiev, this precipitated a series of secret meetings between the Nazi and the Soviet services. Dimitrov was head of the Western European Division of the Comintern: He knew a great deal about the secret Soviet networks in Germany and its "underground." Stalin was afraid of those networks being compromised, although he was relatively indifferent to the downfall of the legal German Party. According to Semerdjiev, the two leading items negotiated in the talks between the two services were a degree of safety for the underground networks, and along with it, Dimitrov's release.

We'll address in a moment the issue of why Hitler would have agreed to join in this seemingly bizarre conspiracy. It is important to note here that though Münzenberg surely knew about the general outline of the deal, he was probably not one of those who hammered out its precise terms. According to Mr. Semerdjiev, that was left to Wilhelm Pieck, and the Central Party Archives contain copies of telegrams that fully sustain his claim. Mirov-Abramov, however, would have known all about them, and Münzenberg was involved in intricate consultations with Mirov all through June of that year, planning strategy for Leipzig. Radek would have known about them *in extenso,* and the Central Party Archives clearly show Radek personally directing important conspiratorial aspects of the enterprise.[23] So would Radek's protégé Otto Katz, who had come to Paris as Münzenberg's first conduit of instructions and information after the fire in March.[24]

Dimitrov himself, from the time of his arrest until the time of his acquittal, was kept constantly informed about events as they unfolded through the thoroughgoing penetration of the prison itself. The apparatus had unseen access all over Leipzig. A copy of *The Brown Book* was smuggled into Dimitrov's quite comfortable cell, and there he read it at his ease.[25] The man in charge of keeping Dimitrov instructed and informed was Wilhelm Pieck, the very man whose behavior had first alerted Ruth Fischer's suspicions in Paris during the London Counter-Trial. Pieck guided Dimitrov through the entire experience of investigation and trial, and it was even Pieck who provided Dimitrov with the substance of his last flamboyant oration before the court, that sudden spontaneous display of courage that had stirred the world.[26]

So the main outlines of the Dimitrov conspiracy have been made much more precise by information from those around Dimitrov himself in Bulgaria. But the confirming piece of evidence came in the end from Babette Gross herself. In Munich in 1989, I sketched again Ruth Fischer's claim, and asked her for her view. She immediately confirmed it. She also noted that certain lawyers active in Leipzig had also been party to the arrangement, and added that in later years she herself had met Torgler, and he had told her quite forthrightly about the details.[27]

So the evidence is very powerful. Hitler's persecution of German communism was almost certainly pursued in full collaboration with Stalin and the full knowledge and direct personal co-operation of the future head of the Communist International, using the Comintern's "anti-fascism" as cover. Almost certainly, the acquittal of Georgi Dimitrov was the result of secret arrangements with the Nazis, and the founding scandal of the Soviet-sponsored anti-fascist movement, one of the leading forces in the moral life of this century, was created in direct collaboration with Hitler himself.

But why? The leading question about this collaboration of dictators concerns Hitler's motivation. What conceivable *quid pro quo* would have induced Hitler to cut loose the biggest communist fish he'd ever caught? Ruth Fischer says nothing on this question. Nonetheless, the political circumstances of that moment permit at least a plausible hypothesis.

From Hitler's point of view, the trial's focus on the communists was a diversion. His real preoccupation at this moment was not so much with his enemies the communists, but with his old allies and comrades in the SA. In fact, in the SA, Hitler and the communists had a common enemy, though Hitler wanted to keep his enmity secret. The central question facing Hitler during the latter part of 1933 was what armed force, what *kind* of police and army, he should develop in order to put totalitarian muscle into his new power. This decision was far more important than his struggle with the communists. On it depended the whole basis for his state terror, while internationally the decision would determine the basis for Hitler's pre-war position in the European world.[28]

His choice lay between the established German army and the SA. On the one hand, as Chancellor he stood at the head of the *Reichswehr,* and it was, albeit mistrustfully, at his disposal. On the other, he owed much to the SA, an untrained gang of paramilitary Brown Shirts, the street army which had been so essential to the Nazi party's rise. The leader of the SA was Hitler's long-term comrade, Ernst Röhm; the two men had been co-conspirators from day one, since 1919. From the start, they had used the SA as their instrument of political intimidation; as the extras in the strutting street theater of Nazism; and as a way of galvanizing the various disaffected, often unemployed working-class German males who formed the basis of the Nazi movement, just as they did of the communist movement. When Hitler assumed power in 1933, the throngs of Röhm's Brown Shirts were what Nazism *meant*. They were one reason Hitler was so frightening.

Prior to 1933, this manifestly dangerous private army of ideological fanatics had no official standing whatever in the German government. Yet its brutalizing shadow darkened every aspect of political life. One of Weimar's most lamentable errors had been to relinquish any part of its sovereign monopoly on armed force by permitting such an organization to exist at all. By mid-1933, Röhm had a million men paid and in uniform; three and a half million more stood in the SA reserves. This made the SA, the private army of a political party, one of the largest military organizations in the world; certainly far, far larger than the German army itself.[29] That menacing fact was not lost on any foreign minister in Europe. To be sure, the *Reichswehr* was still in place, and Hindenburg was still its patron and senior general. To be sure, the SA was not a true army. Not quite. Not yet.

But Röhm had waited a long time for his empowerment and in March 1933, he was pretty sure that the time for his reward had come round at last.

Homosexual, indiscreet, deluded, Röhm had always assumed and been assured that when the Nazis took power Hitler would dismantle the *Reichswehr* and transform the SA into *the* German army, with Röhm himself as commandant. This aspiration was totalitarian on its face. It assumed that the army ought to be loyal not to that vague multifarious entity called the nation, but to a *party* and its ideology; not to a country as a whole but an idea, or rather pseudo-idea—fascism; not the territorial security of a Germany once notable for its variousness, but the enforcement within and beyond the German border of one vile dream: *Ein Volk, Ein Reich, Ein Führer*.

The *Reichswehr* for its part despised the SA. Class played a large role in this contempt. In Germany the army was a privileged occupation actively sought out by upper-class men. Its officers viewed Röhm's cohorts as a pack of dim-witted but dangerous boy scouts and political hopheads scraped up from the under-class. To them it was unthinkable that this sickening posse could claim to stand beside the German army of Frederick the Great, Bismarck, and Hindenburg. For the leader of this establishment contempt was the same Hindenburg whom Hitler was so busy manipulating. And the principal object of its contempt was Röhm, with the result that he was thoroughly despised by a number of people whom Hitler viewed as important to his future.

Internationally, the threat of Röhm caused even greater concern and alarm. To Europe, the ''German threat'' and the SA looked very much the same. Had Hitler fulfilled Röhm's wishes, Germany would have re-militarized in a single stroke, endowed by decree with an immense new army of revanchist fanatics obsessed with conquest, and indebted only to Hitler and Röhm. That such an organization might also prove incompetent would not change much: incompetent armies can be just as dangerous in their way as competent ones. In the late spring of 1933, Stalin, Chautemps, and the British, all three, had an obvious interest in common: to stabilize the *Reichswehr* and prevent the militarizing of the SA. Whatever their other differences, on *that* they agreed.

But the center of the secret is that a militarized SA was a prospect viewed with no less alarm by Adolf Hitler himself. Despite his many promises to Röhm, Hitler did not propose to let them become a reality. The world's most profound political secret of the end of March 1933 was that Hitler had made his own decision: He would go with the *Reichswehr*. And he was therefore in search of a way to rid himself of his old comrade, and be rid of his boy scouts too.[30]

Hitler had a number of reasons. He genuinely feared a pre-emptive French invasion, and he suspected, probably rightly, that militarizing the SA *would* make Germany too dangerous too fast for Europe's nerves. Hitler wished to reassure the British too. In February 1934, he was placating Anthony Eden with a promise to demobilize two-thirds of the SA and open the rest to international inspection.[31] But his truest motive was his simplest: Would Hitler establish Röhm, overnight and by his own decree, as the most powerful man in Europe? More powerful even than himself? Capable, perhaps, of a coup?

On the contrary.

In late 1933 only a minuscule handful of people knew that in absolute secret Hitler had begun to conspire with his newest henchman, Heinrich Himmler, to consolidate his personal control over the German police and military through an interlocking set of new elite corps. These were to be the SS, the SD, and the Gestapo, and they were to replace the SA as the backbone of Nazi power. In fact, the very first job assigned to this new consortium of militarized police would be to serve as Hitler's weapon in one sudden but gigantic act of gangsterism through which the SA would be demolished and its leadership, beginning with Röhm and all his lieutenants, rounded up and slaughtered in the seventy-two hours of infra-government terror that came to be known as the Night of Long Knives.[32]

In my view, this is the key to the entire event. *The secret but true purpose of the Leipzig Trial was to discredit the SA, prior to its elimination.* It was a common interest in which Hitler and Stalin found the basis for a profoundly secret liaison. In the light of this shared interest, the entire thrust both of the Nazi campaign and of Münzenberg and Katz's effort suddenly becomes coherent. The common purpose of both disinformation campaigns was not primarily an attack on each other, though they called each other names. The common purpose, clearly understood by both Hitler and Stalin, was to prepare Röhm and the SA for the slaughter.

Discrediting Röhm was work Hitler could not perform himself without alerting Röhm to his danger. But the communists? Let *them* make the headlines. Let them alarm the world, and the *Reichswehr.* It was the first of a number of arrangements in which both dictators made secret use of each other to discredit their own internal enemies. The entire thrust of *The Brown Books* and the London Counter-Trial was to discredit the SA and in particular Röhm. Interestingly, both *Brown Books* go rather easy on Hitler personally. Of course, the most famous Nazi of all is much vilified, but Münzenberg's campaign was careful never to blame Hitler himself for the fire. On the contrary, the dictator was exculpated, explicitly and often. *The Brown Books* know their culprit: It's the SA, the SA, that's to blame. The SA set the fire. The SA is the polluted source of Nazi violence. The SA is brutalizing German politics with its atrocities—and both *Brown Books* present a long, often accurate and fully damning inventory of those atrocities. Most important of all, the Münzenberg campaign never misses a chance to raise the threat of an SA coup against Chancellor Hitler, or even more alarming, a coup against the *Reichswehr.*[33]

The true target of both dictators was Röhm. They set out to destroy the SA's political base by showing that its leadership was filled with treacherous adventurers and that Ernst Röhm was an unstable degenerate not fit for power.

And who could deny that it was the simple truth?

Early in the morning of June 30, 1934, Hitler flew to Munich. Upon the signal of his plane touching down in that city, the Blood Purge began, and Hitler's newly empowered elite corps embarked upon its first genuine test as an armed fist. Throughout Germany, the principal leaders of the SA suddenly found themselves face to face with something new, a fresh horror emerged whole from the swamp of Nazi intrigue: the Waffen SS. Arriving at the Ministry of the Interior in Munich, the Chancellor stepped into a reception room to behold the floor piled with corpses; the shot, stabbed, and bludgeoned bodies of sundry SA true believers who'd got up early and donned full uniform to welcome their leader ''in state,'' and who now littered the official parquet in their blood-soaked best. Hitler then proceeded to Wiesee, a Munich suburb, where, in a resort sanitarium, the foremost SA big-wigs had forgathered for a special ''conference'' ordained by their Führer. Hitler strode into Röhm's bedroom and roughly shook him awake. ''Bind him,'' came the command. Down the hall, Edmund Heines (a central object of Katz's attack) was found in bed with his own chauffeur. Both men were shot dead as they struggled to scramble free. Up and down the screaming halls the SS went. Hitler then retired to the Brown House, fond venue of so many happy days, while all across Germany the machine guns began to blaze and the co-ordinated wave of peremptory arrests and murders began and went on for the next seventy-two hours.

Back in Paris, this event was viewed with satisfaction, but it was in Moscow that, as we shall see, it was watched with an interest that opened new paths. In this context, it should be noted that the archives show that during the campaign, Radek himself directed his agents in Berlin to find ways of implicating leading figures in the S.A.[34] Immediately after Röhm had been murdered in the Blood Purge, a third and final book was instantly produced, once again anonymously written by Otto, filled with ''documentation'' forged by two literary workers in the *apparat*: Bruno Frei and Alfred (''Konny'') Norden. This was called *The White Book on the Executions of June 30, 1934*.[35]

Katz's *White Book* functioned to cap the arguments of *The Brown Books* and revise the list of prime SA culprits and arsonists in such a way that the Communist version of SA history was co-ordinated with the actual hit list of Röhm's slaughtered lieutenants—Karl Ernst, Walter von Mohrenschild, and others. *The White Book* has the look of an attempt to square all versions of the event and bring the two disinformation campaigns, communist and Nazi, into consonance.

It should be noted that the manuscript of *The White Book* was meticulously edited in Moscow by Dimitrov, and that in those days Dimitrov did very little that was not supervised by Stalin himself.[36]

Though Röhm was the second most powerful man in Germany, until the trial he had not been among the more visible Nazis. Before the Leipzig Trial, he had always ceded the spotlight to Hitler, Göring, Goebbels, and others. But now the leader of the SA was suddenly and unwillingly made world-famous when the news broke that this hero of the new German manhood was a homosexual.

It is quite true; Röhm was a homosexual, though the fact was little known. Münzenberg and Katz made it famous through the device of a little black propaganda and forgery. Here is how it was done.

One of *The Brown Books*' most enduring claims is that Marinus van der Lubbe was a homosexual. The notion survives to this day, something many people have vaguely heard and suppose they "know" about the arsonist: He was a homosexual. There is no evidence anywhere for any such thing. It was a pure fabrication of Katz, concocted sometime in 1933 during a visit to the Netherlands with a Dutch journalist.[37]

The lie had only one purpose. It was to link van der Lubbe sexually to Röhm and thus make the latter's homosexuality news. In 1933 even more than now, serious newspapers would generally not publish information about a person's sexual tastes unless they impinged on hard news. Until then, Röhm's homosexuality had been known to a relatively small number of insiders. But when Katz concocted evidence of what seemed to be Röhm's homosexual fling with the man who torched the Reichstag, the fact was suddenly plastered across the front page of every newspaper in the world.

The device for staging this fraud was a document which the *apparat* either invented or acquired from some interested party still unknown. It consisted of a list of names, mainly nicknames and the first names of boys, and was produced at the London Counter-Trial by a "Herr W. S."—in fact a Katz operative—who claimed to be a friend of a certain "Dr. Bell." It was claimed that Dr. Bell's special task in life consisted in procuring boys for Röhm, but that the physician-pander had prudently kept this secret inventory of their names as his "life insurance."

"Herr W. S." testified that Dr. Bell had told him all about picking up van der Lubbe as a hitch-hiker in 1931. Finding him "comely," Bell claimed to have supplied young Marinus to *Obergruppenführer* Röhm as a sexual partner. It is fair to note here that to judge by the evidence of his photographs, van der Lubbe was an exceptionally homely, really almost repellant, youth. A simian goofiness was plastered on his squinting features. His flabby body dangled and lurched. He looked comical in his clothes. The idea of him as "comely" is bizarre.

No matter. *The Brown Book* proceeds with "Herr W. S.'s" tale:

> Dr. Bell fetched a number of papers from a secret cabinet. He pointed to a sheet and said: "This is Röhm's love-list. If I ever publish it, Röhm is a dead man." He showed me the list, which contained some thirty names. I remember very well that one of them was Rinus, followed by a Dutch name beginning with van der.[38]

The news was sensational, and it ran world-wide.

It was pure fraud. More real but no less conspiratorial was the information purveyed in the *Brown Books* and the Counter-Trial about SA brutalities. This information was often very accurate. It came from many covert contacts, but especially certain leaks within Police Headquarters on the Prinz Albrechtstrasse in Berlin.[39]

Precisely who was pilfering the files in that turbulent place is a little unclear. Several possible sources for the leaks present themselves. One might have been communists still working for the Berlin police. Under Weimar the Berlin Police had been Social Democratic, or "pink"—sufficiently so that in 1933, many communists and sympathizers remained within its ranks. A second possible source might have been the Nazis themselves, insiders tied to the new Gestapo, men with a vested interest in discrediting the SA, especially if they had the nod from Hitler. One such figure was Rudolf Diels, a rapidly rising thug in Hitler's confidence and slavishly operating on instructions from above. A third possibility were non-Nazi conservatives, true believers in the honor of the *Reichswehr*, horrified by what they witnessed every day in this loathsome center of police intrigue and violence. Or it might have been some ingenious combination of all three.

The most famous of these conservatives was a young lawyer named Hans Bernd Gisevius, who during World War II served as a major covert contact for American intelligence and was a crucial conspirator in the von Stauffenberg plot of 1944 to kill Hitler—yet another effort on the part of the *Reichswehr* to reclaim its honor and save the country.[40] In his job on the Prinz Albrechtstrasse, young Gisevius was deep in quiet, angry conspiracy, trying to undermine the SA, working together with his immediate superior, another non-Nazi conservative named Arthur Nebbe. We know that the effort included stealing files and supplying them to the anti-Nazi underground: Much of the stolen information surely appeared in Münzenberg's campaigns. The irony is that if Gisevius was the leak, he was probably playing into Hitler's hands.

In fact, Hitler may even have known what he was doing, and been delighted. Consider the following strange course of events.

One week after the London Counter-Trial ended, Hitler (in real or feigned anger) suddenly removed Rudolf Diels, who was his personal henchman in the Prinz Albrechtstrasse, presumably over the breaches of security that had shown up in the London propaganda. Diels seemed disgraced; Hitler seemed enraged; Diels fled to Czechoslovakia, from which it was rumored that he threatened "embarrassing revelations" if he was not restored to power. And indeed Diels was soon re-instated. To Gisevius and Nebbe, this reversal seemed the end. Diels was their archenemy, and with his exoneration over breaches they may well have caused, they were certain that the charges would next fall on them, and with a vengeance. But no. The day of Diels's return, Gisevius was summoned to his office and greeted with a sudden warmth and friendliness. Astonishing! Gisevius was not to be shot but promoted. To a big new job! Gisevius was to become the Gestapo's special liaison. Where? To the Reichstag Fire Trial!

Now, Diels loathed Gisevius. This promotion and surprise had been ordained from above, during Diels's re-instatement meeting the day before, when the chief of the fledgling Gestapo was given his new marching orders by Hitler himself.

These new orders focussed entirely on the Reichstag Fire, and they undoubtedly included Gisevius's promotion. They ended with Hitler informing Diels that his first, absolutely confidential order of business would be to learn all he could "on Herr Röhm and his friendships." Hitler let that one sink in for a moment. Then he added, "This may be the most important assignment of your career."[41]

Another source for links between the Nazi Reich and the Soviets may have been a certain General and intelligence officer named von Bredow, the then director of military intelligence for the *Reichswehr*. Bredow is known to have had elaborate clandestine contacts with yet another "White Russian" organization, this one located, like Katz, in Paris, and known as the "Guchkov circle." The Guchkov circle was penetrated from top to bottom by Soviet agents. One quite reliable report to the American State

Department of 1940 asserts that Otto Katz had acted as a ''go-between'' for Bredow and the Soviets. This may or may not have been true: It *is,* however, a perfect fit for our available information. The same memorandum asserts, most interestingly, that ''Katz knows the secrets of the Brown house.''[42] As an experienced intelligence officer, not a Nazi, and loyal first to the army, Bredow had every motive to assist Katz, since he knew the secrets of ''Brown'' intrigue in attacking the SA, especially if that assistance were sanctioned by the Chancellor's silent nod—though to be sure, after June 30 such operations would have supplied Bredow with information highly compromising to Hitler among his fellow Nazis. If Bredow believed he was safely on the winning side, he was in error. On the night of the Blood Purge he'd helped create, Bredow walked home, apparently perfectly at ease. At his doorstep, he was met by agents of the SS, who drew their revolvers and without one word, shot him dead.[43]

Another fabrication attacking the SA is a now long-forgotten bit of disinformation known as the ''Oberfohren Memorandum.'' The evidence strongly suggests that this extraordinary forgery was concocted by Münzenberg's old lieutenant, Gibarti, working through a press front he then ran called the German Information Office.[44] The Archives show that the German Information Office was entirely under Soviet covert control, and also indicate an elaborate role for this ''press service'' in campaigns to come.[45]

Dr. Ernst Oberfohren was a German professor of political science who in middle age became a rather dour and unspectacular conservative member of the Reichstag. As a conservative, Oberfohren was hostile to communists and fascists alike, though his party, the German Nationalists, was caught in the gravitational field of fascism and had been an uneasy partner in the right-wing coalition of Hitler's first weeks in power. Oberfohren was outraged by this alliance; vocally opposed to those in his party who imagined Hitler could be brought to heel and ''instructed,'' he seems to have manipulated rather dishonestly to win his point. He was caught out, resigned his seat, and had a nervous breakdown. As all his worst fears came true, the wretched man shot himself on May 6, 1933.

This death in despair of a high insider offered the *apparat* a great opportunity. Safely beyond denial, Oberfohren could be cited as ''source'' for the inside stories about SA perfidy which Gibarti was then planting in the British press, especially in the *Manchester Guardian.* Karl Radek's secret directives now in The Moscow Archives explicitly order his people to make use of the *Manchester Guardian* as a leading press outlet in the campaign. He was undoubtedly making use of contacts already in place and coordinated by Münzenberg's people.''[46] As the high point, the German Information Office released a ''memorandum'' purporting to have been written by Oberfohren (or a journalist close to him) just before he pulled the trigger. In it he recounts all the horrors he has seen. It made very sensational front-page news everywhere.

It was a pure piece of black propaganda, most likely written by Gibarti himself. Like the rest of the campaign, the Oberfohren Memorandum exempts Hitler personally from current evils. It actively promotes and admires the *Reichswehr*, while seeking to show how Röhm and his men are a menace to German legitimacy. It describes Hitler not as the master of the situation but a front man losing control of the mad dogs in the SA.[47] Hitler's alliance with Hindenburg, Oberfohren said, can never survive the fascist hordes threatening them both. Röhm (assisted by Göring and Goebbels) is forever described contriving to rush headlong into a coup d'état against Hindenburg, the coalition, and the *Reichswehr*. Above all, the *Reichswehr*.[48]

This fantasy, that Hitler was somehow not really in charge, proved peculiarly resilient. The same idea was widely believed inside American Intelligence during the war, including by people close to Allen Dulles, and it was swallowed whole by many German insiders as well.[49]

On the day of the Blood Purge itself, while the firing squads shattered the calm in Wiesee and Munich, and grandiose eminences were having their brains blown out in their offices, a leading Berlin police official rushed up to Hitler to tell him that Himmler was a dangerous man, he was killing people, and he had too much power.[50]

One wonders that Hitler did not burst into his celebrated insane laughter.

Two days before Christmas 1933 the world was astonished to hear that van der Lubbe had been sentenced to death in the guillotine, while all the other Leipzig defendants had been acquitted. *Acquitted*! Göring and the Nazi press raged in bewilderment until a new line appeared, claiming that the acquittal was proof of the autonomy of German justice under Hitler. Torgler promptly vanished into a concentration camp. Dimitrov, Popov, and Tanev were removed from Leipzig and conveyed to Moabit Prison, just outside Berlin itself. There they were held, pending their return to the Soviet Union, for two months longer. Meanwhile, Münzenberg continued his campaign and Hitler refined the plot against Röhm. Then, at the end of February, exactly a year after the fire, they were suddenly released and flown in triumph to Moscow.

The work was done.

A rather revealing episode about literature makes a fitting ending for this epochal but still rather mysterious founding event of the Second World War. A few days after the acquittal, two Germans associated with the Committee of Inquiry into the Leipzig Trial—in other words, Katz and some minion—approached André Gide and André Malraux with a proposal for a mission to Berlin. Throughout the Dimitrov campaign Gide and Malraux had been used incessantly in all kinds of capacities, ranging from signing petitions to chairing the more chic protest meetings of the Parisian intelligentsia.[51]

But this new mission seemed more glamorous. Gide and Malraux were to travel to Germany and present themselves (with a mass of petitions) to none other than Hitler himself. Well, if not Hitler, Goebbels—and use their prestige as the most eminent men of letters in Europe to press for Dimitrov's prompt release.

Shrewdly, Katz or his men appealed to Malraux's sense of himself as a swashbuckler, his vision of himself as the Gallic T. E. Lawrence. A persistent identification with the British secret agent and adventurer was an important fantasy for Malraux.

Within a few days, *L'Humanité* had announced that Malraux and Gide, youth and wisdom together, the embodied conscience of Europe, would travel into the heart of the Hitler terror to save brave Dimitrov from his imprisonment. January 2, the night before their departure, Gide dined at the Malraux' with two friends, both very close to the communist propaganda apparatus, Alix Guillain and Bernard Groethuysen. All the gossip was conveyed to Gide's neighbor and his closest confidante, a woman named Maria van Rhysselberghe, or as Gide affectionately called her, "La Petite Dame." La Petite Dame adored Gide; she acted in many ways as a kind of shadow wife to him, his daily companion, the woman with whom Gide could be himself and not be alone. They lived in the same building, and when Gide was in Paris they saw each other several times a day. Back in her own apartment, however, and without Gide's knowledge, Maria van Rhysselberghe maintained a copious diary filled with all his table talk, the entire inventory of his comings and goings. She was an unannounced Eckermann, who left behind a remarkably absorbing and very reliable record of his life.

All that happened around the visit to Berlin was duly inscribed in La Petite Dame's secret journal. Excitement was high.

Though Malraux and Gide probably did not know it, the mission was a fool's errand and a fraud. Once they had left the Gare de l'Est and crossed into Germany, press coverage came to a complete halt. The disappearance of that attention was an exact correlative of the attention of the *apparat*. Katz does not seem to have felt the smallest interest in what his ambassadors might or might not do in Berlin—least of all what they might or might not say to Hitler or Goebbels. All that mattered was that they be *seen* to go. As Katz may even have foreseen, when the two great men arrived in the German capital, not a single important Nazi was in Berlin. Everyone—Hitler and Goebbels too—had adjourned to Munich for a party conference there. Nor was there anybody from the other side, from the Berlin underground *apparat,* to receive or guide them. They simply got off the train, proceeded to a hotel and thence to the Ministry of Information on the Wilhelmstrasse. It was entirely empty save for its secretaries. The two representatives of the conscience of Europe had no official meeting of any kind with anyone.

Malraux and Gide decided instead to leave a letter addressed to Goebbels. Judging from its style, I would guess (uncertainly) that its author was Gide. It explicitly regrets Goebbels's absence, explaining that throughout Europe the fate of the Bulgarians was causing mounting anxiety, and how much it was to be regretted that they could not return to France bearing the news of the Bulgarians' imminent release. No mention of Torgler in his concentration camp appears at all. This letter was handed to an aide, and the two writers left.[52]

As closely as I can reconstruct it, this is what really happened. It is flatly contradicted, however, by André Malraux's own account of the event thirty-eight years later. In an interview with Jean Lacouture in 1972, Malraux insisted that he and Gide had indeed been ushered into Goebbels's presence, where they made their case. Malraux quoted what he claims was the Reichsminister's response. "What you are seeking is justice," Goebbels is supposed to have said. "What we are interested in is something else—German justice," to which nationalistic, phrase-making Malraux claimed Gide bleated a feeble "*Hélas*!"—his sole contribution to the discussion.

So far as I am able to determine, this story is a complete fabrication. That the major Nazis were not in Berlin that day is clear. If for some reason Goebbels returned unexpectedly or had not yet left, there remains the letter itself, the text of which was widely publicized, the whole gambit of which is to deplore Goebbels's absence. All available Gide scholarship, moreover, is unanimous in reporting that the two men met nobody of any political importance. This includes the eyewitness report of La

Petite Dame in her journals, recorded immediately after having herself discussed the event with both Gide and Alix Guillain.

Malraux's account is a fraud.

It is easy to see that a man of Malraux's amour propre might have invented his encounter on the heights of evil to cover the stinging recognition, still perhaps felt forty years later, that in his political vanity he had been used; that his aspiration (shared by Gide) to assume the mantle of Victor Hugo and Émile Zola as the *grand homme des lettres,* conscience of Europe, had been made ridiculous.

Yet it was while concocting the story of his meeting with Goebbels that Malraux confided his suspicion, based on what information he does not say, that while he and Gide were enacting the Berlin charade ''Hitler and Stalin were already entering into collusion.''[53] By 1972 Malraux, Minister of Culture under de Gaulle, was in a position to have pretty good information on this subject.

In any case, Gide and Malraux were in Berlin with time on their hands. Characteristically, Malraux tried to put together an encounter with a great man: Oswald Spengler, author of *The Decline of the West.* But Spengler was out of town. Well, in that case he might try his in-laws: Clara Malraux's parents were German Jews long resident in France. But the Goldschmidts were also not available. It was just a bad time. For the author of *La Condition Humaine,* the mission to Berlin turned out to be a dead loss.

Gide was at least able to go off and spend the evening in a gay bar.[54] He had always liked that part of Berlin life, and even at that late date, six months before the slaughters of the Blood Purge, it was still possible to find it there, a lingering bit of Weimar, under the lindens.

Chapter 5

The Deal

And so the founding event of Stalin's "anti-fascist" campaign was almost certainly cover for the first of several deals with Hitler and the Nazi government. The Dimitrov arrangement was only a first step in Stalin's larger policy. For more was coming, and from both sides.

Shortly after dawn on July 3, 1934, three days after the Night of Long Knives had begun the Blood Purge, Hitler's juddering private airplane touched down at Tempelhof airport in Berlin, bearing the Führer back from his bloody days and nights in Munich. On the tarmac stood a tense committee of senior Nazis, assembled to welcome their now absolutely undisputed leader and greet the new age of gangster politics. At the head of the group, which was divided between murderers and victims-to-be, hovered Himmler and Göring, clutching their lists.

The bleak dawn light was an appropriate violence of red on black. Moving past his mute saluting men, Hitler seemed slack, dazed. He stared into the vacancy. His lips sagged, and as he walked he dragged his feet, as though shuffling through dead leaves, or trash.[1]

In the middle of the very night of June 30, the night the Blood Purge began, Stalin himself greeted the new age with a similar gathering of murderers and victims-to-be. It was after midnight when Stalin summoned the politburo and his intelligence chiefs to the Kremlin for an assessment of the situation. His demeanor in that small-hours meeting was calm, methodical, and entirely unsurprised. His information was remarkably exact, and it had reached his study with amazing speed: As he spoke, Röhm's wailing minions were still being machine-gunned in their beds.[2]

The make-up of the meeting was most noteworthy. To begin with, nobody from the army had been called to hear what Stalin thought about an event that totally transformed military affairs in Europe. It seems Stalin did not particularly want the army to hear what he thought. The group was dominated by people from the intelligence services, including the immediate superior of a man who four years later would defect, Walter Krivitsky. This man's name was J. K. Berzin, and he will later rejoin our story in a position of great covert power during the Spanish Civil War.[3] There were other oddities. For example, seated strangely near Stalin was a conferee whose presence at first blush seemed inexplicable.

It was Münzenberg's old comrade and patron Karl Radek. At that moment in Soviet history, Radek bore the cumbersome title of director of the Information Bureau of the Central Committee of the Communist Party. To the world, Radek looked like a famous Bolshevik who wrote big features for *Isvestia* and appeared at culture conferences. None of that could have placed him so near Stalin that night. The true reason for Radek's presence was not visible.

Stalin opened the meeting with some general observations about Nazi politics. They were based on excellent information, much of it supplied by spies working in Germany as part of the anti-fascist underground. Hitler, he said, was dealing at this moment with various opponents—dangerous, radical opponents—to his "moderate" policies: disloyal monarchist rightists in the army, and Nazi radicals like Röhm. Such people were unable to supply that unequivocal loyalty the rest of the German army was giving their Führer so very impressively.

Fortunately Hitler would definitively terminate these annoyances this very night. As for the Europeans, Stalin predicted (correctly) that their leadership would mistake the change for some sort of weakness on Hitler's part. They were quite wrong. Hitler would emerge from this night not weaker, but the most "mighty" (a favorite word) personage in Europe. The Führer was proving himself. And of course that would have profound consequences for Soviet policy.

Henceforth, Stalin told the meeting, Soviet policy would be bound to Germany. Krivitsky later summarized the dictator's position. "Stalin had always believed in coming to terms early with a strong enemy. The night of June thirtieth convinced him of Hitler's strength." Krivitsky continued: "The course of Soviet policy toward Nazi Germany followed from

Stalin's dictum. The Politbureau decided at all costs to induce Hitler to make a deal with the Soviet government.''[4]

It was—or it seemed—that simple. In the middle of the Night of Long Knives itself, Stalin announced his policy: ''to cut a deal with Hitler regardless of setbacks of rebuffs.''[5] Five full years before the pact, the course was set. The room took it in. Krivitsky does not indicate that Karl Radek, leader of the anti-fascist movement, who was sitting near Stalin, showed the faintest flicker of surprise at that moment.

Radek showed no surprise because he felt no surprise. He was among the few who had known the true policy from the start: that Stalin's dual policy toward Hitler consisted of overt anti-fascism *plus* secret appeasement. In fact, Radek may have been the only figure who was fully aware of the double game. He was the senior Bolshevik most associated with the anti-fascist campaign Münzenberg was orchestrating in the democracies.[6] He was also Stalin's secret emissary for negotiations with the German ambassador seeking to appease Hitler and prepare for the pact. And why not? What better cover for such an emissary than ''anti-fascism''?[7]

Radek was an old friend of Walter Krivitsky. Both were Jewish Poles in a Russian world; both were protégés of Felix Dzerzhinsky. Radek used to come around to Krivitsky's office in the Lubyanka for half-indiscreet chats, and some of our best information about Radek during this changing and deceptive time comes from Krivitsky's account. Krivitsky does not seem to have known that Radek was already negotiating with the Germans, but what he did learn would have come as a jolt to the thousands of people in Europe and America who were committing themselves and not infrequently sacrificing their lives to the campaign against Hitler and Hitlerism.

''Strategic Eyewash for fools'' is what Radek called that campaign in Krivitsky's company. As for Hitler's attack on German communism, only ''idiots'' imagined that ''Soviet Russia should turn against Germany because of Nazi persecution of Communists and Socialists.''[8] The anti-fascist campaign was a mere maneuver, ''a matter of big politics.'' Stalin ''had not the slightest intention of breaking with Germany.'' Indeed, Krivitsky claims that in 1933–34 nobody in the upper reaches of the apparatus—presumably including Münzenberg—''dreamed'' of a genuine break with Germany.[9] To be sure, the anti-fascist campaign had its strategic purposes: It galvanized the left, it induced the democracies to re-arm, it formed the emotional basis for renewed loyalty to the Soviets. But what Stalin really sought, and almost from the beginning, was alliance with Hitler.[10]

Alliance with Hitler? In 1939, when the defecting secret agent told this to Western intelligence services he was brushed aside as almost mad. When Krivitsky was rebuffed by governments, he went public with his information. His articles were greeted with unrelenting vilification from the left and gasps of disbelief from everyone else. *Alliance with Hitler!* This was lunacy, stuff for derisive laughter, absurd, proof that Krivitsky was a fraud and probably a monster.[11]

Then a few months after Krivitsky published these claims, the Nazi-Soviet Pact was signed in Moscow, exactly when he predicted it would be signed. Absurdity had become prophecy.

The prophecy was remarkably accurate, and since 1939 the years have further confirmed most of Krivitsky' s other claims. For example, in 1939 he gave in broad but precise outline the Cambridge Conspiracy of Philby and Blunt. He also sketched in general but exact terms, the *apparat*'s penetration of the New Deal, both enterprises conducted under the auspices of the ideals Radek dismissed.

Throughout the summer of 1934, intelligence reports about the Blood Purge kept rolling in. Stalin read them all, totally absorbed. He meticulously studied every document. Famous for his *Sitzfleisch,* the schoolboy of terror was doing his homework, page by slow page. As he planned great things, no detail was too slight. Every scrap mattered. His diligence would mature in the Kirov murders and the Great Terror, events that would make the Blood Purge seem small.[12]

In that slow rumination lies an important difference between the two monsters. Hitler's tyranny was defined by impatience. He was fast, and speed was his strength. He disarmed his enemies through the theatrical lightning of his violence. Stalin on the other hand was slow—slowness itself. Hitler acted soon, Stalin at last. Stalin's was the soul of the bureaucrat, Hitler's, of an actor. Stalin's terror owed nothing to effect; its whole power lay in immovable, faceless implacability. One is told that it was rare, during the thirties, for Muscovites to pronounce his dreaded name, whereas Hitler's name was spouted in the ghastly Heil Hitler! salute every time people met. For Stalin, patience was murder's highest instrument, and his vengeance, not one whit less cruel than Hitler's, could wait forever. They were the tortoise and the hare of totalitarianism.

And now the tortoise was considering his next slow step.

The use of the anti-fascist campaign as cover for the appeasement of Hitler and negotiations for the pact is one of the most daring and, in its vile fashion, brilliant acts of duplicity in the history of politics. It was indeed so absolute in its betrayal of the most essential moral issues in modern politics that even a half century later it is difficult to grasp. Yet it is essentially very simple.

Stalin pursued a dual policy, seemingly contradictory, but in fact consistent. Once Hitler held power, Stalin's policy was to stabilize his Eastern border by directing Hitler's aggression toward the democracies. If there was war, he wanted it to be between Germany and the West, while he waited out a bruising conflict safely allied with Hitler. Stalin seems to have assumed that Hitler's evil would be as cautious as his own. He was completely convinced that the Germans would never embark upon a two-front war. Of course, despite his considerable admiration for the tyrant in Berlin, Stalin did not want to see Hitler *win*. The idea was to destroy both Hitler *and* the democracies in a Second World War that would end with Stalin moving a fresh Red Army west, into areas prepared for him by his secret services, only after the real fighting was over, when he could stab his battle-weary ally in the back, gangster to gangster.[13]

So the aim was dual. First, to direct German aggression westward. For this, Stalin needed to rouse the democracies against the German threat. Hence, the anti-fascist campaign.

Second, in order to assure that Hitler really would turn westward, he needed absolutely secret negotiations arranging for a stabilized division of Eastern Europe, mutual assistance, and eventually a reliable alliance. Hence, Radek's missions with the German Ambassador. Of course neither position was ''sincere.'' Questions of sincerity did not enter Stalin's thinking.

As for European socialism, one might assume that the Comintern's every resource would be consumed by the crisis Hitler was creating for it in Berlin. Not altogether so. Stalin viewed events in Germany from a very different perspective. He did not feel the sense of anger and peril one might assume the world's leading communist would have experienced over the rise of Hitler.[14]

And of course, Hitler's murder of German democracy troubled the Soviet dictator not at all. On the contrary. He had abetted it from the start. Even Hitler's assault on German communism was not a cloud so impenetrably dark that Stalin could not discern a little silver peeking through. True, Gestapo rifle butts were battering down communist doors, and the German leadership was being rounded into concentration camps. True, the gangs of street hoods who had been the muscle of the German Party were pulling on their brownshirts and strutting in a new parade.

But was this new enemy absolutely unwelcome? Not absolutely. The

German communists were not likely to take power legally, and even if they did, the wrong kind of communist Germany might prove dangerously independent. On the other hand, a proper understanding with Hitler would help purge German communism of that wrong kind. Let Hitler do it. Besides, Stalin believed that his kind of power in Europe required the collapse of the established "bourgeois" order. He believed, correctly as events proved, Germany would be his only *after* a war. Stalin was a Marxist-Leninist, after all: He assumed that whatever destroyed that order helped him.[15]

It was an exceptionally penetrating and far-sighted scenario for the Second World War. Its resemblances to the Second World War that really took place are of course numerous. But there was one great oversight, so typical of the tortoise's about the hare.

Stalin simply did not expect Barbarossa. At least not so *quickly*.

Captured Nazi foreign ministry documents reveal that Stalin began highest-level and absolutely secret approaches toward the Nazi government almost immediately after Hitler assumed power in 1933. The discussions took place with the German ambassador in Moscow, not through Stalin's foreign ministry but a more select emissary, outside the bureaucracy. This emissary was Radek.[16]

Before Hitler took power, Stalin's public anti-fascism had been muted and ambivalent, as had both Marxist theory and its accompanying cant. Fascism was a symptom of bourgeois society tearing itself to pieces, capitalism unmasked and destabilized, moving toward its revolutionary death agony.

Stalin put this familiar theory into practice. He foresaw great things in the demolition of Weimar. Like a devout Bolshevik, he followed Lenin's Zimmerwald policy to the letter, giving no quarter to any non-Soviet party of the left—"social fascists" all, which he marked for destruction. And if Hitler could do the job, so much the better.

There was even some prospect of Soviet military aid to Germany. All through the twenties, and until May 1933, both secretly and publicly Stalin had supplied Germany with a brisk exchange of military assistance. After May 1933, Stalin terminated the aid, but Radek was nonetheless authorized to keep alive the prospect of Nazi-Soviet military collaboration. Indeed he waxed effusive and sentimental over it. "There are magnificent lads in the SA and the SS," Radek told his German contacts. "You'll see. The day will come when they'll be throwing hand grenades for us."[17]

. . .

Even after anti-fascism became a dominating communist preoccupation, it passed through differing phases and served differing ends. The anti-fascism of *The Brown Book* may seem very like the anti-fascism of the Popular Front, and to the outsider, they must have looked identical. They were not identical. The earlier anti-fascism, for all its deceptions, was a genuine instrument in Stalin's carrot and stick policy toward Germany. The Popular Front was more radically deceptive than that. To be sure, the idea was still to pressure Hitler toward the all-desired alliance. But it added to the Big Lie in Europe a sinister domestic agenda that was no less important.

To a very significant degree, the Popular Front was a propaganda front for the Great Terror. Stalin's campaign annihilating every vestige of independent political thought inside Soviet Russia coincides precisely with the campaign proclaiming democratic pluralism and openness in the West. This coincidence is of defining importance for understanding them both. The Front and the Purge were prepared simultaneously. The heyday of both was 1936 and especially 1937. By the spring of 1938, with the Moscow murders mainly complete, Stalin began to wash his hands of the propaganda operation. By the summer of 1939 he killed it dead.

The instigating event of the Terror was significantly modelled on the Night of Long Knives and on the wave of fear that followed. In the middle of the night of December 1, 1934, six months after Stalin had buried himself in study of the Blood Purge, all of Moscow was suddenly roused by wailing sirens and frenzied searchlights raking the sky. On the radio and from loudspeakers in the streets, came the echoing announcement: Stalin's beloved comrade Sergei Mironovich Kirov had just been murdered in Moscow. The deed was part of a vast conspiracy against the Revolution.

The Leninist world was about to be torn apart in public, and millions would die. People long proclaimed as the saviors of humanity would soon be grovelling before the Soviet courts proclaiming themselves monsters of evil, begging for death. Stalin clearly understood that this awful spectacle would need some smoke-screen in the West, some propaganda force to counteract the waves of doubt and revulsion that were sure to come, even among the most devout. This was one of several reasons why the Popular Front "tactic" was proclaimed at this time, promoted as the indispensable bond uniting all people of goodwill against fascism. This would be the new bond to the Soviets. The Popular Front was what no decent person could turn against, *in spite of the trials*.

Stalin's propagandists wrung their hands. Surely these killings, so public, so extreme, will alienate the innocents. Stalin brushed them aside. "Europe," he snorted, "will swallow it all."[18]

He was right again.

The center for managing the European aspect of the Terror was Paris, though its focus soon shifted to Spain, where it expanded to really large-scale killing of the undesired left under the cover of the Spanish Civil War. Before then it included work ranging from forging disinformation to arranging a select array of machine-gunnings, decapitations, strychnine poisonings, axe murders, and garrottings of redundant revolutionaries throughout Europe and the Americas. The targets were often communists or former communists. There was of course Trotsky. Another victim was Ignace Reiss—"Ludwik." When his hour came round at last, Münzenberg was almost certainly present himself. While the Popular Front prepared itself to carry Stalinist righteousness politics to new heights, and millions in the Soviet Union died, these would be the new and the true tasks of the *apparat*.

Stalin was preparing himself for September 1, 1939.

Karl Radek was the invisible eminence for all these large events as they led up to the war: the anti-fascist movement, the search for the pact, the Terror. Within the Kremlin, he was also the guiding hand in what we might call intellectual Stalinism. Catharine Karolyi remembers him at a very grand reception for George Bernard Shaw at the British Embassy in Moscow in 1931, "leaning over the balustrade in a black Russian blouse" deep in conversation with Lady Astor, "very pale with an Abraham Lincoln beard and the aspect of a French *communard*."[19] Gustav Regler remembers him from 1935, drinking hard at a reception in Maxim Gorky's country villa, ripping open his shirt at the banquet table, fascinating Malraux and the visiting literary celebrities as he plunged forward with . . . dangerous talk. His Bolshevik colleagues sat by, frozen with fear.[20] From his revolutionary youth, Radek had been tight with a kind of ferocious eagerness, but there was also something jeering, abrasive, cynical about him. His mind was marked by a rather special weld of cynicism with certitude. Like Brecht and his own protégé Katz, like many of the most knowing liars, Radek's rationalizations convinced him that everything important, really important, was based in falsehood. As a result, falsehood became for him a kind of truth. To Radek duplicity was the last word. This contradictory but potent point of faith left him arrogant, installed in a perpetual easy victory over the stupid credulity of the innocent. Life, he was sure, was a lie. And that, he believed, made him always right. He was Stalin's ideal intellectual.

For he was an intellectual, a real one. In a circle filled with tenacious boors and clever thugs, Radek was a quite genuine literary-political man in the classic European manner. Polish and Jewish, his manners and outlook were those of a German cultural revolutionary, albeit one with an exceptionally conspiratorial penchant. Conspiracy was Radek's school: He became a hot revolutionary handyman for Felix Dzerzhinsky when he was 18 years old. His connection to the founder of the modern police state was the defining relationship of his youth.[21] Then came Lenin: Even before the Revolution, Radek was not only Lenin's press advisor but also his political fixer in German politics. After the Revolution Radek was among the founders of the Comintern, entrusted with special attention to propaganda and its secret service.

Radek was now at the center and at the top. But then he made a gross false step. Following Lenin's death he supported Trotsky against Stalin in the struggle for power, and this blunder ended his successful first phase. In November 1927 Stalin had him exiled to the little town of Tomsk, cast to the extreme outer edge of Soviet political life. Radek was not made of very stern stuff; exile soon broke his defiance and he began a concentrated search for Stalin's forgiveness, which worked at least to the degree that he managed to worm his way back to Moscow. But it was not a glorious return. He was relegated to a squalid, freezing flat in the basement of a slum. Radek was a man very nearly at the end of his resources. His boyish buoyancy was gone. He grew stooped. His walk shambled, dragged. He was going to die in that basement. Something more was needed.

In 1930 that something was found, and Radek's fortunes absolutely changed. From his basement hole he moved to Dom Pratisetsvo, an apartment building reserved for the most important members of the government. His flat was magnificent. It featured a dazzling view of the Kremlin and the Moskva. It also featured a direct line to Stalin's study.[22]

Precisely how Radek thus transformed his status is not known, but the trick must have been impressive. The strongest rumor is not accepted by all scholars, but asserted by Trotsky and vouched for by his highly reliable secretary van Heijenhoort. It claims that Radek used his basement and his previous bond to Trotsky to act as a decoy for Trotskyites still in Moscow, above all a senior NKVD official named Blumkin, the better to betray them to the firing squads.[23]

However he did it, Radek regained Stalin's favor to a spectacular degree. By 1933 and 1934 it would be hard to find anyone in more intimate confidence with the dictator: mastermind of the anti-fascist line; ultra-secret emissary to the Nazis; inside advisor in all matters of cultural politics; and his secret right hand in foreign policy. But despite a title and a major role at *Isvestia,* Radek mainly stayed in his apartment often reclining on an enormous couch set before his view of the Kremlin towers, doing what he had always done best: reading everything, and calculating every angle. Around him were strewn magazines, newspapers, and manuscripts in five languages. Radek would calculate the line on everything from James Joyce to the NKVD; from Malraux's relation to Aragon to the latest conspiratorial ripple among the German refugees. Nothing passed him by. He read and calculated. And above all else, he waited for that special phone to ring.

It rang constantly. Radek had become Stalin's private answer-man, the most witting insider of them all.

Meanwhile the Terror was gathering. Seen from outside the totalitarian perspective, the *logic* of the Terror seems impenetrable. *Why?* A regime wishes to replace one set of politicians with some more satisfactory set. Very well: Why not fire them, replace them, disgrace them if necessary? It would surely have been easy enough for Stalin to divest his bypassed comrades of their power. Why *kill* them—and in the process begin a wave of murder in the millions spreading through the society. *Why?* The Terror joins the Nazi Holocaust as a prime example of motiveless malignity.

But that is to see the questions of power, the human city, and guilt from the religious or humanist perspectives which the radical ideologies of this century seek to destroy. An essential tenet of the NKVD was that the system *needed* the arrest, torture, and death of thoroughly obedient—therefore "innocent"—people, since without random terror, the innocent would never be afraid, and (even ideologically) the Soviet state was made coherent by fear. From this perspective, some of that motiveless malignity falls into place.

There is of course much more: For example, it is plain that Lenin's totalitarianism encouraged a certain kind of political personality to flourish, and Stalin's emergence was no accident in the annals of evil. The Marxist-Leninist system was based on police terror, denunciation, and absolute power, and had been so from the beginning. There was never a moment when these did not dominate the political culture, and it was a culture which naturally favored and advanced Stalin's kind of sensibility: an intensely intelligent conspiratorial mind, obsessed with a sadistic and paranoiac need for vengeance, dead to all human warmth, and convinced that the only meaningful human motives are greed and fear.

But Stalin's thinking, especially about the Terror, was also informed by ideology. Even in its "pure" form, Marxism-Leninism necessarily sanctifies Terror, as the Leninist cult of Dzerzhinsky made plain well before 1930. Like all the Bolsheviks, Stalin saw Terror as the Revolution's tool.

He seems also to have followed Marxist theory in his belief that individual talents and commitments are relatively without meaning in the grand dialectic. Since individuals do not make History, the special qualities of individuals are unimportant. Everyone is replaceable. If the autonomous system happens to brush this or that person onto history's ashheap, what of it? The loss of an individual is meaningless.

Thus, if Field Marshall Tuchachevsky is brilliantly, too brilliantly, galvanizing the Red Army for a confrontation with Hitler, it is *right* that he be shot. Hitler is appeased; a threat to the system is removed. The very next morning the Red Army will have another perfectly good Field Marshall at its head, without the capacity to stand against the Party and its leader. Who could object? It was merely Marxist theory radically applied.

It was also an unstoppable engine for mediocrity and murder.

After Kirov's murder the Terror gathered its forces secretly. To be sure, the first big targets, Kamenev and Zinoviev, were arrested immediately, but their trials were not held for a full year and a half afterward: August 1936. In the interim, relative calm prevailed. To be sure thousands of "unimportant" people—i.e., non-Party people—were being disposed of in a set of largely unnoticed bludgeonings, basement murders, firing squads, and general round-ups. But apart from their unnoticeable demises, 1935 was a calm year.[24]

In that false calm, the Popular Front was created.

The Popular Front was the Comintern's anti-fascist alliance with the non-Stalinist left, and Dimitrov himself proclaimed it at the VIIth Congress of the Comintern in August 1935. Since the delegates had spent years sabotaging and defaming the "social fascists" they were now ordered to embrace, he was obliged to define its essential mendacity at the start. "Comrades" he confided to the huge restless hall, "you will remember the ancient tale of the capture of Troy. . . . The attacking army was unable to achieve victory until with the aid of the famous Trojan Horse, it managed to penetrate to the very heart of the enemy camp."[25]

And so the Popular Front was trundled into place and, irresistibly noble, it was left parked in the Western dawn.

The celebration over the era of good feeling this peace offering created was ebullient and irresistible. In Paris, New York, Hollywood, and London a new variety of Stalinist righteousness became the dominant cultural chic of the era, and left hardly a single cultural figure untouched. Stalin had been right again: Resisting the Front would look indecent, like endorsing Hitler. The wishfulness of an age was tapped.

In Paris the cultural spectacular of the year was the Congress in Defense of Culture at the Salle Mutualité in June 1935. It seemed to marshall every literary celebrity in Europe, from E. M. Forster to Pasternak to Malraux, and was perhaps the greatest showcase of the era for the War of Ideas. The Mutualité Congress *looks* like the culminating collaboration between Gibarti and Münzenberg, those two inventors of the politicized writers' congress, but Babette Gross denied with vehemence that Münzenberg had anything to do with it, and I have found no evidence that either Gibarti or Katz were on the scene. The secret funding seems to have come through Katz's friend and Stalin's intimate Mikhail Koltsov.[26] Certainly, it was not *overtly* connected to Münzenberg, and he may even have been kept out of it because French Intelligence watched him too closely, and he was too visible a lead. Certainly, it was crucially important that Soviet sponsorship be secret, and communist presence minimized, even though the place was packed from wall to wall with all the "usual suspects."

Gibarti and Katz were nonetheless major invisible presences in the Popular Front, from London to New York. In London, the Left Book Club was summoned into existence under Otto Katz's wise guidance and probable secret funding.[27] Meanwhile, Otto's friend Claud Cockburn founded the small but tremendously influential newssheet, the *Week:* Cockburn was certainly guided by Katz, and the *Week* was almost certainly a funnel for information supplied by the *apparat.*[28]

In high politics, the tragic crucible of the Front was Spain, where leading Münzenberg-men like Katz and Julio Alvárez del Vayo played large roles. Because Spain was a Popular Front war, it was also the Terror's principal European outpost.

In Franco-Soviet relations a high point of the Popular Front was André Gide's propaganda tour of Russia. This coincided exactly with two events: the installation of the Blum government in Paris and the death of Maxim Gorky, possibly by murder, followed by his state funeral in Moscow during June 1936. For both, every stop of the War of Ideas was pulled, as the dictator prepared for the show trials of Zinoviev, Kamenev, and their fellow "conspirators" in August.

With this event, the Terror began in earnest. The trials were a great success: Zinoviev and Kamenev read their lines perfectly. Their "confessions," quite without parallel in the literature of abjection, formed the basis for new purges, imprisonments, and executions. The two had been promised their lives for co-operation, but of course as soon as the show was over, the death squads were sent to take them to the basement. When the soldiers stepped into Zinoviev's cell, he instantly grasped the truth. He flung himself on the floor, made some desperate plea in his high-pitched voice, and gave the impression of hysteria. This induced one of the young NKVD men to pull his revolver, force Zinoviev into an adjacent cell, and shoot him through the head then and there. Hearing of this scene greatly impressed Stalin. He gave Zinoviev's killer a medal.[29] In later years, Stalin got into the habit of having his valet, a man named Pauker, re-enact the old revolutionary's terror in caricature at the late-night drinking parties that were his kind of fun. He especially loved to watch Pauker crawling on the floor and clutching at chairs while he mocked the singsong of Zinoviev's Jewish accent, breaking into a parody of Hebrew prayer, "Hear O Israel!" during the begging part.[30]

The tortoise was moving quickly now, capable of surprise, capable of sudden terrifying turns. Within three weeks of the trial's conclusion on September 27, 1936, came one of the most sudden.

Karl Radek himself was abruptly but secretly put under arrest. A few days later Münzenberg arrived in Moscow. Instead of his usual meeting with Radek, he was informed, in absolute confidence, that he would be seeing Radek no more.

As Münzenberg listened a new kind of fear must have dropped into his soul.

Karl Radek was a very shrewd man. He certainly knew in detail the treachery of his great patron. Even before his arrest, he seems to have contrived some sort of scheme that would serve as his "life insurance" against his own liquidation. In the Lubyanka, he resolutely resisted his interrogators. When his blackmailed co-defendants asked him to co-operate, he answered that he would only with assurance from Stalin himself that he would not die.

At this point Radek sat down in his cell and wrote a long letter. It was for Stalin's eyes only and its contents are unknown, but it was powerful enough to bring Stalin personally to the NKVD building the next day. There Stalin and Radek held a prolonged conversation behind closed doors. What was said is also unknown, but when it was over Radek was a changed man. Radek obviously had convinced himself that Stalin feared him dead more than he feared him alive. Some deal for his life had been cut.[31]

From the moment Stalin left the building that day, Radek became a totally co-operative witness. At his trial three months later, in January 1937, he played his role as abject with special relish, correcting Vyshinsky when the hard-drinking prosecutor fumbled his own lines, enthusiastically condemning himself. His testimony was watched with special interest by all-knowing insiders, most especially by an unusually attentive delegation from the German Embassy. His testimony was real insider's stuff: bellwether for the Terror's next turn.[32]

The verdict condemned everyone in the dock to death—everyone except Radek. Radek was given ten years' imprisonment. At that moment Radek turned to the courtroom, broke into a shy grin, and with a shrug lifted his hands: "Who knew?"

Who indeed? The true targets of the trial of Radek and his fellow "conspirators" were not merely Radek, but the Terror's next victims, Nikolai Bukharin and Field Marshall Tuchachevsky.

Tuchachevsky concerns us most. Radek was accused of being a German spy, a device with the special merit of explaining Radek's actual, and fully authorized secret contacts with the Germans, just in case Nazis or anyone else tried to use them in some embarrassing way. In his testimony, Radek planted an ostentatious disclaimer. Radek assured the court in his broadest strokes that Marshall Tuchachevsky knew nothing, absolutely nothing, about his own exchange of "certain materials" with the Germans. This plant was an as-yet-undelivered death warrant. Reading the story in the Western press, months before Tuchachevsky's arrest, Walter Krivitsky turned to his wife and told her Tuchachevsky was doomed.[33]

At that very moment, in a Gestapo laboratory documents were being forged purporting to show Marshall Tuchachevsky conspiring to storm the Kremlin with a renegade unit of the Red Army, murder Stalin, and seize the Soviet government.[34]

The sources of this disinformation were the Soviet secret services working in conjunction with the Gestapo. As usual, both governments were served. Hitler would use the forgeries to rid himself of certain *Wehrmacht* personnel he found insufficiently devoted, while Stalin would be supplied with all he needed to round up the general staff of the Red Army and shoot them all. Why shoot the Red Army general staff? Partly to placate Hitler, and partly for reasons of his own.[35] At the same time Stalin would rid himself of a threat to his German policy, and a threat to himself too.[36]

Marshall Tuchachevsky was a very remarkable man. Though born to the minor Tsarist aristocracy, he was a dedicated communist. No non-Stalinist information has ever been produced to challenge his loyalty to the Revolution. He was cultivated, multi-lingual, intellectually playful, with an ironic turn, easily the most intelligent Russian military man of his generation, and so among the most intelligent people in the entire government. He had travelled widely: He knew Germany and its army intimately, and that knowledge had become the strongest single Soviet voice for full preparedness and early confrontation with the Nazi threat. As such he was in the dangerous position of holding views unwelcome to both Hitler and Stalin. In 1935 and 1936 he was swiftly galvanizing the Red Army. He was tremendously popular in the ranks.

Each had his own reason, but the dictators agreed. Tuchachevsky must be dealt with.

And dealt with he was.

As the Popular Front was parallel to the Terror, so the War of Ideas in Paris ran parallel to conspiracy, with anti-fascist discourse proceeding while the secret services saw to it that the lethal exchange between the two dictators was *absolutely* reliable, foolproof, and untraceable.

The plot against Tuchachevsky was instituted with the Soviets, but Hitler decided to participate sometime near the end of 1936. This was right around the time Radek cut the deal in his prison cell. Stalin himself had already planned the route of the Tuchachevsky dossier.[37]

In December 1936, Walter Krivitsky met in Paris with the senior NKVD executive then in Europe, a man named Slutsky. They met on the terrace of the Café Viel on the Boulevard des Capucines, near the Paris Opera. At this meeting Slutsky ordered Krivitsky to throttle down his anti-German operations. "We have set our course toward an early understanding with Hitler, and have started negotiations," Slutsky said. "They are progressing favorably." As for anti-fascism, Slutsky added, "there's nothing for us in this rotting corpse of France, with its *Front Populaire*."[38]

Then came a special part of the assignment. Krivitsky was ordered to select two agents who could successfully impersonate German officers and have them on hand in Paris. Krivitsky was not told that these men would be used to assassinate one of the most well-known NKVD targets of the time, a leader of the White Russian emigration in Paris, who went by the name of General Miller, and that General Miller's death would be used in the Tuchachevsky murders.

The material incriminating Tuchachevsky was provided to Reinhard Heydrich through the Soviets in Paris immediately after Radek's trial. The German forgeries based on them were made under Heydrich's supervision in Germany after Radek's trial was over. Hitler was personally shown the forgeries by May.[39]

These transactions naturally required absolutely reliable secret agents working in deep compartmentalization. In Paris, one center of Soviet-Nazi intrigue was a confederation of the politically lost known as the Union of Tsarist Veterans, a group of old soldiers clinging to the ever more threadbare honor of the army and society the Bolsheviks had destroyed. The Union's leader was named General Miller, who was committed to the sabotage of that irreversible victory and managing of that defeat. In predictable fact, Miller's organization was multiply penetrated, a playground of European conspiracy. It was laced through with Soviet agents, some of whom appear to have been linked to Katz.[40] Miller's second-in-command was a certain General Skoblin, whose wife was a famous Russian torch singer named Nadezhda Plevitskaya. Both were Soviet agents. Skoblin, moreover, was a Soviet agent whose specialty was contact with the Nazis.

Skoblin's first task was to get into Nazi hands the lie that Tuchachevsky was conspiring with the German general staff. When this bit of information found its way to his office, Heydrich immediately recognized it as a lie, but decided to use it as disinformation against some local enemies. The principle of the Leipzig Trial was becoming habitual.

Meanwhile, information damning Tuchachevsky, information even beyond the forged dossier, was concocted. It too seemed to have Nazi sources. It was fed into the networks to be passed on to Stalin, and along the way to various people in European politics who might be usefully deceived. The route was a revealing and curious one: the Czech intelligence service of President Edvard Beneš.

Beneš was an indiscreet politician who could be relied upon to talk before he thought. A diplomatic joke of the era held that the three best ways to get information around Europe were "telephone, telegraph, and tele-Beneš."[41] When his intelligence service, assisted by his right hand, Hubert Ripka, gave Beneš the disinformation, the credulous Beneš pounced: What was this? Treason? In the Red Army?

Beneš rushed to inform Stalin, and French intelligence as well. No matter: Stalin was delighted to have the French think the Tuchachevsky fraud was authentic. Meanwhile, he listened to Beneš's warning in solemn wonderment.

Beneš's conviction of Tuchachevsky's guilt was not a minor force in European politics at that time. According to Sir Isaiah Berlin, even a figure so little trusting of Stalin as Winston Churchill himself was persuaded that Tuchachevsky really had been a traitor, and was persuaded on the strength of Beneš's word.[42]

But how was Czech intelligence apprised of the story? Who managed the flow?

We know the route was Paris; the "source" was portrayed as the German anti-fascists. This means that the agent would be based in Paris and be known to be connected to the anti-fascist underground. He should operate at a high level and yet not be seen even by the informed as in the NKVD. It would help if he were already an old hand at this kind of clandestine Nazi-Communist collaboration, as from Leipzig, and it would not be surprising if the man were a protégé of Radek.

The number of secret agents in Paris answering to even many of these aspects in the profile was not all that large. But only one answered them all, including the clinching crucial detail of being a trusted supplier to Czech intelligence and confidant to the people closest to Beneš, men such as Beneš's prime minister, Hubert Ripka.[43]

I would remind the reader of Babette Gross's response to my question about Otto Katz's possible role as a Nazi agent; her assertion that he was close to Hubert Ripka at the appropriate time.[44]

The precise role of Münzenberg in this policy of Nazi appeasement is murky. Babette Gross dates March 1936 as the time of Münzenberg's recognition that the Popular Front was a fraud. But surely the suspicion dawned before then. Ignazio Silone, who knew him quite well, used to argue that despite his appealing personality and the fervor of his anti-fascism, Münzenberg was "just as cynical as the rest of them."[45] Certainly he was no friend to democracy—and in 1935 and most of 1936, he still put the Revolution before everything. Did he know of Stalin's secret diplomacy?

With Radek talking relatively freely, with Krivitsky witting, with Katz a probable participant, it seems probable that he did. Did he know everything? As much as Katz? As much as Reiss? That secret probably died with him.

But on the practical level, from the moment Radek was arrested, Münzenberg understood that the Terror was now moving in his direction. He lived with a new fear, in a new relation to power. He was no longer serving the Revolution. He was attempting to save himself from it.

The last time Willi Münzenberg ever saw Otto Katz was during the pact. Münzenberg had made his break and, with great caution, was edging toward open opposition, living in Paris and editing *Die Zukunft*. He was protecting himself with conspicuousness.

One day as Münzenberg was sitting in a Montparnasse café, Otto Katz happened to stroll in. Münzenberg did not let the moment pass.

"Otto Katz!" he called out. His voice was loud.

Katz stood still. Then the tirade began: within the hearing of everyone in the café, Münzenberg began to "shower him with mockery," and then ended with a question. Who are you working for these days? Is it Stalin? Or Hitler? Or is it perhaps—*Beneš*?

Katz went white, turned on his heel, and left the café without a word. This tongue-lashing certainly suggests that Münzenberg was to some degree witting about the secret course of events. It was their final meeting.[46]

This much is certain. During the mid-1930s, the two totalitarian states under the cover of their mutual hatred were negotiating moving toward an alliance in order to position themselves for the war to come. *As the anti-fascist War of Ideas took shape, the two secret services used that struggle to supply each other with disinformation against each other's domestic enemies. Thus, Stalin used the Gestapo to discredit and destroy Tuchachevsky and the Red Army general staff, while Hitler used the Comintern and the Münzenberg operation to discredit and destroy Ernst Röhm and the SA.*

It was a deal, and its cover was "anti-fascism." Morally, it was a betrayal of everyone who had been enlisted into the anti-fascist struggle through fellow travelling. And politically, it was part of the larger deal that led to the Second World War.

Radek's ending passed unnoticed. On January 30, 1937, he was led from his Moscow courtroom and never publicly seen again. There are various accounts of what happened next. Solzhenitsyn reports that despite Radek's real or imagined hold over Stalin, he was simply shot. Alexander Orlov, a senior NKVD man close to the events, says Radek was at first set up in relative comfort, so the appearance of a lenient house arrest could be used to persuade Bukharin to co-operate in his own demise. For Bukharin was arrested just as Radek's case was closed. If so, the improbable leniency lasted only so long as it took for Bukharin to swallow the improbable bait.

Another version has it that Radek was removed from that place and dispatched to one of the most bleak and sunless sub-arctic slave labor camps of all. There he sank into the faceless squalid prisoner's world, freezing, starving, amid the rats, the bugs, in rags. He is said to have survived two years.

The exact manner of his death is debated.[47] One story holds he was murdered in a brawl with a prison thug. This version has a suggestive variant. When Lenin and Radek took power, the Bolsheviks embarked on a series of experiments intended to stamp out that bourgeois excrescence, the family. As a result of this policy, complicated by the Civil War and natural disasters like the Volga Famine, Soviet Russia began to fill with packs of pauperized, parentless, sociopathic orphans, desperate marauding packs of children, the *bezprizornii*. They lived by begging and thievery and worse. During the 1920s visitors to the USSR repeatedly spoke of seeing the starving bands of little beggars shoved from station platforms by the rifle butts of Red Army soldiers.

Those who survived grew up. The bands of marauding children became sociopathic packs of adults: brutal, uncontrollable, murderous, real threats. Stalin dealt with them in various ways. Sometimes the NKVD simply rounded them up and mowed them down with machine guns. Sometimes they were sent to the more remote arctic camps to die as slave laborers.

The story has it that sometime in 1939, one such pack of the Revolution's monsters cornered Karl Radek in the prison yard. He was far from history now. The killing winter was all around him and he was alone with the Revolution's wretches, nameless. Someone flung him to the ground. Then, following the impulses by which they lived, the *bezprizornii* were all kicking together, smashing out the brains of this brain-proud man against the tundra.

Nemesis the goddess is fierce. Fierce—and ingenious.

PART TWO

The Case for the Traitor

Chapter 6

Cambridge West

The Courtauld mansion on Portman Square in London houses one of the world's great institutions for the study of the history of art. Though the building is very grand—it has eighty rooms—its architectural discretion makes it an ideal example of that restrained aristocratic elegance which the British Empire installed in the heart of its capital during the middle of the eighteenth century. In such a house, the Earl of Chesterfield might have attended upon the graces. Under its neo-classical portico there are two doorbells. One is simply for entry to the Courtauld Institute. Another, set apart, is marked "DIRECTOR'S FLAT."

On the morning of April 23, 1963, a man named Arthur Martin, an investigator for the British counter-intelligence service, stepped up to the door and rang the bell set apart. At that moment the director of the Courtauld was a thin, cold, composed, intellectually very impressive art historian and connoisseur who had been in charge since 1947. He would remain so until he retired, covered with honors, ten years later in 1974. He was named Sir Anthony Blunt.

This was by no means the first of Sir Anthony's decorous chats with British counter-intelligence. Dull encounters like this one had been going on for twelve wearisome years, ever since the disappearance of two men, Guy Burgess and Donald Maclean, whose defection to the Soviet Union in 1951 had instantly become one of the enduring sensations of modern politics.

They were an odd pair, Burgess and Maclean. Both had known each other from their university days at Cambridge, but they had never known each other very well, and in truth they had never much liked each other. At Trinity College, Cambridge, Donald had never been quite fast, flashy, homosexual, or important enough for Burgess. He struck Guy as big and boring, out of it, uncertain, tight with sexual anguish and his Scots-Presbyterian compunction. Yet in his staid, suffering way Maclean had gone on to become the greater success. In 1951, Burgess was a brilliant but increasingly seedy presence in the upper-middle reaches of British literary life, broadcasting, and politics, while in that same year, Maclean was doing better. Until recently Maclean had been serving as a very senior member of the British diplomatic community in Washington, a principal advisor to the ambassador, with access to the most sensitive information in the special relationship between the United States and London.[1] As it happened, during Mclean's tenure Guy Burgess had himself inexplicably been dispatched to the American capital, as if to extricate him from a series of mild-to-intolerable muckings-up in various branches of the London establishment. In Washington, Burgess spent a number of months as a loud, drunk, dirty hanger-on at the middle levels of the British diplomatic community, generating disgust and being impossible wherever he went. He lodged in the basement of yet another Cambridge friend, whose innocent wife Burgess drove straight round the bend with his sickening personal habits. This friend, however, was a man Guy really *did* feel close to. He was Kim Philby.

When Donald was rather ominously recalled to London, Burgess arranged to go back home as well. Maclean knew, but was not supposed to know, that he had been recalled because he was under investigation as a Soviet agent, and Guy Burgess knew it too, since the entire British plan to arrest Maclean was in itself penetrated, very near the top, by the Soviets.

On the night of May 25, 1951, Guy and Donald were together as Guy drove Maclean to a late-night ferry about to cross the Channel from Southampton to Saint-Malo. May 25, as it happened, was Donald Maclean's 38th birthday, but the two men were not in a festive mood. They were running from a warrant for Maclean's arrest. Not the arrest of Burgess—only Maclean. Little was as yet suspected of Burgess. Burgess's task was simply to get Donald to Southampton and set him on the first leg of the rescue.

When Burgess picked up Maclean at his suburban house outside London, Maclean's wife Melinda was preparing a private birthday party for two. She had never before laid eyes on their scruffy, unannounced, and surely none-too-welcome visitor. Here was the man with whom her husband's name was about to be wedded forever. Donald, fearing an MI-5 bug in the room, introduced him as "Mr. Stiles," whom he said was "from the office."

Melinda was on the spot: There was nothing to do but ask "Mr. Stiles" to join the birthday dinner. As the meal neared its end, Melinda stepped out of the room for a moment, and Burgess turned to Maclean, reverting to a harsh, too-familiar tone. He informed him that his hour had struck. They were to leave at once, now, this minute. It was not a suggestion but a command. When his wife of the last twelve years returned to the room, Donald Maclean stood up and excused himself. "Mr. Stiles and I," he said, "have to keep a pressing engagement, but I don't expect to be back very late. I'll take an overnight bag just in case." Then they were gone, leaving Melinda Maclean standing bewildered over the crumbs of the birthday cake.[2]

What those two fated men said to each other on their dark drive south can only be imagined. It was a wild ride: they almost missed the boat. Though their names *are* wed, Burgess and Maclean, after their university coolness, had become more and more bound together in the sick union of their mutual secret and their mutual loathing. Burgess's powers of verbal sadism were legendary, and he had grown more and more blackmailing and abusive toward Maclean as time went on. By now the diplomat had ample reason to fear and hate his old university companion and fellow spy.[3]

When they pulled into the parking lot at the Southampton docks, Burgess more abandoned than parked his rented car and rushed Maclean to a waiting ferry called the *Falaise*. The boat churned in the dark, wide and heavy, about to push off. At this point, Burgess's part in the escape was supposed to end. Back in Washington Philby's instructions had been clear. "Don't you go too, Guy!" Burgess hustled his very tall companion toward the waiting boat. Beside him, Maclean was huge and hunched: tight-lipped with fear. Burgess seemed in charge. He tossed half a crown to the garage attendant, hollered "we'll be back on Monday!" and then as the departure whistle screamed they raced to the gangplank.

The *Falaise* was the night's last ship out. Just as the gangplank was lifting, Burgess acted on an impulse he'd been nurturing for days, his own last-minute addition to the intrigue. Quite unnecessarily Burgess jumped on board too, and as the British coastline began to recede into the dark, history changed a little.[4]

. . .

Thirteen years later, the authorities still simply would not let up on Sir Anthony. All that time after Burgess's defection, Blunt was still hearing from boring policemen like Mr. Martin, for no better reason than that Guy and he had once been friends. Intimates, even. They had known each other ever since Cambridge, when Blunt had been a very young don at Trinity College and an even younger Guy Burgess had first come sauntering down the High Street, already a dazzler, equipped with the last word, a lethal condescending smile, and the unstoppable flow of an intellectual patter that would make him "the best of the slick Marxists around London."[5] He was also already a drunk, but while alcohol would at least leave Burgess a sodden, self-pitying wreck, at Cambridge drink only made his undergraduate splendor shine the more. He seemed destined for everything remarkable. The young Anthony Blunt was only one of many to think that Guy Burgess was among the most brilliant and compelling human beings he had ever met.

But that was the past. An innocent association of Sir Anthony's youth. Sir Anthony had gone on to more serious things. How many dull, dreary times over did he have to explain that yes, he'd once found Guy a fine intellectual companion; and yes, Guy's reckless glamour had once appealed, but that he knew nothing about Burgess's secret political commitments. Nothing about his subversions (if subversions they were) at the BBC. Nothing of betrayals or espionage inside British intelligence, though to be sure Sir Anthony himself just happened likewise to have served in British Intelligence during the war. Nothing about Burgess's activity as high-level staff to a member of Clement Atlee's cabinet. Every bit of it was guilt by association. Blunt had denied it all so often that he seemed to batten on denial. With every visit this connoisseur of snobbery grew more amused, more arch, more theatrically patient as the weary old questions grew easier to turn aside. Now Arthur Martin was at the Director's Flat once again, and the tiresome, tolerated little ritual was about to be replayed.

Blunt admitted his guest. Martin sat down, uncomfortably, across from him. Blunt had always intimidated him a little. Between the two he set a tape recorder.

Then Martin moved quickly. The British security services, he said, had recently come into possession of quite unequivocal information proving that Blunt had acted as an agent of Soviet espionage during the Second World War. Blunt answered that no such evidence could possibly exist for the simple reason no such activity had ever taken place. Martin persisted. He was just returned from the United States, he said, where he'd had a protracted interview with Mr. Michael Whitney Straight. Blunt absorbed this information with a level, unflinching gaze and complete silence. He showed no reaction. Martin later recalled the moment: "I think I said something like 'I saw Mr. Straight the other day, and he told me about his relations with you and the Russians.' " He then outlined precisely what Michael Straight had told him those relations were.

Anthony Blunt continued to sit very still, looking at Martin without any sign of fear, except perhaps in the too-tight immobility of his poker face, that narrow shield. One of Anthony Blunt's worst fears had just become real. He was suddenly without his easeful answers. He said not one word. Blunt was thinking as fast as he could, and probably was waiting for Martin's next move. Arthur Martin likewise sat silent. When their silence had gone on so long that Martin was sure Blunt wasn't going to break it, the interrogator leaned forward and said directly into the tape-recorder, very slowly and distinctly, "I have been authorized by the Attorney General to give you a formal immunity from prosecution."

Blunt's expression remained one of calculating reserve. With immunity, a prime fear—prison—had been dispelled. Blunt's best rationale against telling the truth—self-protection—was gone. After a few moments he stood up, poured himself a very large drink, and went to a window. There he stood for a rather long time, surveying with his cold expert eye the budding springtime down in Portman Square. It would be interesting to know what options, what fears, what memories of ruined passion may have flashed through his mind as the moments prolonged themselves. The tape-recorder turned in the silence. Behind him, over his fireplace, hung Poussin's *Eliezer and Rebecca at the Well,* which Blunt had discovered misattributed in Paris and bought with money from his intimate friend Victor Rothschild.[6] The Poussin was—apart from his secret—his most precious possession. Martin was not going to speak again. At last Anthony Blunt took a long sip from his glass, turned to his accuser, and said simply: "It is true."[7]

The Cambridge Conspiracy is the most voluminously examined penetration of any government known to modern history, and the most famous episode in the history of espionage. More members of the circle are unmasked almost every year, yet in contrast to spy stories in which the motives are money, or revenge, or mere mean nationalism, the power exerted by this set of double lives over the public imagination seems never to be lost. This may have something to do with the fact that their secrets came from so very near the top. Donald Maclean, had he not been uncovered, might very possibly have become British Ambassador to the

United States. A success of the 1989 West End Theater season was a plausible play showing Anthony Blunt in a long, dodging dialogue with the Queen. The story of the Cantabrigians' unmasking seems a perpetually renewable drama of concealed hatred and lurking truth. Each new identification—the third man, the fourth man—seems to bring a new shock of recognition.

It is often asked, apparently in genuine perplexity, how so many of these privileged Englishmen could have been "traitors to their class." This is to misunderstand both their treason and their class. Münzenberg's apparatus reached into every country of interest to the Bolsheviks: Germany, France, England, the United States, the Low Countries, the Scandinavian democracies, and many more, and in all those places it sought to organize the intellectual elite, particularly wherever that elite was in formation, for example in colleges and universities. Precisely the same people who instituted the Cambridge penetrations supervised parallel operations in New York and Washington, in the Ivy League and at the *École Normale Supérieure,* from Paris and Berlin. The International really *was* international. The obvious yet rarely understood stroke of secret service genius behind all such operations was the simple recognition of an essential bond between the so-called "establishment" (by which is meant little more than the elite of a given society), and what Lionel Trilling called the "adversary culture"—that part of society which, by virtue of its superior education and critical equipment, develops for itself a leveraged position within the middle class, based in ambiguity and the perspectives of criticism and argument, insight and protest. The adversary culture is a branch of the middle class; usually its most vigorous intellectual and artistic wing. It is drawn, albeit ambivalently, to radicalism; radicalism is part of its vision of freedom and truth. The radical solution, it imagines, would tear aside the bourgeois facade; radical insight, it suspects, reaches the deepest truth. In fact the ability really to grasp, if not embrace, radical insight is what the adversary culture believes sets it apart from the vast hypocritical and second-rate middle class to which it belongs but also wishes—understandably, properly—to distinguish itself.

The recruitment of the Cambridge spies and similar agents in all the democracies was based on this simple insight: The adversary culture *is* an elite. That is what a prime manipulator of the Cambridge group, Theodore Maly, one of the greatest of the "great illegals," the Hungarian mafioso *par excellence,* understood and created as a network. And so it was with that resident of the International who instructed the youthful Whittaker Chambers in the New York Public Library. Elite youth can be best discerned in the *quality* of their protest. They are likely to carry the presumptions of that protest into middle age, and into authority. Catch that protest in its school days. Develop it properly. Deepen it, convince it, frighten it, blackmail it, network it. Then you will have forged the unseen "revolutionary" bond between Bohemia and power.

If we trace the unseen moral motivations of the Cambridge spies, those engagements emerge as a kind of map, and moreover a remarkably clear map, of advanced British intellectual life in their era. It is a composite portrait, albeit one in shadows, showing the elite of the generation that inherited Bloomsbury culture, that dynamic and difficult group of people whom Noel Annan has given a name that both mocks and manifests a certain smugness: "Our Age." Here were the children of Bloomsbury coming into their maturity, and into power. Theirs was a curiously stereotyped, although very classy, typicality. The Bloomsbury spies manifested many of the best traits of their adversarial time; they made an almost too-natural fit with the generation that preceded them. They were high Bloomsbury's children. The circle emerged especially from that crucible of Lytton Strachey's cultural strategy, the Cambridge discussion club, "the Apostles." Blunt was one of Virginia Woolf's young friends; he also had been the college lover of her nephew, Julian Bell. Guy Burgess, who in one sense might be called the ultimate British Münzenberg-man, was for many years one of Harold Nicolson's young friends. He was not (it seems) one of Nicolson's lovers, but Burgess was Nicolson's comfort and company, bound to him through the sexual-social bond that Sir Isaiah Berlin has called in another context the "homintern." Guy Burgess steadily exploited his friendship with Harold Nicolson to effect his own rise, and one reason for Burgess's stellar success in that effort was that he was so entirely congenial to the Bloomsbury sensibility. He advanced in the world of the British media in a fashion which Strachey, master manipulator of the Cambridge elite during the previous generation, would have thought to the manner born.

But this very typicality is in itself typical of *apparat* recruitment, and is no less true of American recruitment, from Washington and Hollywood, though in the American capitals the protean elite appeal assumed a Washington or Hollywood face. It was likewise true in France. It was true of Otto Katz himself. I have said that Otto was a classic vanguard intellectual of his time and country, the very type of Weimar, manifesting its presumptions, the moods and modes of Piscator and Dietrich, of Brecht and Feuchtwanger, in all he did and even in all he concealed. Otto began his life wishing to be an artist in Weimar, and he failed. He was at heart not much more than a shrewd dilettante with some extra fire. He lacked what it would have taken to brush anywhere near the greatness of Kafka; even the minor distinction of his friend Kisch was far beyond him. Otto had to settle for being a spy. But he was the perfect spy, and in espionage rather than art, he embodied his age.

In a similar way, the moral history of these concealed idealists for the Revolution—a remarkable number of whom were recruited under Münzenberg's auspices—necessarily includes a great people who manifest many of the best insights, talents, and values to be found in the advanced culture of their time. The right wing (and even others) has the tendency to condemn the adversary culture wholesale, not least because a set of fellow travellers, spies, and traitors emerged from it. This is worse than absurd. In most of the liberal democracies, the adversarial culture includes much that is best in the whole society: most alive, most probing, most inventive, most conscious. It was so on the Left Bank of André Malraux; it was so in the Bohemia of Greenwich Village, where the recruiters for the *apparat* reaped such a rich secret harvest. It was so in the rooms of Trinity College, Cambridge, where in 1938 Anthony Blunt did his quiet recruiting. That best must be remembered.

By making this claim I do not in the least intend to invoke some countercultural sentimentalism to excuse these wretched men and women. The Cambridge spies were servants of Stalin, and they were Stalinists. So were their cohorts in France, the United States, and the other liberal democracies. There will be no historical forgiveness for them. Nothing can erase their infamy. Their service to the tyranny and its lie was probably in secret truth even more iniquitous than the damning array of betrayals and acts of cruelty already known to have been performed with their willing assistance. And yet, and yet . . . they approached and succumbed to their aspiring evil driven by a set of concerns that were, and remain, admirable and even indispensable: indispensable to the society, and to us. It is very true, they were despicable. Yet they should also be seen in the light of Rebecca West's observation: "There is a case to be made for the traitor. He is a sport from a necessary type." From Prague to Hollywood, it was so.

Münzenberg understood this juncture of radicalism, elitism, and power from his earliest days. That is what motivated sponsorship of major exhibitions of, say, Dadaist art. Münzenberg had himself photographed admiring Dadaist exhibitions which under his master Stalin would have been grounds for execution. That is why he had his people distribute sixteen-millimeter prints of Soviet cinema by Eisenstein and Pudovkin to every college campus in the West. This procedure brought in a broad harvest of high-level sympathizers, and from that wide gathering also came, especially from its upper crust, a few true agents-to-be.

In that light, it should not be surprising to know how ubiquitous were the Münzenberg-men in the initiating phases of the great espionage stories. The ferment of Münzenberg's radical opinion-making moved by natural progression toward secret service work. Kim Philby was dispatched straight to Gibarti and Paris carrying a letter of introduction from the Münzenberg-men in charge of the League Against Imperialism at Cambridge. He was inducted into secret work through Gibarti and the World Committee for the Relief of the Victims of German Fascism. Guy Burgess was connected to Münzenberg's Paris operations all through the thirties. Blunt sought, once he was unmasked, to disinform British intelligence with diversionary tales about Otto Katz. Likewise, Otto Katz was a contact for the novelists Josephine Herbst and her husband John Herrmann, busy in the Greenwich Village Bohemia in the year that John Herrmann began to be a courier for a network of witting sources for Soviet espionage among the officials of the New Deal in Washington, two of whom were, almost certainly, Alger and Priscilla Hiss. They in turn were part of the Washington network run by another Hungarian *mafioso* using the name Jay Peters, organized in Washington by a young American named Harold Ware, who had been a Münzenberg-man since the mid-twenties, who had entered the American government in service to the apparatus, and was by 1933 a fully engaged spy. But the Münzenberg connection was if possible even more powerful in France. During the Second World War, when André Malraux met Charles de Gaulle for the first time, he told the general that in the thirties the French tradition of Voltaire had been taken over and run by one Willi Münzenberg. It was a name the general had not heard before.[8]

So the Cambridge spies, despite the British tenor of their treasons, were quite precisely reflected by opposite numbers among the American political elite. When the story of Burgess and Maclean's defection broke, right in the middle of the Hiss case, most observers obscurely felt a similarity between the unmasked British diplomats and the accused American. Nor was the parallel lost on the principal players themselves. In the last days before his flight, drinking compulsively and at the point of cracking, Donald Maclean slurred a confession to a then uncomprehending Cyril Connolly: "*I* am the English Hiss."

Less obvious is the fact that the transformations of these idealists into spies necessarily involved a slow psychological task of initiation and deepening, and this required the collaboration of those in the apparatus involved in shaping opinion—that is, Münzenberg and his people—with the silent, faceless, unseen men of the deep-cover *apparat*. They worked together. The covert actions of which we speak began in ideas and in ideals. Noel and Herta Field, Anthony Blunt and Donald Maclean, and (as I think most probable) Alger and Priscilla Hiss never would have entered the world of espionage and betrayal except through a portal they saw as one opening onto the very highest moral commitment.

This fusion of public opinion and secret action is nicely illustrated by the intersecting paths of two men. One was an American: Noel Field himself—a verified State Department mole, about whom, in contrast to volumes about Alger Hiss, it seems nobody has two words to say. The other is a Hungarian *mafioso*: Theodore Maly, an agent who must rank as one of the greatest of the great illegals, a founding father of the secret service of the NKVD, one of those acolytes of Felix Dzerzhinsky and Saint Terror whose lives make it possible to see how the founders of the Soviet services really could believe they were laying the foundations from some grand new edifice of human good.[9]

These two men both very gentle, both very cruel, are linked. Field's recruitment, or at least his development as a Soviet agent in Foggy Bottom took place in Washington. Yet it was supervised by Maly when Maly was in Europe, before he himself took command of the Cambridge Circle. There was a juncture between Washington and London, and Maly was fully party to it. In fact Maly's fondest dream was to be granted a ''transfer'' from England to America. The reason was simple: The woman he loved was in New York.

The Ariadne whose thread binds Cambridge and America, ''anti-fascism'' and ''espionage,'' and leads from Maly to Noel Field was a German communist close to Babette Gross and Willi Münzenberg named Hede Massing. She knew Babette and Willi from the earliest days: The friendship with Babette antedated Hede's work as a spy and also outlasted it, persisting right up to the end of Hede's life. As a young woman, Hede was an actress. Also a flirt, a woman with a roving eye. She married three times, and each of her husbands turned out to be somebody in or near the apparatus. The first was none other than Gerhart Eisler, the brother of Ruth Fischer, and a first-tier *apparatchik* who (especially in America) would work in close collaboration with Otto Katz. Her second husband, a man named Julian Gumperz, was a left-wing publisher linked to the Münzenberg Trust. Hede's third husband was a scholar and writer named Paul Massing, who became part of Willi and Otto's anti-fascist enterprise in Paris.

While she was living with Paul Massing in Paris, Hede made the transition of which we are speaking: The transition from propaganda to fully covert work, operating under the cover of Willi and Otto's "anti-fascism" and directed by one of the great illegals and an intimate associate of Theodore Maly: the great master-spy whose code name was "Ludwik," whose true name was Erwin Poretsky, but who is best known as "Ignace Reiss."

During the summer of 1933, everything was coming together. The Leipzig Trial, and the London Counter-Trial were about to take place. Willi and Otto were consolidating their new task. "Anti-fascism" was taking shape. In England, Maly and his colleagues were successfully perfecting the networks spun from Cambridge. And in America the New Deal of Franklin Roosevelt was in its first hundred days.

In response to all this, "Ludwik's" top-secret apparatus in Paris was itself beginning to move in some new directions. Willi Münzenberg and Ludwik, representing respectively propaganda and deep cover, were personally close, but their operations were compartmentalized. Babette had been instructed never to show the smallest flicker of recognition if their paths chanced to cross those of either Reiss or his wife, though they were all old friends.

Such was the context within which Ludwik summoned Hede to him one summer day with instructions for a new assignment. She was to prepare for a meeting with a "most important comrade." "Try to look your best," Ludwik told her. "Don't be as flippant as you usually are. . . . Show more respect for important people."[10]

Ludwik escorted Hede to a café near the Opera called the Café Scribe. Hede and Ludwik took a table, ordered an *apéritif,* and made small talk, waiting. A few minutes later, there materialized at their table "a tall, lank, elegant man of about forty-two. His face was tanned, strangely ascetic, his eyes deep and sad. His hands were the long, narrow, aristocratic kind."

It was Maly. Hede did not know it was Maly. She may never have known. She certainly did not know it when she wrote her memoirs. But Maly it was.

The elegant agent sat down and without introduction addressed Hede by her first name. He told her he was known among "our people" in the apparatus as "*der Lange,*" the Tall Man. So why didn't Hede call him that, too: the Tall Man.

At this point, Ludwik slipped away.

Maly had arranged this meeting to preside over a radical change in Hede's life as a spy. Though Massing knew nothing of Maly's work in England, the Tall Man was proud, even a little vain, about his British connections, and Massing sensed they were important. "I gathered," she later wrote, "that he was the head of some apparatus, probably the GPU in England, *and that he was slated to go to America in a similar post*" (my emphasis). "Felik" [Ludwik's assistant] had probably mentioned the fact that I was a genuine American citizen with a genuine American passport; that I was on my way to the United States; that I had been working for Ludwik and might be worthwhile looking over."

So what brought this secret eminence of the Cambridge Conspiracy to the Café Scribe were *American* concerns.

Der Lange leaned back in his chair and suggested they have a night on the town. "He was suave, worldly, spoke fluent English. 'It takes an Englishman like me,' he said, pointing to his exquisitely tailored clothes with a wink of his eye, 'to know Paris.' "

The rest of the night was like some wistful little date, less like a rendezvous for spies than a scene from Ernst Lubitsch's film comedy of romance and revolution, *Ninotchka,* recast in a chronically melancholy key. Hede and the Tall Man had dinner in a Norman restaurant, and ended up at 4 A.M. in the Melodie Bar, listening to a black jazz band while, over their sad brandies, *der Lange* grew confidential with her. He confessed that he was a man in love, that he was trying to be transferred to America so he could rejoin a woman in Ludwik's network named Gerda Frankfurter. The Tall Man loved Gerda, but she was lost to him. The apparatus had ordered her into the American operation. He did not know if he would ever see her again. The gloom thickened as the evening ended and he lapsed, as he would again, into "depression fits of self-accusation."

Hede was being sent to New York, using that precious *real* American passport of hers, there to engage in an important new phase of secret work. In fact, in America Hede would get to know Gerda Frankfurter well and would work with her often. Maly took out a cigarette box—"it was a rather primitive method, I thought,"—tore its top in half and told her that she would know her American contact when she was handed the other half.

A few weeks after Hede Massing arrived in America, a man came to the door of the apartment she'd found in New York. He was stout, vulgarly dressed, self-important, stupid. He announced that he should have the torn top half of the cigarette box, but he had lost it. Here was a prime example of the NKVD's new breed, and he blustered in with his orders.

Working under her new cover as an "anti-fascist" journalist, Hede began to frequent left-wing circles in New York and Washington, a witting agent making contact among the "innocents." One of the people for whom Hede became a link to what was called the "anti-fascist underground,'' and was in fact the *apparat,* was Josephine Herbst, a novelist and journalist from the circle of Ernest Hemingway. It appears to have been through her contact with Hede (and very possibly a meeting with both Münzenberg and Gibarti) that Josephine Herbst was sent to Germany on what has every appearance of a mission for the Münzenberg underground, the first of what would be a number of covert actions she and her husband would perform for the *apparat.*[11] (The co-operation between Hede and Gibarti on Herbst's assignment in Berlin incidentally illustrates the close collaboration between Willi and Ludwik's branch of covert work.) Right around this time, Herbst also became either a good friend or an important political contact, or both, for Otto Katz. That was a friendship Josie kept well out of public view, guarding the secret for the rest of her life. Meanwhile, Herbst's husband was being prepared for serious work in Washington espionage. This was John Herrmann, a not-very-successful novelist who had served as Hemingway's drinking pal from Paris to Key West. Herrmann would soon find himself working in espionage against Washington, right around the time that Hede herself moved to the capital to begin a top-level mission of her own.

Herrmann's work in Washington was to help manage the network created by Harold Ware, a network that includes, I believe, Alger Hiss. Hede Massing was assigned to cultivating a rising young star in the Department of State named Noel Field. Her task, so she thought, was to guide him, oh so gently, through the secret door. Herrmann and Massing were working side by side. They were operatives together in Cambridge West.[12]

Hede Massing does not seem to have known that in 1934 Noel Field was already very much in Moscow's eye, and had been for some time. Noel's mother, a devout Quaker woman, was often in Europe and had repeatedly worked as a courier for Ludwik. Mother Field was passionately opposed to Hitler; the missions she ran for Ludwik in Germany were protected by her frank American face and her precious American passport. I have never seen the claim made that Noel Field's mother was anything other than a sincere but naive anti-fascist. Nonetheless, she seems to have preceded her son into secret work, and it was secret work for Ludwik. Couriers—note well—are often selected precisely for their innocence. The reason is simple: The ignorant, if caught, will have nothing to say. We might add that it seems that Madame Field senior's brisk rectitude and purity of righteous passion, albeit useful, rather got on Ludwik's nerves.[13]

Whether the apparatus found Noel through his mother or the reverse is an unanswered question. But back in America, Noel Field was already secretly involved in communist activity, and probably had been so since 1926 or 1927.[14] He appears to have been inducted into the American Party at roughly the same time that Whittaker Chambers was meeting with his ghost from the Comintern at the New York Public Library. Note that these men were *not* first recruited out of fear of Hitler; the date is much too early.[15] And just as Donald Maclean had been told he could best serve the Revolution in the British Foreign Office, so the young Noel Field was to serve the Revolution as an American diplomat.

Hede's account of guiding the seemingly innocent Noel Field into espionage is one of the most complete reports of these seductions we have. Her first assigned task was to become the Fields' friend. Accomplishing that proved easy. Hede genuinely liked Noel; she also liked his wife Herta. Massing was lonely in America; she found the couple comforting, ''almost European.'' In fact Herta Field was German-born; and Noel, born in London, came from an American background that was ''cosmopolitan'' in something like the old Henry Jamesian mold. Hede found Noel dreamy, idealistic, impulsive. He was also destined for great things at State. In the not-too-distant future, Field would be offered a job in charge of State's German desk, no less.

Thirty years later, Noel Field's publishing colleagues in communist Hungary would fall silent when Noel Field approached them in the halls; they were afraid of being reported to the Committee as the horror-hardened Stalinist passed them by. What a different story it was during that Washington springtime in Roosevelt's first term! As a youth, Field seems to have been, if not exactly charming, at least a likable type. Somewhere there exists a snapshot of the young Noel taken by Herta in a woodland spot a mere ten minutes outside central Washington. Field is beaming at the camera, and buck naked. The picture was taken to prove how swiftly the young diplomat could get from the Seat of Government to the State of Nature.

On another occasion, walking late at night on the Mall, high on wine, Noel paused before the Lincoln Memorial, spread his endless gangling arms wide and began to serenade the great Daniel Chester French statue with the *Internationale*. Honest Abe looked down on the chanting Quaker.

Hede's task was to coax and set the steel in this rather winning and seemingly romantic soul. Her job was to watch and report every tiny surge that rippled across the hidden surface of Field's good but ingenuous mind. She was to probe and toughen his idealism, win his trust, and locate his capacity for betrayal. Hede had to think with Herta and Noel, feel with Herta and Noel, breathe as they breathed.

Field loved Wagner, and he assumed that his German anti-fascist friend Hede must love Wagner too. Hede detested Wagner. Night after night, once Noel was home from another day on the rise at State, Hede would join the Fields in their apartment for some of Herta's *gemütlich* cookery. After supper, it never failed: Wagner. Hede would sink back on the couch, feigning joy as the curly-haired Quaker's son stretched out and rolled his eyes over *Lohengrin.* On and on and *on* it went. At last silence let Hede prod things back to earth with some serious talk about anti-fascism; about the awful struggle going on in Europe; about the Revolution. Above all, Hede would harp on the troubling question of what a merely bourgeois administration like Roosevelt's could really do against the threat. After all, Roosevelt was part and parcel of the capitalist system that had spawned fascism. He was part of the problem, as good revolutionaries like themselves knew. Good intentions were not enough. It really was to the Soviet Union, to Marxism-Leninism, that one must look for the way out. But how? With what help?

It isn't clear exactly how long it took Noel Field to become a true Soviet agent. I myself do not entirely discount the possibility that Field may already have been fully witting and inside the apparatus by the time Hede entered his life. Field may have been more knowing about Hede's maneuvers than he let on. After all, he had been a secret member of the Party for years. Massing reports that Field originally hesitated to steal documents directly from State. She says that her recruit at first preferred to write summaries of important documents, summaries he would bring home and then read aloud to Hede, who would take them down in shorthand. Massing suggests this caution was born in Field's moral compunction—as if shorthand took him only halfway to betrayal. The argument is not persuasive. Field's caution seems far more likely to have been an elementary but shrewd self-protective measure, a way of assuring that the Soviets would get their material without any traceable written link to him. If Alger Hiss had insisted that Whittaker Chambers take shorthand notes, rather than let Priscilla type *his* summaries on the family typewriter, the Hisses might never have been exposed. Who then was the naïf? Hede or Noel?

But then all the accounts of Noel Field's espionage work, without exception, are peculiarly contradictory. Evidence available for many years has made certain conclusions about Field inevitable. Those presumptions as I write, appear to have found full confirmation in the Archives of the Ministry of the Interior in Budapest.[16] But it is plain from other sources that by the mid-1930s Noel Field was an active witting source for Soviet espionage in the Roosevelt State Department; it is likewise clear that when he proceeded to Europe after that time, he remained under Soviet discipline throughout the war, and in fact almost certainly until the moment of his arrest in Budapest in August 1949, after his colleague in espionage Alger Hiss was being accused by Whittaker Chambers in Washington.

Some say Field was a reluctant agent, filled with compunction and divided loyalties. It is claimed that in 1936 Field was about to be promoted to that plum job at State's German desk, but turned it down, quit the State Department, and proceeded to Europe for work at the League of Nations, not in response to Soviet needs but because he was still ambivalent about espionage and couldn't square betraying the American government while actually working under its oath. (Betraying the League, it's implied, would be a more acceptable proposition.) Yet other good witnesses describe Noel Field the secret agent as exceptionally eager; burning to go the whole distance from espionage to assassination. In this version, it is the apparatus rather than Field that is ambivalent: the apparatus turns down *Field,* despite all his eagerness. In fact, all accounts of Field's career repeatedly show the young American on the sinister inside of events, in political places where dabblers were not allowed. During the peak of the Terror, for example, he was safe and influential in Moscow, enjoying all kinds of privileges that Stalin did not ordinarily grant to Americans who prated too much about mixed loyalties in his service.[17]

In short, a confusing and minimizing fog of ambivalence surrounds all our knowledge of Noel Field; smoke from what I'd guess is a smokescreen, which clouds our view of Field's real political work at every step. And a very substantial amount of the fumes seem to come from a part of the apparatus run by Ludwik and Krivitsky. Even after Field's death, the fog continued to spread. Karel Kaplan, the Czech defector who was the Dubcek government's investigator into the Slansky Trials, reliably told me that the records he had seen in Prague indicated that after 1938, Noel Field was "mistrusted" by the apparatus—because he had been too close to Krivitsky. I strongly suspect that this claim was intra-apparatus cover, and that it had been provided to Field for many years.

It is true I come to this suspicion from inference and not hard evidence. The evidence is contradictory. One version says Field was outside the apparatus because he was too close to Reiss and Krivitsky. Another says he was outside the apparatus because Reiss and Krivitsky would have nothing to do with him. This incessant slippery talk about ambivalence strikes me as wholly misleading. The dossiers of Field's debriefing, purportedly discovered in the Hungarian archives in 1993, are said fully to sustain the darkest view of Field's sinister commitments in his life as a secret agent. According to Maria Schmidt, Field did indeed go the whole distance from espionage to assassination.* But even without the Budapest file, some evidence already before us is plain. Field was *in* the apparatus. He was in Washington. He was in Paris. He was in Marseille. He was when he approached Allen Dulles, and he was when he worked for Münzenberg's people in Europe. After his release from prison after the Terror enacted in his name, he remained a Stalinist of such absolute devotion almost as to defy belief. For example, he claimed that on the day of their release, he and Herta were told for the first time that Stalin had died while they were in prison, an event which so overwhelmed them both with grief that they fell into each other's arms and "heaved with sobs." From the very beginning, claims about the hand-wringing compunction of such a figure sound very fishy. Let us suppose Field really had just turned down a straightforward order to use his desk at State for espionage—on the grounds of divided loyalty, no less! Is it even imaginable that the Soviet residents would meekly accede and suggest instead an extremely sensitive European slot where the reluctant spy might muse on his doubts?

This scenario, I submit, is absurd. Of *course* Ludwik would have refused to employ such an obvious security risk in Europe or anywhere else. He would have refused to let him into his presence. Yet we know perfectly well that Noel Field *did* go to Europe under Soviet sponsorship; that he *did* meet with Ludwik there, and that he became well known to Krivitsky. We also know that he went on to become—to *remain*—an undercover *apparatchik* demonstrably in good standing for many years.

In fact, none of these accounts dwelling on the ambiguities of Noel Field are plausible, or in my opinion true. Apart from Hede Massing's account, no persuasive evidence suggests that Ludwik felt ambivalent about Field or that Field felt ambivalent about Ludwik. I do not believe that Field refused to spy at State, or that Ludwik refused him employment.[18] I think it much more likely that Noel Field did, always, precisely what he was told to do. I think that a refusal to do so would have put him definitely out of the apparatus and made him a man in trouble by late 1934 at the latest.

Our best evidence on this subject actually comes from Whittaker Chambers. Krivitsky explicitly told Chambers, long before Field was in trouble, that the apparatus had forthrightly ordered Field to turn down his State Department promotion and proceed instead to the League and thereby enter the European arena.[19] The importance of this seeming step

* Here I must caution the reader again about this as yet untested, but very interesting source. See footnote on page 91.

down can be measured by the role Field later played in "anti-fascist" networking of the apparatus in the true focus of interest: Eastern Europe. Field's supposed (and in my opinion non-existent) compunction on the subject played no role. It is true that Hede Massing's account is out of phase with this view. My guess is that Hede Massing was as much the innocent as Field himself, and that she was simply out of the loop on this decision, being confused by some smoke of her own. Evidence supporting this hypothesis is that Massing was never even told that Field, a man she supposed she was coaxing out of a soft, merely moralistic, anti-fascism, had been a secret member of the Party for many years and was fully under its discipline. The innocent who lay there rolling his eyes over *Lohengrin* may have understood more about the secret strategies of the friendship than Hede imagined. Who was watching whom? My guess is that they were watching each other.

"Oh, Hede! Hede!" So sighed Babette Gross when we discussed her old friend. Naive, sad, driven soul: That was the implication. Yet naive Hede finishes her account of her recruitment and link to Noel Field with a fascinating final note which deserves further investigation. "I think there is much more to Krivitsky," she wrote, "than he wrote in his book *In Stalin's Secret Service*. I believe that if Noel Field is ready and able to tell his story, the tragic dual role of Krivitsky will be understood much better."[20]

This comment strikes me as one that might very well prove prophetic for research. To it I can only add a footnote of my own. The Noel Field who persuaded Hede Massing that he was such a very gentle soul, so filled with exquisite moral compunction, is very reliably reported to have boasted, more than once, that he had assisted the NKVD in tracking Ludwik to his hiding place in Switzerland after Ludwik broke with Stalin and tried to get his family into hiding. Field regarded it as a point of solemn pride to have given assistance to the team that managed to find the old spy in Lausanne, entrap him there, and machine-gun him down.[21]

Ten years after Ludwik was murdered, the events of the emerging Cold War suddenly turned Noel Field into a spy very much in the cold. Field had spent the war as a Soviet agent working in the "anti-fascist" cadres Stalin had spread all through Europe. Here is the true point of intersection between propaganda and deep cover. The "anti-fascist cadres" running all through Europe had, as we have seen, a number of purposes beyond resistance to fascism. They were in fact networks created to destroy the opposition, including other anti-fascist opposition, and lay the groundwork for post-Nazi Stalinist power in Europe. This is where the Münzenberg networks, and particularly Otto Katz, played their politically most decisive role, and it is also the arena within which Noel Field came into his own as a secret agent. It is plain that working with these groups was Field's specialty in the Soviet services, for which he served as a prime American contact.[22] This dear friend of Otto's had now passed far beyond dictating summaries of State Department cables to Hede Massing. Working in close conjunction with the Münzenberg operations, and under cover of his seeming role as a leading American do-gooder in the world of European refugees, Field from this point forward played a large role in the fate, and in fact even the survival, of countless political refugees all around Europe. This was the entire non-Nazi political class of the continent. As Field and his masters knew full well, it was to these frightened and competing people that power in the post-Nazi world would be allocated. And it was Field's task to help assure that it would be Stalinist power.

In that capacity Field performed another clandestine task of great value to the Soviets. In Switzerland he had approached his acquaintance Allen Dulles, an old friend from his early days at State, and who was now in charge of the OSS station in Geneva. Noel Field persuaded Dulles that Field's work at the League and later with the American Friends Service Committee and similar organizations had given Field first-rate contacts with important anti-fascist groups who otherwise mistrusted the Americans. Field offered himself as a liaison. He would quietly watch out for American interests, ensuring Dulles was fully informed and keeping all the right people in touch. It is plain that Field saw himself as under Soviet discipline when he made this offer to Dulles, and it is no less plain that Allen Dulles, in what many see as a typical lapse of judgment, fell for the "offer" like the proverbial ton of bricks. Whereupon Field became one of Dulles's advisors on anti-fascist politics, and American intelligence was once again penetrated, at a senior level, by yet another double agent in Stalin's service.[23]

Not bad work for somebody who, we are asked to believe, played no role. Once the war was over, Field was in search for a new role until that dark day in 1948 when Whittaker Chambers accused Field's fellow mole at State, Alger Hiss, of being an underground agent. The moment he read this headline in Paris, Field understood his old life was over. With Chambers exposing the Ware network, Field knew it was only a matter of time until the thread led to him. An American subpoena, even one summoning him as a witness rather than as a target, had to be avoided at all costs.*

---

* Of course, if (as is sometimes claimed) Field really had been a double agent working for the Americans, he would have needed only to contact his control Allen Dulles to be granted ironclad protection from the events unrolling in Washington. But American protection is precisely what Field did not seek.

He naturally turned at once to the Soviets. And of course, the NKVD chief Beria and the apparat quite agreed with him: He must not fall into American hands. But the Soviets did not choose to rescue Field in the same way they had rescued Maclean. There would be no apartment or dacha. Not yet. First Noel Field was to be arrested, as were his wife, his brother, his adopted daughter, and beyond his wretched family a very large number of other people.

Field was directed to Prague. He went to Prague. And at that point Noel Field vanished from the face of the earth.[24]

Field had in fact been taken to a safe house outside Budapest, where he was held prisoner under elaborate surveillance. There the new role Field was seeking in the Soviet services was revealed to him. He was to become the man whose accusations would provide the basis for a new wave of mass arrests and purges all through Stalinist Eastern Europe.[25]

Field was now to adopt a new pose, and adopt it he did. It would be announced that all through the war he had acted as a kind of American super-agent and master-spy, a highest-level conspirator and double agent working on orders from Allen Dulles. It would be asserted that in this conspiratorial capacity he had devoted his life to subverting the Revolution, and above all that he had drawn a large number of traitors into his web, turning seemingly good communists into American spies, Titoists, Trotskyites, and other scum.

In fact, the people thus accused were in fact merely communists Stalin wished to liquidate, a large percentage of whom had been active in the cadres of the anti-fascist movement in Europe in the days leading up to and through the war. It is plain that Stalin had decided the time had come to roll up the anti-fascist cadres once and for all, and cover their tracks with a vast new round of show trials. Field was the ideal mouthpiece for this purge, since he was both an American and one who had been ubiquitously active among these cadres from 1936 onward. As he had known everybody, everybody could be killed in his name.

Thousands died.

And so, in Noel Field's name a new intra-party purge and general political Terror began in Budapest and eventually ran through every country in Eastern Europe, culminating in the 1952 Slansky Trials in Prague and their many victims.

One such doomed soul was Field's old friend and mentor, Otto Katz.

Exactly how fully co-operative Noel Field was in this enterprise is somewhat unclear. He was unquestionably being held as a prisoner in Budapest and so was his family. He was relentlessly interrogated, as was Herta, though the records of Field's debriefing, made at the time of his release, are said to show him a fully, even enthusiastically, co-operative collaborator with the secret police.[26] He seems to have been tortured. Yet even from the earliest stages of the operations, Field was an oddly co-operative prisoner, and his sufferings did not leave him a simple victim. One fact is salient above all else: *Field was not executed.* Thousands of others were put to death in his name, but the great ringleader of ringleaders was left alive. Why? It would have been so easy to put him to death. In later years, Field was among the first to be "rehabilitated." Why? It would have been so easy for him to tell the world the truth, expose the lie.

But Noel Field did not expose the lie. He was provided with protection and advancement by the Hungarian Stalinists for the rest of his life, and for the rest of his life, this "innocent," so famous for his compunction and ambivalence, served them with a devotion unmarred by the smallest expression of doubt.

We know only a few of the scenes from Field's imprisonment. Noel Field was being held in that cottage when the very first victim of the new Eastern European Terror was brought to the same place to be accused, interrogated, tortured, and made to confess. His name was Tibor Szonyi. Szonyi was no innocent: He too was a practiced builder of Stalinist cadres in Europe, a covert operator whose life had been lived inside the Party. He supposed himself to be an admired leader in that Party; empowered and trusted soldier of Stalinism, just like his good, good friend Noel Field.

The first step in the demoralization of Tibor Szonyi was to slap him in the face with a charge of high treason. He was an American agent, a tool of Allen Dulles and the OSS, and the master-spy Noel Field was his go-between. Szonyi naturally denied the charge. He laid down his denial as if he was producing his Party card, proof positive. This was a member of the Central Committee speaking, a man who had given the Party everything, whose loyalty had been proved by years, a lifetime of service.

Then, like a horror in a dream, Noel Field himself stepped out from an adjoining room. Tall, American, with a large lantern jaw and enormous eyes, this Quaker son of puritan success must have borne an alien air to the Hungarian's eyes. That air now became nightmarish. Field stood before the gaping *apparatchik* and proceeded to repeat the entire accusation. Compelled or not compelled, Field was at this early point working *with* Szonyi's torturers. He repeated it all: Yes, Szonyi was a tool of the Americans. Yes, he had often been the go-between for Szonyi's treasons with Allen Dulles. Yes, Szonyi was a traitor to communism, a linchpin in the evil Noel Field network.

Challenged by this surreal presence, Szonyi's sense of himself must have trembled. Field was putting together shreds of truth reconstituted as bizarre inversions of fact, an ultimate paranoiac vision, politically empowered. Of *course* Szonyi had worked with Noel Field. What undercover European anti-fascist hadn't? They had worked together in Europe—*for the Party*. They both were completely loyal servants of the Revolution. Noel Field, master-spy? A lifetime of absolute commitment was being turned into a tale of absolute betrayal.

When he was finished, Noel Field left the room, and Szonyi's real "interrogation" began. It was conducted less with questions than with rubber truncheons. Within a few hours, the once-proud member of the Central Committee, who had served the Party so well and so long, was crawling around the floor babbling confession after confession about his conspiracies with Allen Dulles, the OSS, and Noel Field.

Though Noel Field was of course not personally present at them all, this was only the first among hundreds of such "interrogations." What began in Budapest now spread across all of Eastern Europe. One Party official after another, almost all of them people who had been active in those anti-fascist cadres in Europe before and during the war, confessed to having conspired with the arch-demon Field, and prior to being killed, participated in ripping their own lives into a mound of shredded falsehoods.[27]

In effect, one prime purpose of the Eastern European Terror purges of 1948–52 was to round up the old Stalinist anti-fascist cadres of the war and pre-war, cover their previous work with a set of judicial lies, and kill them all. Exactly what crimes and compromises Stalin was covering in this slaughter of his own anti-fascist underground in Europe must be a matter for scholarship in the years to come. It has not thus far been seriously explored in the literature known to me.[28] We know one of probably many dark secrets Otto Katz took to the grave: that the Reichstag Fire Trial, the founding event of "anti-fascism," was a collaboration with Hitler. But the documents suggest that Katz may well have been privy to many other secrets of anti-fascism: It's said he knew "the secrets of the Brown House"; he may well have known the secrets of Tuchachevsky's downfall and the murder of the general staff; he certainly knew many of the secrets of the Terror in Spain, and in this context it should be noted that the prime targets for Stalin's round-up and elimination of his own people were the anti-fascist cadres in Spain. Finally, Otto may have been aware of how the Czech secret service was used in the bloody business of putting in power the government which was now obediently condemning him to death.

America's entry into the Cold War precipitated a crisis in the secret world. Hiss and Chambers were cracking open the American networks that had been founded under the auspices of the same "anti-fascism," whose European cadres were being rolled up in the East, all operations which surely helped pave the way to Yalta and Stalin's political conquest of Eastern Europe. For Stalin, like the Western democracies, had much to defend in Yalta.

A multitude of sins had been committed in the name of Stalin's "anti-fascism." Philby and Burgess were especially well placed to accomplish this kind of treachery, because both had insinuated themselves into the Special Operations Executive. Special Operations Executive, or SOE as it was invariably called, was the branch of the British secret services set up to assist resistance fighters on the ground in Europe, most of whom naturally turned to the British for help. Inside SOE, Philby and Burgess were in a position to subvert and destroy those among them not in Stalin's game-plan. Some are known. Many have probably not yet been uncovered. There is the black tale of how the Cambridge group betrayed the Mihailovich resistance fighters in Yugoslavia.[29] It is probably only the tip of the iceberg.[30]

Yet if Stalin and the British had secrets to keep about the treasons of "anti-fascism," so did the Americans. And Noel Field probably had a pretty good idea of what those secrets might be. A mystery worth exploring would be the relative silence of the American intelligence community on the subject of Field.[31] The reluctance of the senior diplomatic advisors to Truman, the so-called "Wise Men," in attacking Hiss may well have been doubly potent in the case of Field, all the more so because Field's work had been so richly abetted by the bad judgment of Allen Dulles, at a moment when Dulles was the number two person, about to become number one, in the newly formed CIA. The communists were able to accuse Noel Field of having been an American agent for the simple reason that he was. Serving as an OSS liaison to anti-fascist resistance fighters in Europe, Field may well have done damage to non-Stalinist anti-fascists very much along the lines of Philby's efforts at SOE.

This was surely not a story which Allen Dulles was eager to see in the form of headlines. If Stalin was looking for a way to embarrass and inhibit the American shake-up of his apparatus which came with the Hiss case, he may well have found that way in Noel Field. When Alger Hiss was compromised by the Americans, Stalin may well have felt he had an American card to play in defense. That card, I conjecture, may have been Field.

The new Eastern European Terror lasted from 1948 to 1952. During it, Noel Field was never publicly produced. He was never tried, even *in camera*. Nor was he executed, though untold numbers of people in his so-called "ring" were hanged or shot or died in torture, doomed by his "confessions." He and Herta were held in prison until November 1954, a total of six years. They were then released. The date of their release, interestingly, was exactly the day of Alger Hiss's release from Lewisburg Penitentiary. They were "rehabilitated"—even though nobody had ever admitted they were Stalinists in the first place.[32] Thus was Noel Field freed from an ordeal of world-wide political importance which, more perfectly than any living person, he knew to have been based top to bottom on lie piled upon lie.

The large lanky American never looked back. One might suppose the experience could have left an "idealist" like Noel Field with a second thought or two about Stalin's justice. Not at all. While Hungary slowly de-Stalinized, Noel lived on in Budapest, more loyal than the regime. He never returned to the West, even for a short visit, even when it would have been perfectly safe for him to do so. He never gave any historian or journalist an interview about his life, no matter what the writer's political persuasion. He never made the minutest effort to explain or even clarify his own role. The steadfast tin soldier of Stalinism worked for the rest of his life as a middle-level executive in Hungarian publishing. Until the end he was feared by his co-workers. And with what reason!

Herta Field outlived Noel: She died only in the 1980s, near the time that Hungary at last began to emerge from its decades of oppression. The repressed by that time had begun to return. The great public manifestation in Budapest celebrating the fall of communism was designed by Lazlo Rajk, the son of a leading Hungarian communist sent to his death through the "confessions" of Noel Field. By the time Herta expired, it was not easy to scare up many Marxist-Leninist true believers left in Budapest.

But Herta was one of them. Gathering before her coffin, the people who came to Herta's funeral were told that as the occasion ended they would be asked to rise and sing the *Internationale*. Herta would have wanted it that way.

People glanced at each other in embarrassment. They shuffled to their feet, and in *a capella* voices, quavered through the old anthem, stanza by stanza, to the bitter end.[33]

. . .

The Cambridge spies, incidentally, were obsessed with the Hiss case. A fascinated Burgess saw it "as a battle of good and evil in which all good was on the side of Hiss and all evil on the side of Chambers." This might seem merely the standard left-wing line—until he added (it was the *echt* Burgess touch) that even in his goodness Hiss was probably guilty. Sublimely, superbly guilty—since only a communist would achieve the seamless perfection of duplicity which the life of Alger Hiss must be if Chambers was right.[34] Maclean was in America when the Hiss case broke. Donald publicly adopted the familiar pose of outrage: Hiss was an innocent progressive victimized by fascist America. Yet it was Maclean who blurted to Cyril Connolly, at the end of a drunken evening: "*I* am the English Hiss." Over breakfast the next morning, just to be sure nobody mistook his small-hours claim for alcoholic bravado, Maclean returned to the subject. "What would you do if I told you I was a communist agent?" Connolly stared back. Maclean ended the discussion with a taunt: "Go on—report me."

Donald was getting very near the edge.[35]

The Cambridge Conspiracy was *almost* a total success. With just a bit more luck, every one of the Cambridge spies might well have retired undetected to Kent and their knighthoods. Donald Maclean was exposed only through a flukish episode in what is called Sigint, or signal intelligence, and by some particularly resourceful and intelligent work done by the FBI.[36] Had it not been for the good luck of the code breaking known as the "Venona Intercepts," there is nothing at all fanciful about picturing the Kennedy era with an undetected Donald Maclean, Soviet agent, serving as British Ambassador to the United States; Kim Philby, Soviet agent, directing British counter-intelligence, or perhaps as "C," running all of British intelligence; Guy Burgess, Soviet agent, very senior at the BBC; and Anthony Blunt, Soviet agent, confidant to many of the most elevated personages in British political life, from the Rothschilds to the royal establishment. Stalin's recruiter at Trinity College had packed in a good day's work. And it might well have stuck, unless some waverer in the group such as Goronwy Rees had been brought at last, like Whittaker Chambers, to tell the truth.[37]

But we must return from Field to the great illegal agent who sent Hede Massing to him: Theodore Maly. Anthony Blunt many times told Arthur Martin and Peter Wright that he and his friends could never have been seduced into the lives of secret work by the kinds of canny but brutal dimwits Beria dispatched into the democracies during later years.[38] But Maly was different. Maly was a man of moral feeling. Maly touched the high serious.

And so he did. The man who had sent Hede Massing to Washington was yet another member of the Hungarian Mafia, fully familiar with all the many covert operatives from Budapest we have been discussing. He was an intimate colleague of Dzerzhinsky: a companion of Saint Terror. He was also the elegant Hungarian *par excellence;* smooth, multi-lingual, cultivated, and knowing, a man with a multiple and nuanced mind. He had many names: lots of people called him "Teddy," others called him "Theo"; depending on which country he was passing through, he used many other aliases as well. He often went under the name "Mr. Peters," an alias intended to confuse, since his opposite number in New York, another member of the Hungarian Mafia, also used the alias "Peters," until "J. Peters" was deported to Hungary as a result of the revelations of Elizabeth Bentley and Chambers, there to work the rest of *his* life in Hungarian publishing, perhaps alongside his old recruit Noel Field. Another of Maly's aliases was "Paul Hardt." Finally there was the nickname Hede Massing heard: *der Lange,* "the Tall Man."[39]

That Maly was fully witting about the American penetrations is shown by the American mission he gave Hede Massing that night in the Melodie Bar. But further evidence of the link between Cambridge and Washington is found in the career of Michael Straight. It was at Maly's suggestion that the American Michael Straight was recruited at Cambridge, and it was with Maly's permission that Straight was sent back to America for work in the capital.

Michael Straight was brought into the apparatus by Maly's man in place, Blunt; and as we have seen it was a recruitment Blunt would live to regret. It is important to note that from the beginning, Blunt made it plain that he intended Straight to enter the *American,* not the British, apparatus. The Cambridge circle and the Washington penetrations were linked.

Here is how Straight himself tells the tale.[40] One day in 1937, shortly after his closest friend John Cornford had been killed in Spain, Michael Straight was asked to drop by the rooms of the brilliant young don Anthony Blunt "in the loveliest court in Trinity."

In 1937 Straight, who was already a committed student communist, was in the midst of his grief. Part of his conversation with Blunt that day was over what Straight might do in John's memory. As they talked, Blunt asked what Michael planned to do when he left Cambridge. Well, Michael had been vacillating; he did not know. In any event he thought he would become a British subject.

At this point Blunt adopted the cool controlling tone of which he was lifelong master. "Some of our friends," Blunt told Michael Straight, "have other ideas for you."

"Other ideas?"

Blunt maintained that same tone of incisive authority.

"Your father worked on Wall Street," Anthony continued. "He was a partner in J. P. Morgan. With these connections, and with your training as an economist, you could make a brilliant career for yourself in international banking."

"I don't want a brilliant career in international banking," I said. "I have no interest whatever in becoming a banker."

"Our friends have given a great deal of thought to it," Anthony insisted. "They have instructed me to tell you that is what you must do."

"What *I* must do? . . . What friends have instructed you tell me?"

"Our friends in the International. The Communist International. . . . My instructions are to inform you of your assignment, and to assist you in every way that I can."[41]

Straight protested that he could not tolerate a life on Wall Street. Blunt agreed to convey Michael Straight's *cri de cœur* to "our friends." In due course Maly informed Blunt that while it was still essential that Straight go underground in America, his family connections in Washington would serve as well as those on Wall Street.

For one thing, Michael's family owned the *New Republic* magazine. Did it not?

It did. Maly was very well informed about Straight's opportunities in Washington. And indeed Michael Straight would return to America and become the editor of that journal. While he was editor, Straight's sister Beatrice Straight would marry a man named Louis Dolivet, who in turn had been a Comintern agent, and one of Münzenberg's most important protégés. It is perfectly possible he was still under Soviet discipline when he married Beatrice. Certainly Dolivet was wonderfully close to many of the leading actors in our tale. Dolivet had been a close associate of Otto Katz. While on Soviet assignment in Geneva before the war, he had also shared an office with Noel Field. During that same time he was extremely close (and possibly a case officer) to Noel Field's mistress, a woman named Herta Tempi, who was likewise a Münzenberg agent.[42]

Maly had made a very deft placement. Within days after his arrival in that city, before he'd even made contact with his Soviet control, Michael Straight was in the second-floor sitting room of the White House, having tea with the Roosevelts.[43]

But what sort of man was Theodore Maly, this recruiter for Saint Terror, this master of the "idealistic" spies?

Theodore Maly began his life as a servant of God and ended it as a servant of Stalin. That trajectory defines much in him. He was present at the founding of the NKVD—then called the Cheka; a close associate, friend, and protégé of both Mikhail Trilisser, the founder of the foreign wing of the NKVD, and Dzerzhinsky himself. Maly's life followed a path that instructively describes the ethical consequences of Dzerzhinsky and Lenin's vision. Maly was a man whose nature was by every account exceptionally pure, gentle, cultivated, and kind. No reporter fails to note these qualities. Yet this gentle being was present at the creation of totalitarianism, and his life is a demonstration of the union between radicalism and terror.

He was best remembered by his friends for his intelligence, his blue eyes, the shy sweetness of his smile, and his shrewd kindness. Back in Budapest, the Tall Man had begun his career in the priesthood, and he made the crucial transition from religion to revolution, from faith to terror, only after being tried in the crucible of the First World War. When that war broke out, Father Maly had enrolled as an army chaplain, and worked among the troops on the Eastern Front of the Carpathians. There he was taken prisoner, and spent the rest of the war huddled in prisoner-of-war camps, witnessing horror after horror, watching soldiers dying *en masse* from typhus and frostbite, trying to bring them the final consolation of the faith while their bodies crawled with vermin.

Given the experience through which this young priest found his initiation into hell, it would seem grossly presumptuous, an act of pride, to suggest that for all his gentle brilliance, Maly was a weak man. Who would dare call anyone weak in the face of such things? Yet there *are* people whose faith and humanity are strengthened by horrors no less awful.

They broke Maly.

"I lost my faith in God, and when the revolution broke out, I joined the Bolsheviks. I broke with my past completely. I was no longer a Hungarian, a priest, a Christian, even anyone's son. I was just a soldier, 'missing in action.' "

This path to anonymity, the choice of despairing dissociation, is one of the most important moral byways of the modern experience. His wish to be good led Maly down the path to dehumanization, though it was a path he saw as redemptive. Wrapped in the facelessness of his annihilated faith, the newly atheistic Maly joined that "guardian of the revolution," the Cheka, the first incarnation of the NKVD. His new sacramental task was to remake the world. One of his early assignments was to move with the squadrons of the Cheka through the terrain of the Civil War.

Strange to say, this gentle person discovered himself yet once again in an arena of indescribable brutality.

"We would pass burning villages which had changed hands several times a day. . . . Our Red detachments would 'clean up' villages exactly the way the Whites did. What was left of the inhabitants, old men, women, children, were machine-gunned for having given assistance to the enemy. I could not stand the wailing of the women. I simply could not."

When that wailing of the women began, Maly would pretend to have diarrhea—and then, as if in confirmation, he developed a case of quite genuine dysentery. While the Cheka's machine gunners stood in the squares mowing the people down, Maly, favorite protégé of Saint Terror, would run to hide behind a truck. There he would double over in an agony at once intestinal and ethical, hands not over his gut but his ears.

The Terror worked. The Civil War ended, and the Cheka had made the Revolution safe. Except that its cruelties were soon followed by the collectivization of the Russian peasantry, with *its* murders *en masse*. And strange to say, the gentle Maly was once again on the scene.

"I knew what we were doing to the peasants, how many were deported, how many were shot. And still I stayed on. I still hoped the chance would come for me to atone for what I had done."

Atone? Atone while remaining in this secret police? It is an arresting misuse of the notion of atonement, all the more so coming from a former priest. It takes no very advanced theology to grasp that before any sinner can hope to atone he first must cease to commit his sin. The person who wishes to atone for murder must first stop murdering, stop being party to murder, and stop absolutely, without equivocation. In the absence of that turning back, there can be no atonement. Nor can there be forgiveness.

But Maly was lost to forgiveness. When he entered Dzerzhinsky's world, when Maly chose to become an instrument of the Revolution's annealing Terror, he enlisted his soul in a political system which bound the Good to Terror. "*Evil, be thou my good.*" For all his sweetness, *in* his sweetness, Maly had become a protégé of that Faustian vision for which the great collective expression in this century has been the revolutionary ethic. Noel Field too, was a sweet man, notable above all for his gentleness. And like Maly, Field too had a recurrent way of finding himself smack in the middle of cruel brutalities.

In his book *Witness,* Whittaker Chambers speaks of the man who served the Revolution faithfully, until one night in Moscow, he heard screams. Just that: *He heard screams.* And he broke. Father Maly also heard those screams, but he could not see the way to turn back or anywhere to turn.[44]

Why? It seems a fair guess that the sadistic conflicts of this gentle human being were inscribed in his commitment to Dzerzhinsky's vision of sanctity. Yet "atonement" filled Maly's mind, and in his search for it, he embarked on a strange, secret, private campaign.

One day there appeared before him a peasant woman pleading for the life of her husband, a man who had been sentenced to be shot for stealing some potatoes to keep his family from starving. This was the collectivization: hundreds of thousands were being killed. In the eyes of the Cheka, this doomed son of mother Russia stood no chance whatever. He was a "class enemy"; his life was meaningless and worthless. The Cheka was not protecting potatoes: It was ridding the regime of an unsubdued, therefore "enemy" *class.* The *idea* was to kill men like this man. The poor man's wife was appealing to the old set of values, as if the theft of the potatoes was a "wrong," and its punishment might be mitigated by mercy. She stood before Maly making her peasant plea for an old thing called the Right.

As a good Marxist-Leninist, Maly of course understood that "right" or "wrong" were moralistic trifling in the large plan of the Revolution's purge of capitalism's evil. Besides, Maly wasn't sure he even had the authority to save the wretch.

Yet then and there Maly decided that—as his "atonement"—he would act. Somehow or other, he would rescue just this one lost little human life. He would gather together all his power, all his persuasiveness, all his pull, everything he had all to save this one utterly innocent potato thief.

He went to his NKVD superior, another member of the Hungarian Mafia, and marshalled his best. Miraculously, it worked. The chief listened, had compassion, and agreed. Together the two men commuted the man's sentence to imprisonment. Just like that. It was done: an act of mercy, a personal intervention, actually performed. And so simply!

At this point Maly happened to be called away, dispatched somewhere else on a two-week assignment.

"When I got back, the first thing I did was look for my case. I could not find the file. I ran to my chief. He did not know what had happened, and both of us started to hunt for the file. We finally found it. Scribbled across it was one word: 'Executed.' "

"This time," Maly said, "I did not get a belly ache."

Instead, he walked in a blank daze to his quarters. When he stepped into the room, Maly discovered that it was his cat that had suffered from a cramp and done the soiling while he was away, leaving its mound right there on his bed. Very quietly, the former priest picked up the offending animal and on the spot strangled it with his bare hands. Then he flung his pet's corpse out the window.

By the next morning, Maly knew that he could no longer live in Soviet Russia. Once again, rather than turn back, he turned—outward. He proceeded instead to headquarters and requested a foreign assignment he had often turned down many times before, even though work in European espionage was a much less bloody business than the NKVD's heavy daily task at home. His superiors were delighted. They had always thought Maly's talents were wasted on the crude slaughters of collectivization.

Trilliser's successor directing the NKVD foreign wing, a man named Slutsky, had always admired Maly for his smoothness, his easy command of many languages, his good looks, his tact and social skill.[45] He promptly gave Theo a foreign job worthy of his gifts. It would lead to his subtle work in England.

When Maly sent Hede to America, he was a man in love, though he was never able to arrange his own assignment to America so he could rejoin his beloved Gerda Frankfurter.

In 1938, at the height of the Terror, he was recalled to Moscow. He was commanded to leave his work with the Cambridge group; that was turned over to a new control, the sinister assassin Alexander Orlov.[46] Everyone knew this recall meant the end, and Maly knew it best of all. He proceeded to Paris and there, en route to the slaughterhouse, he paused. His friends in apparatus warned him again. Returning to Moscow was suicide. Find some other way. The man of atonement demurred. Come, come. What were his chances of outwitting the assassination squads if he tried somehow to hide in Europe? Even America? Maly considered his choices.

There was also discredit. If he fled, Maly knew Yagoda's men would use his years in holy orders to create his final portrait as a traitor—and nobody would ever be able to untangle the lie. His agent's honor, his seriousness as a revolutionary, would be smeared beyond repair, forever. To save that honor, Maly wanted whoever in the future might know or care to know that he had died obedient to the Revolution.

Maly went to the Gare de l'Est and boarded the train.

In Moscow, he was assigned a desk job for a few dull months. He sat at the desk and shuffled papers. He read *Isvestia*. He stared out the window into Dzerzhinsky Square, out onto the colossal statue that had been erected there of his old friend and mentor—the same statue which in the great days of August 1991 would be torn down at last by the jubilant crowd. As I write, there is talk of erecting on that spot some appropriate monument, perhaps a huge cross, to serve as a sentinel to the millions dead.

Gazing out on Iron Felix's statue, the Father Theodore Maly that was sat waiting to join those dead. He did not wait long. One fine morning his desk was empty. He was never seen again.[47]

The original spy who knew too much. Walter Krivitsky explains the Nazi-Soviet Alliance a few months before his sudden demise. (*UPI/Bettmann*)

Karl Radek, cynicism's sage, just before his arrest. (*UPI/Bettman*)

Willi Münzenberg in Moscow (far left), about to be empowered, 1921. (*Photo ABZ: Berlin*)

Maxim Gorky and H. G. Wells with Moura Budberg, the spy they both loved. (*University of Illinois Libraries*)

The Princess Maria Pavlova Koudachova, Soviet agent, around the time she began to manage the life of Romain Pollard.

Willi and Babette. (*Literary Estate of Margarete Buber-Neuman*)

Gorky returns to Russia. (*UPI/Bettmann*)

Münzenberg in Berlin, after Lenin gave him his mission. (*Atlantic; Berlin*)

Otto Katz. The lieutenant—and one of the most complex secret agents of his era. (*National Archives*)

The death of Weimar: the Reichstag burns on February 27, 1933.

Marinus van der Lubbe in the dock.

Dimitrov, Popov, and Tanev confidently await trial.

Babette Gross with Arthur Koestler in 1955. (*Courtesy of Peter Gross*)

Josephine Herbst and John Herrmann en route to Russia. (*The Beinecke Library*)

André Gide and André Malraux prepare for their delusive "Mission to Berlin"—the occasion that led Malraux to suspect a conspiracy. (*Giselle Freud*)

Ella Winter, whom Gibarti called a prime Party agent on the West Coast, with Lincoln Steffens and Sinclair Lewis.

Above: Harold Ware — American Münzenberg man turned American spy.
Left: Dorothy Thompson in Red Square.
(*Dorothy Thompson Papers: Syracuse University Library*)

Liston Oak (second figure from left), propaganda agent in Madrid, with literati; Ernest Hemingway, oddly clean-shaven, stands beside Oak. (*Joan Worthington*)

Above: Hede Massing, Noel Field's guide into secret work and sometime wife of Gerhart Eisler, testifying in Washington after her break. (*UPI/Bettmann*)
Left: Alger and Priscilla Hiss at the time of his trial in New York. (*UPI/Bettmann*)

Chapter 7

Bloomsbury and Espionage

Theodore Maly and the Hungarian Mafia's great achievement in Europe and America was to find a wedge into power within the elite of the adversary culture, and especially of the modernism that was at its center. Of course this is a much wider matter than the meaning of treason. To a very remarkable degree, the elites of the twentieth-century democracies chose to define their taste and language through the language of revolution and the dissociation of sensibility. Picasso would hang on bankers' walls.

It is in this deeper sense—in the bond between the language of the democratic elites and the language of revolt—that espionage is tied to culture.

And it is in this sense—that the Cambridge spies might more accurately be known as the "Bloomsbury spies." Or perhaps one might more accurately speak of them as the spies who were Bloomsbury's children. One of Anthony Blunt's first lovers was Virginia Woolf's nephew, Julian Bell; it was Blunt and his people who guided Julian Bell toward Spain, where he was killed. Blunt likewise recruited Michael Straight in the midst of his grief over the death in Spain of John Cornford, who was likewise the son of two academic members of the coterie, Frances and Francis Cornford. Burgess and Blunt were raised in the atmosphere of Bloomsbury. Add to this Burgess's intimacy with Harold Nicolson. The Cambridge spies were in Bloomsbury's second generation, and must be counted among its heirs.

. . .

Our understanding of Bloomsbury has become so dominated by the presence and genius of Virginia Woolf that it is sometimes forgotten that the coterie was less her creation than that of her intimate (and one-time fiancé), Lytton Strachey. Strachey always saw himself as an "animateur," a man with a mission. He came to great clarity about that mission very early in his life. Seizing on the question of taste, Strachey proposed to redefine the ethic and nature of the British elite. While he was still an undergraduate at Cambridge, and later, in and around the First World War, Strachey set his essentially Oedipal task: To define a new era in British opinion by organizing the most shining offspring of the eminent Victorians into a group bent upon destroying the philistinism, hypocrisy, and repression which, he claimed, defined the loathed and loved world of their parents.

In practical fact, what Strachey summoned up in the Bloomsbury coterie became a kind of intellectual mafia created to allow the offspring of the British establishment to join the adversary culture without any sacrifice to their status in the hierarchy into which they had been born. The Bloomsberries correctly understood the modernist revolution to be the greatest cultural force of their time, and they also believed it was a challenge to everything their parents had thought important. Strachey showed his followers how to join that culture in such a way that their elite standing would be enhanced. This was not easy, but Strachey, greatest offspring of a British family notable in all its branches for molding and manipulating British opinion, accomplished it. His purpose plainly was to reinforce rather than undermine the aristocratic status into which the coterie's members had been born. Plebeian or non-U types, no matter how impressive, had no place in the network. The need to knock his parents off their pedestal was not exactly D. H. Lawrence's problem. Bloomsbury therefore treated Lawrence as a parvenu, and rejected the "underbred" James Joyce, until the genius of both had become so successful they could only make themselves ridiculous by denying it. Bloomsbury was an in-house operation of the British elite.[1]

Strachey himself was a rather nasty item. Julian Bell's brother Quentin Bell describes him as "a creature torturing and self-tortured, slipping from one agony to another, a wretched sighing hand-wringing misfit, a quite impossible person."[2] Though time has partly justified Strachey with Bloomsbury's many triumphs of taste and influence, one must note that apart from Virginia Woolf Bloomsbury produced almost no artists who can hold their own in the true first rank. Following Strachey's lead, the coterie remained far too preoccupied with questions of mere taste to touch real greatness. As for debunking the Victorians: One also can't help noting that a quintessential Victorian, George Eliot, wrote far more intelligently and with far more real feeling about sex than the modernist Virginia Woolf.

Still, Strachey's subversion of middlebrow mores needed doing. There was power, inevitability, and great beauty in the modernist experience. Only in retrospect do Strachey's disingenuousness and intellectual perversity seem to dominate his struggle to provide his allies with an ever-more-secure platform for despising the British middle class.

For the coterie's rationale Strachey borrowed a cult of "friendship" from the Cambridge philosopher George Moore, so that to this day E. M. Forster's silly pseudo-thought (it was borrowed from Moore: The business about having the guts to betray one's country before betraying one's friend) is almost invariably raised in any discussion of the Cambridge spies. And when your "friends" are collaborating in the deaths of hundreds of thousands of people who do not have the privilege of your acquaintance? What then?

Yet for all his talk about the sanctity of "friendship" in the Bloomsbury group, Strachey protested much too much. The reverse is more like it. As we know from the incredibly voluminous documentation of every shiver and sigh of every single member of the coterie, there was nothing so wonderfully amiable in Bloomsbury conduct. Even by the ungentle standards of most literary cliques, Bloomsbury was exceptionally malicious within its own ranks, and with outsiders cruel to the point of systematic sadism. All the talk about "friendship" concealed quite different interests.

Paul Johnson describes it well: "Not for nothing was Strachey the son of a general. He had a genius for narcissistic elitism and ran the coterie with an iron, though seemingly languid hand. From the Apostles he grasped the principles of group power: The ability not merely to exclude but to be seen to exclude. He perfected the art of unapproachability and rejection: A Bloomsbury mandarin could wither with a glance or a tone of voice. Within his magic circle exclusiveness became a kind of mutual life-support system. He and [Leonard] Woolf called it 'the Method.' "[3]

Friendship was not the true motive, any more than the long-term aim was a social club for bright undergraduates. Strachey's legacy was to show how elite standing could be encoded in anti-establishment contempt—always in the name of friendship, friendship. Nonsense, of course. First, last, and always, the real politics of Bloomsbury was a search for elite cultural power in England.

. . .

In the first generation, few members of the Bloomsbury coterie were fellow travellers and fewer still were true Stalinists. Leonard Woolf's soft-left writing on Imperial policy is more like it, even though the Woolfs' political mentors, Sidney and Beatrice Webb, became more or less abject Stalinist propagandists. But Strachey's legacy, which placed the new mandarins throughout British publishing, broadcasting, academia, and intellectual life was, to say the least, fertile ground.

Which is where Blunt came in.

On the public level, the move to Stalinize Bloomsbury taste was led by Otto Katz and the Münzenberg apparatus, using British fronts such as the Left Book Club and its many appendages. Covertly the process was led by Blunt and his gofer, Burgess, guided by Maly and by Ludwik's Recruit in the London offices of the Secret Intelligence Services (SIS), silently sustained by the talent-spotters throughout the universities and in the Münzenberg-Gibarti propaganda network, and tied to the Soviets through a dual NKVD-Comintern network running through Amsterdam, Berlin, and Paris. The process was in motion by at least 1927, when Ludwik set up shop in Amsterdam. Hitler had nothing to do with its founding. It was complete by 1935, and it culminated in Spain, where certain observers such as George Orwell began to dare to dissent.

Back at Strachey's Cambridge, the obvious heir to all this was Blunt. For the Cambridge spies were Bloomsbury's heirs by direct line of descent. The crucible for both was the "Cambridge Conversation Club," the Apostles, a long-established campus secret society for aristocratic young intellectuals: Tennyson and Hallam had been members. Strachey and Leonard Woolf had taken over the Apostles for their own political purposes before the war, and a generation later Blunt and Burgess remade it for theirs. It was Blunt who saw what rich possibilities were waiting to be used by the *apparat* in the Apostles.

A secret club of brilliant young men: The Apostles had been the ideal venue for Strachey's mingled fantasies of sex and power, played out among corrupted tousle-haired youth. By only slightly modifying Strachey's essential principles, Blunt transformed it into an equally ideal arena of *apparat* recruitment. It was elite, secret, and bound by its own loyalties.[4] Controlling it, Blunt and Burgess were able to capture the imaginations of Bloomsbury's children, while preparing them, as Strachey had prepared their parents, for lives of leadership nicely fused with scorn for the established order. Within Strachey's supercilious view of the British middle class was encoded an assumed right to rule that class. This was precisely the contempt which Blunt found so congruent to his own disdaining soul, and so *very* useful as a political instrument.

One link was Blunt's early love affair with Virginia Woolf's nephew, Julian Bell, who ten years later died in Spain. Julian wrote home to his mother in some detail about this adventure (his sexual initiation), the high point of which was Blunt spiriting Julian away to a culture conference in a French town called Poitigny, run for fellow travellers by a complex Soviet sympathizer close to the original Bloomsberries: Prince Dimitri Mirsky.[5] In fact, Prince Mirsky may well have been the inventor of the culture conference as an instrument of elite propaganda. Prince Mirsky died, mad, in the gulag.[6]

Anthony Blunt's affair with Julian Bell ended when Julian proceeded to a relationship with a woman, and then "a series of mistresses." But while it was going on, he wrote to his mother, "I feel certain you won't be upset or shocked. Still, don't let it go any further, or it might get round to Virginia, and then one might as well put a notice in the *Times*."[7]

Once exposed, Blunt did not defect to the USSR, and it is clear that unlike Philby he despised the mere thought of life in the Utopia he served. But then, what did Blunt not despise? Though his suits fitted perfectly and though he hated the socialist motherland, he was a hard-core Stalinist *apparatchik* quite without conscience toward either of his countries, his "ideals," or his friends. Least of all did he care for that abstraction, humanity. He despised "humanity." His snobbery was absolute. He was a manipulator of genius, with a talent for subtle intimidation and for measuring the vanity of his victims that makes the efforts of Guy Burgess seem amateurish fumblings. His chosen role was to be the most sublimely placed insider of all, the perfect Prufrock of the British establishment. "Deferential, glad to be of use/Politic, cautious, and meticulous," Blunt was invariably to be found just a step behind and a shade to the left of power, the associate and even intimate of principal figures throughout British life, from the royal establishment, to the Rothschilds, to the highest levels of the intelligence services. Most intellectuals are involved in what might be called powerless power. Blunt wanted more: He sought covered but real command, power he could exercise *without seeming to*. He was made for duplicity.

His relation to women—some women at least—seems to have been that of a needy penitent. As exposure drew near, he became genuinely, even childishly, terrified at the prospect of losing the good opinion of Queen Elizabeth, the Queen Mother. Once, quietly drunk in a taxi with Rosamund Lehmann, he suddenly burst into tears, and incomprehensibly began to beg her forgiveness—though to be sure this bizarre display may actually have been a charade used to test what Rosamund's lover, Goronwy Rees, as someone who knew about Blunt's ring, may have confided in their pillow talk.

Toward men, on the other hand, Blunt's attitude was one of hard, suppressed, controlling rage, and a silent but relentless search for the point of vulnerability. This he customarily found, not surprisingly, in the secrets of either ambition or sex, standing or shame. Better yet, both.

He was really a very high-class blackmailer. It all swung on a kind of sado-masochistic hinge, which is in some way reminiscent of Strachey's ethic of ambiguous contempt. Blunt invariably put himself in a position to despise those he served. He despised the sleek and fluting members of the establishment, whom he viewed as history's fools, doomed to be swept away. He likewise despised the Soviets who ran him, and whom he brushed aside even as he obeyed. Bumblers, clods, boors. In the void between servility and loathing Blunt found power.[8]

That so many of the Cambridge spies were homosexual can likewise be traced to Strachey and Bloomsbury. Strachey's cult of "friendship" was in practice a cult of homosexuality. Strachey genuinely believed that as a homosexual he belonged to an erotic elite that had passed beyond the crudity and grossness of heterosexual manhood into the realms of finer feeling. In a letter to Keynes, Strachey speaks of Cambridge, with its "sad atmosphere of paradox and paederasty" as the ideal place to launch his critique of English life, a critique that was simultaneously contemptuous, masochistic, enraged, and (seemingly) passive.[9] Yet, he went on, "we can't be content with telling the truth" even though "we must tell the whole truth and the whole truth is the Devil. . . . It's madness for us to dream of making dowagers understand that feelings are good, when we say in the same breath that the best ones are sodomitical . . . our time will come about a hundred years hence."[10]

Maly must have been especially shrewd on this score. Communist morality and Marxism-Leninism in general have been relentlessly hostile to any variety of homosexual freedom. Whenever the subject is raised, it has usually been inside a dank fog of talk about bourgeois decadence. My suspicion is that Anthony Blunt and Guy Burgess used their own great shrewdness to make their Soviet controls see how a homosexual coterie based on Strachey's model could be exploited, both in its unstated loyalties and its unstated possibilities for blackmail, and thereby form the basis for an espionage ring. I have no evidence to prove it, but some such conversation may well have taken place, and if so, it must have been an interesting one. In the files of the former Soviet Union, there exist shrewd, most farsighted assessments of the role played within the ring by homosexuality. They are explicit about the ways the half-seen sexual bond held Burgess and the stress in the unity of their alienation. Similar reports are no less insightful about the long reach into the elite that this sort of ''homintern'' bond provided. (Bear in mind too that certain members of the ring were not at all homosexual. Kim Philby was certainly not in the least homosexual, and the self-tortured Donald Maclean can be called homosexual only rather tendentiously.)

Certainly there was very little tolerance for homosexuals in Stalin's apparatus, though of course there were plenty of homosexuals in it. Young radicals of the early thirties clutched the fantasy that communism meant sexual freedom—and in the privileged West, in some sense it partly did. Certainly, radicalism and Bohemianism were intertwined, joined in that angry righteous perspective of the intellect that seeks compensation for feeling at once set apart, different and shunned.

But inside the *apparat,* communist puritanism and the almost incredible bigotry of Stalin's entourage meant that most homosexuals and bisexuals lived if anything with more furtiveness and self-contempt than their non-communist brothers and sisters. One thinks of Whittaker Chambers's agonies over his homosexual yearnings, or Louis Aragon, poet of sexual freedom, suppressing his desires while Elsa Triolet was alive, only to emerge as a flamboyant embarrassment to the Party once she was dead.

Naturally, none of this meant anything to homosexuals who had the misfortune actually to live in Utopia. At the very time that Amabel Williams-Ellis, Lytton Strachey's cousin once removed and sister of John Strachey, was singing the praises of the White Sea Canal, Stalin had dispatched three thousand homosexuals to the agonies of slave labor and early death in that project.[11] Visiting fellow travellers were often manipulated sexually. André Gide was surrounded by attractive sexual partners and seduced into compromising situations. These were used first to manipulate him, and later for the invective against him when he produced *Return to the U.S.S.R.*[12]

Yet Countess Karolyi records with what whoops of laughter the *apparat* heard of Gide's plan to plead for homosexual liberty during his ludicrous (and, for Gide's honor, mercifully never held) audience with Stalin.[13]

Münzenberg made the universities a center of his interest in order to touch the adversary culture in the place where it was shaped. In Cambridge, he and Gibarti were represented by the League Against Imperialism and by the two dons closest to it: Roy Pascal and Maurice Dobb. These two teachers had a profound effect on all the Cambridge conspirators.[14] But after 1932, Otto Katz also made England one of the bases of his power.

In fact, in the summer of 1933, Otto's English was strangely proficient as he set foot in London for what seems to have been the first time. I can find no evidence that Otto had ever lived before in any English-speaking country before then; yet from the moment he set foot in Dover, probably incognito, his English was at least workable and wisecracking. It was imperfect, to be sure; filled with all kinds of Teutonic errors, but fluent. Where did he pick it up? As a schoolboy in Prague? Perhaps some sort of training in Moscow? Wherever he learned it, Otto could say pretty much what he wanted to say in English. And he wanted to say a great deal.

He had arrived at a moment of special richness in the history of totalitarianism. Theodore Maly was by then well established in England. Maly had come to England well after Ludwik had placed his recruit in the upper track of British intelligence, back in 1927. Maly and Ludwik worked together, from London to Amsterdam. Maly remained in England through most of the thirties, operating now and then from an office next door to the one used by Gibarti's propagandists in London, an outfit known as the Anti-War International, which was in fact the British office of Amsterdam-Pleyel. The front man for the Anti-War International was a Münzenberg-man recruited from the Bloomsbury elect, Lytton's cousin once removed, John Strachey. As usual, propaganda and espionage were functioning hand in hand.

As his train pulled into London, Otto had many friends already waiting for him. Friends *and* the British secret service, for Otto was under the surveillance of SIS "watchers," probably from the moment of his arrival.[15] In later years Otto made it plain that he was fully aware of this surveillance from the moment it began. One wonders exactly who or what made him aware of it.

Katz's immediate task was to stage the show of the Reichstag Fire Counter-Trial, assisted by an unstoppable ball of English political fire, none other than Red Ellen Wilkinson. Ellen Wilkinson was a driving force in Labor's left wing; she had also been a hard-left collaborator with Willi and Louis in many a radical effort gone by. To some not quite discernible degree, this founding personality in the British Labor party must have been conscious of Otto's true role. Only a fool in her position would have failed to guess that Otto was a Soviet agent, and Ellen Wilkinson was nobody's fool. Or rather she was *almost* nobody's fool.

She had been, for a while, Stalin's fool, though she later became a staunch anti-Stalinist, and Otto fooled her sufficiently to use her anti-fascism as cover for the arrangement with Hitler. But then with that, he fooled the world. Ellen remained under Katz's spell through Munich. It has been suspected that he had an affair with her. Certainly they were close. He guided her through Spain. Even the summer of the pact, Ellen quite contentedly paid a visit to Otto on the Riviera.[16]

Another contact waiting for Otto in England was the lifelong Stalinist and propagandist, Claud Cockburn. Cockburn had first encountered Otto at least the year before at Amsterdam-Pleyel. In years to come, Cockburn and Otto would work together in many an adventure—in London, in Spain, and doubtless in America as well. Their link would peak in surreality during 1952, when Otto stood wavering in the dock in Prague, mouthing his "confession" and covering for some important secret service tracks. In his speech Otto told how he had betrayed the Revolution by serving Trotsky and Lord Beaverbrook in conspiracy with (among others) that ruthless agent of the Imperialists, Claud Cockburn.[17]

What was their real connection? By a curious coincidence, sometime between Amsterdam-Pleyel and the day Otto arrived in London for the Counter-Trial, Claud Cockburn had summoned up a London rumor sheet, an insider's political rag known as the *Week*. The idea behind the *Week* was to publish for the select few a weekly paper filled with the very best political gossip, all carefully but ingeniously arranged to serve the hard left and Stalinist position at any given moment. It was plain that the *Week* could and should not have a mass or even a large circulation. The gratifying sense of being in the select number of those truly on the inside does not flow from reports in *Time* and *Newsweek*. The *Week* has been called a "conspiracy theory bulletin." Its targets were precisely the insiders it was designed to reach: a splendid strategy. For a number of years, Franklin Roosevelt based many of his most important decisions on information about British and European politics he'd found in the *Week*. He never missed an issue.[18]

But where on earth did Cockburn pick up this stuff? There were plenty of lies in the paper, but much of its information was dead-on accurate, and often *very* much from the inside. From which desks were these sizzling tales lifted? Cockburn always shrugged off the question. He got his stuff from pals, he said; he had all kinds of pals. Nothing much more than the babble of the boys in the pubs of Fleet Street, where to be sure Cockburn was an inveterate habitué. That and certain . . . well, let's call them "correspondents" in Germany. Certain "friends" in Paris. You know. People. Here and there.[19]

Perhaps. But the *Week* was founded very shortly after Cockburn had a high-level meeting in Berlin with Willi and Otto. Its appearance in London political life coincides precisely with the period of Cockburn's most significant intimacy with Katz. Is it mere coincidence that Otto was a witting agent of both the Comintern and the NKVD, trained by Willi and Radek for precisely this kind of information and disinformation? Can that fact really have no relevance? More likely, some significant part of the rumors Cockburn spread in the *Week* originated with the *apparat* and were supplied by Claud's best guide through that wilderness of mirrors, Katz.

A suggestive ripple among the shadows that cover Otto's relation to the *Week* is a vague rumor of the time that there be a New York edition of the *Week* financed by Ralph Ingersoll. Ralph Ingersoll was an influential friend and colleague of Henry Luce, who in the 1930s became the lover of Otto's devoted political protégé, and dear friend, Lillian Hellman. Not only was Ingersoll besotted with Hellman, but under Hellman's guidance the political life of this senior executive in the Luce organization assumed a decidedly Stalinist cast. He soon became a sponsor and money-man of pro-Soviet publishing in New York. [20]

Ingersoll became publisher of the Stalinoid newspaper *P.M.*—a classic Münzenberg-style daily. Here too, Otto may well have had his unseen place. Ingersoll was guided through every step of this enterprise, practically every paragraph, by Lillian Hellman and Dashiell Hammett. Hammett regularly interviewed prospective editors in his room at the Plaza Hotel, and in the paper's first months, every word that appeared in *P.M.* had been approved in advance by Hammett or Hellman, either in New York or at Hellman's farm in Westchester County.[21]

P.M. was slated for large circulation, a close American cousin to the Parisian Stalinist daily *Ce Soir,* a paper for which Otto was certainly a covert control, run through Otto's protégé Paul Nizan, and fronted by yet another literary celebrity close to him, the Stalinist poet, novelist, and abject, Louis Aragon.[22]

Did Otto play some similar role at *P.M.*? Was *he* at the Westchester County farm too? It is perfectly possible, even probable, but must rest unproved. Certainly it is true that high-level agents of the apparatus, from Katz to Louis Dolivet, could be found hovering near *P.M.* throughout its existence.[23] Whatever the game, it would have been scrupulously clandestine.

And Claud Cockburn himself? It's frequently been suggested, by Peter

Wright among others, that Cockburn may well have been a colleague of Otto Katz in the secret service of the International.[24] By the time the Spanish Civil War rolled round, it is certain that Cockburn was quite consciously fabricating disinformation for Otto.[25]

Well, *was* Cockburn *Nash*: "ours?" Maybe and maybe not. Finally, the distinction does not strike me as presenting a very meaningful difference. Cockburn spent his adult life as the most visible and best-connected Stalinist journalist in England. He was the perfect incarnation of a certain glib tone of sneering condescension—the Cockburn tone was Bloomsbury vulgarized—fused with a wholeheartedly Stalinist soul and mind. Guy Burgess talked very much the way Cockburn wrote. In Claud Cockburn, Stalin was in full and public possession of his man.

In the fall of 1933, the Counter-Trial had made its headlines and served its purpose. Anti-fascism was becoming the central issue that the age demanded, and London was following Paris as its capital. But there was more to be done in England than to stage the Counter-Trial.

Among the means used to promote the Stalinist chic was the Left Book Club, in which Katz played a large role. It will be remembered that Münzenberg was one of the inventors of the book club in its modern form—and that a year and a half before he dispatched Otto to Moscow in 1929, Willi assigned his man to be administrator and agent-in-place at *Universum Bücherei,* his book club in Berlin. The Left Book Club was more or less a cookie-cutter version of *Universum Bücherei.*[26]

The front men, of course, were English: John Strachey, Harold Laski, and Victor Gollancz. Of this trio, Strachey was a witting agent; Victor Gollancz almost certainly so, and Laski a very sophisticated innocent.[27] With Sidney and Beatrice Webb, the intensely ambitious Strachey became the leading publicist for Stalinist intellectual chic of England and front man for the the Anti-War International.

Strachey's biographer says Strachey invariably consulted with Harry Pollitt and "the British communist party" before making his selections for the LBC.[28] No doubt, but Harry Pollitt was a notoriously rough diamond. He knew nothing about the rarified literary and intellectual politics in which the Left Book Club trafficked. The man who really understood these matters was Katz, and from its very first listing the Left Book Club's agenda was a direct reflection of the current concerns of Münzenberg's Paris office, which Katz ran: a book by Rudolf Olden—a longtime Münzenberg collaborator—and a British translation of Malraux's *Days of Contempt,* which had been written to order for Münzenberg with the steady "assistance" of two Otto Katz minions, Manès Sperber and Willi Bredel.[29] Besides this, under a number of pseudonyms ("O.K. Simon") Otto also wrote a number of the club's featured, though long-forgotten, selections.[30]

So Otto was at the least a tutelary spirit for the LBC, and probably more.

The name—Left *Book* Club—misleads a little: Like *Universum Bücherei,* it was much more than British communism's bookshop by mail. It was how Stalinist opinion was "networked" in England. The Club offered Münzenberg's familiar array of camps and conferences and propaganda tours of the USSR, and it organized the usual cadres for directing opinion in every area from the theater and art to sports. Whenever propaganda required, the rabbits of protest would leap from the clandestine cap. There were clubs to celebrate Soviet cinema, Soviet art, Soviet anything—joined to the usual untiring search for intellectual legitimacy. This craving for the prestige of cultural big names amounted to an institutional neurosis for the *apparat.*[31] Nor was the church forgotten: Gibarti was particularly proud of how effectively he dominated the political attitudes of the Right Reverend Hewlett Johnson, Dean of Canterbury Cathedral.[32] (Johnson was never the Archbishop of Canterbury, incidentally, though credulous Continentals often jumped to that conclusion, and Gibarti was delighted to have it so.) Johnson was a genuinely contemptible creature, mindless and cheerful in his Stalinism, a cleric who could be relied upon to rain blessings on any act of cruelty or tyranny that Louis Gibarti told him to bless, while denouncing as un-Christian any challenge or question put to the dictator's power, wherever it might appear.[33]

One bit of Ariadne's thread linking propaganda and espionage can be picked up in the youth of Rosamund Lehmann's brother, the publisher and poet John Lehmann.

In 1933 John Lehmann was a promising and glamourously well-connected young man of letters who had just stubbed his toe against the ego of Virginia Woolf. The result was a painful but brief hiatus in what would become one of the most distinguished careers in modern British publishing.

John Lehmann came straight down from Cambridge at the turn of the decade, and was introduced to his trade by taking on the slightly dangerous job of assisting Leonard and Virginia Woolf at the Hogarth Press, to which he had been sent for the interview by his great friend, the Woolfs' nephew and Anthony Blunt's lover, Julian Bell.[34]

Leonard and Virginia were delighted with Lehmann, and he got the job. He served his apprenticeship with such success that by 1932 or so a certain inevitable friction began to emerge. John Lehmann was much more than merely a bright young man. He soon showed a very genuine and specific aptitude for publishing. Leonard and Virginia were able to leave everything in his hands; for the first time in years, a holiday was possible—days, whole weeks of freedom. Lehmann was no mere gofer. Not only did he have taste and intellect of his own; he was beginning to put the stamp of a new generation on something that had always been absolutely and uniquely theirs.

Despite her quite unfeigned fondness for this golden boy, and she *was* very taken with him, Virginia especially disliked the new note. A fresh generation of anti-poetic realists was emerging, a generation for whom Virginia Woolf was an institution but not a model. The writers of the thirties were assuming their identity: John Lehmann was their man at Hogarth. Virginia watched it all through somewhat narrowed eyes. As the inevitable confrontation drew nearer, things grew rather tense at the Hogarth Press.

At this point, Lehmann decided that the better part of valor was to slip away from Tavistock Square for a while, and join his friends—friends he'd been bringing to Hogarth: Christopher Isherwood, Stephen Spender, W. H. Auden—in German-speaking Europe. *The* place to be. Yet though he does not say so in his beautiful memoir *The Whispering Gallery*—he makes only one passing remark about "the swirl of . . . underground . . . anti-war and anti-fascist activities"[35]—John Lehmann did not go to Vienna spontaneously. He was sent.

Who sent him? As things grew sticky at Hogarth, Lehmann had gone for advice to John Strachey. Strachey listened and understood perfectly. He quite agreed: the situation with the Woolfs was becoming strained. Why not take some time away, let things cool down. Visit the Continent. How about Vienna? After all, many of Lehmann's friends—Isherwood, Auden, all sorts of fascinating people—were heading there that summer. And Strachey knew just the way to make the trip worthwhile. Why not travel under the auspices of a splendid radical organization which Strachey ran; surely John had heard of it? The Anti-War International? The Anti-War International was more than merely idealistic. It was in the thick of the *real* anti-fascist fight. And Strachey could tell him, confidentially, that the real anti-fascist fight was about to be in Vienna. Vienna would be *the* place to be this summer. The young man's blood raced a little when Strachey suggested that Lehmann travel to Austria as a "secret correspondent."

. . .

And was Vienna the place where the "real" anti-fascist fight took place? Not precisely. Vienna is where the *illusion* of the anti-fascist fight would be played out. It was an illusion created to serve ends very different from the defeat of Adolf Hitler. In 1934, the apparatus selected Vienna as the scene of an important "anti-fascist" campaign mixed with covert action. Gibarti was almost certainly a principal actor in the propaganda effort, while the chief of "underground" action, working on espionage and subversion, was a decidedly murderous operative named Alexander Orlov, who after Vienna moved on to England, where he took over directing the Cambridge group, while after London he moved on to larger things in Spain.[36]

The aim of the Viennese anti-fascist campaign of 1934 was not, at any point, to oppose Adolf Hitler. On the contrary. Its function was to undermine the two leading parties of Austria. One of these was on the far right, the "clerico-fascists." The other, on the left, was a Marxist but non-Stalinist Social Democratic party. Both of these parties were detested by Stalin and Hitler alike. And the two dictators' shared motive in Austria was to use the "anti-fascist" campaign to provoke them both into mutual destruction.

In Vienna, the anti-Stalinist Marxists, socialist city-dwellers mainly, were led by Otto Bauer. The arch-conservative countryside of the "clerico-fascists" was led by the Austrian premier, Engelbert Dollfuss. Note well: "clerico-fascist" though he was, Dollfuss was every bit as roundly detested by Hitler as the Marxist Bauer was hated by Stalin. That is the crucial point. Both dictators wanted both parties destroyed. Neither Dollfuss nor Bauer had ever done his act of submission to his respective totalitarian leader, and the aim of the campaign in Austria was simultaneously to serve both the Nazis and the Soviets by destroying them both.[37] They only seemed to take sides with their apparent ideological allies. A year later Dollfuss would be assassinated not by communists but by the Nazis. Stalinist "help" tore Bauer's non-Stalinist party to shreds. A campaign that would destabilize Bauer and Dollfuss was therefore a welcome event in Hitler's eyes, and Stalin's secret service eagerly took on the job. In 1934, Dollfuss had set out to tear down the very real achievements of Bauer's Social Democratic government. At this moment, Stalin saw the opportunity to wreck the hated Social Democrats under the guise of help.

Gibarti and Orlov set out to create a high-visibility "anti-fascist" campaign, mingling propaganda and covert action, sabotaging and discrediting Bauer's non-Stalinists under the appearance of "aid" while generating one of the dominant and most destructive political clichés of the 1930s. This was the notion that the social democratic left, and the democracies in general, were too weak, too ambivalent, too much of a divided mind really to fight Hitler. For that, decent people would have to turn to the hard left, and to Stalin. But they would be brought to this change by an "anti-fascist" campaign that in reality posed no challenge at all to Hitler and was in fact perfectly welcome in his eyes.

This lie about the feebleness of democracy, and the campaign that promoted it, were a great success. By the time the effort was over, the combined brutalities of the *apparat* and the Austrian clerico-fascists left Austria's entire non-Stalinist left dispersed, converted to Stalinism, or in jail. Many of Bauer's naive young supporters ran for their lives to their "friends" in Russia: The Soviets gave them a parade, then sent them to the gulag.[38] Simultaneously, and to the Nazis' delight, Dollfuss was destabilized and discredited as well, and by the end of the year the Nazis had assassinated him. He was replaced by a bewildered, weak, utterly intimidated government of the anti-Nazi right, cowering in an effective squeeze between the two dictators. And when Hitler at last moved into Austria in the Anschluss of 1938, Stalin's protests were strictly perfunctory.[39]

All this had required a lot of smoke and mirrors. Bookstore windows groaned with titles on Viennese outrages; the press was drenched in Austria's agony. Naomi Mitchison was dispatched to Vienna by Victor Gollancz, with a "generous" advance to write what became her *Vienna Diary*. Mitchison, an inveterate fellow traveller, was greatly flattered by being made a courier. "I was carrying papers," she proudly wrote, "from socialist friends to their British comrades in my thick woolen knickers."[40] From Stephen Spender and W. H. Auden to Hugh Gaitskell, the fellow travellers were made to converge *en masse*. Strachey was right. Vienna was *the* place to be.

Meanwhile, John Lehmann took up his job as a "secret correspondent," typing up innocent but fervid "anti-fascist" articles. Presently he was approached by a "swarthy" comrade, casually introduced, who insisted upon getting together privately with Lehmann. And what did he want to talk about? Politics. Serious politics.

The chat at this sort of recruitment rendezvous was notable for being at once very probing and distinctly evasive. At last the stranger had a suggestion. Up until now Lehmann had merely been writing articles—wisely suggested by the International—and placing them in various publications back home. Wonderful, brave work. But there was other work to do for anti-fascism. Even more important, more serious work. Special work.

Like?

Well, it dealt with . . . "other political information."

Other information?

Precisely what "other information" remained unclear, but the swarthy visitor was persistent, "refusing to take 'no' for an answer."[41]

"My 'recruiting sergeant' was very pressing, but extremely vague about what he exactly wanted me to do."

Lehmann became uneasy. "I smelt a rat . . . that is, I decided he would finally reveal that he wanted me to become a Soviet agent." At this point, still deep in his "secret correspondent's" innocence and a little scared, Lehmann turned for advice to John Strachey. What passed between Strachey and Lehmann is not recorded. Lehmann releases only the information that their talk "convinced me I was treading on too dangerous ground." After his conversation with Strachey, "the mysterious gentleman" who had been so very persistent "vanished from my life."

Lehmann ends his mini-confession with a sigh: "Of course I see now that I was peculiarly vulnerable, and perhaps lucky to swim past the lobster-pot as easily as I did."[42]

This heir to Bloomsbury has been standing at the precise point of intersection between propaganda and espionage. Münzenberg's Anti-War International *was* the propaganda branch of the Soviet espionage apparatus. Lehmann had been sent to Vienna as a recruitment test, and in his squeamishness and probably partly false naiveté, he had failed that test. It was an examination that others passed, and passed brilliantly. One successful candidate, for example, was Kim Philby.

But the mingling of propaganda and espionage among the Bloomsbury spies is best illustrated in the relation between Blunt and Burgess. Once exposed, Blunt held a "press conference" over smoked trout in the board room of the London *Times,* during which he claimed to have been led and run for the *apparat* by Guy Burgess. It is true that Burgess seems to have recruited Blunt. And what a very discriminating choice it was. Yet they all worked together, with Philby playing a decisive role and Blunt coolly guiding and tempering Burgess's inveterate enthusiasms and excesses.

Though the entire circle was under the control of the NKVD, it makes some sense to call Burgess the "Münzenberg-man" in the group. His career—his work in broadcasting, his "circle"—form a classic British reflection of the Münzenberg style. Burgess knew the Münzenberg legals very well, and was often in Paris, showing off in front of Goronwy Rees by invoking the kind of cultural pull only the Paris office could arrange: dinner with Theodore Dreiser, for example, when the apparatus trotted out the author of *An American Tragedy* for yet another culture conference. I've heard it claimed that Burgess was actually presented to Willi. This is perfectly plausible, though I have seen no proof of it, and Babette Gross could not remember.

In effect a "Münzenberg-man," Guy surely knew Otto reasonably well; yet he was also an agent of espionage under control. In the early days, Maly ordered him to pose as a convert to British fascism, working and sleeping with a fascist fellow traveller and Member of Parliament named Captain Jack Macnamara, an obvious assignment in covert work, as was Burgess's war-time work in SOE. That Burgess could be that, *and* simultaneously be so much the Münzenberg-man indicates precisely the interpenetration of propaganda and espionage services which is so often denied. Burgess moved in the worlds of *both* Maly and Gibarti, and simultaneously.[43]

Poor Burgess seems to have been guided at the deepest level by the cruel muse of failure. He is one of the great and instructive human wrecks. Such people are often enough found in secret services. The life of achievement in art and the intellect is not a very forgiving one. What begins as brilliant youth can very easily sink into some awful region between the second and third ranks, the anonymous place where so often even the best of the quite good sinks and drifts forever. In 1931, it was generally assumed that Guy would become one of the great academics of his era. Given how Burgess ended—bleary, sentimental, slobbering—it is difficult to grasp how many serious people thought Guy Burgess the youth one of the most brilliant, compelling, promising human beings they had ever met.

In preparing this book, I have met many agents of influence who worked for various governments within the Münzenberg tradition. More than one has left me with a troubling, nameless afterimage, the sense of some shadow hovering over our talk. I'm tempted to call that lingering shade the ghost of Guy Burgess. Repeatedly, it comes cropping up again: the same glib charm. The same startling but too-glancing erudition and intellectual range. The same enthralling capacity for gossip; the same breezy knowing of everybody and everything. Often, the same elegance—though often a failed elegance, grown a tad seedy, a little dirty, or sloppy, or out of date, or somehow off. Often the same sexual gamesmanship—

whether heterosexual or homosexual is incidental. Often, a similar river of alcohol flowing nearby. These men (the ones I've met have all been men) who began life dazzling everyone with their promise. Like Guy, they set out with the very grandest connections in the world of politics, the intellect, and the arts. And then—

We might call it the Burgess curse. The same desolation, often accompanied by alcoholism. The same deepening obscurity covered by one lurching move from one doubtful option to another, and the same shabbiness of promises worn down, then worn thin, and at last worn out. They strike one as men whose double lives were born in a fatal disjunction between their great expectations and their true secret selves. For them, failure began virtually at the moment of early success, back when splashy debuts look like achievement. Their failure would be failure felt before it was seen as promise and loss mingled in bafflement.

For many such people, work in the secret world can be wonderfully restorative. It places them in the realm of power; it locates them, albeit secretly, in a network of larger importance, a role like the one which hope once offered. Once again, their hand is on the pulse. Secretly, they can feel it, there again. Except that by that time, the work of ruin is very nearly complete. Those whom the gods have wrecked with promise, they next make spies.

But if Guy Burgess was failure's tragic creature, Blunt was spiritually tied, and absolutely so, to success. He could not, would not, did not fail: ever. His driving demon was not the muse of failure but the wish to be connected to the network of power. Success defined Blunt's life as surely as failure defined Guy's. It may well be that the secret of his prolonged shadowy love for Burgess can be located in this odd coupling of shabby ruin with the impeccably achieved.

In a BBC dramatization of the defection made in the 1980s, the screenwriter has Burgess warn Blunt that he is going to run to Russia with Maclean by mailing Blunt a note containing nothing more than some numbers. The numbers are page references to some lines of poetry, a stanza from Robert Browning, a ballad entitled "Waring," about a once-exciting youth turned failure, who finds he can no longer endure being what he has become. As the poem begins, Waring has decided at last to leave London without so much as a goodbye. He is running, and he will run to . . . Russia.

In the film, Blunt gets the note, opens it, and sees the reference. Browning? "Waring?" Perplexed, he takes down his copy of the poems, leafs through the book until he finds the place, then reads, *sotto voce:*

What's become of Waring
Since he gave us all the slip,
Chose land-travel or seafaring,
Boats and chest or staff and scrip,
Rather than pace up and down
Any longer London town?

In a moment, Blunt takes it in. It comes as the shock of recognition, and we see him absorbing it. Guy? "Giving us all the slip?" *Guy is defecting too.* Then, enraged—at once betrayed, bereft, and very much endangered—Blunt flings the book across the room. I've not seen any evidence that this incident really occurred, but it is a brilliant, genuinely moving screenwriter's touch, and *ben trovato.*

At the height of his adventures in London, Guy Burgess lived in two successive flats there. The first, from the thirties, consisted in the top floor of a place in Chester Square. The second, where he lived during the war, was a large, pleasant place leased through Victor Rothschild on Bentinck Street. The two places seem likely to linger in the iconography of espionage as two *maisons de rendez-vous.* Both have been vividly described several times, notably by Goronwy Rees and Malcolm Muggeridge. In Bentinck Street especially, the muse of history seems to have decided to play one of her periodic pranks: Outside number 9 Bentinck Street is affixed a blue-and-white plaque indicating that here once lived Edward Gibbon, author of *The Decline and Fall of the Roman Empire.*

In Chester Square, Burgess held court, usually in bed like a squalid Louis Quatorze, receiving visitors in rooms filled with the "indescribable debris and confusion from the party that had taken place the night before."[44] Beside the bed were piles of books—Burgess seems to have read and re-read *Middlemarch* almost continually through his adult life—and many liquor bottles, variously knocked back. Also near at hand was a frying pan brimming with the nauseating slop of a kind of homemade stew which Burgess concocted each week-end as a somewhat less liquid fortification for all the alcohol, and in order not to waste any tiresome time at a stove. "An evening at Guy's flat," writes Goronwy Rees, "was rather like watching a French farce which has been injected with all the elements of political drama. Bedroom doors opened and shut; strange faces appeared and disappeared down the stairs where they passed some new visitor on his way up; civil servants, politicians, visitors to London, friends and colleagues of Guy's popped in and out of bed and then continued some absorbing discussion of political intrigue. . . ."[45]

The Bentinck Street flat was Guy Burgess's home during the war. As the Allies' capital, London was the capital where all the conspirators came to roost. Many roosted, at least now and then, at Bentinck Street. It was a delightful place, very much a step up, even luxurious; testimony to Blunt and Guy Burgess's increasing influence over their good friend Lord Victor Rothschild, who had sublet it to Burgess for a song.

If one could capture who, and what, passed through Bentinck Street during those years it would be possible to reconstruct some grotesque but remarkably full secret history of the Second World War. It would be political Proust belated by a quarter century, the cataclysm of the age as viewed by Jupien. Bentinck Street became a kind of salon, in which Burgess gathered the homosexual underworld of London together with some of the most devious and despicable political operatives then at work. I'm thinking for example of the Baron Wolfgang von und zu Putlitz, along with a distasteful creature from the upper anonymity of French politics named Edouard Pfeiffer. All this was crowned by the Bloomsbury elite.

Malcolm Muggeridge describes a visit there even more memorably than does Rees. Muggeridge was a middle-class boy. In this passage one can hear his own bitter, anomalous protest against Bloomsbury and its snobbery:

> There we found another gathering of displaced intellectuals, but more prosperous, more socially secure than the *Horizon* ones—John Strachey, J. D. Bernal, Anthony Blunt, Guy Burgess, a whole revolutionary *Who's Who*. It was the only time I ever met Burgess, and he gave me the feeling, such as I have never had from anyone else, of being morally afflicted in some way. His very physical presence was, to me, malodorous and sinister; as though he had some consuming illness—like the galloping consumption. . . . The impression fitted in well enough with his subsequent adventures; as did this millionaire's nest altogether, so well set up, providing, among other amenities, special rubber bones to bite on if the stress of the Blitz became too much to bear. Sheltering so distinguished a company—Cabinet Minister-to-be [John Strachey], honored Guru of the extreme left-to-be [J. D. Bernal], Connoisseur Extraordinary-to-be [Blunt], and other notabilities, all in a sense grouped around Burgess; Etonian mudlark and sick toast of a sick society.[46]

One of the Bloomsbury grandees well known to Burgess was Harold Nicolson. Nicolson met Guy Burgess in the early thirties, and Nicolson's biographer cites Burgess as one of the young men who held some grip on the feelings of Nicolson all through this period. Whether they were lovers is unclear and doubtful, but they obviously became close friends. It is clear that Burgess used his friendship with Nicolson as part of his rise. It was through Nicolson's influence that Burgess joined the staff of the BBC in 1936; in fact, much of Burgess's rise through the British establishment took place under Nicolson's sponsorship. Nicolson shared none of Guy's political values; the bond was not political in the large sense, but in the more narrow Bloomsbury sense, and it was bound to the old code of Bloomsbury assumptions.[47]

Burgess was guided into broadcasting, obviously, by his "friends" in the *apparat,* but only after a year or two posing as fascist fellow traveller, working in the office and bed of Captain Jack. Simultaneously Burgess took a job directing public relations for a Nazi fellow-travelling front, the Anglo-German Fellowship, a group Philby was likewise ordered to join. Both men were active members for two years, spouting the line. That this fact alone did not automatically disqualify them for any place whatever in war-time British intelligence has never been explained. Indeed it is overlooked in almost all the discussions of their rise, yet short of a brass band, it is difficult to know how a gross risk to British security could have been more blatant. Membership in the Fellowship forthrightly proclaimed Nazi association. No matter. Both men were shoehorned into the most sensitive areas of the British services by their untiring admirer within the services, a major figure in the history of British intelligence, Guy Liddell.

Guy Liddell is one of the enduringly mysterious figures in the history of secret service intrigue. He was from the mid-1920s until he left the service in the mid-1950s probably the most important single figure in either the British or American services to address himself primarily to the question of covert Soviet activity in England and outside Russia. Virtually everything known by the American State Department about the *apparat* prior to the founding of the OSS had its origins in memoranda forwarded from London and Liddell. He was one of the most beloved and entirely trusted figures in the British services. For years, the slightest hint of compromise attributed to Liddell's name awakened the flashing ire of committed emeritus members of the service: the late Sir Dick White, for example.

Yet it is also true that virtually every significant advance in the British secret services made by members of the Cambridge group was made under the patronage of Liddell. His assisting hand can be found in every significant move they made. Liddell has repeatedly been proposed as a possible mole within the services: this charge has repeatedly been turned aside. The most significant such accusation comes from Burgess and Blunt's college friend Goronwy Rees, who was himself recruited into the apparatus around this time and broke with it at some uncertain date:

possibly the Nazi-Soviet Pact. Rees considered Blunt's entire career both before and after exposure to have moved under Liddell's collaborating protection.

The question of Liddell will only be answered in the archives, and I predict his mystery will prove even more persistent than that of the Hiss case. While we wait for the necessary research to be undertaken and completed, the case against Liddell must rest as eloquently made and then doubted again by Mr. John Costello.[48] I have little to add, except to say that I regard the circumstantial evidence against Liddell and in favor of Rees's accusations to be so massive and so compromising that, once it is known, it becomes almost impossible to return to viewing Liddell in the simple light of simple innocence. More investigation is needed. But as one shrewd observer put it to me: ''If Guy Liddell was *not* a Soviet agent, he was just wasting his time.''

On the very long list of compromising truths known about Liddell is that he was a regular habitué of Burgess's salon on Bentinck Street. Bentinck Street was a place that a shrewd child could spot as packed to the walls with security risks. How a senior official in British counter-intelligence would have chosen it of all places to let his hair down beggars inquiry. Liddell was also directly responsible for placing both Kim Philby and Guy Burgess into their first jobs in the British intelligence services. This took place shortly after both men had left membership in and service to a well-known Nazi front, many of whose members were by war-time directly chargeable with treason. To be sure, by 1936 Philby and Burgess had dropped their fascist pose. What of it? The gross security risk remained, staring out. Either Liddell didn't know about their old commitment. In which case he was failing in his job. Or he knew they had been posing. In which case he knew they had been Soviet agents. Or he knew the truth and thought it didn't matter. In which case he was an idiot and an incompetent. And nobody thinks Liddell was that.

Harold Nicolson, on the other hand, was a major broadcaster,[49] a power in the BBC: during the war he became the BBC's political head, with full access to Churchill, as well as parliamentary secretary to the Ministry of Information, which ran the secret services. And of course he was a legendary personage in the Bloomsbury group, husband of Virginia Woolf's lover Vita Sackville-West, and a very notable diarist, diplomat, and arbiter of taste.

Nicolson's numerous published diary entries on Burgess are anything but complete or candid. After 1952, Nicolson plainly did his best to cover this ill-favored and credulous union with the spy. The full story in its emotional and political dimensions has never been seriously explored, though an exceptionally meticulous historian of broadcasting, Mr. W. J. West, has studied its consequences for the BBC.[50]

Under Nicolson's patronage, Burgess advanced spectacularly through the Bloomsbury networks; he was soon the most influential political producer in the entire BBC, where he introduced Soviet propagandists and fellow travellers wholesale. These naturally included Anthony Blunt, whose many appearances at the BBC were most useful in his rise. For Blunt's kind of ambition, the scholarly reputation needed the added luster of a little popular chic.

Meanwhile, Burgess exploited his role at the BBC with subtlety and dexterity.[51] But there was more to it than that. As Nicolson's biographer laconically notes, "there can be little doubt that Guy Burgess extracted from Harold inside information which he passed on to his masters in Moscow."[52]

When Guy Burgess defected, Nicolson as usual wrote in his diary, and what he wrote is revealing. The entry is filled with anguish. "If I thought Guy a brave man, I should have thought he had gone over to join the communists. As I know him to be a coward"—one wonders how Nicolson knows this, exactly—"I suppose that he was suspect of passing things to the Bolshies and realizing his guilt, did a bunk."

There is something a little repellent in this notation. Anguish—yes: But one also is struck by the schoolboy tone; by the weak-minded, evasive thought about "courage" made in a remark that reveals ignorance of both Burgess's actual courage and his actual communism; by the unidiomatic use of the word "realizing" and finally by the kid's talk about "passing things to the Bolshies," and "doing a bunk." Here was an "Apostle," the very incarnation of Lytton Strachey's ideal, who had spent a friendship with one of the foremost of the Bloomsbury group lying to him in every meeting and using him at every opportunity not for mere crude personal gain—heaven forbid!—but in the service of tyranny. Nicolson had been jerked around and kissed up to and deceived not to make a few pounds or pull off admission to some club. Burgess had stooped to all this in order to betray his country and to serve the enslavement of nations. Speaking of it, Nicolson forgets that he was something more than a friend with Guy Burgess. He was a minister in Winston Churchill's cabinet, a man upon whom the fate of whole peoples, strangers to him, to some measurable degree depended. He seems incapable of addressing any of this. He cannot face a scrap of it; he would not even really face it in the years to come. In his correspondence to Moscow, Nicolson continued to treat Burgess as if he were merely an exceptionally errant friend with whom he happened to disagree. He never could see that this "friend" had used him, his position, his confidence, that unmentionable thing called his political power *and* his political trust to betray his friend *and* his country, along with a number of other countries—most wretched of all—into the bargain. It was all E. M. Forster in reverse, but with a relentless vengeance. Rather than acknowledge such a thing, Nicolson's voice reverts to childish babble. "Did a bunk?" He speaks as if Burgess were a ten-year-old classmate caught cheating at some game, albeit a game on the playing fields of Eton. It makes a nightmarish final twist in Lytton Strachey's malicious, power-driven, angry cult of "friendship."

Yet it would be very wrong to end on a note of mere condemnation of this used and deluded man. Nicolson's diary entry ends on a note of great personal pain. He *is* in agony; he *is* ashamed. "During my dreams," Nicolson concludes, "his absurd face stares at me with drunken unseeing eyes."[53]

Some rough beast, born in Bloomsbury, had slouched all the way home.

Chapter 8

In America

Although the work of the apparatus in the cultural and political life of America assumed rather different forms from those it took in England, there are parallels between its interventions in the two countries. As we've seen, development of the elite spies based in Cambridge and Washington was co-ordinated at the top by many of the same people. Maly sent Hede Massing to recruit Field in Foggy Bottom while he himself stayed in London, occupied with the ring around Burgess and Blunt. The operation had transatlantic reach. While the United States may have had no precise equivalent to the Left Book Club, the quiet interventions of the apparatus reached from its mass culture to the upper regions of its high seriousness, from Broadway, to the modernist Bohemia, to the networked fellow travellers of Hollywood.

In America, we can find the *apparat* monitoring the marriage of Sinclair Lewis, while nurturing the myths of manhood and Bohemia spun by Ernest Hemingway. It influenced the glamour culture of Hollywood, while it ran networks of influence in Washington and reached into the Spanish Civil War. To trace every aspect of this phenomenon would be tedious stuff. Networks can baffle description—which was, of course, precisely the idea. It seems more instructive to follow just a few strands through the fabric of the American century.

We might begin with Sinclair Lewis in Austria. The strand taken up there will lead us through many different artists, and many different spies, before it ends in Washington on a sweltering summer night.

In the years just after Lenin gave Münzenberg his mandate, Sinclair Lewis was the most famous *serious* American writer alive. His international standing in the mid-twenties is hard to overstate. *Main Street* had appeared in 1920; *Babbitt* in 1922; *Arrowsmith* in 1925. His satiric portrait of American philistinism triumphant, so very angry and so very persuasive, had made him seem everywhere *the* truth-teller about our large flat land. By 1926 that enormous world-wide reputation was just waiting for Willi, and a carefully orchestrated effort was mounted to entice Sinclair Lewis into the fellow-travelling network. Its focus became his marriage.

The story begins in Vienna in 1926, where Dorothy Thompson, a compelling young preacher's daughter from upstate New York, was installed as the most rapidly rising star in American international journalism. There was something quite irresistible about Dorothy Thompson in 1926.[1] She was a very nervy young woman, brisk with a certain old-fashioned girl-reporter eagerness, lots of pizzazz, and a drive to get to the bottom of every story, an urgent insistence upon *really* understanding events. But that simple drive was also transposed into a more impressive key. For one thing, Dorothy Thompson was quite exceptionally intelligent. She wrote with an innately worldly sense of style, far beyond the common run of journalism, and was blessed with a not-easily-distracted talent for keeping her focus on reality. Preacher's daughter that she was, she seemed a born analyst of power, politics, and events.

On the night of Dorothy Thompson's thirty-third birthday, July 9, 1927, a number of influential friends arranged a festive dinner featuring some of the most interesting political society in Vienna. One important guest was Münzenberg's favorite aristocrat, Count Karolyi, and the evening was to be capped by the presence of that tremendous celebrity, Mr. Sinclair Lewis.[2]

The occasion turned out to be only a so-so success. Sinclair Lewis did not especially shine that night, but neither did he turn drunk and abusive, as was often the case. In the grand company he seemed pre-occupied, ruminating; he was even charming, though in a rather subdued way. At one point he took pen and paper to sketch a crude floor plan for his dream house, an as-yet undiscovered farmhouse on some as-yet unseen hill in Vermont. The sketch was passed around. People sighed, smiled. It was handed to Dorothy. She took it in. After dinner, Lewis maneuvered Dorothy into a quiet corner. In that moment alone, he leaned toward her and very quietly asked her to marry him.

Dorothy Thompson broke out laughing. "Why Mr. Lewis, I barely know you!"

Then she leaned back and gazed for a short silent time into the face of her future.

Dorothy Thompson and Sinclair Lewis came from roughly the same place in their culture and their era; if one looked only at their public profiles, their marriage was a brilliant and irresistible natural fit. He was, she wrote, "of my own blood, and in many ways of my own nature." Dorothy felt for Lewis that mixed admiration which journalists often feel for imaginative artists, and in her case that admiration helped carry her to love. She was a woman who could not be awed by counsellors and kings, but she was a little in awe of Lewis: she did at first feel a partly frightened reverence for his tortured inwardness and somber power. She found him "stimulating to weariness," and the preacher's daughter added: "He is a very curious and demonic person, hard-drinking, blasphemous, possessed, I often think, of a devil."[3] Lewis meanwhile loved Thompson's manifest openness and her competence: he felt his depression lift a little in the presence of this wonderfully worldly country girl. He loved her energy; loved her mind; loved her love. It was not enough. Lewis was also an intractable alcoholic, and he was a man who felt a wide and tragic margin of loathing for anything or anyone he had the misfortune to love.

Their liaison was the grand testing passion of both their lives. It was commanding and cruel. Its unhappiness was its heartbeat. It was abandoned only after years rendered numb and hopeless by Lewis's addiction. It was a tragic union, but in the eyes of Willi Münzenberg, the romance between these two shining lights was an incomparable opportunity for influence over American opinion.

Münzenberg gave it top priority. Even before their marriage, in the first days of the romance, Willi personally travelled to Vienna—unprecedented!—to consult with his people and arrange a discreet meeting with the happy pair. Not that they grasped whom they'd met, of course.[4]

A propaganda tour of the USSR was promptly laid out for the lovers, a high-profile honeymoon before the fact. At exactly the same time, a winning and rather talented young American journalist named Vincent Sheean somehow materialized in their lives. Sheean was a fellow traveller very much mixed up in the Münzenberg operation. He was certainly an instrument of its manipulations of Lewis and Thompson, though the precise state of his innocence then or later is hard to gauge.[5] In any case both partners soon grew very fond of Vincent, and Vincent became an eager acolyte both to their love and to their trip. He ended as a lifelong friend, and after they both had died, he said goodbye with a rather good book about the marriage: *Dorothy and Red.*

Sheean may have been more or less an innocent. Not so his girlfriend, who was a witting Münzenberg agent, and in deep. Her name was Rayna Prohme, and Rayna serves as another example of the symbiotic link between the propaganda apparatus and the espionage system. She was a hot communist from Chicago, a real fire-eater, the recently divorced wife of the playwright Samson Raphaelson, the author of *The Jazz Singer,* and a man who would later play his own considerable role among the Hollywood fellow travellers.[6]

Rayna had worked for Willi and Gibarti as a propaganda agent in both Europe and China, sometimes with the love-struck Vincent at her side. What did Vincent know about Rayna's "special work"? That is not clear, but he certainly knew a fair amount. In 1927, at the same time that Vincent was shepherding Dorothy and Red through the USSR, Rayna was called "home" to Moscow in preparation for a very big new secret service assignment. And Vincent Sheean was painfully aware that the true reason Rayna was in Moscow was not her love for him. She was there to leave him.

Rayna was about to enter the Comintern's school for covert action, there to be trained as a deep-cover penetration agent, a mole who would be dispatched back in the States. Rayna's step into the next circle of secrecy threw Vincent into despair. She was about to be supplied with a cover *life*. She would be assigned possibly a new name, a new existence. Who she was, what she said she believed, whom she said she loved—all these would be assigned: Plausible lies. Where was intimacy, where was love, in the life of a deep-cover agent? How is one husband to a woman whose life is a lie?[7]

It is plain that Rayna was in the process of rejecting Vincent and his love. She was rejecting him and choosing her secret work in espionage. She did not live to complete her task. While Dorothy Thompson and Vincent were together in Moscow, Rayna was suddenly struck down by a cerebral hemorrhage and died after a few days of agony. Dorothy nursed the young woman through her passage to death; Vincent was at her side. The young man's despair became grief.

The *apparat* buried Rayna in Moscow with Dorothy Thompson walking beside Vincent in the little funeral procession. The hearse crawled through streets piled with snow while Vincent and Dorothy slowly walked behind. Walking with them was none other than Soong Chin'ling, or

Madame Sun Yat-Sen, widow of the Chinese revolutionary. Madame Sun Yat-Sen was a Münzenberg and Comintern operative, one of their most important in the Far East.[8] She worked under full apparatus control, and she had served as the prime patron behind Rayna's rise in the Soviet services.[9] Behind the freezing little cortege of walkers, Madame's vast limousine crept along, attentive and ready in its post-imperial grandeur.

Did Dorothy Thompson grasp how completely her visit to Russia was being run by the Soviet services and encircled by its operatives? Did she plumb the real nature of Rayna Prohme's career; did she have any accurate sense of Vincent's role? Sheean reports that he told Dorothy the whole truth about Rayna as the girl lay dying in Moscow. I very much doubt the reliability of this claim. Dorothy wrote a long letter to Lewis at the time, describing Rayna's death and alluding to her talk with Vincent. The letter gets the real story quite wrong—so wrong that my guess is that Vincent's confession was deliberately misleading.[10]

There were a number of other ways in which the Moscow trip of 1927 did not go well. Dorothy Thompson only nibbled at the bait. The next year she produced a brisk, direct, remarkably well-written book called *The New Russia.* Though written in sympathetic tones, *The New Russia* quite relentlessly identifies the leading deficiencies of the Soviet system, not least of which she defines as a society riddled with a paranoid domestic spy system and the ubiquitous OGPU.[11] Just as Willi had foreseen, Thompson did indeed become the most important American anti-fascist journalist of her generation, but she also became a strong, well-informed anti-communist at a maddeningly early date.

The apparatus had only a little more success in its courtship of Lewis. He continued to be guided by Sheean, and Sheean remained a committed fellow traveller. In the summer of 1939, for example, he joined Clifford Odets and Dashiell Hammett as leading signers of an open letter slinging invective at Walter Krivitsky for his revelations about Stalin's secret services. The ad ran in papers from coast to coast, signed by some four hundred other star culturati culled from the fellow-travelling networks and the Hollywood Stalinists. A principal point was to deride Krivitsky's claims about Nazi-Soviet collaboration.

Bad timing is bad luck. The very same day, in the very same papers, the Nazi-Soviet Pact was announced.

But even guided by Sheean, Lewis never really became a reliable Stalinist after the manner of, let's say, Dashiell Hammett. Lewis dallied as a mere fellow traveller of the fellow travellers—though I fear it was petulance and drink, far more than honor or insight, that spared Sinclair Lewis the disgrace of Romain Rolland.

Lewis balked in his sullen way from the start. At the last minute before the 1927 tour, Lewis announced, typically, that he didn't feel like going. Who the hell needed Russia anyway? He'd come later, when he damn well felt like coming. Dorothy was disappointed, but just as typically she plunged ahead, curious and probing.

In Moscow, Münzenberg had laid on his best—even Theodore Dreiser was summoned from America to provide the visit with the desired literary charisma. Lewis joined the party three weeks late. A lavish great-man reception greeted him. The author of *Main Street* moved through Russia swimming in flattery, banquets, worshipful crowds, and promises of huge editions. Thompson's many letters to him before he arrived are wonderful, not only as records of life on the receiving end of this kind of propaganda operation, but also as love letters. Their tenderness feels fresh as this morning.[12]

Thirteen years later the age of innocence was over. The Nazi-Soviet Pact had knocked away many a mask. Dorothy and Red's marriage was all but dead. Deep in the winter of 1940, at the height of that alliance, Otto Katz arrived in New York in preparation for clandestine work in America. Five days later, Dorothy Thompson picked up the phone, telephoned the FBI, and asked to speak to an agent in charge of espionage. She then provided the Bureau with several of Otto's aliases, told them that she had met him on several occasions, that she knew him to be an agent of the NKVD, and noted especially that he had very close secret links with the Nazis and the German government. Three days after that, the Visa Division of the State Department prepared a memo as close to the detailed truth about Otto as any official American document I have found.[13]

Its final paragraph is particularly impressive. ''According to the information given by an unnamed but reliable source, this person was once known in California as Breda. He has been at various times an international spy, agent of the Soviet government, member of the Gapayu, acted as a go-between for General von Bredow, also was in the Reichswehr Intelligence Service and worked at one time for the French Government *as well as for the Nazi Government. He is said to know the inside story of the Brown House*'' (my emphasis).[14] An unnamed but reliable source? The memo was written three days after Dorothy's tip to the FBI. My guess is that either she was the unnamed source, or that Dorothy directed investigators to that source. In either case, somebody was on to something very big.

Where on earth did Dorothy Thompson pick up this astonishing and uncannily accurate information? I cannot say. Wherever she learned her secrets, they were top drawer, and they went straight to the White House, where the warning was viewed as an irritant and ignored. Though she was at this moment the foremost anti-fascist journalist in English, Dorothy Thompson was far from liked in the Roosevelt administration. A. A. Berle, the assistant to Roosevelt who dealt with the matter, ended his analysis of the material before him with an annoyed brush-off.[15]

As a result, the heat on Otto was very mild, and he was free to spend the next eleven months in New York. It was during this visit that his close friends Lillian Hellman and Dashiell Hammett were central to creating the Stalinoid daily paper *P.M.*, an English-language clone of the Parisian daily *Ce Soir,* a journal for which Otto is known to have been the unseen guiding hand.[16] Otto's remaining time in New York was untroubled, though he and Ilschen went through an odd little dust-up with the Immigration department in early June 1940, right around the time France was invaded, and a few weeks before Münzenberg was assassinated while in flight.[17] Later information, mainly coming from the British, asserts that Otto was very much a party to Münzenberg's murder.[18] Otto himself told Klement Gottwald that he had, in his own delicate phrase, "aided in the struggle against [Münzenberg]."[19] Does that mean he helped organize the murder from that transatlantic distance? In the preceding months, Otto had been close to the British agent who in June would advise Willi on the fatal journey that ended in his assassination.[20] Nevertheless, Otto Katz's exact role in the death of Willi Münzenberg remains mysterious.

A final detail. When Dorothy Thompson made her call to the FBI, Otto gave as a reference an old and close friend. The memos refer to her as "Mrs. John Hermann [*sic*]."[21]

Mrs. John Herrmann was better known as Josephine Herbst. Through Josephine Herbst, we take up another strand in the network of culture and espionage. It is the strand that leads through the life of Ernest Hemingway.

It is an instructive exercise in cultural history to make a list of all the people in or near Ernest Hemingway's circle in Paris during the 1920s who later ended either in or very near the Soviet secret services. The roster turns out to be impressively long. There was Dos Passos himself, along with Donald Ogden Stewart, and their great pal, John Howard Lawson. But there were also many more. One of most interesting of Hemingway's chums from those days of *The Sun Also Rises,* was a half-talented but hard-drinking midwesterner, a would-be writer endowed with much more hope than future, named John Herrmann. And at John Herrmann's side was his more gifted girlfriend and later wife, Josephine Herbst.

Sinclair Lewis may have been famous, but to the people around Ernest Hemingway, he was a famous middlebrow. Lewis never became a member in good standing of the modernist Bohemian elite, the rising twenties' generation of John Dos Passos and Ernest Hemingway. They too had come to Willi's attention; they too were on Willi's list. But the story of their links to the Soviet services makes a more complex tale than the sad story of Dorothy and Red.

The story starts among the ambulance drivers in the First World War. During the two years before Woodrow Wilson brought the United States into the war, gung-ho young Americans hungry for real life were obliged, because of American neutrality, to settle for being mere non-combatants in what seemed to them *the* great event of their lives. The European battlefield was the only place that mattered. Yet for young Americans, the only path to the battlefield turned out to be something like driving an ambulance. And so it was that a generation of young men, including young writers, drove ambulances: John Dos Passos, Hemingway, E. E. Cummings, and John Howard Lawson all became ambulance drivers, tooling and lurching across the torn fields of France in their Model A or Citroën vans, just so they could *be* there.

The war meant real life, of course, but it also meant Europe—and of course the relation to Europe is an indicating trait in the cultural personality of any American. The war offered these young Americans *their* Europe, and their Europe was not the Europe of Henry James, not the Europe James thought had been rendered conscious and beautiful by history, but a Europe of catastrophe and Bohemia, a Europe of war, of revolution, of freedom, of breaking loose. It was a Europe they would use to reprimand and replace that civilized order to which James, as the great expatriate, had consecrated his life.

They made up the generation born around 1895, and they went "over there" looking for adventure, for authenticity, for release from provincialism. They left Europe seeing themselves as cynicism's truth-tellers, the bearers of disillusion's mission, the guys who would salvage *real* life, *real* feeling from all the lies—the bourgeois lies—that had been discredited in the trenches.

The ambulance drivers emerged, almost every last one of them, from the ample American middle and upper-middle class, with its etiquette books, its mahogany banisters, its Persian carpets, its potted palms and urns of polished brass; its libraries with uniform editions of Tennyson and Henry Wadsworth Longfellow and . . . Henry James. Goodbye to all that. The new culture of the twentieth century would use a Bohemian refusal to make a new life.

The ambulance drivers did not create that new modernist life. They discovered it, mainly through other, older Americans already in Europe. The modernist coteries were then composed of a minute Europeanizing vanguard, led especially by Americans from the generation just previous to their own: Ezra Pound, T. S. Eliot, and Gertrude Stein. The generation of 1895 was a latecomers' generation, and it arrived in uniform. Once the war was over, they set out to acquire the coterie taste of a new Bohemianism. They did so remembering the trenches, but sitting at the feet of the arbiters of the new taste, glancing in wonder through flickering light at the Picassos and Matisses that hung from floor to ceiling on Gertrude Stein's walls on the rue de Flerus. Once they got the feel of that modern thing, the likes of Dos Passos and Hemingway were able to popularize the new strain as their predecessors had never been able or willing to do. The ambulance drivers turned "the modern" into the voice of a new generation. They endowed the modernism which had been, before the war, a closed estheticism, with a new and much broader political meaning. They teased the cults of Stein and Pound out of the salons, and they made modernism famous.

That modern achievement of the early twenties is now so withered, so stale, so past even academicism that it is difficult to recall that it too was once fresh as the morning. It is difficult to recall that the *style* of Ernest Hemingway, now so often and so monotonously denounced, and yet still so monotonously imitated, once swept through the mind of a generation like a revelation, proclaiming a new and better way to live, a new and better way to feel, a new and better way to tell the truth. It broke on American ears as an *ethical* voice; it had ethical power, strong with the sound of the new authenticity. From it Hemingway summoned up the myth of a new Bohemian heroism, and through it he made himself the most famous writer in English of this century. Much the same was true of Dos Passos, though of course on a different scale. In *Manhattan Transfer* the nasal music of American talk is captured with a dry sharp exactitude. And it sounds very different from that "civilization" to which Henry James gave voice.

Though they came to Europe at the same time, Hemingway and Dos Passos did not actually meet until 1924. By that time the apparatus was aware of them both, and it was engaged in an effort, metaphorically speaking, to take possession of all that was represented by the *symbolism* of these two men's lives. Between John Dos Passos and Ernest Hemingway, that effort would come to a conspiratorial climax during the Spanish Civil War.

They met in Paris, and at first the two young lions hit it off just wonderfully. They were two ambulance drivers; they were brothers, sons of the same world; they understood each other at once. Pals. They drank to it. Another pal was Donald Ogden Stewart, who in 1924 was still a classic twenties' "sophisticate," Cole Porter all the way, master of the high life, toastmaster general. Donald Ogden Stewart really was quite a good friend of Cole Porter, along with the "socialites" Gerald and Sara Murphy, and Dos Passos used to join Stewart and Hemingway for glorious springtimes at the Murphys' villa on the Riviera. Meanwhile Picasso was dropping by to visit every afternoon. It was vanguard heaven, and Dos Passos would regularly write home all about it to his other pal, John Howard Lawson.[22]

John Herrmann and Josephine Herbst were likewise part of this circle. They were not in heaven, however. As the glamour faded and time wore them down, Herrmann became a spy, and Herbst an agent of influence.[23] In the late twenties, Donald Ogden Stewart, who later became a leading Hollywood Stalinist, had not yet met Ella Winter, who in turn would become one of the most trusted agents in the American propaganda apparatus, and Lincoln Steffens's wife. But Hemingway had met her. A 1926 note from Hemingway to Ezra Pound mentions meeting Ella Winter. It is typically nasty. "You heard of course of Steffens' marriage to a 19 year old Bloomsbury kike intellectual. Last chapter in the book of revolution."[24]

Everybody was getting acquainted.

By 1927, the Sacco-Vanzetti case was making the propaganda operation in New York a vehicle for world-wide attention. But Sacco-Vanzetti was designed for the masses as well as the elite. Certain other efforts were targeted strictly on elite culture. Not surprisingly they reflected the taste of the agents who had helped them into being, and so they favored the Berlin avant-garde. One example was the vanguard of the New York theater, especially a small organization known as the New Playwrights' Theater.[25]

New Playwrights' Theater was a modernist enterprise organized by John Howard Lawson, and its star author was Lawson's fellow ambulance-driver John Dos Passos. Dos Passos was at first enchanted by the offer of working in the theater; he suffered from the novelist's classically unsatisfied itch for the stage. Besides, the little theater in the Village was to be "radical": That is, it would have the "expressionist" look of Americanized Piscator. And of course its politics would be the politics of the Revolution.

Lawson, Dos Passos, and the others at New Playwrights' Theater were unobtrusively supervised throughout the enterprise by the Mutt and Jeff of the American Communist party, two contriving legmen for the *apparat* named V. J. Jerome and Alexander Trachtenberg.[26] Both of these men were *apparatchiki* who took their cues from whichever of Münzenberg's Hungarian mafiosi happened then to be resident in New York. My guess is that at this moment the Comintern representative in New York was Gyula Alpari or Bela Szantil. Certain British intelligence reports explicitly name Gibarti as well. Hungarian mafiosi, all of them.

In any case, the true purpose of the New Playwrights' Theater appears to have been to help Stalinize the New York vanguard while assisting its founders, above all John Howard Lawson and Lawson's political sidekick, Frances Faragoh, make their move to Hollywood. New Playwrights' staged two "expressionist" plays by Dos Passos: *The Moon Is a Gong,* and *Airways, Inc.* The plays had a certain elite critical success, and that success was just enough to launch Lawson and Faragoh, in 1928 and 1929, in the film industry. There they had arrived. There they would embark upon their *real* life's work, which was neither drama nor film, but organizing Stalinist opinion in the American entertainment industry.[27]

And so this odd little theater in Greenwich Village played its little role as a stepping stone. And it left behind a little mystery.

A fourth partner at New Playwrights' Theater had been a curious fellow with the no less curious name of Em Jo Basshe. Em Jo Basshe is a cipher in the history of theater, but he is of great interest to us, because through his fate we can read the intensity of international secret service interest focussed on the small avant-garde cultural scene in which he lived and moved.

Documents in the National Archives of the United States disclose a very peculiar tale about Em Jo.[28] In 1931, two years after Lawson and Faragoh had gone on to Hollywood, British intelligence informed the Americans that during the time of the New Playwrights' Theater and after it, Em Jo Basshe had been a trained and fully witting Comintern agent in place. The information from the British suggests that Em Jo worked in America under the cover of a false identity. A great deal is made of his close association with Willi Münzenberg and Gibarti. The memos assert that Basshe had worked in New York with Gibarti, and that in 1931, he had gone to Europe, there to meet with Gibarti and Münzenberg, to be given his reward and be promoted to a new secret service assignment by them. The British memos explicitly link Basshe to the Berlin apparatus, as well as to Münzenberg and Gibarti personally. They report on Em Jo's movements, conversations, and plans. All the right names are used. The entire account is exceptionally plausible.

But is it true? When I first came across these documents in Washington, the adrenalin surged. Here it was at last—*the* link between the *apparat* and the early Hollywood networks. I seemed to have stumbled by chance onto a forgotten but once smoking gun. Its burnt powder, though half a century old, was still visible on the chamber. Em Jo Basshe: *the* witting agent in the New York theater! Em Jo Basshe. Once said aloud, the name is hard to forget. So this invisible man was Moscow's eye! And not an obvious Stalinist like John Howard Lawson, as everyone supposed.

It was an exciting find. It sent me on a new wave of research. And this research uncovered . . . nothing but difficulties.[29]

I was unable to find anything anywhere else that supported the claims of the British dossier in any way. In fact, everything else *seemed* to contradict them, and contradict them in an oddly suspicious fashion.

The Em Jo Basshe I unearthed elsewhere gave every appearance of having been a classic emigrant. These accounts show an Em Jo brought to America at the unconspiratorial age of 12, part of the vast wave of Eastern European Jewry coming to America from Vilna and the Pale just before the 1914 war. The British information contradicts this story by asserting that Em Jo "gives himself out as the son of David Jochelman," an important hard-left Polish Zionist, who lived and worked in London, a protégé of none other than Maxim Litvinov, Stalin's commissar of foreign affairs, and also serving as an "Official Advisor" to the Bolshevik mission run in London by Leonid Krassin. As Jochelman's son, Em Jo would therefore have been raised in London. His position under the protection of Willi and the Comintern would be traceable to his very elevated Bolshevik connections. He would have come to America not as a child but as an adult, and possibly illegally. In any case the British presented him to State as a ranking agent of a foreign power: "definite information has been received by our friends here" [N.B. "our friends" is a standard euphemism for undercover informants] "that the Central Committee of the Workers' International Relief has recently created an International Cultural Department under the leadership of Em Jo Basshe."[30] Under the leadership of Em Jo Basshe! Nothing less.

Well . . . perhaps. Admittedly, I've found no traces of Em Jo's childhood in New York—though certainly everyone *took* him for an American. A British background is mentioned nowhere. The shadow I find passing through the record is that of a stage-struck emigrant kid beginning his career as an eager but unimpressive hanger-on at Eugene O'Neill's Provincetown Playhouse, both on Cape Cod and later in the Village, where he began to work as a stagehand at the age of 19. Em Jo wanted to be a playwright. He wrote several hard-left expressionist plays, mainly about the oppression of blacks. The critics, I gather, were bored; Alexander Woolcott described one of Em Jo's works as a "tragedy in fourteen intermissions."[31] But at least the plays had politics *à la mode,* and that got Em Jo into New Playwrights'. Not that he was a leading force at New Playwrights'. In fact it seems he was mainly used and pushed around.

Add to this John Dos Passos's version of the story. Dos Passos knew Em Jo well, and left the most complete portrait I know in *Most Likely to Succeed,* a poorly conceived but generally accurate autobiographical novel about these events, written well after Dos Passos had become a committed anti-communist.[32] Dos Passos depicts Basshe as the least hard-line of the entire group around John Howard Lawson, an earnest, half-talented *schmoozer,* a hanger-out with the Yiddish theater at the Café Royale, and in the end a wipe-out as an artist and as a man, a pitiable ruin.

Very much to our point, Dos Passos asserts (novelistically, of course) that when New Playwrights' disbanded, Em Jo argued and broke with his friends Faragoh and Lawson—broke over the Stalinism of their politics. For this reason, when Faragoh and Lawson graduated to Hollywood, Dos Passos shows Em Jo left behind, iced out of the bonanza that had always been Lawson and Faragoh's actual goal. Bereft of Party support, Em Jo turned into a classic and none-too-beautiful loser, slugging back yet another glass of ever-cheaper booze, muttering about how he'd been done in by his old pals, those bastard Stalinists getting rich and famous in Tinseltown.

Now, could the man described by Dos Passos *also* be the fully trained, monitored, and highly placed secret agent described by the British? Conceivably. Mere drunkenness, failure, and an *apparent* break with Stalinism do not necessarily prove otherwise. Guy Burgess was also a drunk and a failure, and he too claimed (now and then) to have turned his back on Stalin. Perhaps Em Jo was the Guy Burgess of the Stage Delicatessen. And yet . . .

The total lack of corroborating evidence is troubling. It is all the more troubling when one reflects that the man who supplied this information to the Americans was almost certainly Guy Liddell.[33]

Repeat: *The man who supplied this information to the Department of State was almost certainly Guy Liddell.*

Here may be a key. Why would somebody who may well have been Ludwik's recruit ostentatiously and quite gratuitously pass on to the Americans the claim that this third-rate playwright was a Soviet agent?

Here is a hypothesis. Suppose Em Jo was not a Yiddish Burgess at all. Suppose that he was not an agent and never was. Suppose Dos Passos's account of Em Jo's fate is more or less accurate. Suppose above all that the wretched man's break with Stalinism was the real thing.

In that case, by 1930 the fourth partner of New Playwrights' would have become potentially a very dangerous man. He might have posed a real threat to Lawson and Faragoh's important new work in Hollywood. Everyone agrees that Em Jo had a loose mouth. Certainly he was in a position to say many compromising things about his old friends. And in his anger he may even have dared actually to threaten them with some such thing. Em Jo would need to be discredited. And maybe scared a little.

How? Well, since we are supposing, suppose Ludwik's Recruit in London were to supply the Americans with sterling, thoroughly credible information naming Em Jo Basshe as a Soviet agent *and* possibly a deportable alien. *That* ought to make the Americans treat Em Jo's boozy stories with the contempt they deserved. Let the threat of deportation make Em Jo watch his mouth. Meanwhile a planted story would distract attention from Faragoh and Lawson, just exactly as it distracted mine a half century later.

This is only a hypothesis, I admit. But it is a hypothesis with the merit of fitting all the known facts.

In any case, whether he was a spy or a simple failure, poor Em Jo Basshe died an early death, seedy, bypassed, and alone. He did not live to see the war.

Meanwhile, Lawson and Faragoh had gone on to Hollywood, and it is to Hollywood that the next strand leads. Another leads to Moscow. The New Playwrights' Theater, a founding model for the Group Theater, closed in 1928. Lawson and Faragoh went to the Coast while Dos Passos proceeded to the USSR on a classic Münzenberg guided tour. All stops were pulled out in the Soviet Union. Dos Passos was put up as a house guest with Stalin's new culture minister, Fadaev. He soon was close with Fadaev's wife, Valia Gerasimova, "a ranking official of the GPU."[34] Dos Passos travelled through the countryside guided by the ubiquitous Stalinist hack

Anna Louise Strong; he met, flattered, and was flattered by Meyerhold and Eisenstein. He was treated like a great man.[35]

Like most fellow travellers, Dos Passos was vain about what he saw as his own skepticism, his independence. He insisted that his was an open mind. He knew these Russkis were laying it on thick. He could see through these guys; he knew this was all just part of their propaganda. And yet, and yet—why *were* the Russians so interested? He wasn't famous, not *really* famous, not like (say) Sinclair Lewis. He didn't have a lot of influence or a big audience. Why roll out this red carpet unless they were really sincere? They really admired him. They must.

Dos Passos is not widely read today. For this reader, the lure of his work, its enduring freshness, is found in its tone, its hard Whitmanian edge, something in its language that is genuinely cutting, convincing, true. Dos Passos heard America not singing but *talking,* and he heard it with more precision and point than Hemingway ever did.

But the visit to Russia revealed a grave weakness in Dos Passos's personality both as an artist and as a man. In his correspondence from Russia, it is a failing that becomes almost painfully obvious, and typically, it too is manifest in his tone. You can hear it. In Russia, the bad-boy sound in Dos Passos's voice vanishes. He ceases to be the jeering wiseguy, cynicism's upstart sage. He reverts to the rather polite upper-middle-class Harvard man he really was, a good boy who, though unlikely to use the wrong fork, was worried about saying the wrong thing, and above all wanted to be fair, fair about this wonderful humanitarian experiment of the Soviets, fair about socialism in Russia. In Russia Dos Passos reverted to his fundamental, and fundamentally uninteresting, middle-class niceness.

At their best, Dos Passos's letters to Lawson, Hemingway, and Cummings make wonderful reading; biting into them, one hears the tart crack of a perfect McIntosh apple from a depression apple stand. Not at their best, they are depressing and juvenile. The tone can become insufferable, a kind of provincial behind-the-barn snottiness. Hemingway's letters are often just as nasty and callow, but Hemingway often managed to invest his infamous sadism with his even more famous elegance. Hemingway's inveterate maliciousness was alien to Dos Passos, who really *was* a good boy, someone who really *did* want to be fair and just, in a way that Hemingway did not.

Leaving Russia, Dos Passos was escorted to the train by the theater director assigned to guide him around, followed by her whole company, who gathered on the platform to bid the great American writer farewell.

Waiting for the departure whistle, the director at last put the crucial question: "They like you very much," she said, nodding to her actors. "But they want to ask you one question. They want you to show your face. They want to know where you stand politically. Are you with us?"[36]

Dos Passos reported feeling "his head constrict and throb. . . . He took another drag on his cigarette, pushed his hat back and rocked forward slightly on the balls of his feet." When he tried to answer all he could produce was an inconclusive stammer, ending with something about how the answer would take too long, there was not time even to begin. At last the train pulled away, prying him free from his admirers.

The next morning, when his train crossed the Polish border, Dos Passos wrote Hemingway that "it was like being let out of jail."[37] Well, in a way he had been let out of jail. It was partly the jail of the regime, and partly the jail of Dos Passos's conflict over the regime: The captivity of the writer's shallow cynicism at war with his no less shallow politeness. Crossing the border liberated him, let him revert to his immaturity. The bad boy could swagger back into center stage, sneering to his pal, Ernie: "Jesus, all you have to do to realize how swell things are in Russia is to take a look at Warsaw—the differences in people's faces, the way they walk talk eat cross the street. Warsaw's a horrible dump anyway."

The only thing wrong with Russia, he reported to Hemingway, is that while you can "get the jack out of the publisher you can't take it out of the country and had to drink it up in vodka and salt herring." Besides, the sunless weather stank. "No wonder they all want to go to America. There may be something in all this talk about God's country after all."[38]

Back in God's country, Lawson and Faragoh were setting up in Hollywood, preparing to develop the networks of fellow travellers that would later, during the era of the Hollywood Ten, become the objects of worldwide controversy.[39]

The naive sometimes ask why the apparatus took such elaborate pains to set up the Stalinist networks in Hollywood. If propaganda was the purpose, surely it failed: Metro-Goldwyn-Mayer was manifestly not producing Soviet propaganda in 1938. This is to miss the point. Of course Willi and Otto did not think they could call the shots at Warner Brothers. On the contrary, they would never have *permitted* their Hollywood people to give away the game by seeking influence in such a stupidly obvious way. Half a century later, sitting with me over tea in Munich, Babette Gross's voice went tight repeating the litany. You do *not* endorse Stalin. You do *not* call yourself a communist. You do *not* declare your love for the regime. You do *not* call on people to support the Soviets. Ever. Under any circumstances.

You claim to be an independent-minded idealist. You don't really understand politics, but you think the little guy is getting a lousy break. You believe in open-mindedness. You are shocked, frightened by what is going on right here in our own country. You are frightened by the racism, by the oppression of the working man. You think the Russians are trying a great human experiment, and you hope it works. You believe in peace. You yearn for international understanding. You hate fascism. You think the capitalist system is corrupt.

You say it over and over and over again. And you say nothing, *nothing* more. "*Ja, Ja.*" She ended wearily. "You say all of that."

The actual mandate in Hollywood was twofold, and it was not directed at the masses but the elite. The aim was never to make Stalinist movies. It was to Stalinize the American glamour culture, while simultaneously giving the apparatus a cash cow capable of producing a large, untraceable supply of much-needed American hard currency to finance various operations around the world. It was also a refuge for favored cultural *apparatchiki* like Bertolt Brecht and Hanns Eisler. To serve these ends, the idea was to help define the Hollywood elite with the right kind of Stalinist chic. Make the Popular Front a central part of the glamour culture. Let the movies be the movies. Let them be rich and glamourous and fun. Of course don't let them seriously challenge Stalin's regime, but that was secondary. Let Hollywood launch its stars, fill its screens with glamour. Let it keep its corruption. Let it stay innocent. That was the paying strategy.

Of course communists in the glamour society were assigned various political missions, or more exactly pseudo-missions, such as founding the Screen Writers Guild. But these efforts were largely pretextual and propagandistic. The masters of the concentration camp at Kolyma, the perpetrators of the Ukrainian Terror Famine did not greatly care how many thousands of dollars a week a set of pampered and self-righteous purveyors of kitsch made on Writers' Row. Their real interest was to divert as many of those dollars as possible into the *apparat*'s covert finances.

The work in Hollywood was essential to the Popular Front and a logical extension of Willi's familiar operations with the literary elite. Forget Peoria. A Stalinized glamour culture must know all the best people, visit all the most interesting places, live in all the most perfect places, wear the most flawless clothes. It must seem to have unlimited money. It must drop names, and drop the very best names, and drop them as if in a carpet-bombing. As Donald Ogden Stewart's friend Cole Porter would have put it, it must all positively reek of class. Does it need intellectual respectability? Fine: Bert Brecht and the Berlin emigration will supply it. The look must wed ideology to high-stepping style; it must be careless, as Tom and Daisy Buchanan were careless, with the look of almost unlimited ease. It must be radiant with allure of effortless success, a matter of sloping lawns and perfect martinis and the best, most delightful company ever.

Be elite. Lay it on. Just so long as the elite burns with injustice and gives its money to combat it.

Which injustice? Why, follow the leader.

''Columbus discovered America,'' Otto Katz used to say. ''But I discovered Hollywood.'' The development of the Hollywood networks was directed at first from Münzenberg's Berlin and Paris offices. In New York, Gibarti's men V. J. Jerome and Alexander Trachtenberg had been present at the creation of Lawson and Faragoh's film careers and worked closely with them on the Coast as well.[40] Otto visited Hollywood for what may or may not have been the first time in March 1935, under an incognito. His mission was to consolidate and redirect the fellow-travelling networks established by the circle around Lawson and Faragoh, retooling them in anticipation of the Popular Front. His alias was ''Rudolph Breda,''[41] and he adopted the pose of an anti-fascist fighter who'd escaped to tell the tale of risking his life against the Gestapo. (In fact, I have found no evidence that Otto himself was in Germany at any time between 1933 and 1939.) Otto had correctly assumed that Hollywood would be a sucker for an aristocrat. Therefore the freedom fighter ''Herr Breda'' arrived with an aristocrat in tow: One Prince Hubertus zu und von Lowenstein. And that really was his name.

Together Otto and the Prince moved Hollywood to tears, and to use its own language, captured its heart. Of course a number of people in town understood quite well that ''Herr Breda'' was a fraud, and not only Faragoh and Lawson. There were also numerous German refugees such as Salka Viertel who had known the real Otto perfectly well back in Berlin. They kept quiet. ''Herr Breda'' was lying, but his was a noble and anti-fascist lie. Wasn't it?[42]

Under Otto's direction, a new front organization known as the Hollywood Anti-Nazi League was created.[43] This became the prime facade for Popular Front activity in the film colony. To kick it off, Hollywood at its most glittering gathered to hear Herr Breda's terrible tale. It offered Otto his great moment as the actor Piscator had never let him be. After first assembling a very grand dinner party for the Hollywood elite in honor of "Breda," a vast fund-raising testimonial dinner was planned, a white-tie, $100-a-plate benefit for German refugees. The guests included the Archbishop of Los Angeles. The master of ceremonies was Donald Ogden Stewart. Stewart describes "Breda" at these social occasions as "irresistibly intelligent and sincere [*sic*]," adding with a typical flick of his antic self-deprecation, "the champagne was very good, too."[44]

Herr Breda began the big testimonial dinner by genuflecting before the Archbishop of Los Angeles and kissing the Fisherman's Ring, politics' homage to the Spirit. Then he rose to speak.

He spoke about the horror going on in Germany. He recounted his (fictitious) struggles against the Gestapo—that same Gestapo with which Otto was in fact almost surely in co-operative contact. He told about the real struggles of his friends, his comrades, against Nazism. He wrapped some terrible truths in some terrible lies.

"It was one of the happiest evenings of my life," Stewart wrote. "Herr Breda gave his moving description of the Nazi Terror, the details of which he had been able to collect only by repeatedly risking his own life. I was proud to be sitting beside him, proud to be on his side in the fight. . . . Here was a man who had devoted his life untiringly and at great risk of death by torture to the principles I in my dress suit was just beginning to fight for."[45]

When Herr Breda sat down, Stewart, moved and touched by that edge of self-contempt that never left him, stepped forward ("I in my dress suit") and in a choked voice first asked, and then answered, the question in everyone's mind: "What can *I* do?"

Do? Out came the checkbooks. Hollywood was going to found, and fund, its Anti-Nazi League.

And beside Otto was the Prince. The Prince Hubertus von und zu Lowenstein was an interesting and slippery character. Otto and the Prince originally had the task of consolidating the *apparat*'s already well-developed networks and giving them their proper new direction as decreed by the Popular Front. This effort would play its large role in American life and political attitudes for the next forty years.

For many years the Prince continued to act as Katz's man in the celebrity culture of both Hollywood and New York, enticing not only the stars, but leading lights among the German exiles as well. Like the Count and Countess Karolyi, like Wolfgang von und zu Putlitz, and the Princess Koudachova, Lowenstein was one of Stalin's aristocrats. He was a skilled and mendacious political "activist" who it seems right to suppose was very much under Katz's influence and control. The grandeur of the

Prince's title and the sublimity of his sentiments made a tremendous impression in Hollywood, though in later years something about him, perhaps his arrogance and indolence, seems to have palled. Still, at first he played well in the film colony. One might imagine that the senior non-communists among the German exiles would not have been so easily taken in as were Irving Thalberg and Norma Shearer, but not so: Even Thomas Mann succumbed.

They succumbed for a rather long time. When the pact and the war came at last, the "anti-fascist" pose of Katz and the Prince was not abandoned, but it became more overtly delicate. A new line had to be invented, one that would protect their old "anti-fascist" credentials while simultaneously protecting the new alliance, and with it, of course, protecting Hitler. To be sure, service to Nazi interests had to be given rather deviously. One means was to divert attention to the democracies as the prime bad guys, along with a quick return to the rhetoric of "Peace." These decadent democracies—there had never been any real difference between them and the fascists. They were all a pack of "warmongers." It didn't matter who won in Europe: The war was a bunch of imperialists tearing each other apart. Americans who wanted to help England during the Battle of Britain were just falling for the Imperialist line. As for the countries being conquered by Stalin, Finland and Eastern Poland, even to notice a problem there was to reveal an almost Satanic lust for war. These adjustments in Eastern Europe made great good sense, though serious anti-fascists should resist any sympathy for places like Imperialist England, which was getting what was coming to it.

It was at this point that Thomas Mann woke up with an angry jolt. In the spring of 1940, Lowenstein and Katz were in New York, working tooth and tong at anti-fascism's new ambidextrous enterprise. Thomas Mann's letter breaking with Lowenstein and cutting himself off from the sundry "leagues" and "committees" the Prince ran as fronts is a memorable and satisfying document in the literature of outrage.

Mann begins by frigidly noting a recent article written by the Prince, questioning British motives in the sea war. He next dissociates himself from its sentiments in a few harsh and unmodulated sentences. The Prince's position is frontally attacked. Then he levels his weapon: "No Nazi—or Stalinist—agent in this country could have sown such evil propaganda against the democracies and the life-and-death struggle they are waging against the German regime, as you do." Next, Mann demands the instantaneous removal of his name from the masthead of an organization run by the Prince—an organization "whose general secretary you are for life, it seems.'' He then ends: ''I regret so harsh an end to relations which for years have been carried on so pleasantly, but we live in a world civil war in which everyone must choose sides, and you have chosen yours.''[46]

The harsh flat fire of this letter bears testimony to Mann's political rectitude. It also bears witness to the power of the Popular Front as the Big Lie. Both Mann brothers had fallen for it: Heinrich completely; Thomas almost completely. The letter refers to ''relations which for years have been carried on so pleasantly.'' The fact worth noting beyond the satisfying ferocity of Mann's language is that what Thomas Mann saw with such clarity in 1940 was something not even Thomas Mann could see in 1935.

Up until the pact, the purpose and the very name of the Hollywood Anti-Nazi League passed through numerous changes to meet Stalin's shifting propaganda needs. Spain soon became an essential part of the agenda, and it next assumed center stage, once again creating an anti-fascist cause which, conveniently for the two dictators, exploited world concern about fascism without ever focussing on Hitler or seriously inconveniencing him in any way. Though most of the Hollywood innocents were genuinely moved by anti-Nazi sentiments, there is ample room to doubt the ''sincerity'' of even such leadership pawns as Stewart and Parker, Hellman and Hammett. Certainly, leading figures within the League—including Parker, Stewart, and Dashiell Hammett—were infinitely more committed to supporting Stalin than they were to resisting Hitler.[47] The truth is that *real* resistance to the Nazis was always a quite secondary concern for almost all of these people. With the pact, that motive vanished in toto. Yet not one leading figure in the Hollywood network defected—though of course the rank and file, in its innocence, pulled out in numbers. Otto Katz had chosen his front people well. With Hitler and Stalin working together, Parker and Stewart and Hellman and Hammett all stayed in place, self-righteous as ever. Discipline held. Not one raised a single word of public criticism. They did not even opt for a decent silence.

The Hollywood Anti-Nazi League immediately changed its name to the ''Hollywood League for Democratic Action.'' Each of its leaders vigorously defended the pact. Each vigorously applauded the joint Soviet-German invasion of Poland and celebrated the start of the Second World War, always under the banner of being ''anti-war.'' Though the Americans did continue to mouth the vague ''anti-fascist'' double-talk consistent with the pact, no serious criticism of the joint Soviet-Nazi military action was ever heard. The League leaders each gave full support to the Soviet invasion of Finland, introducing the sullen contempt audible in Lillian Hellman's attack on the Finns as the Red Army moved through their country. "I don't believe in that fine, loveable little Republic of Finland that everybody gets so weepy about. I've been there, and it looks like a pro-Nazi little republic to me." (Incidentally, there is no evidence that Lillian Hellman ever visited Finland at any point in her lifetime.)[48] Meanwhile, at the height of the Battle of Britain, the Hollywood Stalinists wanted the world to know that the Yanks were *not* coming. In fact, a front organization promptly named itself with those winged words: It was called The-Yanks-Are-Not-Coming Committee. Dashiell Hammett was its leading light.[49]

All of this was symbolically consummated in the marriage of Hemingway's friend Donald Ogden Stewart to Ella Winter.

Very soon after the Hollywood Anti-Nazi League was founded, Dorothy Parker and Donald Ogden Stewart were swept up to San Francisco for a conference sponsored by the League of American Writers, the literary front of the Party.

The San Francisco meeting was held on behalf of Harry Bridges, the Stalinist leader of the San Francisco longshoremen. (Bridges was important to the Soviets because through his control of the San Francisco docks, he could choke or permit American response to a Pacific War if he were told to do so.[50] According to Donald Henderson, Bridges was linked both to the Münzenberg operation and the military *apparat;* many agents were associated with his San Francisco operations, and there were contingency plans for sabotage of any American action in the Pacific not to Stalin's liking. The Central Party Archives have since shown that Bridges operated under full Soviet control.)[51] The San Francisco meeting had nothing to do with writers at all, but it was exciting stuff for the visiting Hollywoodians.[52]

On the platform they were introduced to the crowd by Ella Winter—"our beloved Ella" as she was called. Parker and Stewart were, Ella announced, people who with just a few quips "can help us more than a thousand jargon-filled pamphlets."[53] Then came a revealing moment. Some activist who hadn't yet picked up the beat of the Popular Front, rose to denounce the Hollywood wits as rich party-givers, dilettantes.

Stewart sat on the platform, blushing with his too-familiar shame, but "our beloved Ella" was having none of it. She was not going to sit and listen to some priggish little radical from nowhere jeopardize a catch as important as her Hollywood luminaries. The comrade, with his dreary superseded rectitude, had spoken out of turn, and Winter reeled on him. Stewart was treated to an on-the-spot display of "beloved Ella's" quite stunning powers of verbal sadism. When the tongue-lashing was over, the errant speaker had been reduced to quivering, decimated silence. As the gaping Stewart sat on the platform, listening to Ella rip apart a man who had dared to despise him almost as much as he despised himself, the screenwriter felt something turn over in his heart. Stewart and Winter were married soon after.

As Stewart's wife, Ella Winter would direct his more or less guileless footsteps down the byways of the *apparat* until he died in 1980, just as she previously had guided the steps of Lincoln Steffens.

For Ella's first marriage had been to Lincoln Steffens. As mentioned earlier, Ella had met the famous American muckraker and begun her affair with him at the Paris Peace Conference in 1919, where she was serving as secretary to Felix Frankfurter, a position for which her professor at the London School of Economics, Harold Laski, had recommended her. She met Steffens delivering him an invitation to dinner with the future justice of the Supreme Court. It is easy to see why Steffens fell for her. Photographs of the epoch show a square-jawed, very sexual girl with lots of warmth and intelligence in those "flashing" eyes that made Stewart fall in love. She had married Steffens when she became pregnant with their son—Pete Steffens—and as a matter of principle, they were divorced very shortly afterward, though they lived together until Steffens died in August 1936.[54]

That death was wonderfully convenient. It freed Ella for the new Popular Front tactic, shifting away from the dreary muckraking literature of conscience to her new life as a propagandist in the glamour life.[55]

When did Ella Winter enter the apparatus? A likely guess would be around 1930, during a visit to the USSR from which she returned to the West to all appearances the true and perfect definition of a fellow traveller, the very perfection of the Münzenberg-woman. According to Louis Gibarti, Ella Winter was "one of the most trusted party agents for the West Coast."[56] She had worked closely with him and the Münzenberg propaganda apparatus from at least 1933, and probably earlier.[57] She was, in short, a witting Soviet propaganda agent. She had been a sympathizer since the Revolution, but until the 1930 visit she did occasionally express a vagrant doubt about the Bolsheviks. By 1930, all doubts disappeared. Ella Winter became one of the most ardent and systematic defenders of the Stalinist tyranny in the United States, and she remained so permanently.

As Steffens's biographer rather delicately notes, once Ella Winter became a fellow traveller, she invariably ''led'' Steffens politically. She was his ''instructed agent, his Joshua.''[58] By the time Steffens died, Joshua had guided Steffens to a Stalinism no longer modified by any hint of critical thought, residual morality, or contact with reality. It was simply abject. When the Moscow Trials opened in the last weeks of his life, he proceeded mechanically to their defense, too tired and morally cowed to respond to even the most obvious and elementary challenges to their validity.[59]

And so, only a few months after ''Breda'' left Hollywood, and even fewer after Steffens's death, ''our beloved Ella's'' romance with Hemingway's companion Stewart began.

But let us pick up the second strand from Hemingway's circle, the one left by John Herrmann, and his wife, Otto Katz's hostess, Josephine Herbst. This is the thread that runs from Montparnasse to Washington.

Josephine Herbst and John Herrmann were born into that generation of 1905 for which the great literary star was Hemingway, and it was on Hemingway that the mystique of both their lives was to a large degree focussed. Like him they were classic midwesterners, born Protestant and in small towns, educated in the land-grant universities. Like him they responded to the discovery of some special talent within them by being drawn east, east to New York, east above all to Europe, as if to their destiny. They missed the European war, but both went to Germany after the armistice, where they became, separately, classic postwar Bohemians and modernists. John dabbled in art history, dabbled in literature. Nietzsche was his god. He took to carrying a copy of Gertrude Stein's *Three Lives* as a kind of badge. He wanted people to know that he was part of the new consciousness. Needless to add, he was writing a novel.

Josie was also part of the new consciousness (she'd had a love affair with Maxwell Anderson), and she too was writing a novel. It was called *The Unmarried.* After Germany, Herrmann and Herbst travelled on separate paths to Paris, where John was introduced to Ernest Hemingway by Ford Maddox Ford. Hemingway and Herrmann hit it off right away, another natural fit. John became a hard-drinking member of the circle that would soon be celebrated in *The Sun Also Rises.*[60]

The iconography of *The Sun Also Rises* is likewise what makes John's first meeting with Josie seem to us now picture perfect. They were introduced at the Café Dome, where John sat behind a high stack of saucers, curing a hangover by becoming, once again, interestingly drunk. The two drank together. They soon discovered that they too were a natural fit. They understood each other. They thought alike, and they admired alike. Hemingway's star was rising, and it seemed to them to be their star. Besides, John and Josie really liked each other. Enough to go back to John's apartment together.

John's room seemed to Josie another perfect setting for a kindred spirit. He kept a death mask of Nietzsche, and "like a private shrine" a copy of *Ecce Homo*. Love came quickly. Josie started to call John her "beautiful boy," and John thought he'd at last found the woman who understood. They slept together, drank together, knew everybody together. Soon they left Paris together to set up in a Breton fishing village where they could write together, the ideal advanced young American couple of their time, smack in the middle of their fantasy.[61]

By 1926, they decided the time had come really to begin. Really, seriously begin; take on the big world and conquer what they'd left behind. They made the exile's return, and went back to New York.

The link between modernism and political radicalism which in 1927 felt so natural to the likes of John and Josie has long since grown obscure. We can recall that the "radicalism" of the founding American modernists—Eliot, Pound, and Stein—was much more often on the right than the left, and that by the mid-thirties Stalinist apologists were having trouble hiding their system's inveterate philistinism and loathing of genuine modernist (or indeed any) esthetics. Finally, the modernist esthetic was promoted postwar above all by the so-called "new critics" in American departments of literature. With some exceptions the "new critics" were not very sympathetic to the hard left. They tended to be "apolitical," with a liberal-to-centrist drift, though their numbers also included a fair number of rightists.

But in 1926, the prevailing tone was very different. Among the generation of kids that included John Herrmann and Josephine Herbst, the link between Bohemian modernism and a general leftism called "radicalism" seemed to be two versions of one thing, like breathing in and breathing out.

Radek and Willi clearly grasped that to organize the elite meant organizing the assumption that artistic and political radicalism were really the same thing. In the middle-class democracies, this notion had some shaky validity. In actual Stalinist practice, of course, it had none at all. Still, the point of efforts like New Playwrights', and of the general ferment seeking to "politicize" New York and Parisian literary culture, was to make this weak-minded assumption seem valid. Herbst and Herrmann's return to New York co-incided precisely with the apparatus deciding to take a direct hand in that cultural life, and they were both soon instruments of the effort, classic literary second-raters put on the map by the propaganda apparatus, letterhead celebrities.

Shortly afterward, the Comintern decided to clinch its hold on the cultural front with a vast writers' congress. It was to be held in Russia itself, and it would serve two political ends. The first goal was European: to co-opt the fashions in modernism then at their height. The second goal was more strictly Soviet: to consolidate Stalin's grip on Russian cultural life. In Europe the thing was surrealism, which was to be Sovietized under the leadership of the surrealist seer Louis Aragon, guided at all times by his wife Elsa Triolet, who like Koudachova and Moura Budberg, was another "lady of the Kremlin."[62]

Elsa Triolet was Russian by birth, cultivated and well-educated, born into the Petersburg professional intelligentsia. She was the sister of Lily Brik, beloved of Mayakovsky. Unlike Lily Brik, Triolet left Russia after the Revolution, living first in the Russian emigration community in Berlin, later in Paris. After an unhappy first marriage, she became the wife of the surrealist poet, novelist, and journalist Louis Aragon. In its time, this union was one of Europe's most infamous public affiliations of obsession with opportunity. Manipulating the ever more elaborate myth of her role as the muse of Aragon, whose life and thought in practical reality she managed with an iron hand, Elsa Triolet contrived to become one of the leading cultural politicians of her time. For decades, she was one of the most influential chic Stalinists in Paris. Her services to the regime never faltered either in their grand manner or in their absolute reliability. She worked closely with Münzenberg, Katz, and Mikhail Koltsov, as well as their successors among the Soviet apparatus, and of course with the French Party as well. Did Triolet's file in the NKVD, like that of Koudachova, bear the sinister stamp: *Nash?* "Ours?" It is quite possible, but (as in the case of Claud Cockburn) whether she was or was not an agent under discipline may be a distinction without much difference.

Triolet was no mere factotum to the *apparat.* She was an overt Stalinist, and it was always her habit to locate herself as near as possible to the top. She knew Radek well. She was for many years on the warmest possible terms with Aleksandr Fadaev, even though that bureaucrat was perhaps more responsible than any other for the enforcement of Stalin's cultural policy in its ugliest aspects. The essential psychological fact is that Triolet was anything but a Bolshevik true believer. In a rare moment of weakness she once confided to a Stalinist friend that she had loathed the Bolsheviks from the earliest days in Petersburg. She was bound to the Stalinist tyranny for reasons that remain murky, but bound to it she was. She gave herself to the regime with what at least appeared to be all she had in all her cold heart.[63]

Aragon and Triolet's assumption of their lifelong appointed place on top of left-wing French cultural life dates from the Kharkov Writers' Conference. They stepped into their roles at these festivities. On the week-long train crawl from Moscow to Kharkov, Aragon and Triolet were constant companions of Fadaev, who had just taken a giant step in Soviet power by being asked to head the Congress. For decades to come, right up until the time, after Khrushchev's secret speech of 1956, when Fadaev killed himself, the sweet political fortunes of Triolet and Aragon would be tied to Fadaev's power.

Two Americans who were eager delegates to Kharkov were John Herrmann and Josephine Herbst, and at Kharkov, Herrmann and Herbst were drawn into the company of the German delegation, which was run by one of Münzenberg's close associates, a Teutonic propagandist named Ludwig Renn.[64] The couple's rapid rise in the apparatus following Kharkov may well be attributable to the good impression they made on this very influential member of Münzenberg's operation in Berlin. In any case, Herrmann and Herbst left Kharkov not just committed Stalinists, but Stalinists whose names and hopes were known in the more senior reaches of the apparatus. Back in New York, they were soon admitted to the inner circles of innocence.

This worked wonders for their reputations. The names of Josephine Herbst and John Herrmann were suddenly being mentioned in the same breath with Theodore Dreiser; both were accepted as clients by the literary agent Maxim Lieber, who was also an agent in another sense, and who numbered among his clients none other than Otto Katz.[65]

Simultaneously, Herbst and Herrmann began to be gently primed for covert work. Josie was now regularly used by the Party and its fronts as a journalist. Probably to guard her appearance of independence, she does not seem to have actually joined the Party, though she may have been a secret member. John did join, and became increasingly active as a Party organizer. By 1934 the couple was introduced, in New York, to Münzenberg himself, probably by Gibarti. She was also in regular contact with Hede Massing working under Hede's cover as an "anti-fascist journalist." It appears it was also around this time, perhaps shortly afterward in Europe, that she made the acquaintance of Otto Katz.[66] Shortly after meeting with Münzenberg and Gibarti, Josie was dispatched to Berlin on a journalistic project which also led her to make covert contacts with the

Münzenberg underground, contacts certainly authorized and guided by the Paris office, to which she returned months later. By this time, 1935, they were well known to Otto Katz.[67] It was at this same time that the *apparat* began entrusting John with serious ''special work'': his work in espionage.[68]

Meanwhile, love and art in all their promise were coming unravelled for John and Josie. Like all the Cambridge spies, John Herrmann was an alcoholic. He was also rapidly developing into an obvious failure. He had no meaningful position in the literary world. His entire claim to such a position was one poorly published book and his friendship with Ernest Hemingway. Hemingway, meanwhile, did not take John seriously. It's true, he liked to fish and drink with Herrmann: ''There are no rummies'' Hemingway wrote, ''better than John.''[69] But believe in Rummy John as a writer? Come, come.

Meanwhile, the force driving Josephine Herbst seems to have been a kind of churning ferocity. Personally, Herbst could be quite a nasty item: domineering, abusive, and foul-mouthed.[70] Yet Herbst's archives do reveal a woman riddled with a wish for tenderness, though it was tenderness mingled, lifelong, with anger. She was all need, and as such she habitually saw herself as cheated: cheated in feeling, cheated in sex, cheated in life.

In 1932 all this—Josie's angry dilemma, John's failure, the role of both of the apparatus—came to crisis during a stay at the artist's colony at Yaddo.

During her residency at the famous colony, Josie met a strong, solid, beautiful, intensely seductive painter named Marion Greenwood, a woman who seems to have habitually defined her very real force of personality primarily in sexual terms. Marion immediately sensed the writer's vulnerability and need; it didn't take her much longer to discover the probably quite simple combination that unlocked Herbst's homosexuality. Marion Greenwood introduced Josie to a level of orgasmic pleasure, of voluptuous hope which she had not found either in her promiscuity or her life with John. With Marion Josie let herself know the full gratification of surrender.

This wave carried Josie to the end of her marriage—and then to rejection by Marion, too. In rather sweet-sounding reversion to Utopian type, the threesome, John and Marion and Josie all together, decided to spend a long idyll, getting to know and love each other in Mexico. South of the border, they would learn to be free and equal, and love one another, all three. (Mexico, incidentally, was rapidly becoming a Great Good Place for American radicals and for the Comintern *apparat* in general, and the tendency would come to a political climax during the Second

World War.) The three Americans went to a little town called Taxco, and there in Taxco the capacity of the human triangle to stand up under sexual strain was tested for the trillionth time. For the trillionth time, it failed.

As the weeks passed, everybody tried hard to *sound* free, *sound* loving. The sound grew more and more hollow. John left first, leaving Josie with Marion. Then a perplexed and pained Josie found that her soulful clinging to Marion was getting more and more on Marion's nerves. Things were growing a little unlovely. Josephine headed north, trying to evade the shrug-off that was plainly not far away as Marion turned icy, then turned her back on Josie, then turned "back to men."[71]

When he left Mexico, John Herrmann had fled back into what he called "his work." This was no longer his work as a writer. His work as a writer was nowhere. Whom the gods have destroyed with promise, they next make spies. Herrmann was following an American version of Guy Burgess's path.

His new work, and it was what the Party called "special work," required a move to Washington. In Washington he would be lending a helping hand to a man named Harold Ware. And the task in which Harold Ware would direct him would be espionage.[72]

Up until his death in an automobile accident in 1935, Harold Ware was one of the leading American-born operatives used by the *apparat* in its penetration of the Washington government. He had been born and bred to totalitarianism; he was the soft-spoken son of a very loud Stalinist propagandist who styled herself "Mother Bloor." He was married to a Greenwich Village literary communist and dear friend of the Herrmanns named Jessica Smith. "Hal" had spent most of his young manhood in Soviet Mecca, where he was trained as an organizer and covert operative connected to Münzenberg's networks from virtually the beginning.[73] By 1931 he was ready to be sent back to the States and assignment to Washington. Ware joined the Department of Agriculture, and began his covert career, rising on the Washington scene.

Ware had first met John before the Mexican interlude, when they worked together in the Midwest, organizing propaganda fronts among farmers. When he got to Washington he was made Hal's covert right hand in recruiting and running networks for agents of influence and espionage in the Washington establishment, work that would involve Alger Hiss, and in an adjacent apparatus, Noel Field.

It takes time for marriages to end. When she too came home from Mexico, in spite of what had happened, Josephine Herbst's marriage was both over and not over at all. It was finished, and yet the hope and dream persisted, marked everywhere by all the pathos of the death of faith. Josie was not through with John, not through being angry with him, and not through needing him. She was often in Washington, often with him in the sweltering heat and wretchedness in his one-room apartment on New Hampshire Avenue. And there Josie was, generally speaking, perfectly aware of what her John's "work" really was.

It must be added that Josephine Herbst was sufficiently trusted in this situation to be allowed that knowledge, in a way that neither Melinda Maclean nor Eleanor Philby, for example, ever were. At the very least, Josephine Herbst had guilty knowledge of the Washington espionage operations. She knew about them and she fully approved. How witting was she? Quite. Certainly far more so than she ever publicly allowed.

There is no evidence that she herself was personally active in the Washington apparatus, or for that matter in any espionage apparatus apart from the propaganda assignments she undertook for Otto Katz, working as a "journalist" in Spain, in Berlin, and Latin America. There she was plainly working for the Comintern, and her work was giving satisfaction. Yet while she was trusted with the knowledge of John's work, I have seen no evidence either to prove or refute that Josephine Herbst was an agent in espionage in the same way that Herta Field doubtless was, and Priscilla Hiss almost certainly was.

And yet, and yet: During the Second World War, a rather curious episode did take place.

After Pearl Harbor, Josie applied for and got a job working at the German desk of the newly formed American intelligence service in Washington. This is not in itself necessarily strange. Certainly Herbst was very well-informed on the subject of propaganda and Germany. She had worked for Münzenberg and Katz in and with the propaganda inside Germany and elsewhere, operating both publicly and using clandestine technique. In fact, Herbst was exceptionally well connected with some of the most important people in the field—Soviet agents whose work in this field she knew to have been of the highest importance and political sensitivity. It was very much the sort of information the United States Intelligence Service might well have used in its own struggle with the Nazis.

Except that, curiously enough, nobody in American intelligence knew anything about Josie's previous history in this kind of work, nothing about her expertise in this very field. Josephine Herbst breathed not one single syllable about her special knowledge, even though it was her job to advise the American services on precisely this subject. About her undercover propaganda work in Germany, Herbst said nothing. About her acquaintance with some of the best-placed propaganda agents then at work, Herbst said nothing. About her great knowledge of the entire anti-fascist movement, Herbst said nothing. And about her own former husband's work as an agent for Soviet espionage, in regular contact with senior American officials whom she could confidently assume were at that moment betraying their oath to the Constitution, she likewise said precisely nothing.

Her attitude toward the job was thus remote from candor. It was also short on goodwill. Herbst's main comment on the work in German propaganda by the American service was to jeer at its naiveté. This was no doubt in some ways appropriate: the people involved were surely a bunch of amateurs. Apart from herself, that is. This makes it all the more odd that Herbst did not offer to instruct them. *She* was in a position to bring some sophistication and insight to the work. One might wonder why she did not? One answer might be that she was attempting to protect old friends, and specifically her old Stalinist friends. To which one would have to reply: precisely.

After a year of work handling confidential intelligence documents at the German desk of the fledgling American service, Josephine Herbst was at last spotted as the gross security risk she so manifestly was, and dismissed. The dismissal was based on far less information than I have outlined above, and it was followed by a public mini-scandal over the awful injustice being done to her.

In fact, there was no injustice at all in this dismissal. The silence of Josephine Herbst about her work for the apparatus makes it plain that she had no intention of being either particularly loyal or particularly useful in her service to American intelligence. Yet since she had no interest in actually being useful in the OCI, since she so vocally despised an effort she had no wish to assist, we may well ask why she was so very eager to work there—there and nowhere else? There is no honest or coherent answer to these questions on record. Certainly, after she was asked to leave the American services, Josephine Herbst never again, in any other capacity whatever, performed a single act or gave a single hour to the American war effort against Hitler.

But of course, Herbst was not honest about her politics because Stalinism does not permit people to be honest about their politics. That flaw makes one resist growing sententious over her dilemma as a person. Yet it is a moving dilemma. Here is a gifted woman of her place and time, struggling, struggling hard, to live a life worthy of its American promise;

struggling hard to reach a destiny she hoped might be hers, a destiny of exceptional moral commitment and the life of art. And here is the failure of that effort.

She was desperately unhappy. Seven years before, Herbst had been in Washington for the awful endgame of the fated marriage that had begun so glamourously at the Café Dome. Her biographer cites a letter written to John after the Mexican affair with Marion Greenwood, once she had returned to him and his work as a spy. It was written at 3:30 A.M. on a sweltering Washington night, and left for him on their kitchen table. Reading it, one can feel the heat pounding, feel the failure, feel the suffocating small hour, black and silent.

> I've just called up to find out the time after sitting & walking here & crying. You shouldn't have let me come back here to stay here all alone. . . . If I hadn't been let alone so many times like this . . . I wouldn't have got into the state I've been in the last few months, the most unhappy woman alive. . . . You've been good to me these last few weeks and I love you more than anything else in the world. If I hadn't I would suffer all the time. But you've never bothered much for a long time to take pains making love to me or to call any part of me beautiful. You never really did that, until *she* did, and that's what's so painful . . .[74]

Alone in that Washington desolation, Josie had almost nobody to talk to. Yet there was one man who worked with John in his "special work" and who used to drop by the little apartment. They'd have coffee, and talk. He was a very intelligent literary fellow, though he had a rather mysterious Dostoyevskian manner and an odd, vaguely Germanic accent which many people mistook for foreign. Yet Josie found comfort talking to him. He was extremely well read; he instinctively understood a writer's mind. She confided at least a few of her troubles to him, and he listened gently. He was insightful, careful, good. He was really very decent, very kind.

It was a meeting that would mark the rest of her life, and in it a circle that began with Sinclair Lewis came complete. Josie's visitor called himself Karl, and Karl's real name was Whittaker Chambers.

Chapter 9

An End to Innocence

The unseen bond between the Great Purges of 1936–38, and the Popular Front offers a perspective on the union between innocence and terror that characterizes much in revolutionary and Utopian thought. Innocence and terror: they are intertwined—and they were never more so than during the bleak years that the world was on the path to World War II. To be sure, Bolshevik "idealism" had been bound to brutality from the start. Dzerzhinsky's Terror had always been meted out in the name of "Revolutionary Justice." Through it, the Revolution spoke. But there was a difference between Soviet Terror before 1935 and after it. Dzerzhinsky's Cheka and the GPU mainly killed and destroyed the lives of people in the proscribed classes. They murdered "enemies of the people," losers in the class war, the lost wretches whose class guilt, it was assumed, deserved no pity. They deserved expropriation; they deserved the annihilation of their ideas, their livelihood, and their culture. Should the Revolution find their death convenient, they deserved to die. In working their defeat, the Party was the instrument of History and of its grand impersonal vengeance. To its sublime cruelty there could be no appeal.

But with the coming of the purges, a new element was added, because its intended victims were to be, above all, *communists,* and therefore people who until 1935 or so had been immune to the more arbitrary slaughters of "socialist justice." Until then, perhaps the most precious privilege of Party membership had been its formal immunity to the death penalty. Under Lenin, the Bolsheviks mowed down class enemies by the tens of thousands, but they paused, understandably enough, before shooting a Party member. By 1935, however, the impending Party purge would require the termination of this shining privilege. By 1935 Stalin had made his move.[1]

Ending the immunity of Party members to the death penalty was an important change in Soviet jurisprudence. But the Terror brought with it tremendous philosophical consequences for the system as well. Here is how. The show trials of the Purges not only made Party members subject to Marxist-Leninist terror, they simultaneously raised the Lie, the special place of the Lie itself in communist thinking, into a kind of apotheosis of *visibility*.

This was new. It is important to remember how audaciously the show trials of the Terror were run.[2] It was as if part of their strategy were literally to defy belief. It seems plain that most serious observers, including most serious communist observers, clearly understood that virtually every syllable the chief prosecutor, Vyshinsky, pronounced in those ringing chambers of injustice and fanaticism was false. Of course some largish percentage of the credulous and uneducated actually believed what they were told—or perhaps more exactly, half-believed it. But the politically serious? The shamelessness of this public falsehood meant simultaneously a new kind of revolutionary faith and a new level of public submission. It was to be submission beyond mere obedience. Almost all the important Bolsheviks killed in the purges were fully obedient to the dictator. It is true that in the senior hierarchy there was some resistance to Stalin's policies and self-aggrandizement but after 1928, as a practical matter that resistance was not terribly threatening. No matter. Even the obedient still have, in some measure, their private thoughts. The new dispensation enforced a totalitarian submission that left no room for any residual "privatism." It was not enough for a Galileo merely to recant and forever renounce saying, even under his breath, *"prove se muove."* The Terror would carry the Lie past the mere suppression of speech. Henceforth, Galileo—Galileos by the hundreds of thousands—would be subject to summary execution merely because they *might* notice the obvious, because they *might* think *"prove se muove."* In the ostentatious mendacity of the show trials, Stalin sought to give the Lie a new totalitarian *force majeure* over that defeated thing, veracity. The trials were something new not just in the history of organized injustice. They were something new in what we might call the history of the truth. It was the end of innocence.

. . .

In his novel *The Magic Mountain* of 1924, Thomas Mann grasped the covert connection between innocence and terror and argued it out on the crystalline but tubercular heights of a sanatorium on the icy Swiss Alps. There, in a pseudo-hospital called the Berghof, filled with affluent Europeans suffering from tuberculosis (and often mere neurasthenia), Mann anticipated the force that would find its outcome in the grunting moral squalor of Moscow in 1937. High in their Mountain House, two hypochondriacal intellectuals, each paralyzed in his own brilliant way, engage in a struggle to win the mind of Hans Castorp, a pleasant, earnest, not overly-bright young fellow from that German upper-middle class which Mann saw complacently awaiting the century's catastrophes in the European flatlands below.

On one side of this debate is a liberal, anti-clerical Italian humanist, Ludovico Settembrini. Settembrini preaches the progress of the human community under the sway of reason and the principles of humanistic idealism. He is opposed by Naphta, a Jesuit and master of the higher polemics, a man whose severe discipline within the Faith is sustained by devotion to a vision of a vast, avenging, crypto-Christian communist revolution. At one high point of their debate, Naphta turns all his contempt on Settembrini's soft hopes for peace and light.

> "No," Naphta went on. "Liberation and development of the individual are not the key to the age, they are not what our age demands. What it needs, what it wrestles after, what it will create—is Terror."
>
> He uttered the last word lower than the rest, without a motion of his body. Only his eyeglasses suddenly flashed.[3]

What it needs, what it wrestles after, what it will create—is Terror. Naphta's dry prophecy shatters the calm of the Berghof. As he pronounces it, only a tiny unseen tremor passes through his body to make his eyeglasses suddenly flash. It is the shiver of a cerebral, angry, righteous excitement.

"Naphta sat motionless, flashing like a drawn blade."

It is easy to substitute for Naphta's quivering presence at this moment the presence of Felix Dzerzhinsky himself, or for that matter even Theodore Maly.

Stalin took direct inspiration for his own purges from the lightning strokes of Hitler's Blood Purge of June 1934. Like Hitler's action, Stalin's new policy required the slaughter of his oldest comrades. Not only did Stalin take direct lessons from the Night of Long Knives, he was, as we have seen, almost certainly an active participant in its preparation through his role in the Reichstag Fire Trial. He had been an active participant almost from the moment Hitler assumed power. And once the Blood Purge took place, Stalin immediately began laying his own plans. He studied every report the *apparat* fed him, weighing its value to his own purposes.[4] Six months after the events in Germany, assassins operating under Stalin's covert orders entered the offices of Sergei Mironovich Kirov and shot him to death.[5] This was the first blow in Stalin's own intra-party purge; as Natalia Guinzberg wrote in her memoirs, "the year 1937 began, to all intents and purposes, at the end of 1934—to be exact, on the first of December."[6]

The link between the impending Terror and Stalin's hidden role in the Kirov killing may have been covered by a thousand lies, but something sinister was quite evident to many observers from the start. Among them were the French novelist and communist Paul Nizan who, with his wife Henriette, was in Moscow at the time. Nizan had been the inseparable school companion of Jean-Paul Sartre and Raymond Aron; of these three musketeers, Nizan was the most committed militant. He worked in Münzenberg's Paris operation; among other things, he had helped prepare the French edition of *The Brown Book.* He surely knew Otto Katz very well.[7] In 1934, Paul and Henriette were rewarded for these efforts with a sojourn in Moscow, doing what we might call post-graduate work in revolution, preparing for their chosen role as propagandists among the French.

In her old age, Henriette Nizan recalled the night Kirov was assassinated. She and Nizan had been at the theater that night of December 1. In the middle of the performance, the news of the murder was not so much announced as it began to seep into the hall. Nobody in the orchestra, where Paul and Henriette were seated, had any idea of what had happened, but a kind of deeper silence, the silence of fear, became palpable in the place, while up on the stage, the performance droned on, suddenly irrelevant. Glancing up into the loges where all the important Party members sat, the couple became aware that one by one, the tiers were emptying. "It was a very curious atmosphere, very striking. I remember I said to Nizan that it was exactly like a declaration of war. And in a way it was."

Nor were the Nizans entirely deceived by the nature of this new unseen war. In December 1934, Paul and Henriette Nizan were devoted militants, and they remained so until the pact. Yet Henriette says that at the time of Kirov's murder it seemed perfectly plain to them both that "Stalin had something to do with it."[8]

"Stalin had something to do with it." The Nizans cannot have been alone among those guessing the truth; we must suppose that many intelligent people on the scene had the same intuition. From that moment forward, left-wing innocence would have to proceed in a new relationship with the Lie. Henceforth, Stalin's idealists would know, at least on some vague level of knowing, that the voice of the Revolution was the voice of falsehood. A whole class of educated believers would be obliged to live inside what Orwell called "doublethink."

But the truth is that even when confronted with the obvious mendacity of the Terror, the majority of innocents could still not turn away from their dream. Stalinist cultural politics were never more confident, never more sententious or more devout than during these dark days. "I have had a very corrupting trip," Nizan confided to Sartre and de Beauvoir when he returned to France.[9] It was not so corrupting that it shook Nizan's commitment. The ability to hold truth and falsehood simultaneously in mind is not so remarkable a moral feat as the too-rational may fondly suppose. Most of us are doing it in some fashion much of the time. After his return from Moscow, Nizan continued to rise in Willi's world, becoming Louis Aragon's right hand at a new Popular Front paper in Paris which Otto Katz helped to found, *Ce Soir*. Nizan remained loyal until the pact.[10]

When that event broke upon the world in August 1939, bringing with it the Second World War, Paul Nizan was, like all Parisian intellectuals, in the South of France for *les vacances*—and once again with Sartre and de Beauvoir. When the newspapers with their astonishing headlines reached them, Nizan stood on their summer terrace, so much in shock that the paper rattled in his hands as he read. He was a man in the midst of a revelation. According to Simone de Beauvoir he stood speechless and overwhelmed, as though the lights had been switched on in a room where until then he had been feeling his way. Suddenly he could see the real shapes he'd been bumping into during all those years of his so-called "anti-fascism." For Nizan too, it was the end of innocence.[11]

Nizan broke with the Party that week. He immediately joined the French army. Just as immediately a campaign savaging Nizan began in the intellectual press, led by the columnist Geneviève Tabouis. Tabouis, in turn, was a so-called "independent, anti-fascist" journalist actually under Katz's control. She sold her services to the Soviet apparatus, and for good money. According to Babette Gross, the Soviet ambassador regularly complained to Münzenberg about the high cost of her payoffs. Though costly, she was obedient. According to Elisabeth Poretsky, she often wrote her column taking direct dictation from Otto, without even troubling to reformulate it into her own words. Her *apparat* nickname: "Stalin's Inkwell." Tabouis's attack on Nizan was fierce.[12]

In American show business, the groundwork for the Popular Front was laid in March 1935 when Otto Katz arrived *incognito* in Los Angeles to found the Hollywood Anti-Nazi League.[13] The parallel event among literary intellectuals took place in Paris during the suffocatingly hot June of 1935, at a grand parley known as the World Congress in Defense of Culture.[14] Because this convention was held in a hall called the Salle Mutualité, it has come to be called the Mutualité Congress. The Mutualité is one of the most famous and frequently written-about culture congresses of the era, a carefully staged piece of intellectual theater, designed to prepare the cultural elite for the Popular Front. Its presiding officers were André Gide and André Malraux.[15]

The actual powers organizing the front men on the podium were Ilya Ehrenberg and Mikhail Koltsov, two critically placed Russians, neither of whom was under Münzenberg's discipline. According to Babette Gross, Münzenberg played no role at the Mutualité. That he did not may well prefigure the fate Stalin already had in mind for Willi. The Popular Front was Münzenberg's undoing. Had Karl Radek, and with him Münzenberg, already been marked for liquidation? Was *that* their true role? If so, did Otto Katz know it? He was surely one of the most important secret agents in charge of the Front, and he did strangely survive and flourish after the fall of his two great patrons.

The Terror was being prepared.

Gide's role in the Mutualité Congress is of special interest. The strategy of the Popular Front required the adherence of the entire left wing of the French elite which, in the tradition of Voltaire, was then, as now, especially responsive to the intellectual leadership of whoever was currently the foremost dissident man of letters in Paris. In 1935, that man was André Gide. No matter that Gide was a homosexual; no matter that he was a rich man and delighted to be one—very much the *grand bourgeois*. No matter: In 1935 he was *the* Frenchman on whose shoulders the mantle of Zola was draped. He was the conscience of Europe, the dean of unacknowledged legislators.

The story of the cat and mouse between the Kremlin and Gide is long, dodging, and delicate. It came to its mysterious crescendo in 1936, on the very threshold of the Terror, when Gide visited the USSR in the most widely touted great-man tour of them all. It ended with the author of *The*

Immoralist on a dais near Stalin, delivering the funeral oration over the body of Maxim Gorky.

One instrument in the apparatus's courtship of Gide was almost certainly a young man named Pierre Herbart. During our interview in Munich, Babette Gross told me that the apparatus had manipulated Gide through "various young men" gathered around the master. The suggestion was that, given Gide's homosexuality, these manipulations were partly sexual. But which young men? Babette Gross named no names; perhaps she had never known them. But it seems to me very probable that Pierre Herbart was one of the instruments in the game.

Gide's relation to Herbart long antedated his relation to the apparatus. He had first come upon the young Herbart gracing the entourage of his much-mistrusted arch-rival Jean Cocteau, the author of *Opium*. Pierre was himself seriously drug-addicted and leading the slack life of a handsome hanger-on in the circle of a rich homosexual celebrity. Meeting him, Gide instantly set out to rescue Pierre from what he viewed as the vacuous debauchery of Cocteau's addicted world. He may well have been (briefly) infatuated with Herbart himself. He once confessed to Maria van Rhysselberghe that Pierre had the body he most wished he might have had as his own.[16]

Whatever their sexual connection, Gide did rescue Herbart from the clutches of Cocteau. He paid for Pierre to get treatment in a detox clinic; he persuaded the youth to leave Cocteau's villa in the South of France and enter the more serious precincts of his own household in Paris.[17]

Inscribed all through the life of Pierre Herbart, one senses an insoluble agony over fatherhood. Pierre was himself very much a son of the bourgeoisie; one of his brothers became no less than a director of the Bank of France. But the Herbart brothers were *abandoned* sons of the bourgeoisie. Their father had deserted the family when Pierre was young. Pierre was later asked to identify the corpse of his father, who had been found dead in a ditch, a vagrant.[18]

So it is not surprising that Pierre's relation to Gide should have been less that of lover than adopted son. But there was more to Pierre's Oedipal task than that. In the 1920s Gide had a sexual encounter, once and once only, with the daughter of Maria van Rhysselberghe, Gide's substitute or shadow-wife in all but sexual and liturgical fact. In a unique experience not with "La Petite Dame" but with her daughter, Gide's biological daughter Madeleine was conceived.

At this juncture, Pierre Herbart made his largest single step into the center of Gide's life. He "legitimized" little Madeleine by marrying Elisabeth, although Elisabeth was almost twenty years older than he: Old enough to be his mother, in fact. Pierre thus became at once pretend father and pretend son, and his perverse role became even more deeply bound in multiple ambiguities.[19]

But the rescue of Pierre Herbart also required Gide to provide his protégé with some sort of plausible line of work. To this end, Gide set out to make Pierre into a writer and intellectual. This had a certain dubious plausibility. Pierre was certainly very intelligent; he had good taste; and he did possess a certain narrow competence as a writer. In the effort, Gide and the propaganda apparatus found common terms. That apparatus soon put Pierre on very much the same Party-sponsored literary career track as the genuinely gifted Paul Nizan was pursuing. That meant lots of articles and assignments for various newspapers and magazines of the chic Parisian left, followed by a year in Moscow during much the same time that Nizan and Henriette were there. Thus, Pierre was provided with a career while Gide had acquired a debt to the French Party, its cultural commissar, Vaillant, and his men. As time went on, the apparatus seems to have grown steadily and more confident that it held Pierre firmly in its grasp, and that Pierre was their key to Gide.[20]

In this belief, they seem to have underestimated Pierre's ambiguities. If Pierre Herbart helped to lead Gide into the arms of the apparatus, it is my impression that he also helped lead him out again.

Gide may have been the main French mark of the Popular Front, but the principal and most ominous political event of the Mutualité Congress was, or ought to have been, the curious absence of Maxim Gorky. Gorky had originally been billed as the ''honorary chairman'' of the Congress. But that announcement had been made before Kirov's murder. Sometime in the events that followed that assassination, the arrangement for Gorky's visit was cancelled. Stalin selected Isaac Babel and Boris Pasternak as his delegates in order to replace the grand old man of socialist realism, who was unable to come, the delegates were told, because of his poor health.[21]

The true reason for Gorky's absence in Paris is that like Paul and Henriette Nizan, he entertained suspicions about Kirov's death. From the earliest days of the Revolution, Gorky had been very much part of the Leningrad political establishment. He had known Kirov well, and with his killing, Gorky smelled the same rat the Nizans smelled. But unlike them, Gorky was in a position to make his suspicions matter. And Stalin knew it.

Gorky was an old man, and for all his faults a brave one. He was very ill; his tubercular emaciated face was plainly stamped with the marks of the final days. He was also the most respected spokesman for the Revolution alive. And as we shall see, for both personal and public reasons, he was moving toward disaffection. Gorky had at least reason to believe that Stalin had played a role not only in the death of Kirov, but possibly even in the death of his own son, Max Pechkov, a few months later. His suspicions were visibly mounting. So Stalin considered: Should Gorky be given that podium in Paris as planned? Sent out of easy reach to talk with important European intellectuals?

Gorky's travelling days were at an end. The author of *The Lower Depths* would never return to Europe.[22]

Gorky's absence at the Mutualité was very plausibly attributed to ill-health. Most people accepted the claim without a second thought. The event swept ahead without him. What actually was said in the turgid deliberations of Stalin's Congress in Defense of Culture has been described many times, and it would be silly to rehearse the rodomontade again here. The hall sweltered; righteousness rose up; the hash of innocence was hashed and rehashed. The participants dripped with sweat and struggled with their rhetoric, maneuvering in and out of largely fatuous and always imaginary "positions." The Popular Front strategy required that the guiding Soviet grip on the Mutualité be invisible but firm. The dull results had their occasionally comic side. At one point Gustav Regler made such a shining speech in defense of Soviet culture that the crowd could not contain its passions any longer. It leapt to its feet and burst into a rapturous chorus of *The International.* As Regler swept triumphantly into the wings, an NKVD agent named Johannes Becher greeted him in a rage, hissing "You've ruined everything! You've given us away!"[23]

The only other event of lingering interest at the Mutualité was the case of Victor Serge.

Victor Serge was a French anarchist and novelist whose revolutionary faith took him to Russia to greet the great dawn of October 1917. There he became an agent of the Comintern, and there he entered the conspiratorial world. He always retained his anarchist passions, but he continued to serve the Comintern and to write, in deepening doubt, until 1933, when he heard the knock at the door, was arrested, and despatched to the gulag.[24]

Serge had seen his downfall coming, and as a kind of life insurance smuggled out of the Soviet Union the manuscript of an anti-Stalinist but still devoutly revolutionary book called *Literature and Revolution,* with the request that in the event he disappeared, the book either be published or used as a lever for his release.[25]

Serge then disappeared. His cause was taken up by a number of people, some of them Trotskyists, who co-ordinated their response at the Mutualité. At the end of a long, propagandistic day, a distinguished Italian radical with strong anarchist sympathies, Gaetano Salvemini, stood up. Salvemini had been a leftist senator in the Italian Parliament; he was a fierce and unrelenting opponent of Mussolini. He now taught Italian Civilization at Harvard. Taking the floor, Salvemini demanded that the Congress denounce the Terror in the USSR as well as Germany, and then asked if the Russian delegation could provide an explanation of "the way Victor Serge was being treated in the Soviet Union."

Trouble. Ehrenberg and Koltsov instantly went into a huddle together, plotting damage control. Too late: Another speaker was on her feet, a Trotskyist named Madeleine Paz. She immediately seconded Salvemini and announced to the Congress that she had reason to believe that the distinguished French writer and revolutionary Victor Serge was being held prisoner in the USSR. She demanded to know his whereabouts.

It is a measure of the tender sensitivities of Stalinist cultural politics that this single request provoked absolute consternation in the hall. *Where was Victor Serge?* With this one challenge to the Lie, the invisible hand trembled palpably. A kind of group hysteria swept the room. The delegates, until now so docile, were suddenly shouting at each other. Fists were being clenched. There was abuse and gnashing of teeth. Folding chairs were being picked up and waved in the air.

Gide and Malraux, up on the podium, looked out on this spectacle, and down came the gavel. The session was unceremoniously ended, and the simple question from Salvemini and Madeleine Paz hung unanswered in the emptying aftermath.[26]

The night of the mini-riot at the Mutualité, Gide found himself badly shaken. The next day, he sought an audience with the Soviet ambassador. The interview was refused. The morning after that, terribly agitated, Gide rose early and prepared the first draft of an exceptionally shrewd letter of protest to the ambassador. Gide was careful not to take Serge's part in anything. The letter was, if anything, too courtly. Gide limited himself merely to pointing out the "feebleness" of the Soviet response to the questions about Serge. That feebleness, he said, had left the partisans of the USSR "fatally disarmed and disabled" before its critics.[27]

That evening, Gide read this draft to assembled friends. Alix Guillain, a high-level Stalinist journalist and the wife of perhaps the most influential left-wing academic in France, attacked Gide's letter with all the angry puritanism of her kind. Couldn't Gide see that Serge's defenders were the merest *poseurs?* Just *think* what the enemies of socialism could do with the talk about friends of the Soviet Union being "disabled and disarmed"; Just *think* of how they would twist and distort those words.[28]

Gide listened carefully, said little, and the next day rejected Alix Guillain's advice. The next day he again rose early and personally delivered the letter to the Soviet Embassy.

It is testimony to the importance Stalin assigned to Gide's role in the Popular Front in France that six months later, Victor Serge was released from the gulag. According to Robert Conquest this was "the almost unique occasion on which foreign opinion was able to influence Stalin."[29]

What can be the real reason for this anomaly? The Soviet Union was about to make a really serious move for a large new measure of control in the French government. Some of the move would be accomplished by covert agents; much would be plain to all. The educated classes in France would need to be convinced that this new communist influence was right and wise; and since the French Revolution the French educated classes had been used to giving an exceptional moral deference, not to their government leaders, and not to the Church, but to some pre-eminent literary doyen. Stalin of course could never understand this simple truth, but Radek certainly understood it with complete clarity. France was the land of Voltaire. That deference to the doyen was basic to the sociology of the French elite; It was a habit learned in the *lycée.* As that doyen, Gide was essential to the credibility of the new policy. And Gide knew it. Despite all his agitation before unfolding events, he seems to have taken a remarkably accurate measure of the power which he now found in his grasp, power far beyond that of any literary man of his era.

The next year, Gide would at last consent to make a tour of the Soviet Union. By then, the Popular Front government of Léon Blum, riddled with Soviet agents, was in power, and Gide had been an honored guest at its installation. And by then, the secret service intrigue around the French writer would focus not on Victor Serge, who had been released, but on the mysterious death, perhaps the murder, of Maxim Gorky himself.

Like Gide, Maxim Gorky took his role as an unacknowledged legislator of mankind with ardent seriousness—but unlike Gide, Gorky approached his task not as a fellow traveller but as a genuine revolutionary. Gorky's role in the Revolution dated back as far as Lenin's own. As a writer, Gorky had come to fame early. At the turn of the century, he was one of the most celebrated writers in Russia, and by 1901 his seditious works had got him into fairly serious trouble with the Tsarist regime. By 1905, Gorky had met Lenin and was a committed Bolshevik. He was in fact probably the most famous Bolshevik in the Party. As a friend of Tolstoy, he made a bridge between Russian high culture and the underground of conspiratorial cells, contributing financially to Lenin's operations, enmeshed in the Party's secret fiscal networks. Meanwhile, his own fame spread.[30] Maxim Gorky was not among those artists made by the Revolution. On the contrary, he helped to make it.[31]

And when the Revolution came, he took up the grand task of creating a new culture for the new Soviet man with a pompous provincial grandiosity which might be touching if one could somehow overlook the damage done in its name. Gorky was most unlike Gide in his grandiosity. He had none of Gide's irony, none of his feeling for the private life, none of his taste for ambiguous things. Gide may have taken up the mantle of Zola, but he had tossed it over his shoulders at a loose rakish angle, and wore it with a smile that showed his sense that the "theater of conscience," though important, also had its absurd side.

The relation of Maxim Gorky to Lenin and the senior leadership of the Bolshevik Revolution is a tragic pantomime of the bond between culture and power. When Lenin assumed office, Gorky saw his own place as the voice of the Revolution's humanity, which he proposed to balance against the role of Lenin, whom he saw as the very voice of power. Gorky seems to have viewed himself as the indispensable counterpart to Lenin: goodness to the dictator's strength. If Lenin was to be the new creator and destroyer, Gorky would plead the cause of humanity before this great and final avatar of power.

Precisely this fantasy, in my view, led Gorky into moral bankruptcy. It was also the living paradigm for ten thousand tiresome art-and-politics debates to come, along with the culture congresses and symposia that orchestrate them. These form a large recurrent phenomenon in Western culture for which Gorky's notion of his personal bond to Lenin provides some sort of originating inspiration. Inevitably, during the thirties, Gorky was the patron saint of the countless gatherings devoted to this pseudo-theme. And yet Gorky was a very intelligent man, and not easily deceived. His insight into Lenin's character was sharp. Richard Pipes cites Gorky quoting, without comment, a Frenchman who had called Lenin a "thinking guillotine," and also cites Gorky on the subject of Lenin's misanthropy: "He loved people. He loved them with obligation. His love looked far ahead, through the mists of hatred."[32]

"His love looked far ahead, through the mists of hatred." Gorky had many opportunities to witness that hatred at first hand. He was the house humanist among the Bolsheviks; in this role, he frequently went to Lenin pleading for the lives of various condemned souls. He later wrote that Lenin seemed always a little perplexed during these meetings, as if he found it difficult to grasp why the life of any individual was worth the time and effort. It is not that Lenin thought the people about to be shot were either good or bad. He failed to see how their life or death mattered at all.[33]

We might speculate a little about the psychology of this exchange between Gorky and Lenin. In his chosen role as the Revolution's intercessor, Gorky must have been at least partly repelled by the cold-blooded system on whose altar he laid his appeals. But isn't it possible, even likely, that he was also attracted as well? That he was excited and moved by the awesome spectacle of the Revolution's omnipotent indifference to the "trifling" decencies of justice? Otherwise, why would any artist of Gorky's standing have been so devoted to playing this role? It became a quite explicit part of Bolshevik mythology; in sentimental propaganda films of the period, Gorky is repeatedly shown worshipfully pleading the case of the people before Lenin. It seems to me that Gorky must indeed have been drawn to this part, just as I suspect a very similar unacknowledged attraction to Terror motivating Theodore Maly. Here are two men, Gorky and Maly, who cannot be called "bad" in any simple sense. On the contrary, both were exquisitely riddled with conscience. Is it not possible that both were stirred up by their very distaste to a kind of sacred awe, not before the goodness of the new Leninist deity but precisely its savage indifference to goodness?

If ambiguity like that touched Gorky's feeling for Lenin, what must he have felt for Stalin? The results were appalling. Trying to continue in his classic role with Stalin, Gorky was soon reduced to moral abjection.[34] But it was abjection divided between servility and secret rebellion, as if the cunning spirit of his peasant past had been revived. Gorky was an obedient servant of the Revolution. He loved the Revolution. He believed in its truth. He gladly spouted its Lie. Yet he was serious in his role as "conscience." He "sincerely" tried to defend the victims of the regime. He used his prestige with all the finesse, and more, that Gide brought to his. And near the end, his rebellion grew. Imprisoned in the servile splendor of his mansion outside Moscow, he plotted his counter-moves against the savage god.

Lenin had only limited patience for this game. Early on, Gorky had been a highly visible personality in Lenin's government. But by 1921, at which time the dictator seems to have grown weary of Gorky's fractious devotion and high-flown pleas, he determined to put some distance between himself and the writer. He ordained that Gorky proceed abroad, where his argumentative conscience would help sustain precisely the illusions that Münzenberg was trying to generate. It was one of the best times of Gorky's life. Abroad, Gorky was sought out by the whole Russian intelligentsia, both communist and non-communist. He knew them, invited them into his household, talked and argued with them at length. His life was filled with the flow of foreign gossip, opinion, and commitment. People who would have feared him in Russia came to like and trust him abroad. He was given many confidences, some of which, perhaps even many, were politically dangerous confidences.[35]

Gorky saw himself as a humanist of Revolution, not its *agent provocateur*. Nonetheless, it was Gorky's habit to make extensive notes of these conversations, strictly for his own purposes, and not the Cheka's. These notes became in effect a high-level archive of Russian opinion abroad.[36]

In 1931, the time came for Gorky to make his return to Russia. Though Stalin and Gorky had not got on well during the twenties, the dictator was now disposed to lavish on Gorky everything the Soviet world could offer any writer. Gorky was to have a central position in the new culture. With his return to Moscow, he became the object of what amounted to a kind of literary "cult of personality," which was in certain ways parallel to Stalin's own. Gorky had always lived with every privilege the regime had to offer. He was now installed in something close to grandeur. He was supplied with a palatial country estate and a town house in Moscow. His works were published in huge editions and made obligatory reading. The apparatus at home and abroad treated him as one of the leading geniuses in the history of humanity. Cities, streets, and squares began to be named after him in almost mindless profusion. Gorky's original vision of his role reached a kind of grotesque fulfillment. He was the central literary icon in the Stalinist world.

At the same time, Gorky himself seemed to pass through a dismaying change. He was becoming an utterly reliable spokesman for the regime in all its squalor.

Had Gorky indeed after 1931 lost the small saving grace of his old ambiguities? Had he entirely succumbed to the Lie?

Perhaps not. Consider, for example, the curious tale of his suitcase.

The story of Gorky's suitcase has been recounted in detail by Mme. Nina Berberova, above all in her absorbing book on Gorky's mistress and translator, the Baroness Moura Budberg.[37] That is a book which has its respectable critics; nonetheless Berberova's remarkable tale is sustained by serious evidence, not least of all her own experience as an intimate of Gorky's household, both in Petersburg before 1921, and in Europe before Gorky made his grand return ten years later. It includes a meticulously researched account of Moura Budberg's role in Gorky's life, first in Russia before 1921, then abroad until 1931, and even afterward, when Gorky had returned to Russia, and until his death in 1936.

When Stalin called Gorky back for his triumphant return to Russia, the question arose as to what should be done with the seething records he had made in all his contacts with Russians abroad.

Here is Mme. Berberova's recollection.

Gorky was very clear that archives of this sort could not, under any circumstances, return with him to Russia. Indeed, his behavior over this archive seems to show that in 1931 he clearly understood that his return to Russia meant that he would be willingly ending the intellectual and artistic freedom he'd enjoyed abroad, and that in future his life would be subject to full totalitarian scrutiny. According to Mme. Berberova, as Gorky prepared to vacate his villa in Capri, he went through his entire body of papers, culling out every scrap that might compromise himself or others in Soviet eyes. Berberova herself assisted him in the task. He then packed all the assembled dangerous documents into one solidly filled suitcase, which he closed and belted shut.

This suitcase, Gorky determined, would be left behind, in the hands of some reliable custodian whom he trusted completely. He carefully explained to those around him that the suitcase was to remain in the West, and not be returned to the Soviet Union even if he himself asked, demanded, that it be brought back to him. If at any time anyone heard such a request made either by him personally, or in his name, they should totally disregard it, and deem it false on its face.

And to whom was this suitcase filled with lethal documents to be entrusted? After much internal debate, Gorky decided to put it into the hands of his consort and companion, the Baroness Budberg.[38]

The allegiances, or lack of them, which motivated the Baroness Moura Budberg represent one of the true personal mysteries generated in the Revolution's saga of betrayal and loss. Whom did Moura really love? Whom did she really serve? There is no simple answer, and in fact the life story of this extraordinary mythomaniac challenges the simplicity of the word "real." Mme. Berberova plainly regards the Baroness as one of her "Kremlin Ladies," of the treacherous company that also included the

Princess Koudachova and Elsa Triolet. In my presence, Mme. Berberova has referred to Moura Budberg as a "double agent"—meaning that Moura served both the Soviets and the British Foreign Office—and that is also what I take to be the purport of her fascinating book, though it is a book with its own mysteries.

Moura Budberg was raised in the middle regions of Moscow "society" during the reign of the last Tsar. She married very young, and married up: to an untitled member of the aristocratic Benckendorff family, with whom she had two children. Her husband was in the Tsar's foreign service in Berlin and London; at his side, even before 1917, she had fully embarked on her career as the grand cosmopolitan she would remain until the end of her life.

But Moura's principal career was as a survivor, albeit a survivor at the top. During the Revolution, her husband was murdered by a mob in Latvia; their children barely escaped with their lives, and were separated from her. In Petersburg, the young and terrified widow sought and got the protection of Robert Lockhart, who in 1917 and 1918 was the most important Western diplomat and British secret agent in Russia. She and Lockhart became lovers, and though Moura incidentally married a Baltic Baron in what was strictly a legal charade (though through it she procured her title), the really important man in Moura's life during the Revolution was Lockhart.[39]

At the end of 1917, in the midst of the conspiracies and intrigues surrounding Lenin's maneuvers toward the Treaty of Brest-Litovsk and his response to the allied landings at Arkangelsk, Lockhart was trapped in a provocation exploited by Dzerzhinsky, perhaps abetted by Sidney Reilly. Lockhart and Moura were arrested simultaneously on grave, highly inflammatory charges. That they both would be shot, and shot soon, seemed plain.[40]

But they were not shot. They were released.

Why they were released remains a matter of conjecture. We do know that while the couple was being held in the Kremlin itself, the man in charge of their imprisonment was a handsome but murderous and fanatical onetime London tailor named Jakov Peters, and that Peters was deep in the mysterious events that followed.

Mme. Berberova obviously believes that Lockhart and Moura were released because Moura successfully seduced Peters, that he became infatuated with her, and that by manipulating his jealous feelings, the Baroness negotiated the deal. Perhaps. Whatever happened, it cannot have been a trifling business. Lockhart was released and returned to London. Moura was also released. But Moura remained behind.

It was at this point that the Baroness entered the life of Maxim Gorky. She was sent to live as a "secretary and translator" in his vast apartment in Petersburg. She soon became a central figure in his large and complex household. Gorky plainly conceived a passion for her which endured for the rest of his life, first in Russia, then in Berlin and Capri. It lasted until the end, when Moura was living with H. G. Wells in London, and Gorky called for her from his deathbed.[41]

Was it real love? Like many mythomaniacs, Moura Budberg seems to have believed that she could not afford or even physically survive any too-rigorous distinction between the real and the unreal. There may have been real love between Gorky and the Baroness; at the same time, most witnesses believe she manipulated Gorky's emotions with great calculation. Here Nina Berberova's account should be supplemented with that of Anthony West, the son of H. G. Wells and Rebecca West, to whom Moura in later years was virtually a stepmother. According to West, early in their love Moura turned to Gorky, all tears, and made her "confession." She had not been sent to him as a simple translator and secretary. She was a police spy. She had saved her own life by submitting to this job, this mission: spying on him. Zinoviev, the unspeakable Zinoviev, controlled her. Zinoviev was trying to discredit Gorky in Lenin's eyes. And now she was caught; she loved Gorky, and yet she was their prisoner.

West claims that Gorky was greatly moved by this confession. He regarded it as proof of Moura's love. Instead of shattering Gorky's trust in her, it confirmed it, and he only loved her more. Moura believed in *him;* it was proof that she had risked the vengeance of the *apparat* by telling him the truth. Meanwhile, his new trust provided Moura with permanent protection against exposure. Nobody could tell Gorky anything about Moura that she herself had not long since confided in him.

In 1920, this sexual story repeated itself with a new man. During that year, H. G. Wells, whom Moura had already met in England through the British Russophile Maurice Baring, arrived as a guest in Gorky's household in Petersburg. During this visit, Moura seduced Wells and entered into what became a lifelong liaison with him. According to Anthony West, Moura made the same "confession" to Wells that she'd made to Gorky. It had much the same effect on Wells, binding him to her only more deeply.[42] There exists a photograph of the three of them together. In it, Gorky looks in warm camaraderie at Wells, while with rather heavy lids Wells takes in Moura, and for her part Moura tosses the camera a look of undeniable Russian allure.

Years later, Wells confronted Moura when an unexpected series of events proved to him that Moura remained in frequent contact with the

Soviet apparatus long after he believed she had ended her relations with Zinoviev and his minions. When he confronted her, she told him that "as a biologist, he had to know that survival was the first law of life." Had she lied? Yes, she had lied: She had wished to live, and in staying alive she had paid "the going price." Did Wells not like it? He would have to take her as she was.[43]

West came to believe that his father's last years were poisoned by his recognition that even though he clearly saw his mistress's falsehood and opportunism, he could not bring himself to do without her. Loving Moura in her special dishonesty as he once had loved her in what he'd believed was her special truth, Wells stayed with her to the end.[44]

But all three men—Lockhart, Gorky, and Wells—loved Moura to the end. Gorky called for her on his deathbed. Lockhart continued to love her and never lost contact with her. Perhaps even Peters, the secret policeman at the center, kept the flame. We will never know. Stalin had him shot in the mid-1930s.

When Gorky returned to Russia in 1931, Moura remained behind, and stayed with Wells. Between 1931 and 1935, Gorky's relations with Stalin, despite occasional strains, had been warm. For example, Stalin was a quite regular visitor to Gorky's house—as was the head of the NKVD, Yagoda.[45] But by 1934, Gorky had begun to irritate Stalin with pleas for moderation. The events of 1935 deepened the rift until at last, with Stalin's awareness of Gorky's suspicions, above all about the Kirov murder, their personal relationship came to an end.[46]

But there seems to have been another, more private, dimension to Gorky's mistrust of Stalin. Six months before Kirov was shot, Gorky's own son Max had died unexpectedly, and in circumstances that everyone thought very odd. In contrast to his father, young Max was a systematic lightweight. Conscience of the Revolution? Voice of humanity? Max loved liquor, racing cars, and fun. He had a pretty wife, and two of his favorite drinking pals were his father's physician, a Dr. Levin, and his father's secretary, a man named Kryuchkov. Both these men were agents of the NKVD. Both were under Yagoda's discipline. But besides mere political surveillance, Yagoda had a quite particular and personal interest in the Gorky household, in which he was a regular visitor. For it seems that Yagoda was having an intensely passionate love affair with Max's pretty wife.[47]

And then Max strangely died. The manner of Max's death was that following a bender with his friends the NKVD agents in May 1935, the young man passed out in the springtime snow, and was brought in with pneumonia. Placed under Dr. Levin's care, he did not recover.

In 1938, when the Great Terror was nearing the end of its vast course, Stalin undertook publicly to rid himself of this same Dr. Levin and of secretary Kryuchkov in a show trial that claimed that they had conspired, with their evil master Yagoda, in the murder of both Maxim Gorky and his son Max. They of course confessed, and of course they were convicted and executed.[48]

It is still impossible to prove that either Maxim Gorky or his son was in fact actually done to death by the *apparat*, though among most informed observers suspicions are profound and persistent. Did Yagoda order Max killed? For us, the important issue is less the truth of this suspicion than whether Gorky *thought* his son might have died in such a way. The thought that Yagoda might have been behind the death of his son, compounding his doubts about the Kirov killing, all added to his own obviously faltering health, and might have made Gorky feel that as the voice of the Revolution's conscience, he had very little left to lose.

In any case, six months after young Max died his death from "pneumonia," an enfeebled but still combative Maxim Gorky publicly defended one of those charged in the Kirov murder—Kamenev, who was in fact already designated as victim number one in the Terror to come. This was when Stalin dropped Gorky as honorary chairman of the Mutualité Congress. Attacks on the writer began to appear in the Soviet press. Meanwhile, in complete secret, Gorky had begun a manuscript attacking the regime. He had it with him in his house outside Moscow, and that he could work on it and keep it hidden from the police spies who surrounded him on every side is in itself testimony to his cunning. Spies like Kryuchkov read every letter, received every telephone call, typed every tremulous manuscript page. Even so, it seems that Gorky managed to conceal his new work in some obscure corner of that huge manor house. The NKVD only found the offending pages by tearing the place apart after his death. In his embittered and enfeebled last days, the dying David of the proletariat, his son dead, his dream reduced to squalor, was accumulating a little horde of rocks, hidden from Goliath.

The spies in Gorky's household did not find his manuscript before he died, but they did know about the suitcase, and of course so did Stalin.

The same summer of the Paris Congress, Gorky's wife Ekaterina Pavlova Pechkova (a woman who was herself an agent of the NKVD),[49] while on a trip to Western Europe paid a call on Moura Budberg in London, where Moura was then living with H. G. Wells. During their talk, Pechkova politely but firmly asked—demanded, really—that Gorky's archives be returned to Russia. Moura treated this request by Gorky's wife exactly as Gorky had told her to. To the other woman's outrage, the Baroness politely but flatly refused.

But that was not the end. According to Berberova's account, one year later, during the spring of 1936, when Gorky was near death, Moura received a second visitor from Russia. This time her emissary was a woman who was obviously an empowered agent of the NKVD. She arrived bearing a letter from Gorky himself, in which the dying writer begged Moura to come to Russia one last time and bid him farewell. The letter said nothing about the suitcase. It contained only its unrefusable last request.[50]

There were, however, certain conditions attached to this visit. The NKVD agent explained them with cold care. First, the agent herself would accompany Moura on every moment of her journey both to Moscow and the return to London. Second, the trip would be made in absolute secrecy. Third, their mode of travel would be established by the service. The two women would take an ordinary train to the Finnish-Soviet border, where they would be met by a special train with a private railroad car prepared for them at Stalin's express command. In it, they would travel together to Moscow.

Last and most important of all, Moura was to bring with her the suitcase with Gorky's archives. It was to contain every paper of Maxim Gorky that was in Budberg's possession.

The Baroness gave no answer. She was frightened and needed advice. She may also have felt she needed protection. As soon as she could, Moura arranged a confidential meeting with her old friend Robert Lockhart, who was still very much a figure for the British services. Though he did not offer British protection, Lockhart's advice was firm and perhaps even sound. Clearly, he said, the NKVD wanted Gorky's papers, and wanted them very badly. What they wanted, they probably would get. Moura's first response, her simple "No" to Pechkova, would no longer suffice. By fair means or foul, in Russia or out, the apparatus was going to take possession of those papers. Either Moura would hand them over and do exactly as she was told, or the NKVD would take them, using its own methods. She was being offered a choice within choicelessness. Lockhart in effect advised Moura Budberg to surrender.[51]

She did. Covered under a veil of secrecy which she maintained for the rest of her life, Moura Budberg left London accompanied by her companion from the NKVD. They travelled just as she had been told they would travel, and as they travelled Moura was carrying Gorky's suitcase. When she arrived in Moscow, she was immediately escorted to Gorky's country estate. There, before she was taken to Gorky's sickroom, she was met by Voroshilov, a prime commissar, and Stalin himself, and Moura put the suitcase directly into the dictator's own hands.[52]

The story of André Gide's much manipulated and spied-upon journey to the USSR has been told many times, and told in the first instance by Gide himself in the book he published in September 1936, *Retour à l'U.R.S.S.,* the document with which the old mandarin at last out-maneuvered the *apparat.*[53] It was an attack on the entire Soviet system. Pierre Herbart later described the scene in Spain, in the first months of the Civil War, when he took the galleys to Mikhail Koltsov in his bivouac. The agent was handed the proofs of the *Retour*. Koltsov complacently flipped them open and began to read. After a few moments, he started in shock. He began to turn the pages faster, in agitation. Attack! Gide had written an attack! The expression on his face was pulling into one of rage defined by fear.[54]

Koltsov, incidentally, was not only one of the agents supervising the manipulation of Gide. He was also one of the visitors whose thoughts had been confided to Gorky. Koltsov later perished in the gulag. It may have been at the moment he first glimpsed what Gide had written, he also glimpsed his own fate.

But in June 1936, despite repeated warnings to Münzenberg by (among others) the Count and Countess Karolyi that Gide would never be a reliable fellow traveller, Gide at last agreed to embark, with a retinue of distinguished French intellectuals, on the grandest propaganda tour of all. The apparatus gave Gide the highest priority; They obviously viewed him as indispensable to the Popular Front in France. Gide was greeted everywhere by rapt officials and huge trumped-up crowds. No excess of ingratiation, no form of flattery was spared.

Travelling with him and his retinue was also Pierre Herbart. The cat and mouse of all this was growing arcane. Somewhere along the way, somewhere in his own secrecy, Gide was reaching his own decision to turn against the apparatus. When did he reach this decision? How did he reach it? In Russia, he gave every appearance of being the perfect dupe. Four months later, he produced an important and even noble anticommunist book. However he reached the change, it seems he probably reached it in conjunction with Herbart. The moment, or more likely sequence of moments in which he turned against the system must be left to the imagination. Only traces of the turn have been left for scholarship. It is plain that two months after Gide returned from his Soviet trip, while he was at work on his account, the watchful *apparat* was fully convinced that the book would be totally supportive of the Popular Front. Accordingly, they arranged to make it the bestseller of the year, the flagship book of that phase. But somewhere, somehow along the way, Gide secretly emerged from his pilgrimage of lies. That pilgrimage itself was one in which the most powerful moment, and the low point, had been the death and funeral of Maxim Gorky.

By May 1936, Gorky was obviously dying. That was the time that Moura received the emissary demanding her return and the suitcase. She seems to have arrived in early June, as Gorky lay deathly ill in his country mansion, immobilized by his age, and his long, losing struggle with tuberculosis and a steadily more grave heart condition. At Stalin's command, a highly publicized vigil had been mounted around the country house, a deathwatch supervised by the NKVD. This had a dual purpose. One was propagandistic: Stalin wanted Gorky's death to be world news, the death of the father of socialist realism, an agony in praise of the regime. The other was for security: to see to it the old man said nothing before he died.

It was likewise indispensable that Gorky die on schedule. Stalin had long since set the month of August as the moment when the Terror would be unleashed in full force. It was therefore essential that the conscience of the Revolution be safely entombed, at the very latest, by the end of July. Fortunately that could easily be arranged.

On May 31, 1936, Gorky's doctors (including the bibulous Dr. Levin) assured Stalin that the writer was certain to die soon, soon. Plainly, the dictator no longer needed to fear that any disagreeable prose would be flowing from Gorky's pen. Unfortunately, imminent death did not entirely dispose of the problem. Gorky might not be able to write, but the old boy could still talk. Worse yet, he was trying to talk, constantly asking to see visitors, especially famous foreign visitors, people who would be listened to in the West. There was something he wanted to say. Something important.

The original plan for aligning the Popular Front with the Terror had included an English replay of the Mutualité Congress to be held in London during May. Mikhail Koltsov and Ilya Ehrenberg were once again to be in charge, and almost all of Gide's travelling companions, along with such celebrities as Elsa Triolet and Louis Aragon, were expected to be in attendance. Another honored guest was to have been the celebrated translator, companion of Russian writers, and friend to Russia abroad, Moura Budberg. But when Gorky became really seriously ill on May 31, plans changed.

Koltsov and Ehrenberg now turned their skills to deathbed politics, the diplomacy of the sickroom corridor, played in the Stalinist key. Who, if anyone, was to stand by Gorky's bedside? And when?

Their tactics were pushed by the needs of the Popular Front, and pulled by the Terror. To promote the Front, Gorky's dying scene, as in some grandiose history painting, must seem to make the grieving world of enlightened Western culture gather round. But to protect the Terror Gorky had to be kept quiet. So Koltsov and Ehrenberg were assigned a job: to preoccupy the great and famous with Gorky's dying, while preventing anyone from reaching his bedside prematurely.[55]

Meanwhile, the effects of the Popular Front on European politics had initiated the intended, and some unintended, havoc. Léon Blum's Popular Front government was installed on June 6, 1936. Within days, strikes were spreading across the country. Gide would leave for Moscow from a Paris all but paralyzed by labor unrest. At the same time a Popular Front government in Spain, prodded by Otto Katz's close friend and associate Julio Alvárez del Vayo, had been careening toward the crisis that in July would break out as the quintessential event of the entire Popular Front: the Spanish Civil War.[56]

The push-pull of this situation began to be felt in Gide's life. The resulting dance had its tragicomic side. Four days after Blum became premier of France, Ilya Ehrenberg had dinner with André Gide and informed him that Gorky was very ill and about to die. He urged Gide to put aside everything and prepare to leave for Moscow immediately. Forget the London Congress; hurry to Russia to see the old man before he expired. Gide agreed. That night, he began urgent preparations.[57]

The next day Gide's apartment was filled with people helping him prepare to leave that very day. Humorless and intense, Gide was frantically packing, struggling to maintain order as he readied himself to leave within hours. Meanwhile, in Moscow Gorky had taken a sudden turn for the better. The old man had rallied. He no longer seemed moribund. While he was plainly still a sick man, he suddenly seemed to be doing quite well.[58]

. . .

The French writer Jean Malaquais, who was present that day, recalled that at around 2 o'clock that afternoon the phone rang in Gide's apartment. The room, filled with all Gide's entourage, fell silent. Something had happened. Perhaps Gorky had died. Malaquais picked up the phone.

"It's the eye of Moscow," Malaquais said, mock sinister, to the listening room. There was mild laughter as Gide took the phone. The caller was in fact Ilya Ehrenberg, explaining that despite yesterday's urgency, there had been a sudden change. Gorky was better. Much, *much* better. In fact there was now no hurry at all. This precipitate rush to Moscow was really quite unnecessary. In fact it would be far, far more convenient if the visit did not take place right now at all. Gorky would be all right, and in fact a later date was much to be preferred.[59]

Gide listened. When he hung up the phone, the room was waiting.

Was Gorky dead?

"C'est remis," Gide answered, dryly. ("It's been put off.") The room burst into gales of laughter.

Ehrenberg had in fact presented Gide with a new timetable for his arrival in Moscow. Ehrenberg explained that everything had been worked out quite carefully. The ideal date for Gide now to arrive would be, he said, June 18.[60]

Was Maxim Gorky murdered by Stalin? We do not know. But we do know that Maxim Gorky breathed his last about two hours after Gide's plane touched down in Moscow. It was the late afternoon of June 18. Exactly.[61]

The same sinister shuffle between urgency and delay over Gorky's deathwatch was danced by Louis Aragon and Elsa Triolet, with Koltsov rather than Ehrenberg as their guide. Little though they liked Gide, Aragon and Triolet had been much involved in planning his trip, and they were among those whom Gorky was asking to see. Earlier that spring, Ehrenberg had warned the obedient Elsa away from any too precipitate visit to the dying master's bedside. In June, when the old man's demise became international news, the French couple thought it best to give at least the appearance of hurrying to his side. They actually visited Elsa's sister Lily Brik, who actively encouraged them to delay in Leningrad as long as possible, apparently consciously detaining them.[62]

When Koltsov at last arranged to drive Aragon and Triolet to the estate, he knew Gorky was about to die, though en route, he flattered them with the information that Gorky himself had demanded they be brought to him "the moment they arrive."[63]

The moment they arrive? They had quite intentionally been delayed for days. On the afternoon of June 18, as Gide's plane was touching down in Moscow, Koltsov pulled up before the gates of Gorky's country mansion. At the gates, they were refused admission by the guards. While their chauffeur argued with the gatekeepers, Dr. Levin appeared. Of course the physician was given immediate entry. The French delegation watched him go in. Then they fretted, until a short while later, Levin re-emerged, and Koltsov approached him. The secret agent and the NKVD physician talked quietly together for a few moments. Then Koltsov turned to Aragon and Triolet in tears to say that Gorky was dead.[64]

The national mourning around Gorky's death included a huge state funeral in Red Square. A speech by Gide was to be featured. It was an important part of Popular Front strategy that the leading representative of European literature be on the podium.

Gide and Pierre Herbart (the other writers in Gide's party were still in London, or en route) had been installed in the Hotel Metropole, and there he prepared for his prime appearance of the tour. Koltsov was very much the organizer of this aspect of the event, and it was through Koltsov that Herbart was instructed to pass on to Gide what it was thought would be an appropriate approach in his talk. The subject was to be the fate of the adversary culture under the Revolution. Koltsov suggested the approach deal in a theory of what he called "currents" as opposed to "countercurrents." Put simply, this view was that outside the Soviet Union, outside the land of the Revolution, conscious and enlightened people should be prepared always to go "against the current." Inside the Soviet Union however, because of the triumph of the Revolution, opposition ceased to be admirable or even admissible, and the impulses of adversary culture should be suspended. Inside the Soviet Union, the duty of the intelligent was to go *with*, not against, the current. Because the adversary culture had triumphed in Russia, opposition no longer had any place. See? Simple.

Inside his room at the Hotel Metropole, Gide went to work preparing a speech devoted to this theme. At his side was Herbart.

A word about Gide's relation to Herbart. It seems to me quite possible that the story of Gide's break with the apparatus is somehow enclosed within the untold story of what happened in this relationship during 1936. It is plain that Koltsov and Münzenberg viewed Herbart as an obedient servant of Stalinism. It is likewise plain that despite Pierre Herbart's many weaknesses as a person, they were not entirely correct in that assessment. Herbart had spent the end of 1935 and the first months of 1936 in Moscow, preparing to be a propagandist, probably on much the same track as the Nizans. When he returned in May 1936 to act as Gide's escort to Moscow, it was plain to La Petite Dame that Pierre was no longer an uncritical admirer of the Stalinist state.[65] Pierre spent considerable amounts of time urgently confiding stories of governmental stupidity and cultural censorship to the master. As Gide's visit was arranged, she also became aware of something almost conspiratorial going on between the older and younger man. La Petite Dame, who prided herself on knowing everything, noted that they were now deep in long confidential conversations on subjects unknown to her. Shortly before the June departure, as she sat with Gide in a car while Pierre darted into a store to buy some cigarettes, Gide turned to Maria and said to her, rather mysteriously, "Pierre and I understand each other." And nothing more.[66]

Were the two of them moving toward a break even before the departure? The day before the funeral, June 19, Gide's work on his speech was suddenly interrupted by a knock on the hotel room door. It was opened, and before them stood, to Pierre's astonishment, none other than Nikolai Bukharin. Bukharin was slated to be one of the other speakers at the ceremony. He was already a man marked for destruction, and that destruction did not fail to come. Radek's show trial would lay the groundwork for his demise. It was the show trial in which agents Kryuchkov and Levin would also be tried and executed for the "medical murders" of Max Pechkov and Maxim Gorky himself. But on June 19, 1936, Bukharin, though stripped of power, was still one of the most important Bolsheviks alive, and Pierre at least knew it.

Gide was still deep in his speech, but Pierre immediately introduced him to this very grand personage, trying to convey his role in his introduction.

Gide made the author's assumption that Bukharin was interested in his speech and insisted on rehearsing some of its ideas for his guest. Using Koltsov's suggestion about the "currents" and "counter-currents," Gide summarized his oration—how Gorky with his genius for protest had been a force against oppression, and that indeed throughout the history of culture, that culture now so endangered by the fascist threat, artists had always played a more or less vigorous, more or less veiled, adversarial role. But with the Revolution, something essential in culture had changed. With its triumph, the artist was no longer the adversary of power. His voice now should be a voice of affirmation, sustaining the proletariat and above all its leadership, now that they had inherited the "calm and radiant triumph" which had been made possible by fighters like Gorky.

Gide looked at Bukharin, waiting for approval. Bukharin did not express his opinion. Instead he explained, in French, that he was very desirous of a private conversation with Gide. *Entirely* private.

He thinks I am a police spy, Herbart thought. "No, no," Gide hastily replied. Pierre is not *de trop*. You may speak freely, Comrade . . . Bunin."

Bunin? Bunin was a novelist and poet, a sometime friend of Gorky, not a Bolshevik at all. He was an emigré who had left the USSR well over a decade before.

It was an awful gaffe. It was worse. It was an error to cause despair. Bukharin stood in silence before Gide. Awareness and innocence stood staring at each other. A smile began to play over Bukharin's lips, a smile as Herbart later said, of "unspeakable contempt." He then backed out of the room without another word.[67]

The next day, Gide stood in Red Square and delivered his speech proclaiming the end of the adversary culture to a vast assembled crowd, rapt in mourning. On the high dais stood Stalin himself.

Not far from the dictator's side, in what many would have taken as the greatest honor life had to offer, stood the Baroness Moura Budberg.[68]

Chapter 10

The Spanish Stratagem

The creation of the Popular Front marked the beginning of the end for Willi Münzenberg. All through 1935, Willi's suspicions that the monster might turn its lethal wrath in his own direction still lay quiescent. He remained a major foreign communist. He still held great power. To judge by every appearance, he continued to be trusted. It is true that by 1935, his authority had begun to slip a little. For example, he was not put in charge of the Mutualité Congress. But it was not until a year later, in the middle of 1936, that Willi first began clearly to discern the shape of his real future under Stalin, and to know fear.

During the summer of 1935, a year before Maxim Gorky's demise and the commencement of the Terror, Babette Gross and Münzenberg arrived in Moscow to attend the great meeting which became the last world congress of the Comintern. The VIIth Congress of the Communist International was a brilliant and highly publicized affair, far more so than any previous Comintern congress had been. It took place in the grandeur of the Palace of Nobles, and Georgi Dimitrov, the hollow hero of the Reichstag Fire Trial, now installed in the equally hollow post of Comintern director, delivered the mendacious keynote address. It was on this occasion that Babette Gross glimpsed for the one time in her life the man who ruled her world, and in whose presence Willi had stood so often. Babette found herself on the grand staircase of the Palace of Nobles when suddenly the guards forced her to step back, and Stalin passed her by, a tiny little man, descending.

At the VIIth Congress of the Comintern the Popular Front was proclaimed. Here the assembled revolutionaries were presented with the tactics of the new "anti-fascism." Until now, communists had always been told to direct undiluted venom toward all non-communist anti-fascists, who were to be described as hypocrites, weaklings, and fools, little better than the fascists they falsely claimed to oppose. No more. Henceforth, all those until now reviled as "social fascists" would be flattered and embraced. Henceforth, anti-fascists of all stripes would find friends among the communists. The delegates listened in obedient disbelief. *Co-operate?* Here was the flat reversal of everything Lenin stood for. It contravened the whole hard heart of Revolution. It shrugged off the very principle of confrontational hatred to which everyone there had pledged their lives.[1]

Of course, their outrage had been anticipated; Dimitrov understood that the new line would have to be stroked into place. Revolutionary rectitude would need to be placated. The substance of his address was to reassure the delegates that he understood their surprise. But of course they must all clearly understand that the new policy only seemed to reverse their commitment. The new line was, of course, a lie. The Revolution, the true Revolution, had not been betrayed at all. If we communists talk for the moment about co-operating with the lackies of the capitalists, *naturally* we are deceiving them. He asked the delegates to recall the instructive tale of the Trojan Horse, that hollow offering of peace filled with death, left at the enemy's gates. Ponder the meanings of that gesture, comrades: There is the truth of our new front.[2]

Dimitrov was of course quite right: The Popular Front was always a lie, and a lie directed against the West. What Dimitrov did not bring to the delegates' attention, however, was the lie within the lie. For in fact, the death really lodged inside this Trojan Horse was not intended for the capitalists at all. The death hidden inside the horse was intended for the *delegates*. A significant number of the people then being given revolutionary reassurance in that marble hall were going to be themselves killed by the Terror hidden inside the noble and deceptive edifice of the Popular Front. Many were already marked. One of those many may well have been Münzenberg.

The atmosphere at the VIIth Comintern Congress, like the atmosphere in the whole city of Moscow that summer of 1935, was one of forced gaiety.

Yet already the disappearances and arrests of various communists known to Babette and Münzenberg were making people talk in whispers. One sunny afternoon, Babette sat at a table on the café terrace outside of the Hotel Metropole, with her friends Suzanne Leonhard and Sophie Liebknecht. A more highly placed trio of women among the ranks of foreign communists would have been hard to find. The conversation took a critical turn; there was disapproval of Stalin's new policies, complaint about the quality of life in the USSR. Hoping to lighten the mood, Babette broke in a line she intended to be a quip, a wisecrack. "Don't talk that way," she said. "You'll get us all arrested."

Joke. The line was intended as a joke. Nobody laughed. The three women sat in silence, and something in all their lives changed.

Such was summer innocence in 1935.[3]

But the real business of that summer did not take place in the Palace of Nobles at all. Every day Münzenberg was picked up at his hotel and driven to Comintern headquarters, where he began to be shown the true, unseen, and the new dispensation. Even though the VIIth Congress seemed to represent the apogee of Comintern power, and the Popular Front the culmination of Münzenberg's style of cultural politics, in fact the old system was being systematically dismantled from within. This had been in the works for some time. The Archives of the Central Party contain correspondence between Münzenberg and Dimitrov months before, in which Münzenberg complains of sabotage of his operations from within the Western European Bureau, and is obviously concerned enough to ask explicitly that he "be permitted to retain my functions."[4] The crisis he'd feared now came. In a series of covert actions and bureaucratic turns, the various functions of Lenin's creation were being silently usurped and put under the hidden but absolute control of the intelligence services and secret police. This was an exact bureaucratic reflection of the way the Popular Front was set up to mask the Terror.[5]

Workers International Relief? It was no more. Mezhropohmfilm Russ? The great production house of Soviet cinema, the home of Vertov, Eisenstein, Dovzhenko, vanished into the bureaucratic haze. The old fronts and their networks were to exist under new systems of control, with many of the operations displaced. In the new organizations, Willi would function as "liaison," or "advisor." Gibarti's World Committee for the Relief of the Victims of German Fascism would no longer serve. Despite its many achievements in disinformation and espionage, an entirely new front would now be required. It would be known as the *Rassemblement Uni-*

verselle Populaire, or "RUP." Willi would not be in charge of RUP. It would be run by an unctuous but rising young Rumanian secret service star named Louis Dolivet, a good, good friend of Otto Katz, trained in Willi's shop, and comfortably on the inside of the new arrangements. Dolivet would take the lead. Willi would "advise."[6]

At these meetings for secretly reshaping the International, two men in particular emerged as the new Moscow powers. They were perfect emblems of the moment. The first dealt with Willi on cultural politics and propaganda. This was the repellant Andrei Zhdanov. It was that famous man's first really important senior job. Zhdanov will be remembered as the most brutal of the many brutal people who, from this time until the dictator's death, ran Stalinist culture.[7] Zhdanov was the enforcer of the Terror in art; the secret policeman of socialist realism. When one hears about the horrors visited upon Soviet writers and artists during this period, when one thinks of the hell known to Mandelstam and Akhamtova and Meyerhold and all the uncountable others, it should be remembered that the presiding officer of their anguish was Zhdanov. Even Münzenberg, a man not easily startled, was startled by Zhdanov's gross crudity and virtually total ignorance of Europe. This was the man who would now instruct Münzenberg on all new aspects of Soviet cultural and propaganda policy, the man in charge of those policies during the heyday of communist cultural idealism.[8]

But the meetings were governed by a second even more powerful individual; though this man never himself appeared at the meetings. His directives were conveyed by others; his name was only invoked: "Comrade Moskfin." It may have seemed odd that "Moskfin" avoided the meetings, that he seemed never to be personally present. But so it was. His name was a strange one, faintly sinister, and to Münzenberg, new. "Comrade Moskfin?" It was unfamiliar. Yet by "Moskfin's" command, IWR was finished off; by "Moskfin's" order the assets of Mezhropohm-film Russ were made to disappear.[9]

And who was this Comrade Moskfin? Willi probably did not know that Moskfin was in fact Mikhail Trilliser, the director and founder of the foreign arm of the NKVD and now a senior figure in the GRU. He had come to embody, in fact, the interpenetration of all three services. And under this cover name, the NKVD and military intelligence were assuming functional but covert control of the International. Zhdanov and Moskfin-Trilliser: Here was the new age; here was the new cultural brutality; here was the covert but ubiquitous new role of the secret police. This was the power behind the mask.[10]

And so, when he returned to Paris that summer, Willi Münzenberg, though still a major figure in the apparatus, had been slightly demoted. He may have suspected, but could not have known, that he was marked for the end. He was a little disempowered. His new given tasks were to serve as the leading communist in the formation of the new Popular Front Fusion party of the German left in exile. This job had its real significance, and in it Münzenberg made many of the contacts with non-Stalinists in exile which would serve him three years later, when he himself was edging toward his own break. In addition, many of his old networks still worked under new names, and he remained close to them. Finally, he served as an advisor to Dolivet and RUP.[11]

The *Rassemblement Universelle Populaire* was the social and political instrument of the Popular Front in France.[12] It was not really run by the Comintern at all, but was linked to the apparatus by the Soviet trade unions. Münzenberg was to be its quiet eminence, a liaison with the Russians; not more. It had splendid headquarters on the rue de la Paix; the address was selected for its chic and its name: Paix. Here was the new rich look.

For the Popular Front was very much a matter of style—and in Paris RUP embodied that style. In America at the same time a similar shift occurred, in a move away from ''intellectual'' communism to the new style of the Hollywood fellow travellers. The charmless days of poverty were over. German exiles with their ragged, wearisome moral passions would no longer be the focus. RUP would be social; RUP would be chic; RUP would sport a touch of class. Dolivet was an ideal agent to place among the very rich. For one thing, crypto-communist or not, Dolivet quite unabashedly worshipped and adored anyone and everyone who was what Cole Porter used to call ''rich-rich.''[13] (After the war, Dolivet—then a confederate of Julio Alvárez del Vayo—married Michael Straight's sister Beatrice.) Dolivet was very suave; many thought ''oily'' the *mot juste*. The Swedish banker Olof Aschberg, a thoroughly reliable friend of the apparatus, would serve as RUP's master of ceremonies and financial manipulator. In Aschberg's mansion on the Place des Nations, grand receptions would greet the new age. Parisian money would gather. Elsa Triolet would write malicious novels about the goings-on.[14]

It was a look intended to wed high political righteousness to the drape of a sable coat, the Revolution with a perfect crease, confident with the easy aromatic grace that comes with a look of complete success. This was the heyday of Hollywood communism, the glamour left. Revolutionary congresses would no longer gather in grungy labor union auditoria: From now on Stalin's minions would assemble in Carnegie Hall.[15] Lillian Hellman would appear draped in mink to accept checks for Spanish relief.[16] The Hollywood fellow travellers were expected to look on top of the world, strolling on sloping lawns, and settling in for tinkling cocktails. Theirs was a wedding of the moralism of Lincoln Steffens with the chic of Scott Fitzgerald. On the West Coast, the marriage of Donald Ogden Stewart to Ella Winter made the new symbolism literal. The prevailing atmosphere is captured in Mary McCarthy's short story "The Genial Host," which, McCarthy herself pointed out, was based on a real evening in Lillian Hellman's circle, albeit with the genial hostess herself not depicted. The new taste for luxury was brought to absurdity in the array of champagne dinners and Rolls Royces assembled for a Writers' Congress in Spain at the height of the Civil War.[17] This was the communism of country houses, the anti-fascism of evening gowns. It was all that sparkled in the eyes of Elsa Triolet.

As this new style was taking shape, so was the Terror. In August 1936, eight weeks after the death of Maxim Gorky, Zinoviev, Kamenev, Smirnov—founding heroes of Leninism—were given their show trials, taken into the basement of the Lubyanka, and shot. It had begun.

About a month later Münzenberg was in Brussels with Louis Dolivet, doing some work for RUP. They happened to cross on the street an old friend of Willi, a Dutch Bolshevik who had broken with Stalin and become allied with Trotsky in exile. When he saw Münzenberg with Dolivet, knowing well of course that Willi was still deep in the service of the secret power, Sneevliet stepped directly into Münzenberg's path and said very loud, so everyone could hear: *"Cain, where is thy brother Abel-Zinoviev?"*

Münzenberg could not speak.[18]

Still, keeping silent over the death of "Abel-Zinoviev" was a mere matter of guilt. All the Bolsheviks, Münzenberg not least among them, were old hands at rationalizing guilt.

Fear, fear for their own lives, was something else again.

Shortly after his encounter with Sneevliet in October 1936, Willi was recalled to Moscow for further instructions. The archives show a letter from Dimitrov written a month before, proposing a wide array of new operations submitted for approval.[19] Münzenberg was obviously trying to shore up his position, demonstrate his usefulness. He was now asked to come to consider the results. He was asked to come with Babette. Though it was not usual to be asked to bring his wife, it was not unheard of. The couple went together, travelling somewhat anxiously.

Shortly after he arrived in Moscow, Willi was taken aside and told under conditions of the most absolute confidence that Karl Radek had been secretly arrested and was certain to be condemned.[20]

Willi must have held his breath. Radek arrested! Radek was not only Münzenberg's oldest partner in the apparatus, he was his patron at the highest levels of Soviet power. If the most witting agent of all had fallen, how far away was his turn?

Within days, Willi had evidence that his turn was very near. In that era, the prime instrument of ideological conformity within the Comintern was a body known as the International Control Commission. The ICC was a kind of star-chamber for the apparatus, used to arbitrate genuine problems, but much more significantly to enforce the line and rein in those who might from time to time become forgetful about obedience.

Incredibly, Münzenberg himself was now called before the International Control Commission.[21]

The charges raised against Münzenberg by the commission were alarming by virtue of their very flimsiness. He was charged with having been lax in vigilance. The Falangist mutiny in Spain had broken out two months before. Willi was accused of having permitted a "Franco spy," a typist named Liane, to infiltrate his office. Münzenberg almost laughed out loud. Liane? A Franco spy? He easily showed the Commission had entirely bolixed its facts about Liane. This, he told the commission, was "flea-killing."

But that of course was the problem. The commission didn't particularly care if its "facts" looked right or wrong. And they didn't retreat before Willi's scorn.

On this trip, Babette and Willi had been put up in a new hotel on Red Square: the Hotel Moskva. There they found themselves very much alone. Fear had descended generally all over Russia. Old Leninists were denouncing each other on every side. People were doing anything, anything to avoid arrest; anything, anything to prove their devotion to the regime. Nobody came to call. "After all," Babette said, "we might be among the damned."[22]

So they might. Unconcerned that Münzenberg had made monkeys of them over Liane, the International Control Commission called him back for a second appearance. And then a third.

Münzenberg now understood that his life was in direct and imminent danger. "They were preparing the noose," Babette wrote. "He now had only one idea. To leave Moscow as quickly as possible."[23]

But how could he leave Moscow? Willi knew he would have to negotiate his exit, and with his powers of negotiation rested his and Babette's single hope for salvation. And negotiate with what? Radek was gone. Willi's protector was as good as damned. With Radek condemned, his own prestige was turning to poison. Willi would have to buy out the place appointed for him in the impending purge, and he would have to buy it quickly. With what?

Spain. He would save himself with Spain.

At the very time that the ICC was interrogating him, Stalin for the first time ordered the Soviet Communist party to announce its public support for the Spanish communists in the Civil War.[24] Far more importantly, Stalin signed a secret order increasing the flow of volunteers and covert arms into the conflict.[25]

Yet Stalin absolutely insisted that this flow of arms and volunteers not appear to be connected directly to his government. He was particularly adamant in his demand that money for the Republic not come from Soviet banks. There was to be no Soviet credit for the Spanish Republic. The flow of arms and men would have to come from sympathizers in Europe and America: volunteers. This is where Willi saw his opportunity. He understood that the arms and cash and volunteers Stalin needed for his Spanish policy would have to come from the soft, sympathizing networks he had created. The new order could not be implemented without him. He—he and Otto Katz—had been essential to the covert arms supply and propaganda into Spain from the first days of Franco's rebellion.[26] Spain, Babette later wrote, was "the sheet anchor," and they clutched it to keep from being swept away.[27]

But could that anchor hold?

Münzenberg proceeded to Comintern headquarters for a meeting with Palmiro Togliatti, an Italian communist who was the senior man in charge while Dimitrov was away on vacation. Münzenberg used Stalin's new order to make his case. If the secret edict was to be implemented, Togliatti had better call off the ICC and let Münzenberg get back to work in Paris, because Willi alone could arrange the flow of arms and men without a clear link to Russia. If he absolutely had no choice, he would return from Paris to deal with the ICC—but later, later. Spain needed him now. Willi made this argument with all the force that had made him famous, and it seems to have worked. Togliatti appeared to take his point, and he promised to issue the exit order.[28]

Unfortunately orders from the Comintern no longer carried quite the same authority they once did. Willi returned to the Hotel Moskva. He and Babette prepared to leave immediately. Just at the moment of their departure, a knock at the door brought them their sole visitor. It was Heinz Neumann, Babette's brother-in-law, married to her sister Margarete, and a major figure in the German wing of the Comintern. He and Margarete lived in Moscow, at the Comintern's Hotel Lux. The archives show that Neumann's fall was linked to the fate of Münzenberg. Neumann and Münzenberg had sided together in the intra-party arguments of the German communists as far back as 1932 and the Amsterdam Congress. They usually had been opposed by Wilhelm Pieck and Walter Ulbricht, devoted enemies whom the files show systematically seeking Münzenberg's downfall over many years. As early as February 1935, the dossiers show Münzenberg interceding on behalf of his brother-in-law in a dossier labelled, ominously, "the Case of Heinz Neumann."[29] During the VIIth Congress, Neumann had been designated the fall-guy for the discarded "social fascist" policy, as a result of which he had been relieved of his once-exalted duties and was now working as a lowly translator in the German wing.

Heinz Neumann had come to say goodbye. The three of them talked, anxiously. Then the time for departure came, and in that awkward moment the unsaid obvious surfaced at last. They could not speak. Then Neumann broke down and wept. "We knew," Babette later said, "that we would never see each other again."[30]

Not many weeks later, the knock did indeed come in the middle of the night at the Neumann's room in the Hotel Lux. As Heinz was being taken away, Margarete began to weep. He turned to Margarete in the classic reflex of all husbands before a wife's tears. "Don't cry,"—but then he stopped himself. "Cry then," he said. "There's plenty to cry about." These were his last words to her. He was never heard of again.[31]

Margarete was herself arrested soon afterward. She was dispatched to the gulag, and during the war she would doubtless have perished there had Stalin not turned her over to his Nazi ally. Thus Margarete was transferred from the Communist camp at Karaganda to the Nazi camp at Ravensbrück, one of the many whom Stalin thought it would be slightly better to have the Nazis kill or imprison than himself.[32] There she became an intimate friend of Franz Kafka's great love Milena Jasenska.[33] Margarete managed to survive until the liberation of Ravensbrück in 1945. With the Nazi collapse, certain death threatened Margarete all over again. It appeared she might be "liberated" by the advancing Red Army, and thus fall into Stalin's hands once more. This time she could be sure he would not fail to finish her off. When the gates of the camp opened, she and a friend began to walk, walk, trying to get west. At last, bedraggled and exhausted, she came upon a small band of American soldiers who somehow had commandeered a horse and cart. "Get in," one of the soldiers said. "You've walked enough by the look of you. You're going to ride now." Suddenly it was over.[34]

But in that October of 1936, it was time for Willi himself to escape. Leaving Heinz Neumann behind, he and Babette proceeded to the train station. In those days, visitors to the Soviet Union surrendered their passports to the police upon entering the country and were given them again only when, and if, they were granted permission to leave. They reached the station, but "nobody came to hand us our passports with the exit visas and tickets."

Togliatti's command had never been issued. Or it had been brushed aside.

This seemed truly the end. Babette and Willi could return to the hotel or they could wander through the streets, surely under surveillance. They returned to the hotel. There they sat up in their room through the entire night, waiting for the arrest squad they were sure would come. But when at last the dawn came, the knock had not sounded.

With the dawn, Münzenberg knew that he had at best only one final chance to save himself and Babette. The moment he could, he left for Comintern headquarters and was ushered into Togliatti's office. There, according to Babette, he staged a "tremendous scene." We do not know what happened in this shouting, table-pounding encounter, but it must have been the performance of a lifetime, deploying every resource of persuasion or menace that Willi Münzenberg could possibly command. We know only that when he was through Togliatti, thoroughly cowed, white with fear, lifted the phone and issued the order for their exit visas in Münzenberg's presence. This time it worked.

They left that day.

Their journey home was not peaceful. Crossing the Baltic from Finland they were caught in a violent storm; for two days their ship was battered by the sea. Babette and Willi feared that if the ship took refuge in a port, it might be a Soviet port, and God knew what new dangers that might bring. The couple had begun their new life of peril. They would live it now every moment until the fall of France and Willi's death. For the moment, they at least had their lives, and they were at least on their way back to the West. And they had one thing more: As the Terror raged around them, they still had hold of their sheet anchor, the grappling device to hold them against the overwhelming killing current.[35]

Spain.

The tragedy of the Spanish Civil War, the political event *par excellence* of the Popular Front, has been analyzed and described many times by many able historians.[36] It would be out of place to summarize here the large historical arguments that surround the war. For our purposes, examining the role of secret service work in culture, it seems best to focus on one question and its consequences: the motives of Stalin and his government in the prosecution of that struggle.

It will be my hypothesis here that whatever else may have been involved, Stalin's motive in this terrible enterprise was *not* especially directed toward victory. My belief is that actually winning the Spanish War was always a quite secondary concern in Stalin's strategy. If one examines what Stalin did in Spain, bracketing aside all the fine rhetorical claims his apparatus made on the Republic's behalf, it soon becomes plain that his policy was never calculated to lead to victory or anything that resembled victory for his Spanish allies. On the contrary.[37]

To be sure, one might argue that the Spanish Republic went down to the defeat that was at last complete in March 1939, simply because Stalin was incompetent, a strategic idiot. This seems to me naive and mistaken. The fields of this century are white with the bones of those who underestimated the intelligence of Josef Stalin. Stalin's Spanish policy retains the appearance of being incompetent and self-defeating only so long as one assumes that the Soviet dictator genuinely wanted to win the war, that for some reason he felt a sincere desire for the left-wing Republican government to be the undisputed government of Spain. Yet why would he have wanted that? There are many things that can be won in a war besides victory. So it was, in my view, in Spain.

It is only when the dictator's actual interests have been correctly identified that Stalin's course of action suddenly becomes quite coherent. It was a classic Stalinist performance, shrewdly and successfully pursued. His aim, in my view, was not the victory of the Spanish Republic at all, but its use in a large geopolitical game which meant in fact organizing the Spanish defeat. That policy epitomized the triumph of the Popular Front in all its mendacity. It seems to me plain that Stalin wished to take possession of the Spanish government not to possess it himself, and still less to help the non-Stalinist left possess it. Stalin wanted to possess Spain so he could trade it away.[38]

Here is a quick summary of the course of political events.

Briefly put, in early 1936, a Popular Front government very much along the lines of the ones envisioned at the VIIth Congress of the Comintern took power in Spain, a coalition of the left, under the premiership of a non-Stalinist but *Marxisant* radical named Largo Caballero, a skillful but aging politician with a wide popular following, especially among the anarchistically inclined workers and peasants of northeastern Spain, in Catalonia and its capital Barcelona. Largo Caballero was an honorable man who understood his destiny in the light of the more vague dreams of the revolutionary left. He seems to have faltered into Stalinism, moved and flattered by the vanities of this dream, and he saw the Popular Front as his last chance to become the Mediterranean Lenin he hoped to be. He was certainly not a Stalinist, nor even a Communist in the narrow sense. In 1935 and 1936, the Communists were among the smallest and least-admired parties on the Spanish left. The really large left-wing faction was the anarchist wing, and this was Largo's political base. Of course, despite their small numbers, Stalinist operatives riddled Largo Caballero's government from top to bottom. *Apparat* ubiquitousness in his government was the standard stuff of the Popular Front. It was happening in London, Paris, and Washington too. But in Spain it was writ large.[39]

Once the new Popular Front government took office in Spain, the next phase of radicalization consisted of provocations and counter-provocations from both the left and the right. These were both spontaneous and covertly controlled; they sought destabilization of Spanish society and at the same time responded to it. They were appalling in their violence and cruelty, and they now became a standard feature of Spanish political life. The country became increasingly polarized, and was soon almost hysterically so.[40] Vast demonstrations filled the squares of Madrid; placards with Stalin's face became ubiquitous; the government itself became a vehicle for the rhetoric of revolution.[41] Meanwhile, the Spanish intelligentsia seemed entirely to succumb to the systematic blindness of "politicized" thought, drunk on the ideological elixir.

It was in this atmosphere that on July 17, 1936, a young military officer with a large following made a pronouncement in which he rejected the legitimacy of the government and proclaimed himself the leader of a military rebellion.[42] As such, Francisco Franco became the leader of a forthrightly fascistic uprising against the Spanish Republic. It was civil war.*

*Whether Franco was a genuine fascist in the same sense that Hitler and Mussolini were fascists has been debated. He was not expansionist by ideology, and though he was a military man, he was very little given to typically fascist ecstasies over the joys of war. In fact, he made it his policy to stay out

Stalin's first response that summer was to have Willi and the Comintern make a lot of noise but do very little.[43] The very first representative of the Soviet state to reach the Republican government was André Malraux, sent from Otto and Willi's office, and offering, very covertly, to act as a go-between in the purchase of some French airplanes.[44] At the same time the NKVD apparatus was ordered to start arranging for the covert supply of military material under Soviet auspices to Spain. Stalin had two prime requirements. The first was that any people traceable to the Soviet government stay out of the line of fire, and second that all military purchases be kept secret and not made on credit.[45] The Spaniards and their allies would pay cash on the barrel-head. Malraux loved his job. It was not really very substantive, though it established him as the French pseudo-hero of the new struggle.

Stalin was waiting to see if Franco would win, and win quickly. Franco did not win quickly. Plainly, the Spanish Republic would and could fight back. As the summer gave way to fall, Franco's rebellion was not succeeding. In the passionate slogan of the hour—*No pasarán!*

At this point Stalin decided to take advantage of the situation in a new way. In the early fall of 1936, right around the time that Willi learned of Radek's arrest and felt the Terror brush near, the dictator issued his secret decree ordering new and greater aid to Spain.[46] Meanwhile, the Soviet Party grandly announced its alliance with Spanish communists. This was the moment that Willi appeared in Togliatti's office, making the argument that the Münzenberg offices in Paris were indispensable to the new policy.

In fact, the true substance of Stalin's October 1936 decision was not so much to aid Caballero's struggle as to use his aid as a pretext for seizing total control over the Spanish government, Stalinizing it in its every aspect, and rendering it entirely subservient to his will. That this might undermine the larger war effort against Franco, even doom it to failure, was not really an important consideration in Stalin's eyes. The essential element was that the Largo Caballero government be replaced by people who were really *Nash*: "Ours." Though Largo Caballero was surrounded by Soviet agents and remained intellectually under the thumb of Julio Alvárez del Vayo, the long-standing Münzenberg agent and close associate of Otto Katz, he still fondly supposed himself to be an independent leftist.[47] That was not enough for Stalin. Largo Caballero would have to

---

of the Second World War at all costs. Nor was Franco a racist in anything like the Nazi fashion. Nonetheless, his government was nationalistic, statist, dominated by the reactionary right wing, and an authoritarian police state with strong totalitarian inclinations. It seems to me he can be called a fascist in the more general sense of that dangerous word.

be replaced by an entirely obedient puppet. In November, the *apparat* had made its selection: The factotum would be Largo's Minister of Finance, a corrupt professor of economics named Juan Negrin, and the coup that installed him was carefully timed to put him in power in May 1937. At this same time, the Terror would be unleashed in its full violence in Spain.[48]

Why then would Stalin have been more interested in controlling the Spanish government than in defeating Franco? It is important to understand that Stalin did not undertake to replace Largo Caballero and destroy the non-Stalinist Spanish left because of some purely intellectual or neurotic desire for ideological purity in Spain. That kind of motive would have been much more typical of Lenin than Stalin. Stalin didn't really give a damn about ideological purity in Spain or anywhere else. He wanted control over the Spanish government because he believed Spain would make him a new kind of player in European politics, bargaining between England and France on the one hand, and Germany on the other, and using Spain as his chip. His motivating fear was isolation; his worst fear was that Hitler would simply attack Russia, attack it soon, and attack it successfully. In acting to prevent this, he proposed to bargain with Spain. A communist Spain menaced Hitler. Hitler might well make some important secret concessions to assure that a communist Spain would slowly fade away. For that too was something Stalin could arrange. That would mean Franco's triumph. All right: A fascist Spain nicely menaced France and England, placated Hitler, and tended to turn fascist aggression westward, ringing round France, directing danger away from the Russian border. So—one way or another, Spain could be used. Seen in this light, Stalin wanted Spain not to rule but for the concessions he could extract for it, either by holding it or by throwing it away. These concessions might come from several quarters, but they would come, above all, from the Germans.

This, in my view, is probably the key to his entire policy in Spain. Stalin was not really very interested in having a left-wing government in Spain. Stalin wanted Spain as a chip, perhaps the biggest chip of all, in his response to the German threat.

Stalin's takeover of the Spanish government moved in several phases. First the apparatus had to infiltrate every aspect of the Spanish Republic's base of power, whether political or military. Caballero would have to be removed and replaced with the obedient and corrupt Negrin. At the same time, every possible force for resisting this takeover, any possible opposition in Spanish political life would have to be eliminated or silenced by force. Since the communists were a small minority on the Spanish left, this would require a huge, concerted, and sudden assault using mass terror not against the fascists but most of all against the principal allies of the Republic. It was pointed out to Stalin that this would of course totally demoralize the war effort against Franco. He grasped the objection with perfect clarity. And it did not trouble him at all.

A further piece of evidence suggesting that Stalin was proceeding toward an intentional sacrifice of Spain was his refusal to grant its government financial credit, as Hitler and Mussolini liberally granted credit to Franco, thereby assuring that their client would win the war. Stalin was perfectly capable of supplying at least as good material and credit to the Republic as Hitler was sending Franco. But he knew that a government well-armed and winning with his excellent equipment might not be entirely under his control. Moreover, since he did not intend or expect that the Republican government would last very long, he knew they could never pay back any credit he might extend. Therefore he insisted that his intentionally inadequate trickle of arms to Spain had to be paid for in cash on the barrelhead. To promote this policy, Stalin ordered the apparatus to set up an elaborate world-wide network for private financing of the Spanish war effort. This is where Münzenberg came in, and how he saved himself for a while. To privatize the financing of the Spanish Civil War seems a curious choice for a communist; not that anyone noticed. In the righteousness clubs, the new, ceaselessly promoted test of virtue was giving money "for Spain." "Spain" became the favorite charity of the Popular Front. It became the obsessive concern in all the righteousness fronts of the late thirties. The tragic irony is that all that fund-raising and all that goodwill had been created for no better reason than to enhance Stalin's fiscal freedom to betray that country.

But keeping Spain on a short financial leash was not enough. Knowing that he had the Spanish government at his mercy, Stalin now undertook simply to assume control of their national treasury. Not for nothing had he first served the Bolsheviks by robbing banks. In this tremendous act of international grand larceny, Stalin's principal confederate was none other than Caballero's finance minister, Negrin: Indeed it was by assisting the *apparat* in looting the Spanish treasury that Negrin purchased his hour in the sun as premier.

The robbery of the gold in the Spanish treasury has been described in detail by Krivitsky, who was himself a principal participant. The idea was to loot the country of the gold bullion that was its national treasure and transport it all to the Soviet Union, knowing full well that it would never be returned.[49] How this was accomplished is an incredible tale. Since the days of Philip II, an essential part of the Spanish patrimony had been the accumulation of one of the largest gold reserves in the entire world. Using Negrin and the *apparat,* the Soviets persuaded the Caballero government to transfer huge amounts of this gold to Moscow, partly for "safekeeping" against the menace of a Franco victory, and partly as "collateral" for their "credit" in buying arms. Of course Stalin had no intention of returning anything, ever. The demise of the Spanish Republic only made that refusal easier to defend. The theft of the gold was echoed by many other forms of larceny riddling the Republican effort in the name of "help for Spain." One of the many services provided by Anthony Blunt during this period was to advise the apparatus on the fencing of stolen Spanish art, the proceeds of which were used for the precisely same treacherous purposes as the stolen bullion.[50]

With Spain being used as a card to be played rather than a prize to be won, the conduct of the Spanish Civil War itself took on a curiously propagandistic tone. From the start, the Spanish War was bound in the lie of the Popular Front, and as such it was necessarily based in fraudulence and propaganda.

But the style of things in Spain was very extreme. There are moments when a cynical interpreter might view the Civil War itself as more a literary event than a military one, despite the brutality of the war and its casualties. Since the days when Byron became the hero of European liberalism by dying at Missolonghi for Greek Independence, there had never been a military conflict so richly given over to the rhetoric of the writer-hero. This probably happened in direct proportion to the leading place given in the effort by Münzenberg's apparatus in the earliest days. The cultural politics of the moment culminated above all in one painting: Picasso's great *Guernica.* But the mystique also produced many books of lasting power. At least two very good, and arguably great novels were produced by the two leading literary "heroes" of the hour: Malraux's *Man's Hope,* and Hemingway's *For Whom the Bell Tolls.* As an early negotiator with the Spaniards, Malraux was undoubtedly more politically witting than was Hemingway. Nonetheless, Malraux's presence in Spain was primarily propagandistic, as were his later adventures as an aviator, white scarf flying as he buzzed above the Ebro. Malraux's real service to the Soviets in Spain was to set the tone of Byronic glamour which dominated its image from the beginning until almost the end.[51]

Ernest Hemingway on the other hand came to Spain as part of a film project set up behind a front of famous Americans, a group called Contemporary Historians, consisting of Lillian Hellman, John Dos Passos, Dorothy Parker, Archibald Macleish, and of course Hemingway himself.

The film was to appear under Hemingway's name and came to be called *The Spanish Earth.* The purpose of Contemporary Historians was to deck the picture in celebrity, raise money, and (almost certainly) hide the hand of Otto Katz in its production.[52] But Spain was an irresistible center of all the literati in this period, from W. H. Auden and Stephen Spender to Parker and Hellman. The tendency reached a bizarre culmination with a Culture Congress in Spain in late 1937, notable both for its invective against the traitor Gide and for its extravagance. There the Popular Front's taste for *luxe* and high style was indulged to the point of witless incongruity. With Spain in its agony, the writers toasted their vows to the Republic with champagne, and were driven to and from the conference receptions in Rolls-Royces.[53]

But if the Spanish War sought to wrap Stalinism in Byronic illusion, the deaths died there were real enough. Virginia Woolf's nephew Julian Bell died there, and so did John Cornford, friend of the Cambridge spies. Their youthful idealism, like so much youthful idealism, was at times difficult to distinguish from youthful cynicism. Given the Byronic manner of his end, John Cornford was a curiously direct cultural heir to the great romantic. John Cornford had been christened "Rupert John" after his mother's first great love, the Byronic poet-hero of the First World War and the man Frances Cornford did not marry, Rupert Brooke. Both Brooke and Cornford were, like Byron himself, students at Trinity College, Cambridge. Cornford took his place in a kind of Trinity tradition of early deaths. Byron died in Missolonghi. Brooke died in Skyros. Cornford was cut down in Spain. It is a continuous romantic succession, an "apostolic" succession, of handsome youth dead doing the high deeds of freedom.[54]

But the Spanish War also lives in myth as a last tragic flowering of the revolutionary idealism of the Comintern. That myth had been very much Willi's creation. This too was illusion. On September 14, 1936, Stalin ordered a policy meeting on Spain to take place in the Lubyanka, during which the next phase of Soviet presence in the Spanish War was determined.[55]

Until then most of the Soviet response had been made through the Comintern efforts, both secret and public. It was now decided that all Comintern operations in Spain would be placed under the direct control of the Soviet secret police, and it was simultaneously decided to use that secret police to take over total command of the Spanish Communist party.[56] That would mean the end of Münzenberg's sheet anchor.

And so, following that date, it may be assumed that apparent Comintern operatives in Spain were in fact under the control of the NKVD, including the people in charge of the Comintern's famous legions of foreign irregulars, the International Brigades. Included in this subordination of the Comintern to the NKVD would have been Otto Katz and Otto's closest associate in France, Julio Alvárez del Vayo. In Spain at least, both these men acted under the auspices of the secret police. They were *de facto,* and in all probability *de jure,* its agents. Once this is understood, certain oddities of the scene become quite clear. Among them is the curious difference in standing between Münzenberg and Katz over Spain. To every appearance, Otto was still Willi's lieutenant. It would be my contention that after 1936 the difference between Willi and Otto was more accurately described as the difference between hunted and hunter. After that year, Otto was a covert agent of the NKVD, while Willi was its covert target.*

Otto was on the rise. Willi, though he was being permitted to play out his usefulness in Spain, was slated for liquidation. That is why Otto Katz could spend most of his time in Valencia and Madrid, while Willi never once entered Spain during the entire engagement.[57] It is surely also why Willi specifically warned Babette never to go to Spain, at the risk of her life.[58] Spain may have looked like the land of high deeds for the youth of its time. But the man in charge of fabricating that illusion knew full well that it was an arena for the Terror, and that he himself was one of that Terror's targets.

The politics of all this can be interestingly traced through the destinies of two indispensable secret agents then on the scene. Their names were Berzin and Orlov.[59] We have already come across both men. J. K. Berzin was the senior intelligence officer sitting at Radek's side in the Kremlin when Stalin summoned his officers on the Night of Long Knives and told them the new secret policy toward Hitler. Orlov on the other hand was a protégé of Yagoda, and when he left Spain he went on to England to take over running the Cambridge group from Theodore Maly. Berzin was an

*I should add that in my view Gibarti had also joined the NKVD or the GRU by this time and probably earlier. For one thing, he was being entrusted with very delicate secret work in Spain as late as 1938 and possibly even 1939. To that fact, I add this anecdote. In 1938 Gibarti was in New York, doing business for the apparatus in the German exile community, while collaborating with the German writer Stefan Heym. When I told this to Babette she was for once genuinely surprised. "Gibarti? Working with Stefan Heym?" "Yes," I said, "his partner was plainly Stefan Heym." She became vehement. "Stefan Heym? The Writer? From the DDR? *No!*" I assured her the documentary evidence was indisputable. She was flabbergasted. "Incredible. But that means Gibarti was in the other service! Quite incredible."

old-style Leninist, a military man-cum-intelligence operative, cynical and witting enough to have sat at Radek's side that night, trusted and unmoved. Orlov was a nastier item: a new-style NKVD thug, a graduate of the torture chambers in the basement of the Lubyanka, moving on up.

Berzin and Orlov: Each operated in Spain in great secrecy; each was given tremendous power. Berzin worked under deep cover. His mere presence in the country was a closely guarded secret, known to only a few officials of the Spanish government.[60] He was secretly in charge of the Loyalist Army in all its forms, including those foreign legions of the Comintern, the International Brigades. Because Berzin spoke no Spanish or English, he had to have a translator at his side in all his secret meetings with the Spaniards. This translator was an American, a radical professor of Spanish from the Johns Hopkins University named José Robles Villa. Therefore, whatever Berzin said or heard among the Spaniards, Robles said and heard too. And as it happened, Robles was a close friend, back in America, of John Dos Passos.

Orlov's secret role meanwhile was every bit as elevated as that of Berzin. Orlov was the covert commandant of the secret police in Spain.[61] He was the man Stalin appointed to run the Spanish Terror. Taken together, Berzin and Orlov were the unseen powers behind Loyalist *force majeure.*

Both men clearly understood Stalin's policy. Both knew that their task was to seize absolute control of the Spanish government so it could be used as a bargaining chip with the European powers over Stalin's German policy. Both fully understood the Soviets' true relation to Hitler, and if they had objections to that secret bond they certainly are not known to have voiced them. Nonetheless the two soon came into conflict.[62]

Berzin assumed, plausibly enough, that the Soviet takeover of the Spanish government should not so utterly alienate and decimate the Spanish left that when the job was done, further prosecution of the war would be virtually impossible. After all, Berzin was running an army, and surely Spain's value as a chip disappeared if its army couldn't fight. As a military man he knew what was needed to keep the army fighting. Berzin simply did not believe that Orlov's terroristic and imperialistic tactics were compatible with winning the war.[63]

Orlov and his secret police saw things differently. He clearly understood that if the Spanish government was to be utterly Stalinized, the non-Stalinist left would have to be reduced to submission or liquidated through main force: mass murder, terror, and torture. As to winning the war: Was military strength really so necessary? Perhaps one might as easily seize the Spanish government and meet Stalin's aims through weakness rather than strength.

Both men were right.

Berzin was a good communist. He had no more love for the non-Stalinist left than did Orlov. Orlov was however a man of quite special brutality and cruelty, even by Bolshevik standards. Convinced that Orlov was destroying the Spanish potential to wage war, Berzin wrote a memo for Stalin saying as much and demanding Orlov's recall. The memo was seconded by Arthur Stashevsky, Stalin's prime commissar in Spain, and in further support of it Stashevsky proceeded to consult with Stalin's senior military man, Field Marshall Tuchachevsky, who also agreed with the obvious truth of Berzin's claims. For that matter Stalin himself agreed with the memo, and he explicitly said so.[64]

Agreeing with the memo was not the point, however. What Berzin, Tuchachevsky, and Stashevsky failed to grasp was that Stalin was not only uninterested in a Spanish Loyalist victory, he had no interest even in a really strong military position for the Spaniards. His military advisors may have understood the dual policy, but Berzin, Tuchachevsky, and Stashevsky failed to understand that Stalin was prepared to give Spain away easily and soon. Stalin knew Hitler couldn't be appeased while an array of strong implacable enemies faced him down in the West; he knew any undue growth in Spanish Republican power would only encourage Hitler to strike soon. And avoiding that was the whole point. Stalin could not afford to permit Spanish "anti-fascism" to acquire military substance. With people like Berzin, Tuchachevsky, and Stashevsky pushing too hard for military effectiveness, Hitler would need to be reassured.

So be it. Stalin would reassure Hitler just as Hitler had reassured him on the Night of Long Knives. Stalin arranged to have all three of these trusted senior military advisors arrested, and while fully agreeing with virtually everything they said, kill them all.[65]

Here is the sequence of events. In October 1936, Stalin plotted his course. Two weeks later, Negrin was selected by Stashevsky to replace Largo Caballero. At this point, Orlov began terroristic operations in Madrid and Barcelona. By December *Pravda* had proclaimed that violent purges were the only path to victory in Catalonia. These actions were directed from Valencia, and Berzin was of course fully aware of them. So, inevitably, was his translator, Robles.[66]

In early March, Orlov's brutality among the Spanish leftists was so extreme and outrageous that Berzin sent his alarmed memo to Stalin.

Stalin pretended to take this recommendation seriously, though by mid-March, Orlov felt free to make José Robles Villa disappear—a taste of what was to come. Berzin's whereabouts at this time also become vague. He may well have already been under arrest. In early April, Stashevsky was in Moscow for meetings with Stalin and Tuchachevsky, whom the senior people still believed was empowered, even though Stalin's secret work with the Gestapo, preparing to eliminate Tuchachevsky and decimate the senior ranks of the Red Army, was simultaneously in progress and already well advanced.

At this moment the *apparat* staged the coup that removed Largo Caballero. The public pretext for this move was a demand made to Largo by the Spanish Communist party; a demand which in effect would have meant the liquidation or suppression of virtually all non-Stalinist leftists among the government's alliance. Largo of course flatly refused to approve this passport to certain defeat, and so he was removed as a defeatist and replaced by the "Victory" party of Negrin. The newspeak of Stalinist jargon tells the story. Because he pursued victory, Largo was removed as a defeatist. Negrin, because he was prepared to preside over defeat, led the "Victory" party.

And the new Terror promptly descended. By June the slaughters in Barcelona were shrieking forward in full cry. Many thousands of Spanish anarchists, organized under an umbrella organization known as the POUM, were executed. The leader of the POUM, a man named Andrés Nin, was arrested. When Nin did not "confess" under torture, he was simply murdered in the park of the Prado by Orlov personally, an old hand.

It is plain that by the time Otto Katz's friend Negrin stepped into office, Stalin had already set his course on giving Spain away. It was precisely this decision that Berzin had misjudged, and misjudged fatally.

At this same moment, with Stalin seemingly at the apex of his influence in Spain, and the Spanish treasury safely removed to Russian territory, the Axis powers stepped up their aid to Franco while Stalin began to gear his assistance down.[67] By 1938 Stalin coolly told the Spanish ambassador that his "credit" was "exhausted."[68] In fact the Spaniards had never had any credit. They had paid for their poor bargain with all they had and with that bargain they were assisted to a fore-ordained defeat, which descended on them just two convenient months before Stalin sealed the alliance with Hitler which had been his object from the beginning.

. . .

In the argument between Orlov and Berzin, Otto Katz had chosen with Orlov, and so emerged on the victorious side. Otto was a close associate of Negrin, and in fact served as one of his money-men in the European press.[69] As a Comintern agent flourishing in Spain, he had to be intimate with the NKVD and GRU. It is reliably charged that he assisted Orlov in selecting the damned. His role in these designations for murder was quite well known at the time.[70] Moreover, it seems a plausible guess that Katz, as an intellectual who knew England well, might have played some role in posting Orlov to his new job with the Cambridge spies when Spain had been finished off.

But above all, Katz was a senior Comintern agent running Spanish propaganda in a war defined by a logic remote from the will to win. In this capacity Otto's closest confederate was another Münzenberg trainee, Julio Alvárez del Vayo, who served as Negrin's Foreign Minister while he worked with Katz running a propaganda organization called *Agence Espagna*.[71] After the Spanish defeat, del Vayo went on to the United States, where he worked in various apparatus-sponsored activities, usually hand-in-hand with Michael Straight's brother-in-law, Louis Dolivet, the former director of RUP, who likewise proceeded to the United States once his good work in the Popular Front was at an end. In New York, del Vayo became the person dominating the foreign policy pronouncements of the *Nation* magazine, using his strong emotional influence over its Stalinist editor, Freda Kirchway.[72] But the *Nation* had never failed to have some classic Münzenberg-man in a strong editorial position.[73] Del Vayo replaced a reliable old-line type, Louis Fischer, another close friend of Willi and Otto Katz, who with the Second World War made his break. During Stalin's time, the front pages of the *Nation,* those dealing with politics and foreign policy, were more or less forthrightly Stalinist. The culture section in the back of the magazine was as forthrightly anti-Stalinist. It was a standard Münzenberg tactic to install Stalinists in the front of magazines and Social Democrats in the back. It lent credibility to the look of "independence," and served as a kind of propellant for getting the propaganda to the innocents who were its true targets.

Otto Katz must have been very well informed about the downfall of Berzin, just as he may well have been witting over Tuchachevsky's fall. As we have seen from his role over the Reichstag Fire, these joint ventures with the Nazis were familiar stuff to Otto. But we know that he was well informed about the murder of Berzin's translator, Robles, from a quite different source. And therein lies a tale from the chronicles of American literature.

Here is what happened.

Around 1935, that is with the creation of the Popular Front, the apparatus set its sights on taking possession of the now unchallenged celebrity of Ernest Hemingway. He was an ideal Popular Front personality: In his way, Hemingway was as important in America as Gide had been in France. The directors of the Popular Front hoped to transform him into the biggest literary fellow traveller of them all.

It is hard to overstate, even today, the *ethical* impact of Hemingway's style on at least two generations of Americans. "He liberated our written language": so wrote his third wife, Martha Gellhorn, and though Martha Gellhorn was a woman with few illusions about Hemingway the man, decades later she could still pay him that just tribute in all admiration.[74] In his American way, Hemingway was performing what we might call the Byronic task: He rejuvenated the literary language and infused it with the promise of a hard, credible heroism. It was irresistible. And it was quickly recognized as the tremendously forceful thing that it was. By 1935, Hemingway's reputation had long since passed far beyond its origins in the modernist vanguard. He was by far the most famous highbrow American writer alive, and one of the most admired and influential literary heroes in the world. He had freed up the language, and that accomplishment, joined to his fame, meant that in the logic of things the Spanish War would be Hemingway's war, *par excellence*. In fact, one might almost say that the *style* of the Popular Front had been created with Hemingway and Malraux explicitly in mind. The new look was much indebted to their influence. For example, all three of the principal leaders in the Hollywood Popular Front—Lillian Hellman, Dashiell Hammett, and Dorothy Parker—were writers whose prose was based upon vulgarizing Hemingway's style. In English, Hemingway was the most influential moralist of the Word in his era, passing beyond even Eliot. The apparatus had everything to gain from co-opting him, even though the union of man and machine was riddled with mutual deception and self-deception. Under the influence of that fatal coincidence, Hemingway's enterprise as an artist succumbed to its first really serious public corruption. And he would never again write as well as he had done.

We already have seen how many people in or near Hemingway's circle were in or near the apparatus, and with the creation of the Front, some in innocence, some not, all went into a full court press around their hero. By 1936 the effort was fairly well advanced. Hemingway was becoming a fellow traveller, and his kind of style was very much Popular Front style.[75]

Then, late in 1936, right around the time that Stalin decided to take over the Spanish government, the apparatus decided to sponsor a very high-class propaganda film that could be used to raise money and clinch the heroism of the occasion in Hollywood and the more intellectual capitals. It was thought indispensable to have Hemingway connected to this film.[76] Simultaneously, Hemingway had fallen in love with Martha Gellhorn, herself a fellow traveller, and a remarkably well-connected one: For example, Eleanor Roosevelt felt very particular, almost maternal feelings for Martha Gellhorn.[77] As a result Martha had excellent access to the White House. For every possible reason, Hemingway had to be central to *The Spanish Earth.*

The director was to be a Dutch communist named Joris Ivens, and it would be fronted and funded by a group of famous American fellow travellers: Hellman and Parker, Hemingway himself, Archibald Macleish, and John Dos Passos.

The year 1937 brought the long friendship of Dos Passos and Hemingway into a decisive phase. While Dos Passos had started his career a little ahead, Hemingway's reputation had now clearly bypassed Dos Passos's, and done so forever. To compound this rivalry, Dos Passos and particularly his wife Kate were very fond of Hemingway's wife Pauline, and they had very little sympathy for Hemingway's increasingly callous infidelity to her with Martha Gellhorn. Finally, Dos Passos, who until then had been by far the *apparat*'s favorite American vanguardist, was being displaced in the hard left's hagiography by the much, much bigger star. Dos Passos's psychology, let us recall, was very much that of the good boy. Being good was as essential to his mentality as being bad was to Hemingway's. This meant that when Dos Passos heard serious arguments raised against his beliefs, he tried to take them in and respond to them. And very serious arguments against Stalinism were now being heard, raised especially by Trotskyists in the increasingly harsh intellectual fray of New York. They were the kind of doubts that Hemingway the bad boy dismissed as niggling, intellectual, unreal stuff. Dos Passos on the other hand listened and was uneasy.[78] From the *apparat*'s point of view, he was getting a little unreliable. If things got out of hand, though the apparatus had sedulously built him up, it might be necessary to discredit him. Nonetheless, Dos Passos remained one of the Contemporary Historians. It was agreed that Dos and Hemingway and all the happy band of Contemporary Historians would work on *The Spanish Earth* together.[79]

We have now reached the spring of 1937. Stalin's new policy was fully in place. Madrid had withstood the siege of December, though the Republican government had removed itself to Valencia. Hemingway was already in Spain, and on March 3, Dos Passos sailed from New York for a brief stay in France before proceeding to the war. It was exactly at this time that Berzin wrote his letter to Stalin protesting Orlov's brutality and incompetence. Very soon after, on Orlov's orders, and probably in response to this letter, Berzin's translator and John Dos Passos's good friend José Robles Villa was arrested in Valencia by the NKVD, taken into a basement, and shot to death.[80]

It took Dos Passos about a month to get to Spain, and on April 7 he arrived in Valencia. By this time Berzin was probably under arrest of some sort, but not yet dead. That Berzin remained alive after his translator had been killed suggests that Stalin may still have been maneuvering over Spain, or at the least, still weighing his options.

Of course Dos Passos knew none of this. His first stop in Valencia was with his prime contact there: del Vayo. He presented himself brightly, ready for duty in Spain. The next stop was to see his friend Robles.

Except that for some reason nobody seemed able to tell him where Robles lived. That seemed odd: Dos Passos had understood that Robles had quite an important job in Valencia, yet nobody seemed to have heard of him. Soon Dos Passos found himself knocking on doors in the streets of the town, following vague leads from place to place. At last he came to a poor apartment in a poor quarter. There he found Robles's wife Margare, alone.

Alone and beside herself. José was gone. He had simply not come home one day, and since then she had not been able to get any information at all about where he was. Nobody would give her any help at all. She had been to the police, to del Vayo's office, to every important Spaniard she could think of, and she had learned nothing until just a few days ago she had been told that Robles had been arrested. What could they possibly have arrested him for? José was the most passionate Loyalist alive. Margare was terrified.

We have already noticed how the force of the conventional earnest decencies in John Dos Passos's make-up made him an easy mark for manipulation during his visit to the USSR in the twenties. On this occasion his plain rectitude served him very well. Dos Passos instantly understood that his duty was to help Margare Robles find and defend her husband. He acted at once.[81]

His first step was to return to del Vayo and ask for information. In a flat lie, del Vayo professed ignorance of the entire matter.[82] Dos Passos next proceeded to another old friend, José Quintinilla, a secret policeman who did vaguely admit he'd heard there had been an arrest, but that the matter was minor. It would be cleared up soon, soon.

Julio Alvárez del Vayo at this moment had a great deal more to lie about than Robles's disappearance. Given the secret agenda of the Spanish War and his partnership with Katz, del Vayo's propaganda office was a far more conspiratorial place than a mere bureau for guiding and misguiding the press. Its actual task was the search for ideological conformity. A significant number of people working for del Vayo at this time were actually undercover agents involved in keeping the apparatus informed of any possible deviation from a Stalinist loyalty. I repeat, this was not motivated by a purist's need for conformity. It was motivated by the wish to be sure that in the showdown over the take-over in June, the people being liquidated would not be able to call upon any unexpected allies.

Needless to say, this obsession with ideological conformity is absolutely wrong for any sane politics of coalition, especially in wartime. Winston Churchill was the senior anti-communist politician in Europe, but when the turning wheel made it right, he gladly entered an alliance with Stalin, remarking that to defeat Hitler he would accept help from Satan himself, and even arrange a favorable reference to Lucifer on the floor of the House of Commons. Not so in Spain. Allies with even mildly differing views were to be killed, and killing them was far, far more important than killing the enemy. If this was Stalinist paranoia, as it certainly was, it was paranoia with a purpose: The political method was to assure that when he came to take possession of the Spanish state, he would meet no meaningful resistance. As for weakening the war effort—weakening the war effort was intrinsic to the whole idea. Ferreting out possible opposition was a principal task of del Vayo's office. Del Vayo was almost certainly a member of the *apparat,* but he found it useful to his many deceptions to pose as a "socialist."[83]

In that office there worked two young men. One of them, still only a teenager, was Robles's son Francisco, or "Coco" Robles Villa. Another was a bright young American communist named Liston Oak.[84] Oak had begun in New York as a communist. In New York, he had been drawn into the apparatus and secret work, and his assignment in Spain was a promotion. He was to be assigned to del Vayo's office, where he would covertly assist one of the leading NKVD thugs, a man named George Mink, in ferreting out the wrong kind of Loyalist in the American and English brigades.[85] This he did. A collateral job was to act as a gofer and guide for visiting celebrities in Spain. When in Madrid, he spent inordinate amounts of time in the service of Hemingway, scouring the countryside for alcohol in sufficient quantity and quality for the master properly to hold court at the Hotel Florida.[86]

But marking the doomed was the main part of the job. At first Oak probably did not grasp the purposes to which his quiet reports on political correctness would be put. But he was a very bright fellow. He soon began to discern the pattern. Oak began to suspect he was being used as a finger man in a murder machine. He took to drinking with some of the more garrulous Russian generals, and for all I know, he may even have done it earlier in company with Robles: Oak spoke no Russian. In any case, Oak made it a point to down a pint of heavy cream before he joined these festivities, so he could stay sober while the Russians did not. Increasingly he was leaving the parties knowing the names of the doomed.[87] And somehow or other, sometime in March, Liston Oak discovered the truth about his vanished friend José Robles Villa.

With this knowledge, Liston Oak made what in retrospect was his first small step out of the Lie. He took aside young Coco Robles and told him that he knew, knew for certain, that his father was dead. He had been shot by the NKVD. And he asked that the boy and his mother please, please stop asking so many questions.

Dos Passos meanwhile knew nothing of this conversation. Still supposing Robles to be alive and under arrest for some minor infraction, he proceeded to Madrid, where he was to join his friends among the Contemporary Historians and get to work on *The Spanish Earth*. Hemingway and Martha Gellhorn were staying at the Hotel Florida, basking in all that came from Hemingway's position as celebrity-in-chief, whether it was the liquor brought by Liston Oak, or the publicity he was enjoying over his role as the new hero in what he called "my second war."[88]

When Dos Passos arrived, he was anything but welcome in Hemingway's eyes. As Hemingway saw it, Dos Passos was more interested in stirring up trouble, whining over this man Robles than he was in making *The Spanish Earth*. In addition, Dos Passos's disapproval of the affair with Martha Gellhorn had become fairly obvious by this time. The two motives roused all of Hemingway's vengeful anger. What did Dos Passos know about what real men have to do in real wars? If ever there was an armchair radical, Dos Passos was it. Why the hell did he have to keep yammering on about Robles? Move on. We have a victory to win.

It was into this thickening atmosphere that Josephine Herbst also arrived very shortly after, in mid-April.[89] Herbst was by no means famous enough to be counted among the Contemporary Historians, but she was much more witting politically. My guess is that Herbst was sent to Spain to help monitor and control the American literary celebrities in Madrid. She was inside the apparatus; enough to be trusted with the information that her husband was an agent of Soviet espionage in Washington. She had already done undercover work for the Münzenberg people in Germany, and in all probability had done it elsewhere both at home and abroad. But in truth, Herbst's entire presence in the literary world was essentially a creation of the propaganda apparatus.

Thus, as Herbst arrived in Spain she went immediately to del Vayo and, it is plain that as an insider to the apparatus, the situation was clearly laid out before her. She was forthrightly informed that Robles had been shot, without even a court-martial or any judicial proceeding whatever, as a fascist spy.[90] Herbst was told about the tensions this was causing among the American celebrities. She was consulted on how to handle it. Twenty-five years later, writing about these events in an elegant essay filled with falsehoods and evasions, Herbst claimed that the apparatus wanted her to keep Dos Passos in the dark about Robles.[91] Herbst claims that as a matter of her own conscience she disagreed with this approach, and as Dos Passos's friend, proceeded to act independently, insisting that he be told. This claim is unprovable and as the reader will see, highly unlikely: In my view the evidence suggests that in Madrid Herbst did precisely the job the apparatus wanted her to do, and did it well. In any case, we certainly know that she left Valencia after a forthright briefing by her colleagues in the secret police *apparat,* and that she carried with her a clear mandate to play some part in the mess in the Hotel Florida.

Whatever her stated motives, let us look at what Josephine Herbst actually did. She arranged for the public humiliation and discredit of her dear friend John Dos Passos, while surreptitiously spreading the lie that his close friend in Spain was a fascist spy and had been shot for it. This she did in the midst of a highly publicized series of communist provocations about "fascist spies" in the Republican ranks, then filling every paper and all political talk in Madrid. It was creating general hysteria about "fascists'" penetrating the Loyalist effort. Those charges were being taken in all seriousness by the literary folk on the scene.[92] All evidence likewise indicates that the *apparat* lie about Robles as a fascist, spread in secret by Herbst, was likewise taken as the straight stuff by all the Americans at the Florida.[93] Moreover, though she later claimed to have doubted the truth of the story she was quietly disseminating about Robles, at no point did those doubts soften her behavior or mitigate the virulence of the lie. Certainly she did not allow those doubts to mitigate even slightly the cruel pain and bleak public humiliation her actions inflicted on Dos Passos.

Here is how she handled it. When Herbst checked into the Florida, she was of course promptly drawn into the tensions between the two men, both of whom she knew well. She soon found herself in a situation where she could speak to Hemingway in complete privacy: It was over brandy, perhaps that first night, in his room. Hemingway, like Dos Passos still under the impression that Robles was merely under arrest, embarked on a rant about Dos Passos's meddling. Herbst now made her move, and recalled it later in her own Hemingway-tinted prose. "I put down my drink and said, 'the man is already dead. Quintinilla should have told Dos.' "

Hemingway stared back thunderstruck.[94]

She quickly assured him that she spoke with authority. She had learned the truth reliably in Valencia, but from somebody whose confidence she could not break, someone who in turn had learned it from someone "higher up." Why Herbst could not break this "confidence" is unclear. Why she did not break it thirty years later is likewise unclear. In any case, the lie was safe with her. She told Hemingway that, since she was bound to keep the identity of her informant secret, if Dos was to be told, the story would have to seem to come from somebody other than herself. Using this very curious moral claim, Herbst assured her own anonymity.[95]

Under cover of that anonymity, Herbst next coached Hemingway on how he might handle Dos Passos's dilemma. Dos must be told. Dear friends like themselves could hardly let him remain in the dark. But told how? Where? They contrived not to take the obvious course of simply walking down the hall to Dos Passos's room, knocking on the door, and quietly telling him the truth. They knew perfectly well the story would come to him as a frightening defeat and shock; one might have thought that this was a moment in which the kind gesture called for privacy and discretion. No: Herbst and Hemingway decided to tell Dos Passos the next day, and in quite the opposite context. There was to be a large public gathering of noteworthy Russians and Germans and other foreign VIPs. Everybody would be there, and Hemingway and Dos Passos as the two leading celebrities on the scene would be the center of all eyes. Guided by Herbst, Hemingway decided this would be a far, far better place to tell Dos Passos about the death of his friend. But since Herbst could not be named as the source, who could they claim had told Hemingway the news? They decided to say that a "German correspondent" had broken it to him, right there at the party, on the spot. But what could they do when Dos Passos naturally asked to speak to this German correspondent himself? Well, Hemingway could say that the German correspondent had refused to speak to him.

Such was the strategy Josephine Herbst developed with Hemingway that night. Herbst thought it was a perfectly splendid plan, and she watched with knowing interest as it visibly aroused Hemingway's sadism.[96]

The next day Hemingway plunged into the job with the full vigor of that sadism. The occasion was a celebrity luncheon at the castle previously belonging to the Duke of Tovar, in honor of the Soviet-Spanish International Brigade. The Loyalists were also celebrating Thaelman Day (Thaelman was a German communist, one of Münzenberg's propaganda heroes), and there were many Germans in evidence as well.[97] At this highly political, very public gathering Hemingway swaggered up to Dos Passos in full view of the many people who were gathering round them in circles, and announced as cuttingly as possible that in case Dos Passos was still wringing his hands about his pal Robles, he might want to know that Robles had been found out as a fascist spy and shot.[98]

Dos Passos responded in consternation. Shot? A fascist spy? Where did he learn that? Hemingway instantly produced his and Herbst's lie about the "German correspondent." The "German correspondent" he added was in the room at that moment, but he would not speak to Dos Passos. It seems to me obvious that the plain implication of this lie was that the "German correspondent" saw Hemingway as trustworthy, and Dos Passos as not trustworthy. And so it was surely taken by all the many influential people standing there listening.

Meanwhile, Josephine Herbst stood at a distance, anonymous and safe, watching her handiwork take its cruel effect. Safely apart, peering across the room, she could not hear her two friends' voices, but she could watch Dos Passos's visibly mounting pain as Hemingway cut away at him.[99]

When Hemingway was done, Dos Passos spotted Josephine Herbst and turned to her for help. He approached her "with a little coffee cup in his hand," shaking, manifestly in extreme emotional pain. He explained the situation. Then he wondered again why, if Ernest had spoken to this German correspondent, he himself could not. Fully witting, Herbst calmly told Dos Passos that in her opinion the time had come for him to stop asking questions. She referred him to del Vayo, and with that she left him twisting in the public humiliation she herself had engineered.

Writing about this performance twenty-five years later, Herbst attempted to ascribe her motives to the promptings of her almost exquisitely delicate conscience. These claims cannot even briefly survive serious moral examination. The fact is that Herbst's behavior toward Dos Passos was manipulative and dishonest from top to bottom. Its result was, I believe, its intention: to silence and humiliate Dos Passos while floating the lie, widely believed by almost everyone present, that his friend was a traitor. This was done in such a way as to create the very public impression that Hemingway was a politically reliable person while Dos Passos was not. That the Stalinist apparatus had embarked upon a courtship of Ernest Hemingway while simultaneously undertaking to discredit the too-inquisitive Dos Passos likewise strikes me as not incidental but central to the entire event. As to Herbst's later claim to have doubted the *apparat*'s fabrications about Robles, it seems to me that to have secretly harbored any such doubts in this situation only makes Herbst's the more cynical, and her performance the more entirely contemptible. It seems to me plain that Herbst was doing a job: That job was to spread the lie about Robles in such a way as to cement Hemingway's bond to the apparatus while discrediting Dos Passos as publicly as possible. Moreover, I believe it was almost certainly a job she had been assigned. In any case, it was a very nasty piece of work, and Herbst performed it to perfection.

But there is more. My research has established that a man was staying in the Hotel Florida at this time who, though an intimate friend of Herbst, is nowhere mentioned in her otherwise quite shamelessly name-dropping account. She can't have missed him; she mentions fraternizing with his party. Yet she never mentions this unseen friend in her talk about Spain, or for that matter anywhere in all her writing. Like her own husband, he was a Soviet agent. Once in Madrid, she almost certainly performed that mission in the literal physical presence and probably the collaboration of the NKVD agent who had for several years been her mentor, guide, and quite possibly, control. This man was Otto Katz. It seems likely, virtually certain, that Katz was himself at the Duke of Tovar's castle for the occasion when Herbst set up Dos Passos's humiliation. Everybody who was anybody was, since Otto was there with a number of celebrities whom he was showing Spain as celebrities liked to be shown Spain. Moreover, Otto's cover on this occasion, as it was on many other occasions, might very well have been that of "a German correspondent."

This means that while Josephine Herbst stood at her safe distance watching Ernest Hemingway perform the cruel task she'd set for him, Otto Katz was almost certainly on the sidelines too, likewise watching.[100]

With the humiliation of John Dos Passos complete, with all the assembled cultural grandees in Madrid convinced that his best friend in Spain was a fascist spy, literature was free to rejoin the noble cause of the Popular Front with Hemingway in the lead. Talk about *The Spanish Earth* continued, and Dos Passos even remained in Madrid long enough to give the film-makers and Hemingway a number of suggestions, suggestions which were actually adopted. But everything was ruined. For one thing, stricken though he was, Dos Passos refused to back down. He did not believe the lie himself. He still saw his duty with Margare Robles. His next task, as he saw it, was to return to Valencia, comfort Margare, and extract a death certificate for Robles from the Spanish government, since he knew that the widow could never collect on Robles's life insurance from Hopkins without it. He went to del Vayo, and in another lie del Vayo promised to procure such a document. Of course he never did.[101]

En route to Valencia, Dos Passos ran into another friend from the Hemingway circle, Evan Shipman, who in rather jeering tones told Dos Passos that since his friend Robles had been discredited, he ought to clear out of Spain. In later accounts, Hemingway himself would make much of Dos Passos's "cowardice" in leaving the country. This was another gross falsehood. In fact, from this moment forward Dos Passos's behavior was notable not only for its rectitude but for its courage.[102]

In fact Dos Passos may have been braver than he knew. Events in Spain were now moving rapidly. Berzin was finished, if not dead. In Catalonia, the strategy of the secret policeman was about to reach its triumph. In May, with Negrin in power, the Terror would be unleashed in Barcelona without restraint, and the detested Nin, soon to be murdered by Orlov himself, would be arrested while his cohorts were mowed down. Catalonia and its capital Barcelona would be the scene of this horrible bloodletting en masse, and it was now for Catalonia that Dos Passos travelled, where he happened to meet George Orwell. He proceeded to arrange an interview with Nin himself. The man was to vanish and die a week later.

Then one day in Barcelona, when the new Terror's appointed hour was only a few days distant, Dos Passos was alerted in his hotel room by an almost inaudible knocking. When he opened the door, he confronted the frightened face of Liston Oak, the young American from del Vayo's office who had told Coco Robles the truth about his father, the guy who used to drink heavy cream before carousing with the Russian generals. Oak had taken many steps into the Terror in Spain. Now, just before the full horror, Liston Oak had reached his own fear. He was convinced that he would never leave Spain alive unless he left it now. Right now.

And he had come to Dos Passos for help in the escape. They would never let him leave with what he knew. He was being tracked; if he ran, he would never reach the border alive. Oak had come to Spain as an invisible man, and he knew perfectly well that he could and now almost certainly would die in Spain an invisible man, just as Robles had died invisible—invisible, except for the fluke of Dos Passos's loyalty. His very presence in Spain was a secret. If they killed him now, nobody would ever know or credit the truth, except at best a few friends and abused intellectuals back in New York.

But Dos Passos? Dos Passos was a famous man. The apparatus could not liquidate him without an unpayable price in world-wide publicity. Dos Passos's face had been on the cover of *Time*. He carried the shield of visibility, and Liston Oak knew that he was going to die, and die very soon, unless he had some sort of shield.

In that hotel room the young man whispered because he knew the room was bugged, and in a whisper he pleaded for help.

Dos Passos took all this in and once again acted with clarity and dispatch. He told Oak that he was from that moment no longer Liston Oak from del Vayo's propaganda office, but Liston Oak the private secretary of John Dos Passos. They were leaving together for the French border immediately, that very hour. And on their trip north, Liston was never to leave Dos Passos's side, not once, not for a moment.[103]

And so it was that John Dos Passos left Spain and communism, shielding the terrified young defector not with his body but with his fame, keeping him covered on their every step north. It was not until the two had crossed the border at Perpignan that the young man could emerge from the horror into which they had both been lured, and was free.

Chapter 11

Münzenberg's End

After his escape from Moscow in October 1936, Münzenberg's energies were directed to saving his own life. That did not, however, lead him to anything like a quick or overt break with Stalin. On the contrary. Though Willi knew he had fallen from Stalin's grace, once he returned to Paris clutching the "sheet anchor" of his Spanish operations, he performed some of his most notable services ever to the regime. Yet even as he used Spain to escape from the net of arrests dropping around Radek, Willi understood that henceforth his survival would be a strictly provisional thing, and that the menace of liquidation would become even more dire once his usefulness in the Spanish War came to an end.

Seven months later, during the bloody summer of 1937, that end came at last. The Spanish government was entirely in the hands of the NKVD. The Comintern in Spain, behind its Byronic facade of Popular Front idealism, had become a mere mask for the secret police. Put in personal terms, the process that would separate Otto Katz from Willi was now complete. Put in more general terms, the Comintern, which had always been the base of Münzenberg's power, was being liquidated. For the first months of 1937, Willi retained some measure of influence within the apparatus. He could still protect himself with an uneasy mixture of blackmail, service, and visibility. But in May and June of 1937, it was very clear that he would soon stand in need of a quite new kind of shield.

We have called it "the shield of visibility." For Willi, it took many forms. Around the same time, Whittaker Chambers would call the process of assembling such a defense ''creating an identity.'' But Chambers was a man who had gone underground; he had chosen the invisibility and anonymity of life as a spy, only to discover how easily you could die in that half-light, unseen. During the years after that recognition, Chambers lived in terror, sure he would die as Robles had died, as Liston Oak had feared dying. Safety meant escaping that lethal obscurity. Chambers had to reappear, be seen again. He needed to re-enter the civic life, get a job, a visible job; writing regularly, with a byline for all to see. He had to be known to friends, attend the PTA, live once more in the human sphere rather than in the dank anonymity of conspiratorial hatred.

With Münzenberg, the process was rather different. Münzenberg was in far more direct danger than Chambers ever confronted, but as a leading ''anti-fascist,'' Willi was already a famous man. His safety now depended upon whether he could use his visibility as a shield, even though he was locked in a secret struggle against his old comrades. Not surprisingly, he found his self-defense behind the facade of the anti-fascist movement which he had helped create.

Willi's effort to shape a new and better shield out of his anti-fascism was a perilous course. By 1937, Stalin's search for an alliance with Hitler was already very far advanced, and there was a general understanding among witting agents that the Germans would no longer be the objects of any serious hostile operations. The Popular Front, including the Popular Front's Civil War in Spain, would soon be tossed away.[1] In December 1936, shortly after the Spanish Stratagem was fully conceived and on its way to implementation, Walter Krivitsky had a meeting in Paris with Slutsky, the foreign director of the NKVD. Slutsky's immediate object was to acquire from Krivitsky's networks two young male agents capable of impersonating Nazis over a fairly long period. Krivitsky was not aware of it at the time, but these recruits were to be used in the conspiracy to frame Field Marshall Tuchachevsky and the rest of the Red Army general staff. In his talk with Krivitsky that day, Slutsky forthrightly laid out the state of affairs, some six months before Negrin was installed and the Spanish Terror turned up to full strength.

''We have set our course toward an early understanding with Hitler,'' Slutsky said, ''and we have started negotiations. They are progressing favorably.''

Krivitsky was slightly confused. This was the month after Negrin had been selected as the Stalinist premier-to-be of Spain, and five months before he was actually installed. Krivitsky was well aware that Stalin was seeking an accommodation with Hitler, but the secret agent didn't yet really grasp the link between the German deal and events in Spain. How, he asked Slutsky, could the German conversations be proceeding so very well despite the Spanish imbroglio? Slutsky brushed aside the contradiction. "This time," he said, "it's the real thing. It will be only a matter of three or four months before we come to terms with Hitler. . . . There is nothing for us here in this rotting corpse of France with its *Front Populaire*! . . . I can give you Stalin's own view in his own words. He recently said to Yezhov, in the immediate future we shall consummate an agreement with Germany."[2]

This was in 1936; it was not 1939. Three years would pass before the all-desired alliance really was consummated—at least publicly. Nonetheless, the strategy was in place: deep in their totalitarian collaboration, Stalin and Hitler had set the course that would lead to the Second World War.

Six months later, the Spanish Terror would be fully unleashed. As the Spanish Civil War wound down toward that defeat which Stalin, in my view, had long since chosen for it, the Soviets turned their attention to those spots in Eastern Europe where Stalin expected the largest gains: Romania, Poland, Finland, Austria, Czechoslovakia. The focus of Stalin's interest was moving away from sideshows like Spain to the places he proposed really to hold and really make submit.

This meant that as 1937 gave way to 1938, Münzenberg's usefulness to the apparatus was ominously dwindling toward nothing. At the same time, while Otto Katz continued to move between Valencia and Paris, Otto was less and less concerned with Spanish matters; instead, he was more and more steadily involved in Eastern European politics, especially in the Beneš government, managing the covert communists within the Czech foreign ministry. His role there grew increasingly active and conspiratorial.

From Spain to Eastern Europe; from the Comintern to the NKVD; here were the new realities of the secret world as it moved toward the Second World War. Inevitably, those changes would be reflected, terroristically, within the apparatus. A new and elaborately covered wave of murder and fear within the European and American apparatus was set up, directed against many of the people who had been most instrumental in bringing about the new state of affairs. They began with Berzin's death in (probably) May 1937. Then, after the Spanish Terror in Catalonia, there were many more murders of Stalin's old friends.

The next operation, to which Hitler had been party from the beginning, was the murder of Field Marshall Tuchachevsky and his colleagues on the Red Army general staff, accomplished in part through conspiratorial operations between Stalin and Hitler passing through the Beneš government. Was Katz party to these operations? I think it very possible. Tuchachevsky had been visibly in trouble since May 1937. On June 11, he was arrested and shot.

This made other tumblers fall. It appears that the Tuchachevsky murders provided Ignace Reiss with his motive to turn against Stalin and defect. (Such at least is the received view, and Reiss's real reasons for defection may have been that simple. I do not see that they are self-evidently so. The entire question of Reiss's motivation would, I think, richly repay new study.) In any case, a little over a month later Reiss wrote his letter of defiance, broke, and then ran. He broke after a final meeting with Krivitsky in Paris; his letter to Stalin, filled with enough invective and denunciation to kill him a hundred times over, was dispatched through an oddly insecure source. Reiss fled to Switzerland where, apparently with the help of Noel Field, he was found and killed less than two months later, on September 4, 1937.[3] Shortly after that, Krivitsky himself was looking for shelter.[4]

But these were, on a higher level than Chambers, invisible men. They were underground agents whose whole existence had been contrived to maintain a maximum of secrecy. As with Robles, as with Liston Oak, it was quite possible for them to die unseen, murdered in the shadows where they had lived. In 1937, Münzenberg was no less a target than they were, but because he was a famous man, for the moment he had his shield.

During the three and a half months between Radek's arrest in October 1936 and his trial in January 1937 in Moscow, Münzenberg was maneuvering in uncertainty, trying to solidify his position in Spain by building on his role in RUP and in the new German Popular Front. During this time, it was far from clear what kind of deal Radek would make with the dictator, or what direction the show trial would take. Would Münzenberg be condemned from the dock? It was easily imaginable. Would Radek in his "confession" take Willi down with him? If the deal with Hitler was near consummation, it would be easily imaginable. Could the Terror reach straight into Paris?

When Radek's trial began in January, Münzenberg decided that it would be best for him to become "ill" for the time being, and for purposes of his "health," seek a little seclusion in the country. A cover story was concocted: He was suffering from a "mild cardiac neurosis." There was also a story about a "nervous breakdown."[5] It is plain that there was nothing wrong with him at all. Nonetheless Willi checked into a little-known clinic in the French countryside, secreted on what had once been the country estate of the French romantic poet Chateaubriand. There he submitted himself to the care of a remarkable French physician known as Dr. Le Savoureux.[6]

As best I can determine, the clinic of Dr. Le Savoureux was a perfectly genuine medical establishment. At the same time, it was a safe house in what amounted to an anti-Bolshevik underground. It bore the resonant name ''La Clinique de la Vallée aux Loups.'' There in Valley of the Wolves, near the little village of Châtenay-Malabry, Münzenberg found haven while the Radek trial ran its course.

Dr. Le Savoureux is a (to me) quite mysterious figure. He seems to have been a man of very considerable courage and impressive ideological suppleness. His own nationality, I gather, was French. He was married however to a Russian, a daughter of Plehkanov, a revolutionary and a former companion of Lenin who had become a leader of the Menshevik faction against Lenin in the days just before the Revolution. The doctor and his wife therefore moved along the Russian emigré left—circles famously penetrated by the Soviet services. Nonetheless, the clinic on the estate of the old romantic poet seems to have been safe. At least it was hard to kill people staying there. In it, Dr. Le Savoureux ran a sort of protection service for people in danger.

While Willi was hiding out in the clinic at Châtenay-Malabry, the doctor told him an interesting tale. During the spring of the same year, none other than Nikolai Bukharin, who would succeed Radek in the dock during the next great show trial, had been in Paris during an official mission to the West. This visit to Paris had taken place in the spring, a few months before Maxim Gorky's death.[7] That visit, with the contact Bukharin made with Dr. Le Savoureux, casts an interesting new shaft of light on the old Bolshevik's visit to Gide in his hotel room the day before Gorky's State Funeral, and especially on Bukharin's urgent desire to speak to Gide privately and confidentially. It also casts new light on Bukharin's sudden recognition that Gide was not going to be competent to hear whatever it was the old Bolshevik had to say. That is when Bukharin backed out of the writer's hotel room, mute with what Herbart had called his ''smile of unspeakable contempt.''

Bukharin's official mission in Paris had been to arrange for the purchase for the Soviet archives of major papers in the archives of the German Social Democrats. They included important papers of both Marx and Engels, and this was to be a perfectly legitimate purchase. The discussions were to take place with the Menshevik curator of the papers, a scholar named Boris Nicholaevsky.[8]

Bukharin's conversations with Nicholaevsky soon passed far beyond mere discussion about the possible purchase of the papers. They became confidential, then secret. Bukharin began to speak with great candor on the political machinations taking place at the highest levels around Stalin.* Nicholaevsky's slightly fictionalized report on these conversations, later published as "A Letter from an Old Bolshevik," is a major document. George Kennan has called it "the most authoritative and important piece of source material we have of the purges."[9]

It appears that during this same visit, perhaps through Nicholaevsky, Bukharin was also introduced to Dr. Le Savoureux. It seems that the possibility was at least raised that Bukharin, for whom the Soviet shadows were lengthening at an alarming rate, might defect to the West and become, presumably, a kind of second Trotsky.

Bukharin, at any rate, was with Dr. Le Savoureux when he received his telegram ordering him to break off his discussions with Nicholaevsky and return at once to Moscow. It was obviously a signal of the end, an invitation to an execution. Bukharin was rigid with fear. His voice shook as he spoke; he was white, in despair. It was plain that his life was at an end.[10]

Dr. Le Savoureux tried to persuade Bukharin to refuse this summons. I can only suppose Bukharin and the Menshevik also spoke about what sort of protection Bukharin the defector could hope for, under the threat of Stalin's vengeance. Trotsky's exile was lived, and lived precariously, inside a nomadic armed camp, under security far more stringent than what was then accorded to most heads of state. And even so, within three years, the ice-axe would be driven into his brain.

Bukharin could not, or would not, make that move. He would not, or could not, turn aside this summons to the slaughterhouse. It makes one wonder all the more what message he wished to confide to Gide in those moments before Gorky's funeral.

---

*A glimpse of Radek in these intrigues can be found in Nicholaevsky, *Power and the Soviet Elite,* p. 37. "The Letter from an Old Bolshevik" (Nicholaevsky's representation of his conversations with Bukharin in 1936), suggests both what a senior figure like Bukharin knew, and what he did not know, as the Terror approached. It's an arresting detail that, according to Nicholaevsky, Bukharin believed that the Popular Front had been set up as a response to a secret propaganda network established in the USSR by none other than Ernst Röhm. He was told that a "network" of agents working for the Nazis had been set up by Röhm, dominated by homosexuals active in Moscow cultural life! This all-but-forgotten "conspiracy" was surely a Stalinist canard, but in it one glimpses again several threads we've already seen. The "homosexual conspiracy" of Moscow has the look of an intrigue parallel to the Reichstag Fire Trial—its Russian branch, as it were. It may well have been part of Stalin and Hitler's joint effort to discredit Röhm by focussing on his homosexuality, and thereby prepare him for his demise.

Feigning illness in the Valley of the Wolves, sheltered in Dr. Le Savoureux's safe house, Münzenberg waited for Radek's trial to run its course. He watched every twist, every ripple in the flow of the trial's mendacity. As it moved forward, Münzenberg discovered that he was not being denounced in the courtroom, not implicated. Radek was at last convicted, but mysteriously he was not condemned to death. For some reason, Stalin had decided to delay Radek's demise; for the moment, there would be no bullet behind his ear. This must have been, for Willi too, a kind of reprieve. Münzenberg's jeopardy had deepened, but it was not yet absolute.

With reason. In January 1937, Willi's usefulness to the regime still had five or six months to run. He was still busy with his task, organizing the propaganda networks of the last lying Comintern cause in Spain. Willi's "sheet anchor" still held.

But once the Soviet secret police had completed its kidnapping and capture of the Spanish Republic, Münzenberg lost the last protective device he had to bind his life and safety to Stalin's power. Within a month of the Spanish Terror, the machinery of Willi's undoing began to work overtly. In May 1937, a few weeks after those two classic Münzenberg communists, Liston Oak and John Dos Passos, made their flight to Perpignan, the German Party obediently expelled Münzenberg himself. The rationale for his denunciation was typical Stalinist newspeak. Münzenberg was deemed insufficiently devoted to the Popular Front. In other words, the Popular Front was finished, and with its fall Willi was without his shield.

He would therefore need a new approach. Once Spain was past, Willi's strategy now became to take up genuine leadership in the anti-fascism of the German emigrés, even at a time when the apparatus was withdrawing from that concern. It was the era of what Münzenberg came to call the "Heinrich and Thomas Mann Committees," and Willi's tactic was to manipulate within these righteousness groups so as to keep them constantly alive, while keeping the Party slightly off guard. He was trying to outmaneuver the system he himself had created; Münzenberg had become mongoose to his own snake. As a result, these groups often acquired a more authentically anti-fascist tone then they'd had earlier. Willi was sure that his safety required him to stay continuously involved in the propaganda operations that united his friends and his enemies, both real and apparent. He could not break with anyone, nor could he commit himself to anyone. If the dissociations of terror can be called intellectual independence, now at last Willi was in possession of that "independence," the illusions of which he had spent the previous two decades organizing.

He needed enough distance from Stalin so that he could discreetly disobey; at the same time, he needed to stay close enough to the apparatus so that it could not shoot him without shooting its own foot. So it was a very special dance.

In the archives, for example, there is the report of a meeting of a "Heinrich and Thomas Mann Committee." It took place in 1938. Both Willi and Otto were present, though they were both now deep in the hostility of which I speak. The prime "innocent" present was Thomas Mann. Otto's purpose in the gathering was to suborn one of the righteousness committees with some apparatus money from England. Willi was not going to let him get away with it. The battle flew back and forth, past the author of *Death in Venice,* conducted in double talk. In the end, Otto's effort failed, Willi was left still crucial to the committee, and Thomas Mann departed, dignified but bewildered.[11]

In the old days, Münzenberg had created an ambiguity about secret communist power within the front groups. Now, by moving with maximum dexterity in that same ambiguous space, Willi was finding shelter. His original purpose had been the secret service of the apparatus. Now it was to dodge the executioners.

Meanwhile, the NKVD set out on a systematic effort to lure Münzenberg back to Russia. This was good news; it meant that the shield of visibility was effective enough to prevent simple assassination in Paris. Time and again in communications from Moscow, Willi was asked, ordered, commanded, lured, cajoled, begged. Messengers ranging from Count Karolyi to Louis Fischer, editor of the *Nation,* came bearing the invitations.[12] Time and again, Willi dodged the call. Dimitrov himself sent many requests. At one point a senior NKVD agent named Beletsky, whom Willi knew to be high up in Stalin's political assassination squadron, the sinister Bureau of Special Tasks, personally approached him, all smiles. Come home. Don't be afraid. "Who decides your fate?" Beletsky asked him, in a pertinent question. "Dimitrov or the OGPU? And I know that Yezhov is on your side."[13]

It was a trap of course, and of course Willi sidestepped it. As late as May 1938, three months after Munich, these efforts still were going forward. That month, Louis Gibarti was recalled from his NKVD work in New York and returned to Europe, assigned instead to new work in Spain and Paris. Before Gibarti left New York, he was taken aside and warned by Earl Browder, the chairman of the American Communist party, that he should have nothing to do with the traitor Münzenberg.[14]

When Gibarti returned to Paris, he instantly sought out Willi. They met, curiously, in as public a place as they could arrange: the terrace of the Café Veil. As they sat together, Münzenberg pulled out of his pocket a recent letter from Dimitrov, renewing the appeal to return to Moscow. Gibarti read it, and tried to make the case that Dimitrov was right; there was nothing to fear; it would be perfectly safe for him to return.

Safe? Willi shrugged. If he returned to Moscow, he said, he would be shot like all the others. Ten years later, he would be rehabilitated. And so, he concluded, it was a trip he'd skip. Then Münzenberg folded the letter, slipped it back in his pocket, and while Gibarti searched for an answer, gazed out into the springtime square.[15]

But Münzenberg was a publisher, and to maintain his visibility he needed some public forum for these new maneuvers. He needed a magazine. In 1938, he founded a new and in many ways ground-breaking journal of politics and ideas, a publication which he named, with what must have seemed then quixotic bravery: *Die Zukunft,* the future. *Die Zukunft* was to be a high-level forum for the arguments and hopes of the menaced German left. But it was also intended as Münzenberg's shield. The magazine was a classic Münzenberg-style mix of innocence, intellectual grandeur, and unseen agendas. Its personnel included rebels and geniuses, sympathizers and secret agents. Arthur Koestler and Manès Sperber edited it; the brothers Mann wrote for it; Gibarti worked out of its office, and Otto Katz meddled in it. As the decade now hurried toward its climax in war, almost against its own intentions *Die Zukunft* evolved into something that in retrospect has the look of the first truly anti-totalitarian journal for the senior intelligentsia.

It was a model for publications to come. The manner and even the personnel of *Die Zukunft* suggest Melvin Lasky's post-war publication *Der Monat,* and through that link, the publications of the Congress for Cultural Freedom: *Encounter, Preuves,* and *Tempo Presente*. In the movements of the Popular Front, guided by the life-and-death politics of the Terror, the profile of what would become a post-war anti-communist intelligentsia was taking shape.[16]

Finally, like many people deposed from great power, Münzenberg wrote a book. It was called *Propaganda als Waffe* (*Propaganda as a Weapon*), a skillful and spectacularly well-informed analysis of Nazi methods in the propaganda war. *Propaganda als Waffe* should be viewed as more or less Willi's own, though the real writing in it was much assisted by a still loyal Münzenberg-man, Kert Kersten. Politically, the book is both flamboyant and careful. Very careful. It is relentless on its attack on Hitler; its tone about Stalin is one of bland deference. It slams no doors.

Meanwhile, switching from tones of seduction to the snarl of menace, the apparatus grew more and more frustrated. The Comintern archives contain extensive dossiers laying out the "Case of WM," with the most concentrated work against Münzenberg being supplied by Wilhelm Pieck, the man who was the intermediary in the Dimitrov Conspiracy, and later the first president of the Stalinist East German Republic. In June 1937, a Comintern functionary, Bohumil Smearl, arrived in Paris attempting to retrieve for the Comintern large deposits held in various European banks in Willi's name.[17] Kurt Sauerland, a young writer loyal to Münzenberg, was being held prisoner hostage to Münzenberg in Moscow. He would surrender the deposits, Willi reportedly told Smearl, only if Sauerland were released. Willi was now bartering with lives. (The tactic was a passing success and long-term failure. Young Sauerland's life was spared until Münzenberg was safely dead. Then he was executed as well.)[18] But Willi was not without some threats of his own. It has also been claimed that Münzenberg threatened to go public with secrets of Soviet covert operations if he were expelled from the German Party.[19] That threat failed: He was duly expelled in May 1937.[20] Still, he was threatening to talk. And how much might he tell? A little? A lot? Would he bargain with his revelations? Münzenberg was becoming a really dangerous man.

Meanwhile, the tortoise had lifted his scaly foot and was considering his next step. The next step was the Second World War. After September 1, 1939, it was no longer possible for Münzenberg to remain protected by his ambiguity. In *Die Zukunft,* for the first time, he denounced Stalin. Yet in retrospect, even this performance seems rather mild, a purely moralistic attack. In truth, Münzenberg's response to the pact and the war was as much a matter of covering his own position as a serious assault. And now he would be needing protection of a new kind.

He may have found some protection with the European services. With the war, the secret services of the democratic allies began to gather in Paris. A sometime Münzenberg-man, Paul Willert, was assigned to be the representative of British intelligence in the British Information Office opened in Paris under Noel Coward. It was at this point that Münzenberg began to hold his little lunches.

Once a week, in the private dining room of a restaurant on the Left Bank, Willi would give a lunch for the assembled young secret service agents of the allied forces. During these meals he would systematically analyze the advances of the new Nazi-Soviet allies from his uniquely well-informed point of view. One of those regularly in attendance was Paul Willert. The assembled agents listened like schoolboys.[21]

It was a very ingenious new political device Münzenberg had created. He now knew that he would need to be turning to the allies for his protection, but he also knew that the French, English, and American governments, and especially their secret services, were penetrated by Stalinist agents and sympathizers, and that he could not entrust himself to them. The restaurant room was a good venue. Speaking there, he knew that his views would be heard every week in the English and French chancelleries. At the same time, while he met with these young men behind closed doors, he met with them in semi-public, entrusting his physical safety to none of them. Yet.

The British especially were interested in his fate, and at the senior reaches of the British government, Ellen Wilkinson, now a passionate anti-Stalinist, became particularly interested in Willi's destiny. It was at this time that Münzenberg warned Ellen that she should use the utmost care in any matter concerning either him or Arthur Koestler when dealing with the British intelligence service, that one of his most dangerous enemies was to be found there.[22] It was likewise at this point that both Ellen Wilkinson and her friend Herbert Morrison became implacable adversaries of Guy Liddell, much to the outrage of Liddell's prime protégé in SOE, Kim Philby.[23] In fact it was Wilkinson who now brought an end to Liddell's previously uninterrupted rise in the British security services. Was Liddell the man Münzenberg feared? The record is unclear, but plainly Willi was not quite prepared to entrust his safety to either the British or the French.[24] He felt it was essential to keep his distance from them, while at the same time remaining steadily within their view.

This combination of conspicuousness and concealment could last only so long. In the spring of 1940, the invasions of Scandinavia and the Benelux, followed by Hitler's attack on France, at last knocked the shield of visibility from Münzenberg's hand.

In my opinion, Willi Münzenberg probably met his death at the hands of the NKVD. But the fact is far from certain. As the reader will see, a plausible case can and has been made that Münzenberg committed suicide, hanged himself from a tree on the outskirts of a wood near a tiny town in the Isère valley of the Midi in the early evening of June 21, 1940, the day after the fall of France. And despite improbability, I grant that suicide is at least a possible explanation.

Certain it is that Münzenberg died violently, and by strangulation. I believe the more likely case is political assassination. Most analyses of Münzenberg's death maintain that he was probably killed by an NKVD execution team tracking his flight south during those days of frantic desperation when France was falling. That argument rests upon the certainty that Willi had been an NKVD target for years, and that at this time the Bureau of Special Tasks was regularly exploiting the southward flight of refugees to settle scores.[25] Moreover, in early 1940 Münzenberg had delivered on an old threat to Stalin, publishing in a Belgian paper the names of forty important German communists killed in the Great Terror. This sort of list had never before appeared from such an authoritative source.[26]

But was the end suicide or murder? I am uncertain. The logic of my uncertainty runs something like this. *If* Willi did not commit suicide, he was certainly murdered. *If* he was murdered, he was almost certainly murdered either by the NKVD, or by the NKVD assisted by the Nazis. Moreover, though there is a plausible case to be made for suicide, that case rests almost entirely upon the unsupported word of a prime suspect in the murder. Add to this that Münzenberg was in no way a melancholic or saturnine personality. Nobody among his close associates has ever been able to accept that he could take his own life. His situation on June 21, 1940, was desperate, but not impossible. With really determined effort, he might well have escaped from France. In truth, every single person who was in flight with him, without exception, did reach safety, and they all reached it fairly soon.

Still, at that moment in 1940, Münzenberg understood that he was peculiarly on his own and that he was a hunted man, living under a particular menace of his own. He knew his escape from France, and his future wherever he went, would be shadowed by the secret services of two lethal dictators, both of whom wanted him dead. Here is where suicide seems possible. A certain kind of very dynamic person, cornered, may refuse even at the last to surrender control, and in that defiance may take things firmly back into his own hands, albeit for the last time.

Suicide or murder? Whether Münzenberg died in defiant despair, or was killed cornered, he died the victim of what he had helped create.

Here is what we know happened, with some speculation.

At the beginning of April 1940, the *blitzkrieg* against Norway and Denmark began: By the beginning of May the panzers were rolling into the Low Countries. The French government ordered all German (and American) men not of draft age and not previously interned to internment camps. As the last issue of *Die Zukunft* appeared, Münzenberg had to make his decision. Would he take flight, seeking a way out of France, running presumably toward English protection, on his own? Or should he submit to the internment system, and to the very uncertain protection of the French? It is important to know that in making this decision Münzenberg turned for assistance to his friends in British intelligence. Very shortly before he made his move, he had a meeting with Paul Willert and Sefton Delmer, both of SOE. And he asked Willert and Delmer what they thought he should do.[27]

One need not raise any questions about the reliability of either Paul Willert or Sefton Delmer to realize in retrospect that this was an insecure conversation. For if Münzenberg's path of escape was relayed back to British intelligence in London, as it certainly would have been, the SOE official receiving it in London might well have been Kim Philby. Moreover, even if Philby did not know Willi's path, serious questions have been raised about the reliability of Sefton Delmer.[28] One way or the other, the conversation was quite possibly insecure. In any case, the British agents advised Münzenberg to enter an internment camp, and take that route south.

Thus, on the advice of Delmer and Willert, somewhere around May 13 or 14, 1940, Babette and Münzenberg went to a stadium called the Stade des Colombes, together with throngs of German and American men being gathered to be interned. The German victory grew hourly more palpable. Everyone knew they had to get to the Spanish border, and the path out, probably through Casablanca, or perhaps Marseilles, or conceivably the Swiss border.

Babette and Willi had made exact plans for a rendezvous in the south once they left internment. She was to be interned in a camp for German women near Gurs. But now as the crowd swarmed around them the moment of parting came. They put their arms round each other, and then Münzenberg walked into the throng of evacuees in the babble of German and some American English. They were swept away from each other.

Willert and Delmer had been right: Waves of refugees from the Low Countries clogged every route of escape from Paris to the South. Internment was in a way easier than flight, and everyone expected it to be short. Many saw it not as imprisonment, but as a superior means of escape. The men were separated out into groups of one hundred and sent to various sites. The one chosen for Münzenberg was at Chambarran, south of Lyons. And so Willi departed, part of the anonymous stream.[29]

It has been suggested by some that Münzenberg had a clear destination not in Casablanca but Marseilles, where it is said that he was to meet his old friend Valeriu Marcu, a rich Rumanian emigré, a former communist, and a practiced conspirator and friend of Münzenberg from the earliest days, before the Revolution. Marcu, it is claimed, had a large sum of money for Willi, along with the documentation needed to let him sail out of the port of Marseilles a free man. This rendezvous, if it was ever real, may or may not have been planned in conjunction with the British services. Babette Gross did not believe the story. Moreover, the evidence seems to indicate that in the crisis of June 21, Willi was interested in moving not toward Marseilles but Switzerland, where he and Babette had safe bank accounts. I myself tend to discount the story of Marcu's role in the "rescue."[30]

The camp of Chambarran is an enormous military base near Lyons. The picture we have of Münzenberg once he reached the place is curiously bucolic, given the kind of fear and anguish one would expect the whole company to be feeling. Here is the great tycoon of the secret life, subdued, to be sure, but out in the sun of the fresh springtime, working not unhappily at his assigned job, which was tending the camp commandant's garden. For the first time in his adult life, Willi was out of touch with power. For the first time in his adult life, he was neither more nor less than a man among men, chopping away at the French soil, planting beans. Reports differ slightly, but he does not seem to have been particularly depressed. True, he was—small wonder!—downcast, introspective. He drifted into uncharacteristic silences. His talk was filled with worry about Babette.[31] Yet depression is not the word the witnesses used.

The men interned at Chambarran were mainly middle-aged German exiles, many of them members of that German left which Willi had been so instrumental organizing as the Popular Front. In fact, the company was distinguished. With Münzenberg was Kurt Wolff, the great German, and later American, publisher: Leopold Schwarzschild, the liberal writer and editor. There were many others. These were among the leading lights of that German civilization which Hitler was murdering. It must be added that in all the camps—Chambarran, Le Vernet, Le Cheylard, and others, the apparatus had its cadres well in place.[32]

Typical of such cadres was the person who appeared on the scene next. The newcomer was especially noticeable among all those middle-aged men because he was so young. He appeared among them one fine morning, looking like he was in his early twenties. The fellow had, it was universally recalled, red hair. Let us call him the "Red-Headed Youth." The Red-Headed Youth had a strange tale to tell of having been a communist in a Nazi concentration camp, from which he had managed to be released. Released, he had made his way to France, and now found himself in Chambarran.[33]

This unexpected newcomer, whose name remains completely unknown, was peculiarly interested, even pre-occupied with Münzenberg. He worked hard, and conspicuously, at winning Willi's trust. In her interview with me, Babette remained highly suspicious of anybody who, like the youth, had a communist affiliation which made him so obviously dangerous. Nonetheless, according to all reports, from the start the Red-Headed Youth finagled his way steadily, and finally successfully, into Münzenberg's daily presence. This accomplished, he ingratiated himself with Münzenberg at every opportunity. In early June he began to insist, with tiresome, untiring, and finally successful persistence that he be transferred to the hut where Münzenberg slept. Soon he was in Münzenberg's company all the time, and Willi seemed to accept him. The youth was eager and helpful and always there; a strong young arm.

But the French capitulation drew very near. Münzenberg began to be very much concerned with the next step in his escape. He was in possession of a map of the area between Grenoble and Valence, and after studying it carefully he undertook to convince various acquaintances in the camp to join him on a flight together toward Switzerland—the nearest neutral border. An especially enthusiastic voice behind this idea was the Red-Headed Youth.[34]

There were others, however. Among the older Germans Willi attempted to enlist was a rather well-known Social Democrat trade unionist, a non-communist, even anti-communist, known to Willi from the Popular Front days in Paris. His name was Valentin Hartig.

It must be said at once that Valentin Hartig's behavior on the scene, and above all his subsequent political history, can only be viewed with the most intense mistrust. It is plain that the man who most encouraged Münzenberg in his ill-fated plan to strike out for Switzerland was Hartig.[35] It is equally plain that on June 21, 1940, Valentin Hartig abandoned his fellow refugees, and did so without explanation. He separated from them there and headed—where? When he left Münzenberg and his companions Hartig ran not south but *north*—north to Paris, there to join the conquering Nazis. Where he was welcomed. Though historically very much a man of the left, Hartig there became active in the conquerors' collaborationist trade union movement.[36]

This sinister turn, combined with Hartig's association with the Red-Headed Youth, make me view him with the bleakest suspicion. Babette Gross, after corresponding and meeting with Hartig extensively after the war, was at last convinced that he was entirely innocent in Münzenberg's demise. I do not share that confidence. Possibly he gave Babette some accounting never made public. If so she did not reveal it in our conversations. Certainly Hartig's behavior has never been satisfactorily explained in any document or report known to me.[37]

By June 18 it was plain that total French capitulation was only days away. On June 21 at 5:00 in the morning, the commandant of Chambarran called the men together in the camp yard. According to one report, the gates of the camps were simply flung open and the men set free. According to Helen Wolff, many of the interns, including Kurt Wolff, were herded onto buses and dispatched to another internment camp further south, deemed more secure.[38] Not so with Münzenberg. It appears that Willi and a large number of other interns were ordered to form a column and begin marching on foot, headed toward a camp to the southwest which they were not serious about reaching: Le Cheylard.[39]

It seems that among those on this march were Hartig, Leopold Schwarzschild, Hans Siemsen, Klement Korth, Paul Westheim, Münzenberg, and crucially, the Red-Headed Youth. It has been claimed that Kurt Wolff was also on the march: Helen Wolff assures me that her late husband's diaries flatly disprove this claim.

Unlike Kurt Wolff and others, who left on buses, Münzenberg and his group set out on foot, following highway D20 south, toward Marseilles. By the afternoon of that day the men had trudged perhaps fifteen, twenty miles. They stopped to rest in the lovely spring-green valley of the Isère River, a place where three tiny hamlets sit clustered together on the verge of a great European forest, the Forest of Caugnet. The three towns live as one: Saint Marcellin, Montagne, and Saint Antoine—tiny hamlets all, with only Saint Marcellin big enough to have a mairie and a post office. They are hamlets built around twelfth-century churches, places where people marry the same people with whom they learned to walk and talk. It is a town where the cemetery is as familiar as the school, where one can speak—without inexactness—about what the whole town knows.

The German refugees stopped in Saint Antoine and there, near its ancient church, decided to spend the night. Everyone was very tired; no one wanted to go on. Nonetheless, Münzenberg continued to argue for the break toward Switzerland, though he was still getting no real volunteers for the venture except, it seems, the Red-Headed Youth. And Hartig. In the process Münzenberg claimed that he had on his person 2,000 French francs—a huge sum for any refugee to possess at that moment. As the men were settling in and resting, Willi announced that he had learned from Hartig that there was a car for sale over in the next town, and that he proposed to go there with this money and buy it. He was quite sure there was a car there: Hartig, honest, honest Hartig, "already had reconnoitered" the scene, already had been over to the town. And with a car—think what they could do with a car! There it was, so temptingly, just a couple of kilometers away.[40] They could easily walk there in under half an hour. Willi, typically, decided to act at once. He would walk over to

Montagne and try to buy the car Hartig had found. It was understood that whether this effort succeeded or failed, he definitely planned to return to the others left behind at their resting place. Of course the situation was fluid, but there is no evidence that anyone thought Münzenberg and his friends were embarking on their flight then and there. Valentin Hartig, everyone agreed, should go along because Hartig knew where the car was, and because he spoke such good French. In Montagne they either would or would not buy a car, and then they would return.

Among the others who went with Hartig and Münzenberg was the Red-Headed Youth. Why? The youth was among those pressing hardest for the Swiss scheme, and buying the car would have clinched that plan. Perhaps he also knew how to drive: It is not at all clear that either Willi or Hartig did. (Münzenberg had always been driven by his chauffeur and bodyguard, Emil.) In any case, he seems to have been one of those going to Montagne, apparently along with another of the younger men in the group, though this latter fact is murky.

So off they went, either three or four together. "I can still see him," Siemsen later said, "waving his hand as he went off across the fields."[41]

With this wave, Willi Münzenberg vanishes from history.

He never returned. More to the point: *Not one of his companions ever returned.* Not one. Westheim, Siemsen, and the rest, sat waiting in Saint Antoine and they waited in vain for any one of them to come back. All four (if they were four) men vanished without trace.* But by nighttime, all four men were gone, gone without a word of explanation or clue as to their reasons for flight.

This simple raw *donnée—not one came back*—is the single indisputable assertion we can make about the whole mystery, the unique point of firm ground in a shifting tale. Münzenberg: vanished and dead. The Red-Headed Youth and possibly another young companion: vanished. Valentin Hartig: A man of the left, vanished, only to reappear in Paris under Nazi auspices, during the alliance between the communists and fascists.

If just one of Münzenberg's companions—*any* one—had returned to Saint Antoine, with or without a car, in whatever state of perplexity, to explain whatever disaster or slip-up, the entire matter would have a very different look. *Somebody* would at least *look* innocent.

---

* According to one report, Hartig did briefly reappear before the group that evening, but he reappeared (if he did) without the others, without the money, and without any explanation of anything, and after this brief contact proceeded to disappear again, this time definitively.

. . .

We know the four men reached Montagne without incident. The road ran close along the edge of a dense wooded place called the Forest of Thivolet. This they passed and then they were seen and heard in the town, negotiating hard for some deal on a car: to buy or rent made little difference. The first such effort failed, but the men were directed to another person in the town, a Mme. Gorbetier, who had a car she might be willing to sell. Mme. Gorbetier later recalled that a visitor did come, alone. The stranger who approached her, she said, spoke easy fluent French, and there was no deal over the car. Because of the fluent French, it is plain that Mme. Gorbetier's visitor was not Münzenberg. It has to have been Hartig.

But why was Hartig alone? Was he negotiating for the group, while they rested back at the café? Or was he possibly negotiating for himself, for his own escape? Was Hartig himself carrying the 2,000 francs, or had the money been left with Willi? We know only that the elusive Herr Hartig was seen again later that day by Mme. Gorbetier, but this time in the late evening, eight miles away in a third village, Saint Marcellin. Once again, Hartig was quite alone. After this last sighting on the scene, Valentin Hartig also vanishes, en route to Paris and the Nazis. And by this time Münzenberg was probably dead.

But here is the crucial truth. With Hartig away first trying to buy the car, then having disappeared entirely, Münzenberg had been left alone with the Red-Headed Youth—and the second young man. The three sat waiting in the Montagne café, and were observed there. It is said that Münzenberg sat so utterly exhausted by the day's exertions that he was reluctant to go on. But at this moment the sequence becomes very murky.

In 1987, a controversial book made a large impact at a Münzenberg Congress which took place in Zurich. The book was published in the East German Republic by a man named Gerhart Leo, who held a quite high-level journalistic position in the Honecker journalistic world. It claims that Gerhart Leo's father, a certain Wilhelm Leo, was one of the two young men with Willi—whether he was red-headed or not is unclear—and that Wilhelm had confided the whole truth of the events in Montagne to Gerhart in 1945, when the family returned to Stalinist East Germany to take up residence.

According to Gerhart Leo, once Hartig had left the group and Münzenberg was left alone in the Montagne café with his two companions, Willi was in despair. He also claimed to be ill, and in such a state of demoralized exhaustion that he could not possibly go on without a rest. He urged his two companions to strike out into the forest ahead of him, and he would try to catch up. They obediently left him, though precisely how Willi was to pick up their path through the woods is quite unclear. More to the point, strike out for what destination? The Swiss border? The men were exhausted. Night was falling. They had no car. Hartig had not returned, and he may have had their money. Obviously, the only sensible action would have been to return to their fellow refugees, still camped out, ready to spend the night beneath the stars, a very few kilometers away—fellow refugees who in fact all, every one, eventually reached safety. But there was not even a message sent to the people still waiting in Saint Antoine. Instead, madly, the two young men struck out into the woods.

Leo claims that his father and the other youth waited in the woods for their improbable rendezvous with the "rested" Willi. Except he did not come. After the appointed hour was long past, Leo claims the Red-Headed Youth and the other man returned to the edge of the wood. There they found Münzenberg. He had hanged himself with some rope used for baling the local tobacco, found on the ground.

Babette Gross had read this book several times, very carefully. She viewed it with the utmost suspicion. First of all, she viewed its source, a committed communist journalist publishing with a state-sponsored house in the DDR, as rendering it unreliable on its face. Moreover, she claimed to have no knowledge of any Wilhelm Leo among the German exiles, though her knowledge was encyclopedic. That the elder Leo had been known to Münzenberg she flatly denied. Moreover, she could not believe that Münzenberg would ever have trusted his life to these two obviously untested and unknown men. It obviously would have been far, far better to take his chances with the long column of refugees, trudging south to safety. Münzenberg always intended to return to his friends in Saint Antoine, either with a car or without one, either to pick up passengers or to spend the night under the stars and then rejoin the march. Why then, in the midst of his despair and possible illness, would he reverse himself and say he would try running, on foot, to Switzerland? The idea that a man so utterly grounded in reality as Münzenberg would have even considered embarking on such a trek, walking, at nightfall, without a clear path, in a state of complete exhaustion, unprotected, and in the company of two young communists, struck Babette as preposterous. And so it strikes me.

Add to this the mystery of long silence. Why did the younger Leo and his family wait for almost half a century to clarify one of the most persistent mysteries of the Second World War? Rather lamely, Gerhart Leo claims that the Ulbricht regime disliked former German exiles like his father and disliked Münzenberg even more: Willi was a non-person in the DDR virtually until the younger Leo published his book. Leo claims the regime would have opposed letting this story be known. This is a little difficult to believe. In the West, that Münzenberg had been murdered by the apparatus was almost universally believed during the Cold War, a famous black mark against the NKVD and the German Party. An incontestable demonstration that the assassination theory was false, false and better yet paranoid, could only have been welcome propaganda for the East German government. Yet it took until 1987, after Hartig and many other witnesses were safely dead, for Leo's story to be allowed to surface.[42]

Babette Gross regarded the Leo book as worthless. Though she did not use the word with me, I think it fair to say she saw it as disinformation.

To return to June 21, 1940. Sometime after Münzenberg and his two or three companions had grasped that there would be no car in Montagne, one of two things happened. Valentin Hartig disappeared from the scene, for reasons unknown. He probably never returned to his companions in Saint Antoine, either to return Willi's 2,000 francs, which he may have had in his possession from the visit to Mme. Gorbetier, or to explain what had happened. He simply departed, glimpsed that night in Saint Marcellin, hurrying back to his soon-to-be protectors, the Nazis.

This left Willi alone with one or two young men, one of whom may or may not have been Wilhelm Leo. And it is quite possible that an exhausted and despairing Münzenberg then and there may have impetuously taken his decision, dispatched the two young men into the woods, and once he was alone, gone to the edge of the forest himself, found the farmer's baling cord on the ground, and rigged up the noose with which he hanged himself. I do believe this is psychologically possible. I know it is physically possible. Willi knew how to tie a hangman's noose. A family story recalled that when he was a little child, in the midst of a ferocious argument with his abusive and alcoholic father, the boy threatened to kill himself, and climbed up into the attic of the family tavern with a rope. There he tied the noose, and then sat considering the ultimate act. While considering it, he fell asleep. He was later found there, asleep, using the noose as his pillow.[43]

Now in 1940, he may have tied the noose again. And he may have used it.

But there is another scenario, at least as plausible, for murder. When the first effort to acquire a car fell through, Hartig may have departed on his visit trying to buy Mme. Gorbetier's car, possibly even in possession of the

2,000 francs. It is obvious that Münzenberg trusted Hartig. While he was gone, Münzenberg and the young men rested in the café, awaiting his return. But Hartig did not return. It is possible that by pre-arrangement everyone supposed Hartig would rejoin them with the other refugees in Saint Antoine. In any case, the three were left alone there. It was getting dark.

At this point Willi and the two youths stood up and left. They were seen to walk away from the café together—another refutation of Leo's claim that the two youths left Willi behind in the café. The three were certainly not about to do anything so foolish as set off for Switzerland on foot in the gathering night. Quite obviously, they intended to return, without the car, and without Hartig, to their refugee friends just a few kilometers away. That is the direction they took. They would have to hurry to arrive in Saint Antoine before dark. The road ran past a quite small stand of woods.[44] They may well have thought that by cutting through it they would have a short cut. In any case they entered it.

Münzenberg walked into the rustling obscurity only a few hundred yards at most. He was with the two youths. They were now out of sight. And whatever happened next must have happened very quickly.

If Willi Münzenberg was murdered, as I myself believe he was, the method was probably one common among assassins. A firm cord, strong enough to be called a rope and capable of holding the suspended weight of a man's body yet supple enough to be coiled around the killer's hands, is made into a largish loop. The victim is approached from behind, and the loop is suddenly slung around his neck while the killer pulls the crossed strands back and apart with all his force and at the same time drives his knee into the victim's back. That hard forward thrust of the knee, snapping against the violent backward garroting of the rope, breaks the victim's neck in a single looping blow and produces immediate strangulation. The victim cannot fight back. Death, if not instantaneous, is very swift. The killer would have to be a strong, skilled, probably young man, and the result would be all but indistinguishable from death by hanging, except perhaps for a bruise from the knee in the middle of the victim's back.

If this is indeed what happened to Willi, it would have been a simple matter for the killers to then tie the rope into a noose, hoist the already dead man onto a tree, and leave him turning there while they disappeared.

Task one in any assassination plan would have been to get Willi alone, to lure him away from his fellow refugees; to get him alone with his killers. It was Hartig who convinced him to leave the group in search of that irresistible car. That done, it was Hartig who arranged to go off and leave

Münzenberg alone with the two youths. Whereupon Hartig left the scene, en route to Nazi protection. If Willi was killed, he was surely killed by the two youths, assigned to the job by the NKVD. Babette is right. Münzenberg would never have trusted the young men without Hartig. They were obviously dangerous. But Hartig? He trusted Hartig. He thought Hartig was safe—no communist, a Social Democrat, a reliable man, with no ties beyond what could be seen.

That was the part I think he got wrong.

I concede that Hartig *may* have fled north in simple cowardice, leaving Münzenberg behind with the young men for reasons unconnected to the killing. Babette Gross may well have been right to conclude that he was innocent in the death. Nonetheless, in the absence of other evidence, I continue to find Hartig's behavior suspicious. Certainly if Münzenberg was killed, Hartig's behavior was strangely and sublimely convenient to the killers.

Münzenberg's possibly fatal error was to trust that Hartig was what he claimed to be: a "Social Democrat." He was not; he was a man of the left who felt free to entrust himself to the conquering Nazis in Paris, in exactly the same way that Julius Alpari, Willi's old contact man in espionage, high inside the Soviet apparatus, felt perfectly safe with the arrival of the *Wehrmacht*. I submit that posing as a Social Democrat, Hartig was ideally placed to extend his double life to the services of both dictators. I do not say that he did; we are speculating here. But if Valentin Hartig did collaborate in the killing, then it seems to me possible that Münzenberg's end was itself a collaboration between the Nazi and Soviet services.

It may well have been a last lethal clause in the fine print of the Deal.

It was October by the time the corpse was found. The leaves were falling fast, though they had not covered over Willi's decomposing body when it was discovered by the dogs of some autumn hunters. The rope that had held him to the oak tree probably broke quite soon: when the corpse was discovered it was in a sitting position, knees up, under the tree. There was no money on his person, but a valuable watch was on his arm. In his pockets was a postcard addressed to Babette, a letter on the letterhead of the Paris PEN Club, and some papers that could not be distinguished.

The men who found the body raced to the mairie in Saint Marcellin to report their discovery, but before they did, while the hunting dogs yelped and whined around their gruesome find, each man clipped a small piece of the rope from around the corpse's neck. This was peasant wisdom. For some reason, it was thought that a scrap of rope from the noose of a hanged man brings hunters' luck.

Epilogue

> Some communist in trial for his life in Prague has suddenly confessed in open court that I gave him written instruction to be a British agent and that I was in a superior position in the British Intelligence Service. His name is André Simon, and I vaguely remember meeting him in Paris in 1940. Wanted to reply to the Press that, owing to recent dental surgery, my lips are sealed.
>
> —*The Diaries of Noel Coward,* November 5, 1952

Ten years after Willi's death, by 1950, America had made its entry into the Cold War, and Otto Katz was back in Czechoslovakia, where he stepped forth from the shadows, out into the dim new totalitarian light, a powerful man. During the war itself, Otto had been kept well away from direct hostilities. Spies tend to step aside as armies advance. He had made his headquarters in Mexico, exiled but far from idle, involved in many political maneuvers.

One small service Katz had been able to perform during the war was to spread disinformation about the death of Willi Münzenberg. To this end, Otto made use of his ''Free French'' mouthpiece Geneviève Tabouis, the corrupt and avaricious journalist whom the English and Americans quite mistakenly saw as a sort of heroic truth-teller with the inside word on the French debacle. In her book, *They Called Me Cassandra,* Katz was able to promulgate what became the standard Soviet lie about Willi's end, which naturally claimed that Willi had been a fascist collaborator. In fact, much of the posthumous disinformation about Willi can be traced to Otto. In the very last hours before his own execution, Otto produced, as proof of his loyalty to the Party, the claim that he had been one of those who contrived to bring his old friend down.

Then, in 1944, as the war was ending, Katz suddenly left Mexico City and travelled with his sidekick Kisch back to Prague. There both attended upon the creation of the new Czech state, present and accounted for, standing ready to receive their reward for a lifetime of conspiracy.

Before the Czech coup, during the late forties, Katz seems to have spent some time in that country's Ministry of Information. Heaven knows that ministry, combining as it did propaganda and the secret service, would have been his natural habitat. More visibly, he was made foreign editor of the national newspaper, *Rude Pravo*. He began to write its most conspicuous political column, ''André Simone Speaks.'' Otto was at last fulfilling himself in fame.

Not that he had given up secret work. So long as the Beneš-Masaryk government remained in place, the covert work needed to prepare its downfall must have required all sorts of unseen effort.* After the coup, Katz was important to a sitting government for which conspiracy was a substitute for thought. So one way or another, Otto was in his element.

Yet he had changed. The once-subtle charmer now turned coarse with power. There had been a time, on Norma Shearer and Irving Thalberg's terrace, when Katz had made magic happen with the purr of that Sudeten voice. He now grew arrogant and vulgar. His vanity, once so shrewdly deployed, turned clamorous and shrill. An American leftist remembers attending a Paris ''Peace Conference'' in 1946, when a taxi screeched to a halt beside him on the street. Leering from the open cab window was Otto; he had made the taxi stop merely to drop the name of the big shot he was going to see: Maurice Thorez.[1] Even Otto's modesty took on a posturing and boastful tone. After a meeting of East European grandees in Prague, Katz held back, imparting that he did not want to ''give the impression of being the power behind the throne.''

As for the coup, Otto grew only more influential during February and March of 1948, when Stalin decided to end his charade of collaboration

* Katz's role in the Czech coup is not certainly known to me. Much has been said about that role, but until reliable scholarship examines the archives with real care it would be foolish to go much beyond the supposition that Katz was very unlikely to have been passive as events unfolded.

with non-communists in Czechoslovakia and dispense with the government of Beneš, which had been established in Yalta. For three years, Katz had served as watchdog and penetration agent in this government.[2] But in the winter of 1948, the Czech coup produced the triumph of truth over appearance. The Beneš government, with which Otto had had such long and complex relations, had been built upon that fantasy of coalition between democrats and communists which had been the specialty of Münzenberg's brand of illusion. The apparatus was now commanded to tear this illusion to bits, and to establish a fully totalitarian state. Beneš's government was demolished; Masaryk was "suicided." The Stalinist leader, Klement Gottwald, drunk with power (and also just plain drunk), assumed absolute command, teetering into his place at the head of a government entirely obedient to the Dictator of the Proletariat.[3]

With this new government, Otto would seem to have fulfilled his secret life in some ultimate way, and fulfilled it in overt authority. He could at last leave behind the old covert networks of America, France, England, and Mexico. In the country of his childhood, the socialist paradise had been born; that inevitable Utopia for which Otto had spent a lifetime lying had at last begun to install the reign of materialist perfection. Did Otto—could Otto?—still believe in its dream? Did decades of lying for the truth leave him capable of knowing whether he did or did not? Not that his belief mattered. The sincerity of Otto's faith was quite irrelevant to the fate that was now being prepared for him.

There was never any real safety in Utopia, even for the most obedient servant. If nothing else, there was always Stalin's fatal gratitude to fear. Otto Katz had seen and said many complex and compromising things during those decades. Who could say what in his new life might tempt him to grow talkative? The Dictator might well avoid that risk by consigning Otto to terminal discretion, the silence no interrogator can break. Yet in the end, something more meaningful than Stalin's recompense brought Otto down. He was destroyed by a crisis in the secret world, one that involved all those old networks in the West in which he had played his mercurial role.

The crisis to which I refer came from America with the explosion of the great *cause célèbre* of the era: the Hiss case. It was an event which reached deep into American politics. But it also reached deep into Czech politics, and because it involved such a large number of his old American contacts, it reached all the way to Otto Katz. It reached him, above all, because of Noel Field.

The Hiss case broke in America before the House Un-American Activities Committee in August 1948, triggered by the testimony, above all, of three spies: Elizabeth Bentley, Whittaker Chambers, and later Hede Massing. All these people—Chambers, Massing, Bentley—had entered the apparatus through the Münzenberg fronts, and though Münzenberg's name never surfaced in their testimony, what they said jeopardized many of the networks which had been formed and run in America, and especially in Washington, under cover of Münzenberg's "anti-fascism." The moment of their revelations came six months after the Czech coup, and took place in the marbled swelter of official Washington, at the start of Harry Truman's shaky presidential campaign, at the very moment when the masters of the old Roosevelt coalition had every reason to fear that their political base was about to fall apart. In HUAC's off-season, obviously politically motivated inquiry heard testimony from a courier and contact man for Soviet espionage well known to Otto and all the Hungarian mafiosi in New York, a runner who thirteen years before had been the contact in one of the most important of the D.C. networks. He now stepped forward and began to talk. The witness was Josephine Herbst's old confidant "Karl." Thirteen years before, disguised by his alias, by his Dostoyevskian manner and an indefinable Germanic accent, "Karl" had sat cooped up in the loveless swelter of John Herrmann's tiny Washington apartment, listening kindly as Josie told him the broken tale of her unhappiness. But now "Karl" had stepped to the microphone in his mere American identity as Whittaker Chambers and begun to tell as much of the truth as any American had ever told about what it is to work in the *apparat.*

Because of this action, Chambers would be subjected to a lifetime of public vituperation—but for the moment, what he was saying was electrifying. It was also terribly dangerous—and to more than one side. If Chambers was telling the truth, all kinds of people were at risk, including and especially the networks created in America and in Europe under the cover of Münzenberg and his men. These were networks which throughout the war proceeded under their "anti-fascist" cover to penetrate the allied governments and any number of right-thinking organizations, all in a concerted move to prepare and secure the seizure of Soviet power in Eastern Europe and Germany. And now, at the very moment of the triumph of this secret service policy, Chambers was revealing information which could lead to massive exposure.

A prime example of an agent who stood in the direct path of that peril was Hede Massing's old pupil in espionage, Noel Field. Field was put all the more urgently at risk when Chambers made his most inflammatory statement of all: the claim that one of the people serving as a witting agent of Soviet espionage inside his Washington network was none other than Alger Hiss, an important figure in the American diplomatic establishment. Chambers claimed that Alger Hiss, with his wife Priscilla, had been in service to the Russians since at least the mid-1930s.

It was of the utmost importance that Field be removed from American reach, and the Russians acted accordingly. As the Chambers revelations entered the world headlines, Noel Field happened to be in Prague. He was "frantic" about the events unrolling in Washington; he sought, and soon had, contact with his Soviet controls.[4] He was afraid that either Hiss or Chambers, or perhaps another figure in the Washington penetrations—the lawyer Laurence Duggan, for example—might expose him at any time.[5] As the American revelations moved forward, Field was summoned to Budapest, where he suddenly disappeared. He had been "arrested." And so were Herta Field, Noel's brother Herman, and Noel's "adopted daughter," an entirely undaughterly and fully adult hard-line German communist named Erica Wallach.

These "arrests" were partly genuine incarcerations, and partly a matter of theater. Field and his family were imprisoned all right, and they were not at liberty to leave. Among other things, their confinement made it easier for Soviet apologists in the West to endow them with the necessary image of innocence, making them appear to be victims of the regime rather than the fully active collaborators they really were. But the true theater was to come: In response to the Hiss case, Noel Field was about to be cast in the role of a ubiquitous American "master-spy," whose "testimony" would now be used to justify a vast new wave of Terror running through the Eastern European communist world. This was the myth of Noel Field as the master manipulator of a vast network of traitors to the Revolution running through all the communist parties of Eastern Europe, all of them manipulated by Allen Dulles in the service of capitalism and the worst evil schemer of all, Stalin's new arch-demon, Tito. The traitors were servants of the imperialists, plotting to destroy the Revolution. They were going to restore capitalism. It was the pretext for a vast intra-party Terror that would run through every country of Eastern Europe and be the basis for the execution of thousands.

It is plain that the Soviets co-ordinated the Terror created around Noel Field with the Hiss case. Field was arrested a few days before Hiss's trial for perjury began in New York; he was released from prison the day Hiss left Lewisburg Federal Penitentiary. Meanwhile, in the United States,

Field slipped out of sight and largely out of mind. He and his family of spies dropped from the daily frenzy of press attention, and the tangled tale of the Eastern European trials was replaced by the homegrown sensation of the Hisses, and the tiresome high drama of claims and counter-claims about their innocence or guilt.

Priscilla and Alger responded to Chambers's claims with adamant, absolute, outraged, politically inflamed, and lifelong denial. It was all a lie; every word a loathsome paranoiac falsehood; a despicable fabrication invented by the cold warriors and their rightist cohorts to discredit progressive diplomacy in the United States. In the ensuing drama of charge and counter-charge, no aspect of American political opinion was left untouched. As Diana Trilling has remarked, "for years, the Hiss case represented, in small, what the Dreyfus case had represented for France."[6] The ramifications would run through American political opinion for the rest of the century. As the Fields faded away behind the "Iron Curtain," the Hiss case became the American controversy of the era.

The murderous theater played out by Noel Field at last faded entirely from view. But the controversy over whether Whittaker Chambers was or was not telling the truth about the espionage of the Hisses has never died. As of this writing, the pendulum has begun to swing faster and faster, energized by discoveries in various archives. At the time of writing, I for one have been brought close to certainty, on the basis of archival information, that Chambers was telling the truth.

Near the end of 1992, the director of the Soviet archives, General Dimitri Volkogonov retracted an ill-considered statement made shortly before in which he asserted the absence of any evidence in the Archives of Russian Military Intelligence indicating Hiss's guilt, or for that matter that Chambers ever had been more than a mere member of the Communist party of the United States. Volkogonov's first statement had naturally leapt to the front page of every newspaper in America, and for a moment or two it was taken as the last word, until the general made a retraction, claiming that Hiss's attorney, a man named John Lowenthal, had been "pushing me hard to say things of which I was not fully convinced."[7]

How were Alger Hiss and Noel Field connected? Definitive answers will have to wait for further opening of the Russian and Eastern European Archives, not least for access to the dossiers said to be in the Hungarian Ministry of Information in Budapest, made at the time of the Fields' debriefing in 1954. Even without the Budapest dossiers, however, we know that the Hisses and Fields were socially fairly close in Washington, back before the war, during the sunny days of young New Dealers chatting around the swimming pool. During the war, and up until the time of Field's exposure as a Soviet agent, the two men stayed in co-operative contact. But well beyond these friendly associations, it's plain that Field's search for shelter in Eastern Europe was provoked by the events of the Hiss case. Herta and Noel began their horrendous odyssey through the initiating terror of the Cold War bound to Hiss. Not surprisingly, that is also how their odyssey ended: bound to Hiss. The Fields were released from their Hungarian prison the day—the day exactly—that Alger Hiss completed his tcrm in Lewisburg Federal Penitentiary.

We have already seen how in 1935 Hede Massing acted as the guiding contact for Noel Field in espionage, while Field still was in the American State Department. Simultaneously, in a separate network, John Herrmann and Whittaker Chambers were running the ring of penetration agents to which Hiss belonged. In her book, *This Deception,* Hede Massing describes how in 1935 she became aware that Hiss was putting pressure on his good friend Field, to leave her apparatus and join his network of agents. Field was considering doing so, partly on the grounds that he and Hiss were so very congenial, and worked so wonderfully well together. This caused pressures, and a meeting at the Fields was arranged between Hiss and Hede Massing, in which Hiss and Hede sparred together over whose espionage organization should take the lanky Quaker as its prize.[8] According to Maria Schmidt, the Hungarian archives fully confirm Massing's account of this event.[9] Field's debriefing with the secret police in 1954 is said to be filled with information about Hiss's espionage because he knew it well, and from the earliest days.

And so the fate of the Hisses and their Washington friends the Fields were bound together in the high politics of their era. So were the respective trials convened in their names. Lying for the truth, and (I believe) lying to the end, all four of them were tortured and emblematic mixtures of good and evil. It was their fate to have the secrets of their duplicitous hearts transformed into images necessary to the various visions of good and evil in their time.

The Terror trials built around Field, one of the most terrible and revealing episodes in the history of modern Europe, are still very little understood. They spread through every capital of Eastern Europe save

Belgrade. In Hungary, Rajk was tried and killed; in Czechoslovakia, the premier, Slansky and many others went to their deaths. And it was in this latter trial that Field's good friend Otto Katz was sentenced to death.

In her memoirs, Lillian Hellman sighs that Otto had been executed because "the regime" wanted "to kill his independent spirit."[10] This is nonsense, as is the parallel claim, often made by apologists for the regime, that Field was really a plain and simple victim of Stalinist oppression at the time of the Rajk-Slansky Trials. In truth, Otto was a fully obedient servant of the regime until the last minutes of life. As for Field, while it is quite true that his work as an agent had been compromised by the visibility and immanent exposure of his activities in the West, in fact he acted throughout the era of the Rajk-Slansky Trials as an entirely co-operative fingerman and provocateur, playing the role of the "American master-spy," whose "testimony" could be used to put to death un-counted numbers of similarly compromised agents and comrades from the anti-fascist movement. Ms. Schmidt insists the documents of Field's 1954 debriefing fully support this view. But Field's collaboration was already evident from the simple fact that he was permitted to live and go on to "rehabilitation," while literally thousands of his comrades in the old movement were "liquidated" at this time, and in his name.

It is important to remember that the people condemned in these trials were not necessarily in any way dissidents or adversaries of the regime. To believe they were is to miss the point. These were not doubters, not the Bukharins of Eastern Europe. Almost every one was a fully committed Stalinist. Rajk, Slansky, Reicin, Katz: These were good and faithful servants, all of them. They did not go to their deaths because they opposed Stalin. They died because they had obeyed Stalin in a manner which it had now become expedient to terminate and silence. Reicin, one of the leading Czech victims, was no tender advocate of liberty. He was a notoriously ruthless NKVD agent, and almost certainly directly involved in Masaryk's demise.[11] Rajk, in Hungary, had been a devoted Stalinist inquisitor, whose many acts of oppression included involvement in the torture of Cardinal Jozsef Mindszenty and the oppression of the Roman Catholic church.[12] To be sure it would be a reckless calumny to suggest that all the wretched creatures brought into the docks of these proceedings were collaborators in Stalin's crimes. Not at all. Many were innocent communist idealists. Many were ordinarily decent or venal government officials who happened to be in the wrong place at the wrong time. Or they were simply Jewish, since Stalin's Terror had now taken on an overtly anti-Semitic character. Nonetheless, it should be remembered that Stalin never viewed his closest henchmen as allies. They were always potential enemies, traitors waiting to happen. And in his show trials, the dictator was as often settling scores with his allies as with his enemies. He was also, almost always, covering tracks.

But of course the Rajk-Slansky Trials had a far wider meaning than a simple response to the crisis in secret life created by the exposure of Hiss. The bleak wave of Stalinizing conspiracy which in these last years of the forties successfully swept away everything except communist power both in Eastern Germany and in Eastern Europe must be viewed as a culminating triumph of two decades of the conspiratorial work which after 1945 was enforced and kept in place by the Red Army. And tragically, among the many covert operations used to co-opt, subvert, discredit, cement, and annihilate any political faction not obedient to Stalin, the networks of the anti-fascist movement must be considered the most important. Within the services of England and America, in SOE and OSS, from Kim Philby to Jürgen Kuczynski, penetration agents used their positions to discredit and destroy factions in Eastern Europe and Eastern Germany that were unacceptable to Stalin.[13] In the corridors of the OSS and the British Ministry of Information, people whom we now know to have been penetration agents, people whose prestige came from their history of "anti-fascism" of the sort devised by Münzenberg, arranged to have their perfectly genuine, but non-communist, anti-fascist colleagues cast into outer darkness, discredited, and declared by official testimony "unreliable." It is a nasty irony that the work of discrediting the political motives of other anti-fascists was conducted by agents of a political apparatus which until a very short time before had been in active and overt alliance with Hitler, and for a long time before that had been using its "anti-fascism" as cover for secret bonds to the German dictator. But that irony was lost on almost everyone. The strategy worked. The work of the Cambridge moles in devastating the Mihailovich faction in Yugoslavia is only the best explored and well known of these betrayals. There were many others, originating within both the American and the British services.[14] The cup that was at last filled up in 1948 was a bloody and very capacious one.

And so, with the Hiss Trial, a new Terror began. Show trials for liquidating superfluous Stalinists were now set up in every one of the satellite states. In Hungary, Lazlo Rajk, the most popular communist in the country, was arrested and taken to a bungalow outside Budapest which was in fact a prison and torture chamber. There he was personally confronted by Noel Field, who was being held prisoner in the same place, and who personally insisted upon his role as the American master-spy.

The Terror trials moved through Eastern Europe in succession. They began in Albania and Bulgaria, then gathered strength in Hungary and reached their climax in the terrible Slansky Trials in Prague. There, focus was precisely on those obedient servants who had been most active in the Stalinist cadres of both the anti-fascist movement in Europe, and in the Spanish stratagem. Why this should be so has never, so far as I am aware, been fully explored.[15]*

Then in November 1951 the Prime Minister, Rudolf Slansky, was arrested along with many other important members of the government, most of them Jewish. Katz was not in the very first round-up of victims. Our last glimpse of him as a free man is standing on a streetcar, where he happened to meet the terrified wife of Otto Sling, one of the arrested men. He is said to have tried to comfort her, rather gently.

It was a little after this talk on the streetcar that agents of the apparatus he had served all his life came to take Otto away.

The account of how the confessions of these show trials were extracted from their prisoners comprises one of the many terrible documents of witness in this century. Artur London's *Confession* and Eugen Löbl's *The State of My Mind* are accounts of how every conceivable device of physical agony, gross humiliation, untellable abjection, exhaustion, terror, release from terror, false promise, false camaraderie, and then terror again were brought to bear in systematic and invincible orchestration. Everyone confessed. To anything, everything.

Otto Katz? According to Löbl, he confessed the moment they came for him. He offered no resistance whatsoever. ''He confessed,'' said Löbl, ''in the elevator.''[16]

And in late November 1952 Otto stood in the dock and read exactly the lines required. His confession does not particularly dwell on Noel Field, but it is interesting instead as a kind of grotesque parody and contortion on his life as a secret agent. Since the Prague Trials were overtly anti-Semitic, Otto dwelt on how as the son of a rich manufacturer he had always been drawn to ''Jewish bourgeois elements.'' He confessed to having been a ''Trotskyite'' since his days with Piscator. During the pact he had become a Zionist agent, through the evil influence of a Jewish

* It is an interesting sidelight to the Slansky Trials that in June of 1951, on their flight to the USSR, Guy Burgess and Donald Maclean made a fairly protracted stop in Prague. This was during precisely the time that the trials were being prepared. Who did they meet with? Why were they there? We do not know.

member of Daladier's cabinet, Georges Mandel. He made a point of having conspired with that reactionary, Beneš. In America he conspired with Louis Fischer and the "Jewish nationalist," Felix Frankfurter. In Paris, Noel Coward and Paul Willert recruited him for British intelligence. In America the "agent of capitalist Jewry," David Schoenbrun, had brought him into the American secret service and worked with the Israelis. He had been influenced by the monster, Earl Browder. He had worked for the Zionists in Mexico. He had been bag man for Slansky and other "conspirators" among foreign journalists.

Many years later Löbl would recall that Katz's confession had a peculiarly histrionic tone, and recalled Katz speaking of "no tree high enough to hang me from."[17] Löbl wondered whether Katz had perhaps been signalling all his friends in the West through irony, or whether he simply went to his death, rather as he had lived, a "*poseur*."

Without answering this question, the transcripts as published suggest something slightly different. Arthur Koestler was convinced that Otto's confession was a signal to him, from across the lines, and that its language was written in direct imitation of the confession of Koestler's hero, based on Bukharin, in *Darkness at Noon*.[18] As he came to the end of his confession, Katz spoke of his life as a writer. "I am a writer, supposedly an architect of the soul. What sort of architect have I been. . . . Such an architect of the soul belongs to the gallows." Then, like many of the defendants, he embarked upon a plea for the death penalty. "The only service left to me is to warn all who by origin [*sic*] or character, are in danger of following the same path to hell."

Then he proceeded: "The sterner the punishment . . ." and then, in mid-sentence, something in Otto betrayed him. *The sterner the punishment* . . . but as he spoke, his voice collapsed. His lips continued to move, but his plea for death fell into an unintelligible whisper around the words, a kind of gasping.

Katz was hanged the next morning.

But before the executioner came for him, before dawn, Otto knelt on the floor of his cell and having been given some paper, he concluded his life, as he had lived it: writing. He first composed a long letter to Klement Gottwald, the president of the country, renouncing his confession and making a case for his own integrity. The letter is a coherent and highly intelligent performance, very remarkable given the circumstances under which it was written. It is filled with lies, to be sure: But it is fluent and even glib; a considerable document, and in some ways a persuasive one.

Next Otto turned to write a final letter to his wife. She had been permitted a final visit to him in his cell earlier that morning. This was to be his written goodbye. After he was led away that morning, the guards found left behind in his cell a pile of pages, false start after false start to this letter, along with the draft he at last completed. "My dearest darling Ilschen," Otto begins, and begins, and begins again. He struggles to work in a phrase: "I devoted all the inner forces of goodness I had to our relationship"—but time and again he stumbles over it, and has to take a new sheet of paper. At last he gets it down, and adds: "Remember that, and forget everything else about me." Using the past tense, he speaks of their work as socialists in language that edges toward religious rhetoric: "I have had enough time to think about the future, and I saw it in all its glory. I saw a place reserved for you . . ." Did he write believing or disbelieving, for her eyes or for the eyes of the apparatus? He himself may not have known. He repeats the dream. He urges her: "forward, forever forward," and then kneeling on that floor, Otto repeats the plea: Forget me. Forget me. Live and forget me.

Otto Katz's hanged body, like that of Slansky and their fellow prisoners, was burned.[19] The ashes and bones were put in sacks, and a couple of secret police agents were assigned to take them out of the city and get rid of them where they couldn't be found. Some appropriate valley of desolation had been named, but the drive all the way out was long and dull. Besides, this business with the sacks was a pointless chore. Who cared? Who would ever care? Or know? On a desolate road outside Prague, the agents simply pulled over to a ditch filled with trash. They tossed the sacks onto the rubbish and drove away, leaving them to the oblivion of the blowing winter wind.

A Note on the Archives

This study of the links between the Soviet secret services and the larger intellectual life of the West was begun around the time Mikhail Gorbachev embarked upon *perestroika*. As I worked, my research in many archives and interviews was naturally illumined, albeit in flashes, by the tremendous events which at last reached their climax in August 1991. Yet during those years most of the state archives of the Soviet Union, certainly those of greatest importance to me, remained firmly off-limits to Western scholars. Since 1992, however, considerable though limited access to the historical documents of the fallen regime has made it possible to dig quite deeply into the record. This is especially the case in what are called the Central Party Archives, or more formally The Russian Center for the Preservation and Study of Documents of Modern History, on the Pushkinskaia in Moscow. These Central Party Archives are the principal repository for the annals of the Comintern, or Communist International. Since the Ariadne's thread I follow here was left by Willi Münzenberg, a founding father of the Comintern, the amount of material useful to me in the Central Party Archives is voluminous. I want to take this occasion to thank my researcher in Moscow, Prof. Roman Shenin, along with Mr. S. Todd Weinberg, Prof. Harvey Klehr, Mr. John Costello, and Mr. Alan Cullison for their generous assistance in helping me address and understand the vast amount of material that suddenly became available in late stages of my work. I wish also to thank Ms.

Patricia Kennedy Grimstead for her admirable and candid advice as I approached this task, and to commend her indispensable writing on the subject to any researcher-to-be.

I am happy, and not a little relieved, to report that many months of digging in the fonds of the Central Archives, where most records of Münzenberg's enterprises are kept, have thus far (apart from nuance) confirmed or been consistent with my prior research. In addition, certain of my leading inferences have been corroborated. For example, until January 1993 I was confident through inference, but not sure—not "sure-sure"—that the senior Bolshevik directing Münzenberg over the Reichstag Fire Campaign was Radek. Now I am sure. Until 1993, my research outside the archives had left me morally certain, but without ultimate proof, that during the Dimitrov Trial in Leipzig, the unseen intermediary between Stalin and the Nazis was the German communist Wilhelm Pieck. *Double Lives* was already in galleys when a certain top-secret telegram, intended for Stalin himself, was uncovered in the Pushkinskaia. Pieck was the go-between all right. And for sure. Some significant nuances have changed. I had known, for example, that the "Comrade Moskfin" who in 1935 divested Münzenberg of many of his enterprises was in fact the high-level secret service executive Mikhail Trilliser, and that the event in question was part of the final covert seizure of all functions of the Comintern by the Soviet secret police. I mistakenly assumed Trilliser was acting for the NKVD. In fact it was the GRU. This is a distinction with some difference, albeit not a momentous one.

Most importantly, two premises governing this study have been amply reinforced and placed beyond dispute by this material. The first such postulate may look simple, but it has acquired the candid aspect of the obvious only in retrospect. When I began my work it took strenuous and worrisome exertion to test and demonstrate even my most basic premise: That Münzenberg's enterprises were not in fact "independent" or "spontaneous" political effusions, but propaganda initiatives of the Soviet government, usually masked behind a facade of "independent leftism." The Archives of the Central Party should at long last bring this antique dispute to an end. They show, and show in abundance, that Münzenberg's many enterprises were controlled in toto through the apparatus of Stalin and his dictatorship. It is plain that everything he undertook, from the Sacco-Vanzetti campaign, to the Peace Movement, to the propaganda for the Spanish Civil War—all were performed in stringent coordination with the regime.

To be sure, this will not come as an arresting surprise to most scholars of the subject. Given Münzenberg's public place of leadership in the German Communist Party, his celebrated personal bond to Lenin in Switzerland, and his place in the inner circle of Bolsheviks even before 1917, not to mention his explicit fiery partisanship of the Soviet cause all through Weimar, one might suppose his subordination to the International might be taken as a given. Not at all. Among sympathizers of the sort of work he did, Münzenberg's subservience to the regime has always been routinely denied. Understandably. After all, Münzenberg organized and ran the great networks of fronts and pro-Soviet fellow-travellers. Precisely that denial, precisely that claim to political "independence," is the *sine qua non* of all fellow-travelling, all fronts. Up until the end of the eighties, the Stalinist management of Münzenberg's enterprises continued to be denied in outrage, particularly (and I suppose necessarily) by apologists for the Popular Front. Even quite sophisticated observers continued to discern "independent leftism" and "spontaneity" behind such phenomena as the "Peace Movement" of the late 1920s and early 1930s. The archival record requires that such views be revised. Of course such movements were composed almost exclusively of "innocents" motivated by sincere ideals. But the "Peace Movement" manipulated the fear of war that was so common in Europe and America after 1918 through an unseen political apparatus in the service of Stalin. And the true policies of that apparatus were remote indeed from maintaining the peace.

But it was so with all these propaganda campaigns. The Central Party Archives show a plain, simple truth behind the smokescreens: Münzenberg worked in obedience to the Soviet government. His enterprises were controlled by that government. The only archival surprise on this score—and it is a mild surprise—has been to discover the level of minutia to which Münzenberg submitted his work to supervision in Moscow.

A second large premise confirmed in the Soviet Archives is one which emerged only after I was quite far along in my research. Not only did Münzenberg work in obedience to the Soviet government, but his enterprises were coordinated with the Soviet secret services and penetrated by those services from top to bottom. This covert dimension began within the Comintern but also extended far beyond it. The Archives clearly show that Münzenberg and his lieutenants always coordinated their work with the secret service of the Comintern, known as the "OMS," and with its director, Mirov-Abramov. They also indicate that those lieutenants were covertly attached to other secret service arms of the government: to the foreign wing of the secret police (the "INO" of the NKVD-KGB) and to the GRU, or Military Intelligence.

Some of this secret work should come as no surprise. It is to be expected that a propaganda apparatus such as Münzenberg's would be designed to purvey disinformation. Of course it did. It did so at all levels, from simple planted false news stories to the subtlest manipulations in the most exalted areas of government chancelleries. But there was much more. Münzenberg's fronts, however "idealistic," however crowded with "innocents," were conceived and steadily utilized as cover for the more sinister aspects of secret service work: for espionage, for covert action, for agents of influence, even for sabotage.

In retrospect, it is difficult to see how it could have been otherwise. In the fonds of the Central Party Archives, the dossiers of "legal" and "illegal" work mingle together, hardly distinguished. Working with the OMS, Münzenberg was affiliated with the Comintern's training schools for undercover agents and spies. His enterprises and people were deep in recruitment for espionage. I am exceedingly grateful to that indefatigable researcher Mr. John Costello, who at an early stage shared with me discoveries from his own archival study of Alexander Orlov and Kim Philby which confirm my understanding of the role played by Münzenberg fronts as recruiting centers for secret agents, and especially my inferences about the place of Münzenberg's senior advisors in recruiting Philby. Archival discoveries most generously shared with me by Harvey Klehr of Emory University bring to new clarity the Comintern role in, for example, the espionage rings run by Jay Peters in Washington during the 1930s—rings in which Münzenberg people played a formative part. Meanwhile, the recently published work of M. Thierry Wolton, likewise based in archival research, has uncovered material indicating how Münzenberg and his people were engaged in the pre-war penetrations of the French government which are touched upon in my discussions of the *Rassemblement Universelle Populaire*, and the events around Gide's trip to the USSR discussed in Chapter 9.

This material is vast and indispensable. Its evaluation and publication have only begun. Meanwhile, the most sensitive material remains out of reach. Since 1992, it has been frequently supposed that the Archives of the Central Party are fully open and that its "secrets" are all about to be disclosed. In fact, very little really sensitive material concerning Soviet espionage anywhere in the West has yet been released. Even when that material passed through the Comintern, it has been removed to the Archives of the KGB and Military Intelligence, not to mention the ultra-secret ''Presidential Archives'' now maintained, rather spookily, in Stalin's old apartments in the Kremlin. The present Russian Intelligence Service has continued to put very strict limits on what it will reveal. A number of the most conspiratorial issues addressed in *Double Lives*—the Dimitrov Conspiracy, the full story of Walter Krivitsky, the truth about the death of Münzenberg, the intrigue attending Maxim Gorky's death, the events in Spain surrounding the liquidation of J. K. Berzin, the possible role of Guy Liddell—all these have been partly illuminated by new material, but they have been illuminated, as it were, indirectly and marginally.

I should add a word about Alger and Priscilla Hiss. Not the last word of course; there seems never to be a last word on the Hisses. As the reader will see, in my view a final key to the Hiss case will come only with a full understanding of the political careers and the work in espionage of Noel and Herta Field, and full clarity about the Fields will not come without access to the archives of the satellite states of the former Soviet Union. In the book itself, I already have discussed in some detail the odd episode of 1992, when a senior member of the Russian government, General Dimitri Volkoganov, made and then retracted a statement, produced under what he later claimed was pressure from representatives of Alger Hiss, asserting that he had no evidence showing Hiss to have been a spy. This unfortunate episode only demonstrates the limitations of relying upon the statements of government spokesmen rather than open scholarship. The truth is that, as an archival matter, the Hiss case has not yet been openly or systematically addressed, and it will not be so until the relevant files of Soviet Military Intelligence are open for direct examination by scholars. Meanwhile, the nonarchival evidence indicating that Alger and Priscilla Hiss were witting informants for Soviet espionage remains massive.

But all the most ''sensational'' disclosures of recent times have appeared piecemeal, and always connected to some high-level government decision, the political motivations of which have usually not been far to seek. The opening of the true historical record, with genuinely free access to scholars, has only begun. Some efforts of the Russian government thus far, and above all of many committed Russian scholars and archivists working under appalling conditions, are to be warmly applauded. But the process is still in its infancy. As I write, new dangers confront it. I might add that Russian movements toward openness might well be echoed in the West; in England, in France, and in the other liberal democracies. Nor should the United States be thought too advanced to join in this new wave. The Freedom of Information Act has served scholarship admirably, but most researchers agree that its implementation has been hamstrung by many absurd and antiquated restrictions. In truth, a new spirit of openness on every side is indispensable to that free and newly energized post–Cold War historical discourse, within which, I hope, *Double Lives* may play some role.

STEPHEN KOCH

Notes

Chapter 1: Lying for the Truth

1. The life and death of Willi Münzenberg have been treated by many writers. By far the most important is Gross, *Münzenberg*. Other useful books are Wessel, *Münzenbergs Ende*, and Kerbs, *Münzenberg*. Also noteworthy are Carew-Hunt, ''Münzenberg, and Kersten, ''Das Ende Willi Münzenbergs.'' Indispensable articles are Schliemann, ''Münzenberg,'' and Gruber, ''Münzenberg.'' A significant, if controversial, text is Leo, *Frühzug nach Toulouse*.

Noteworthy personal and political memoirs of Münzenberg appear in Koestler's autobiographical volume, *Invisible Writing*; in Regler, *The Owl of Minerva*; and in Sperber, *Ces Temps-là*, especially in *Le Pont inachevé*. Also important to the events and people around Münzenberg is Buber-Neumann, *Von Potsdam nach Moskau*. The Count and Countess Karolyi in their memoirs, *A Life Together*, and *Memoirs*, both include revealing portraits. Münzenberg himself wrote an autobiographical article ''Die Dritte Front'' and an account of the founding of WIR: ''Five Years of Workers' International Relief.'' Information on Münzenberg revealed through the Freedom of Information Act (dossier #105-54056), regarding information to be in the files of the United States State Department, or the FBI is surprisingly meager and ill-informed, in notable contrast to similar records about many personalities close to him. American officials seem to have known vastly more about Münzenberg's lieutenants than they ever knew about him. (I should note that a large number of files on Münzenberg remain classified, and inexplicably so). Still, a very useful and well-informed ''Memorandum on the Workers' International Relief: Based Exclusively on Communist and Soviet Sources,'' was prepared for the Division of Eastern European Affairs of the United States Department of State, December 16, 1932, and one can hope, albeit wanly, that this excellent document was widely read in the government (National Archives of the United States).

Information pertaining to Münzenberg in the archives of the Communist International in Moscow is massive. See my ''Note on the Archives.''

2. Gross, *Münzenberg*, p. 47.

3. See Tuck, *Engine of Mischief*.

4. See Chambers, *Witness*, p. 6. See also Slonim, *Soviet Russian Literature*, p. 68.

5. Whether Maly lapsed from Protestantism or Roman Catholicism is unclear from published accounts. By far the best of these, however, is Poretsky's *Our Own People* (London, 1969; Ann Arbor, 1970). Poretsky says Maly was a "priest." Other sources, such as Orlov (in *The Secret History of Stalin's Crimes*), refer to him as a "pastor."

6. Information to the author from Mrs. Diana Trilling.

7. For a discussion of Dzerzhinsky's role under Lenin, see Pipes, *The Russian Revolution.*

8. Koestler, *Invisible Writing*, pp. 250–251.

9. For the Kuczynski family's multifarious life in espionage, see Glees, *The Secrets of the Service*. Robert René Kuczynski's relation to Münzenberg is mentioned in Gross, *Münzenberg*, p. 158. The best scholarly volume on the Eisler family is by Peter Lubbe. Ruth Fischer's *Stalin and German Communism* is a major work.

10. Information to the author from Ms. Ruth Price.

11. Except where otherwise indicated, direct quotations from Babette Gross, as well as paraphrases of her views, are taken from my taped interviews of July 1989.

12. Information to the author from Mr. Paul Willert.

13. Münzenberg, "Mit Lenin in der Schweiz," p. 1838, as cited by Gross, *Münzenberg*, p. 59.

14. With this assistance, Münzenberg wrote many articles and speeches. The only book under his signature is a remarkable study of Nazi propaganda techniques: *Propaganda als Waffe*. Willi was assisted in its composition by Kurt Kersten.

15. The Archives of the Central Party, on the Pushkinskaia in Moscow, are formally known as the "Russian Center for the Preservation and Study of Documents of Modern History." I will hereafter refer to them as the "Central Party Archives," or "CPA." The CPA's Third Division is devoted to the records of the Communist International and its successor organizations. It contains their own records, and records of those organizations' ties to various foreign communist and socialist parties. In addition, and as part of these liaisons to foreign parties, the Communist International maintained a working and very active secret service, known as the OMS (the "Department of International Ties"). Many but not necessarily all records of the OMS are also in the Central Party Archives, though as of mid-1993 access to these files remained restricted. Nonetheless it is very clear that Münzenberg worked in close, steady collaboration with the director of the OMS, Mirov-Abramov.

Münzenberg's political activities, both legal and illegal, even the simple management of fellow travellers such as Barbusse, were routinely referred for review in Moscow. (A typical example can be found in CPA fond 495.19.213, in a dossier of material from Henri Barbusse concerning management of fellow travellers connected to the Comintern in Spain, including Ellen Wilkinson.) The records are filled with budgetary requests for fellow-travellers' propaganda trips, reports on relatively small glitches in press coverage, nuanced evaluations of work by "innocents," careful records on all front committees and their functioning, proposals for propaganda initiatives, both covert and overt, in every major country.

Familiar bromides about the supposed "independence" of Münzenberg's political work and that of his fronts must be laid to rest after examination of the Archives. When the work of the fronts became politically sensitive, as it did repeatedly, no detail seems to have been too small for Münzenberg to forward to the Executive Committee for direction "from Moscow," with financial records kept to the penny (e.g., CPA fond 495.292, files 242a, and 244a, among many other examples). Indeed, remarkably fine points of propaganda and organization were submitted for personal approval by Stalin himself (e.g., CPA fond 495.19.243).

As for Münzenberg's personal "independence," he was given deference as a senior figure, but that he was a servant of the larger enterprise, that he was expected to be, and was, obedient to the commands of its leadership, is perfectly evident. [Typical examples along many of this kind can be found in CPA fond 495.19.337, and fond 495.73.26]. This dimension of Münzenberg's relation to the ECCI [Executive Committee of the Communist International] stands out in special relief after 1936, when other members of the German Communist Party, notably Wilhelm Pieck and Walter Ulbricht, set out to discredit him, and Münzenberg's response is filled with protestations of his long and obedient service (e.g., the Secretariat of G. Dimitrov, CPA fond 495.74.; files on "the Case of WM.").

The inter-penetration of Münzenberg's activities by the other intelligence services of the Soviet State, especially the INO, or Foreign Wing of the Soviet Secret Police (OGPU-NKVD-KGB), and the Intelligence Wing of the Red Army, (GRU), is evident throughout the records of the Central Party, frequently showing high-level intelligence officers, such as Abram Slutsky (director of the INO), present at meetings in which his activities were under discussion. (A typical example can be found in the minutes of a meeting of the Executive Committee of the Comintern on the German situation conducted under conspiratorial conditions—with most participants using pseudonyms—with Slutsky in attendance, September 7, 1933. Multiple other examples can be found, *inter alia*, in the Secretariat of Osip Piatnitsky, Central Party Archives fond 495.19, files 216a, 217, 347, 357. All these show Slutsky, or some other representative of the GRU or NKVD secret service, repeatedly in attendance.)

16. Regler, *The Owl of Minerva*, p. 170.

17. For Münzenberg's use of this phrase, see Gross, *Münzenberg*, p. 133.

18. Koestler, *Invisible Writing*, p. 382.

19. The most reliable account of the Comintern in its early stages is Lazitch and

Drachkovitch, *Lenin and the Comintern*, vol. 1. An indispensable volume by the same writers is *The Comintern: Historical Highlights: Essays, Recollections, Documents*. Likewise essential, compiled by Lazitch and Drachkovitch, is *The Biographical Dictionary of the Comintern*. For a useful survey of its activities and role, see Heller and Nekrich, *Utopia in Power*. I have relied as well on Krivitsky, *In Stalin's Secret Service*, and Kennan, *Russia and the West*.

20. Payne, *The Life and Death of Lenin*, p. 510.

21. Ibid. p. 213.

22. Because of his conspicuous public role, Münzenberg avoided contacts that might jeopardize his appearance of operating apart from the *apparat* or the secret police. Nonetheless, the CPA contain a great deal of material indicating that the Münzenberg operations worked in close proximity to the sundry Soviet secret services, not only the OMS, but also the INO (the foreign wing of the NKVD-KGB) and the GRU. (See CPA fond 495.19.213; 495.19.246; 419.19.247; 495.19.357; 495.19.392., *inter alia*.) Babette Gross asserts that Münzenberg consciously kept himself ignorant of details; these were entrusted to others or to the memory of his confidential secretary, Hans Schulz or to operational agents. Nonetheless, Münzenberg's intimate institutional bond to Mirov-Abramov, as well as to Radek (who retained always a high-level involvement in secret service work, especially regarding German affairs) is plain from all accounts and from the files (CPA fond 495.60.244a). See also Gross, *op cit.* on Mirov: pp. 130; 262–265; 293; and on Schulz: pp. 227; 262–266. In addition, we must assume that following classic secret service compartmentalization, Münzenberg would often have been informed only on a need-to-know basis.

23. That Otto Katz was a member of the NKVD, or the GRU (Soviet Military Intelligence), as well as of the Comintern secret service is a conclusion widely shared by those who were close to his activities. Certainly he was so regarded by Babette Gross; such was also the view held of him by many others, including Koestler, Regler, and Ruth Fischer. Koestler claims that Münzenberg spoke openly of Otto having been planted "to spy on Willi for the *apparat*" (*Invisible Writing*, p. 236), noting that this recognition contributed to the generally patronizing tone Willi adopted toward his right-hand man. Certainly from the time of his original mission from Moscow to Paris in 1933, Katz was entrusted with work far more characteristic of the NKVD than of the Comintern. The secret work in the Reichstag Fire campaign required undercover technique and witting involvement at a high level. More significantly, Katz rose to the apex of his influence after 1935, the date after which the familiar distinction between the Comintern secret service and the NKVD and GRU ceases to have practical meaning. That Katz belonged to one of these services strikes me as probable to a very high degree.

Though Katz's involvement in the illegal enterprises of the Communist International were intricate, prolonged, and not infrequently quite public, files documenting his movements turn out to be rather meager—at least in the Central Party Archives. This scarcity is itself suggestive. The most probable is that the files were purged of material dealing with Katz. What remains seems to be material that is either innocuous, and in which Katz played a minor role (cf. CPA 495.73.26), or he is engaged in highly sensitive work, but under one of his cover names, which might have been missed by those clearing the files (cf. Katz engaged in secret conversations with Torgler's attorney, Alfonse Sachs, September 8, 1933: CPA 495.292.244a, in which Katz participates under his cover name ''Breda''). One might contrast the scarcity of records on Katz to the expansive paper trail found there on his more visible master Münzenberg: Willi's thick dossiers line the dusty fonds. Another plausible reason for this paucity of Comintern paper is that Katz was a GRU or NKVD agent, and part of the Comintern only in the eyes of outsiders. If so, we may not see his dossiers soon. The records of those agencies remain obdurately shut away. In fact, the work of Otto's unseen hand may well have been of such sensitivity that his records may be kept in the ''Presidential Archives,'' where the most sensitive documents of the regime are kept in rooms that once served as Stalin's private Kremlin apartment—certainly an *occultum occultorum* chosen with uncanny symbolism.

The question of whether Louis Gibarti (or to use his real name, Ladislas Dobos) was in the NKVD as well as being a ''Münzenberg-man'' is more debatable. When I met Babette Gross, she did *not* view Gibarti as having been an NKVD agent. She viewed him as temperamentally unsuited to secret work. ''He was much too outgoing.'' Nonetheless, when I outlined information about Gibarti's activities in New York during the 1930s assembled through the Freedom of Information Act and at the National Archives of the United States, she came to the conclusion that Gibarti, like Katz, had worked for ''the Russian service,'' or as she sometimes called it, ''the other service,'' by which I take it she meant the GRU or NKVD. Though she found the fact ''astonishing,'' she seemed to view it as quite clearly the case. In addition, I am informed by Mr. John Costello, whose research on the senior NKVD operative Alexander Orlov is based upon access to the relevant archives in Moscow, that the archives support my inference that Kim Philby began his secret service work in Europe through Gibarti's World Committee for the Relief of the Victims of German Fascism. For that reason, the Committee plainly served as an NKVD as well as Comintern front, with Gibarti a witting participant in espionage recruitment.

24. Knightley, *The Master Spy: The Story of Kim Philby,* pp. 36–37. The World Committee for the Relief of the Victims of German Fascism, the organization which dispatched Philby to Vienna immediately after he left Cambridge, was run by Gibarti. The World Committee was a legal front, as we shall see, for illegal activities. (See also, note 20.) Philby was referred to Gibarti by a Cambridge don, Maurice Dobb, who was a talent-spotter for the Soviet services and was active in another of Gibarti's fronts, the League Against Imperialism. (See John Costello, *The Mask of Treachery,* pp. 162-167.) In fact, Philby's trip through Paris on his way to Vienna serves as a useful illustration of how the stages in the recruitment system worked. I am grateful to Mr. Costello for his permission to cite the archival material referred to in these notes.

25. An example of this fusion of bookselling and espionage is recounted by the noted New York bookseller Walter Goldwater, a former communist who during his days with the Party was asked to open a bookstore near Columbia University to serve as a front for espionage activity. (Walter Goldwater, interview in a series of interviews on the advanced intellectual culture of New York, courtesy of Diana Trilling.) The rationale for using a "Press Agency" as a cover for espionage work is easily seen: Both are in the business of transmitting information. The "independent reporters" filing their stories can be made difficult to distinguish from other kinds of informants, while mingling legal with illegal information can be inconspicuously done. Examples of this are the Continental News Service in which Kim Philby worked with the Austrian Soviet agent Peter Smolka (also known as Peter Smolka-Smollett) and the American Feature Writers Syndicate which Whittaker Chambers founded in New York at roughly the same time. FOIA information suggests that a pioneer in this particular device may have been Münzenberg's man Louis Gibarti.

26. See part II, chapter 8, for an account of the life and death of Rayna Prohme. See also Vincent Sheean, *Personal History*, chapter 6.

27. FOIA dossier on Louis Gibarti, #61-6629, section 3. Deposition of Louis Gibarti before Special Counsel to the United States Senate, Robert Morris, Esq., and United States Senators Willis Smith and Homer Ferguson, Paris, August 28, 1951. Question 65.

28. Gross, *Münzenberg,* p. 133.

29. See Caute, *The Fellow Travellers.*

30. Gross, Münzenberg, p. 220.

31. The phrase is taken from an unreliable portrait of Gibarti found in a book called *Crime without Punishment,* by Guenther Reinhardt. Reinhardt was a decidedly unsavory character, a stringer for the FBI, who did manage to insinuate himself into Gibarti's company in the late 1930s. It is clear that he knew Gibarti; it is likewise clear that his portrait is sensational and false in a number of demonstrable ways. The quotation about "rabbit breeding" is, however, at least plausible. I should in fairness add that Mrs. Gustav Regler assures me that Reinhardt's account of her own husband in this book is entirely accurate, and indeed it was Margaret Regler who recommended the book to me.

32. Gross, *Münzenberg*, pp. 216–221.

33. Berberova, *Histoire,* p. 260.

34. An excellent example is a dossier of letters of Romain Rolland and Henri Barbusse on the preparation of the Amsterdam Congress in CPA fond 495, which can be compared to the revealing letter from Rolland to Barbusse published by Babette Gross, *op. cit.*, pp. 224–225.

35. Koudachova's role manipulating Rolland's intellectual life has been extensively documented, sometimes sympathetically, as in David James Fischer, *Ro-*

main Rolland. Her managerial role guiding Rolland's Stalinism was noted very early by insiders (Eugene Lyons, *Assignment in Utopia.*) By the time of Koudachova's death it was quite widely assumed that she was a member of the apparatus. (Information to the author from M. François Fejtö.) In her conversations with me, Babette Gross unequivocally stated that Koudachova was a member of the apparatus, explicitly assigned to managing Rolland's life. A glimpse of Rolland's working relation to Gibarti may be had in Rolland's journal, *Inde,* though the reader should note that this volume was edited by Koudachova herself, and the entry tends to demonstrate Rolland's "independence." A less attractive side of Gibarti's relation to Rolland is documented by Gross, (*Münzenberg*, pp. 224–225). The claim that Koudachova was trained in Moscow for her role in Rolland's life is found in Guillbeaux, *La Fin des Soviets*, in a chapter entitled "Romain Rolland's Marriage of State: Prisoner of the Kremlin." But Guillbeaux is a very dubious character; an obviously compromised reporter and a distasteful personality to boot. In his book of 1937, he gives the impression of having very nearly become a fascist fellow traveller. In any case, he cannot be viewed as reliable, though he plainly knew Koudachova well in their early days in the USSR. He claims to base his account in part on information from Gide and Victor Serge.

36. Gross, *Münzenberg*, pp. 224–225.

37. See Desanti, *Les Clés d'Elsa.*

38. See Justin Kaplan, *Lincoln Steffens*. For the challenges to Steffens's support of the Terror, see Hook, *Out of Step*, pp. 204–205, 569.

39. Stewart, *By a Stroke of Luck*, pp. 233–242, esp. 234.

40. FOIA dossier on Louis Gibarti, #61-6629, section 3. Deposition of Louis Gibarti before Special Counsel to the United States Senate Robert Morris, Esq., and United States Senators Willis Smith and Homer Ferguson, Paris, August 28, 1951. Question 72. Ella Winter's tie to Katz can be seen below, in my discussion of Katz's role in founding the Hollywood Anti-Fascist League.

41. Lazitch and Drachkovitch, *Lenin and the Comintern*, vol. 1, p. 174.

42. On Münzenberg leaving the Communist Youth International, see Gross, *Münzenberg*, pp. 99–109.

43. Paul Johnson, *Modern Times*, p. 714.

44. Gross, *Münzenberg*, p. 118.

45. Payne, *The Life and Death of Lenin*, p. 538.

46. Conquest, *Harvest of Sorrow*, p. 53.

47. Gross, *Münzenberg*, p. 113.

48. Willi Münzenberg, as quoted in Schliemann, "Münzenberg," p. 71.

49. *Saint Anthony's Papers*, no. 9. Issue on International Communism, chapter

on Willi Münzenberg by R. N. Carew-Hunt, p. 75. For Gorky's relation to Münzenberg, see Gross, passim.

50. Conquest, *Harvest of Sorrow*, pp. 55–56.

51. Bertram D. Wolfe, *The Bridge and the Abyss* (New York: Praeger, 1967), pp. 114–115.

52. Payne, *The Life and Death of Lenin*, pp. 537–538. An account of the lower-level political forces surrounding the famine can be found in Conquest, *Harvest of Sorrow*.

53. Gross, *Münzenberg*, pp. 120–121.

54. Koestler, *Invisible Writing*, p. 253.

55. References to Louis Fischer's close connections to Münzenberg and Katz can be found in many sources, including Fischer's own account of the late thirties, *Men and Politics*. See also Gross, *Münzenberg*. For del Vayo's connection, *Münzenberg*, see Gross, pp. 82, 306, and Koestler, *Invisible Writing*, p. 401, and many accounts of the Spanish Civil War. For an admiring account of del Vayo's role advancing Stalinist policy at the *Nation*, see Sara Alpern, *Freda Kirchway*. I am also grateful for information from Mrs. Rae Bernstein, widow of del Vayo's American collaborator and translator, Joseph Bernstein, who also worked closely with Otto Katz.

56. Gross, *Münzenberg*, p. 126.

57. Ibid., on the Moscow-Volga Canal, pp. 262–263.

58. Ibid., p. 251. See also Paul Johnson, *Modern Times*, pp. 274–275. For an account of the White Sea Canal, especially the propaganda campaign involving Soviet literary figures in the summer of 1933, see Aleksandr I. Solzhenitsyn, *The Gulag Archipelago*, vol. 2, pp. 80–102.

59. Stalin's epithet is reported by Krivitsky, *In Stalin's Secret Service*, p. 74.

60. For Münzenberg's reaction to the United States, see Gross, *Münzenberg*, p. 270.

61. The state of the American Party following the Bridgeman, Michigan, raids of 1922 is explored in Draper, *American Communism and Soviet Russia*, pp. 1–51 and passim, and Klehr, *The Heyday of American Communism*, pp. 3–27.

62. In addition to Gross's comments on Münzenberg's role in the Sacco-Vanzetti case, Münzenberg himself pointed with pride to his achievement with Sacco-Vanzetti in *International Press Correspondence*, no. 1, 8, no. 42, August 1, 1928, "Five Years of Workers' International Relief," pp. 1044–1045. See also Russell, *Sacco and Vanzetti*.

63. *Inprecorr*, loc. cit.

64. Lyons, *Assignment in Utopia*, p. 32.

65. Russell, *Sacco and Vanzetti*, p. 13.

66. Lyons, *Assignment in Utopia*, p. 13.

67. Ibid., p. 31.

68. Russell, *Sacco and Vanzetti*, p. 222.

69. Ibid., p. 29.

70. An interesting although problematical account of the Red Aid's sweeping control of the propaganda campaign over Sacco and Vanzetti has been documented, and in detail, from a communist source: Zelt's *Proletarischer Internationalismus*. Zelt wrote after being granted access to the archives of the Comintern in Moscow, and his purpose was to claim credit for the International in the campaign, downplaying the ''bourgeois'' contribution. His book's account of Red Aid's organization and control over the campaign is remarkably detailed. Interestingly, while the book outlines and lavishly praises the effectiveness of the operation, it at no time lets slip the name Münzenberg. At the time Zelt wrote, the guiding spirit of Red Aid was a non-person in the DDR.

71. Russell, *Sacco and Vanzetti*, p. 119.

72. Ibid. For Cannon's knowledge of Sacco's guilt, see p. 133. The organizers' doubts are cited on p. 140.

73. Porter, *The Never-Ending Wrong*, p. 27.

74. Russell, *Sacco and Vanzetti*, p. 117. Russell relies, in part, on Zelt.

75. Gardner Jackson's close association with Louis Gibarti is documented in dossiers now in the National Archives of the United States, 800.00B, dossier on Louis Gibarti, document #37.

76. That Parker was secretly a CP member was told to me by Mr. Steve Nelson, once a senior member of the American apparatus, in an interview of August 1989.

77. Meade, *Dorothy Parker*, pp. 181–186.

78. See Baker, *Brandeis and Frankfurter*, for an account of Marion and Felix Frankfurter's relation to the Sacco-Vanzetti case.

79. See Russell, *Sacco and Vanzetti*, pp. 133–134.

80. Ibid., pp. 141–142.

81. The orchestration of the ''Peace Movement'' through the Münzenberg fronts and their associated organization is very visible in the voluminous documentation of the propaganda of the fronts in the period, culminating with Amsterdam-Pleyel. The process of this development, beginning with the League Against Colonialism, its transformation into the League Against Imperialism at the time of the Brussels Congress, and the increasing pre-occupation with ''peace'' which had its culmination in Amsterdam is documented by Gross, *Münzenberg*, pp. 181–227. Confidential information provided to me and pronounced roughly accurate by Babette Gross indicates that the author of the ''peace'' plan was a

French Münzenberg-man named Guy Jerram, whose plan for an apparatus-sponsored pacifist movement was presented to Stalin in 1928, and revised by the dictator personally at that time. The phrase "peace conspiracy" apparently begins with Jerram.

82. CPA fond 495.292.242a. and 244a. These files consist of correspondence concerning the Leipzig Trial with the Anti-War Commission of the ECCI, which in turn had been in charge of the Anti-War Congresses in Brussels and Amsterdam.

83. Nehru's speech at the Bandung Conference is referred to in Schliemann, Gross, p. 188.

84. Joachim Fest, *Hitler*, p. 395.

85. Information to the author from Mr. Herb Romerstein and Mr. Jorgen Schliemann.

86. The CPA contains many archives on preparation for the Amsterdam Congress, including many dossiers of correspondence between Münzenberg and Piatnitsky on the subject. These documents are found in the same fonds (Fond 495.19 especially) as are records of the Anti-Imperialist League, and later the sundry anti-fascist committees, including the World Committee against War and Fascism.

87. For the secret arrangements at Amsterdam, see Gross, *Münzenberg*, p. 227.

88. The Papen coup is discussed by Fest, *Hitler*, pp. 339–345. See also, and particularly, Gross, p. 229. It is very interesting to note that the CPA contains a secret service report to Piatnitsky by a deep-cover informant dated a week following the Papen coup, (July 29) pointing out that events had caused a rift in the Nazi ranks: That Röhm was pressing for a *coup d'etat* for July 31, 1932, and that Hitler was holding out for a legal seizure of power. The letter's context makes plain that Piatnitsky has been steadily informed about high-level debate within the Nazi ranks from this source, whose code name was "your friend Teddy," (CPA fond 495.19.247). "Teddy's" identity is not known to me, but his file is in the fonds devoted to the Münzenberg apparatus.

Chapter 2: Fire and Fraud

1. The standard work on the Reichstag Fire is Tobias, *The Reichstag Fire*.

2. Gross, *Münzenberg*, p. 240. Münzenberg's consultations at this time were with Iosif Piatnitsky, and focussed on the work of Amsterdam-Pleyel, though it should be recalled that Gibarti ran both Amsterdam-Pleyel and the World Committee for the Relief of the Victims of German Fascism. I should note that Babette Gross emphasized that Gibarti's work in Paris was always done away from Münzenberg's Paris offices, obviously to maintain an appearance of separation. The move to Paris was discussed, along with, presumably, the change in Amsterdam-Pleyel that would come with the anti-fascist campaign. Piatnitsky

was very active in secret matters and espionage, and his influence ranged outside the Comintern to the other services. See Poretsky, *Our Own People*, pp. 105–106.

3. Gross, *Münzenberg*, p. 232.

4. See Fest, *Hitler*, pp. 396–397.

5. Tobias, *The Reichstag Fire*, pp. 84–85.

6. Fest, *Hitler*, pp. 474–475.

7. See Paul Johnson, *Modern Times*, pp. 282–283; see also Gross, *Münzenberg*, pp. 227–233.

8. Gross, *Münzenberg*, p. 232.

9. Ibid., p. 235.

10. Hsi-Huey Liang, *The Berlin Police Force in the Weimar Republic*, Berkeley, U. of California Press, 1970.

11. Gross, *Münzenberg*, p. 235.

12. Ibid., p. 238.

13. Ibid., pp. 234–239.

14. A useful summary of these events can be found in Heller and Nekrich, *Utopia in Power: The History of the Soviet Union to the Present*, pp. 322–344. Radek's role is discussed in many authorities. (See Blackstock, *The Secret Road to World War II*.) Indispensable information about Radek's thinking on relations with Germany at this time is found in Krivitsky, *In Stalin's Secret Service*.

15. CPA fond 495.60.244a. Letter from K. Radek to "Vinogradov." April 10, 1933.

16. Evgeny Gnedin, *Iz istorii otnoshenii mezhdu SSSR is fashistskoi Germanii*, pp. 22–27. See also Hilger and Meyer, *The Incompatible Allies*, p. 262.

17. See Karel Kaplan, *Report on the Murder of the General Secretary*, the letter of Otto Katz to Klement Gottwald, p. 276. The connection between Radek and Otto Katz was revealed to me by Mr. Paul Willert in an interview of 1990. Katz was introduced to Willert through connections made earlier between Radek and Mr. Willert's father.

18. Contacts with the OMS (the Comintern secret service, *Otdel mezhdunarodnoi svyatzi*) in support of the anti-fascist campaign in Paris are discussed by Gross, p. 264. This supervision presumably was run by the OMS and the secret service of the Comintern, rather than any of the other Soviet services. Yet such a presumption may be naive. In these years, the functions of the Comintern secret service were increasingly being drawn into the ambit of the other services, usually covertly. If one concedes the probability that Katz was a liaison between the anti-fascist movement and the *apparat*, the thought that Alpari (and others) may have had similar bonds does not seem too loose a speculation. This would

help explain Alpari's survival of the purges, in which most of his senior comrades in the OMS were put to death, and his curious behavior at the time of the fall of France.

19. See Tobias, *The Reichstag Fire*, on Lubbe's arrest.

20. See ibid. on the arrests of Dimitrov, Popov, and Tanev.

21. Humbert-Droz, *Dix ans dans la lutte antifasciste*, vol. 3, pp. 111–112.

22. Information to the author from Mrs. Frieda Marshall.

23. A useful summary of the public and private terms of rapprochement between Hitler and Stalin in 1933–35 can be found in Tolstoy, *Stalin's Secret War*, p. 88 (with its footnotes). Another very valuable treatment can be found in Laqueur, *Stalin: The Glasnost Revelations*.

24. See Hilger and Meyer, p. 252; Conquest, *Terror*, p. 195.

25. See Regler, *Owl of Minerva*, pp. 331–354.

26. See Krivitsky, pp. 9–15.

27. See Heller and Nekrich, *Utopia in Power*, pp. 324–326.

28. Walter Krivitsky, *In Stalin's Secret Service*, p. 70 (my emphasis).

29. Ibid., 72.

30. Ibid.

31. Information to the author from Mr. Steve Nelson.

32. Gide, *Littérature engagé*, p. 335.

33. Regler, *The Owl of Minerva*, p. 170.

34. Gross, *Münzenberg*, pp. 242–243.

35. Regler, *The Owl of Minerva*, p. 164.

36. A revealing account of such a clandestine propaganda mission, run for the apparatus in 1934, can be found in *A Life Together*, the memoirs of the Countess Catherine Karolyi. This account should be supplemented by a report on the same mission made by Count Michael Karolyi in his *Memoirs*. Note especially the two slightly differing accounts of the role played by the French Embassy in Berlin.

37. Langer, *Josephine Herbst*, from the 1985 paperback edition, pp. 206–217.

38. FOIA dossier on Louis Gibarti, #61–6629, section 3. Deposition of Louis Gibarti before Special Counsel to the United States Senate, Robert Morris, Esq., and United States Senators Willis Smith and Homer Ferguson, Paris, August 28, 1951.

39. The procedure for establishing Soviet authority over a local party and its officials was accomplished by a written order, known as a *mandat*, borne by a given Comintern official, such as Gibarti and presented to the local party. The *mandat* had the effect of a command, requiring full co-operation and indeed

obedience from the local party officials with regard to the project at hand. According to Babette Gross, such a *mandat* was given to Vaillant for Münzenberg's Paris operations. Gibarti testified that he also had such a *mandat*, written on silk and signed by Münzenberg himself, which he presented to Earl Browder in New York in March 1934.

40. Gross, *Münzenberg*, pp. 240–242. It is possible that other hands were at work in this co-ordinated activity at a level higher up the *apparat* chain of command than Münzenberg. Who held this authority after Münzenberg's fall from grace is not entirely clear. One would look to Mikhail Koltsov for the more public face of it. There was also Louis Dolivet and the *Rassemblement Universelle Populaire*, or RUP. See below.

41. CPA fond 495.292.244a. Documents of the Anti-War Commission on the Leipzig Trial and the London Counter-Trial.

42. Gibarti's life has rarely broken into the printed record, and the one volume in which he plays a large role, *Crime without Punishment*, by Guenther Reinhardt is not reliable. My principal sources come from interviews, and Gibarti's files in the National Archives of the United States, as well as my FOIA request.

43. See Gibarti, FOIA file.

44. For the League Against Imperialism as an instrument for sabotage and espionage, I am indebted to Deacon's unpublished *The British Connection* especially pp. 112–114. Deacon relies on revelations concerning Percy Glading over the Woolrich Arsenal Case. Deacon's views have been confirmed by Mr. John Costello, in his work in Soviet archives. Mr. Costello has discovered that Maurice Dobb, of the Cambridge University branch of the League Against Imperialism, and Gibarti himself, played a fully witting role in the recruitment of Kim Philby. See Costello, *Deadly Illusions*, pp. 125–126.

45. The myth of Malraux's adventures with Borodin in the Communist underground has been effectively disposed of by Jean Lacouture. (See Lacouture, *André Malraux*, pp. 114–117.) An arresting example of Malraux's fabrications on the subject can be found in the documents included in Edmund Wilson's essay on Malraux collected in Wilson's *Classics and Commercials*. It is perhaps worth noting that Gibarti, as a China hand, knew the real Borodin, who also appears as a character in *Man's Fate*, as that Borodin was (not surprisingly) quite close to many of the founding personalities of the League Against Imperialism. (See the memoirs of Charles Shipman, or "Manuel Gomez.")

46. See Schliemann, "Münzenberg."

47. See Sperber, *Au-delà de l'oubli: Les Porteurs d'eau*, chapter 1.

48. Karel Kaplan, *Report on the Murder of the General Secretary*, p. 276.

49. For the World Committee feeding disinformation to Winston Churchill, see Deacon, *The British Connection*, pp. 105–107. It should be noted that the Duchess of Atholl was a prime "innocent" for the World Committee.

50. The question of whether Michael Karolyi was or was not under the discipline of the apparatus is much debated. *Apparat* insiders in the United States during the late twenties report being told unequivocally that Count Karolyi was under Party discipline. (See Voros, *American Commissar.*)

I myself knew the late Countess Karolyi in the early 1980s. She was then in her great age—over 90—and still a woman of great charm. I owe her a debt of gratitude. I was twice a resident at the artists' foundation she created in the south of France and dedicated to her husband's memory. At that time, I was not in the least conscious of the Countess's special role in the issues under examination here, though I did read part of her memoirs and knew the gossip at the Karolyi Foundation that she had once been a spy. Though it made no particular impression on me at the time, I must have come across Münzenberg's name for the first time reading her book.

On the rare occasions when we discussed politics, the Countess invariably gave the impression of knowing more than she was prepared to say. Her thinking, though subtle and insightful, remained enthralled by the revolutionary myth. I once asked her, for example, whether she regarded the substance of Solzhenitsyn's *The Gulag Archipelago* as true. ''It is true,'' she replied after a bleak, solemn pause. ''It is exaggerated, but it is essentially true.'' I was (and I remain) astonished that a woman possessed of that knowledge could later say in my hearing that though Hungary was a communist country, ''it is not communist enough for me.'' There was something invincible in her innocence.

The Countess made an instructive contrast to her no-less-intelligent but more politically hard-headed and more flexible contemporary Babette Gross, whom she somewhat resembled and had surely known well.

51. See Elizabeth Bentley's account of her work in the New York office of the League Against War and Fascism, in *Out of Bondage*.

52. See Costello, *Deadly Illusions*, pp. 125–126.

53. See Anthony Boyle, *The Climate of Treason*, p. 108.

54. Gross, *Münzenberg*, p. 264.

55. For Gibarti's contacts with Alpari and Fried, see the interview with Louis Gibarti in the David Dallin Papers, Special Collections of the New York Public Library.

56. Information to the author from the late Babette Gross.

57. Information from Babette Gross. See also interview with Louis Gibarti, in the Dallin Papers, New York Public Library.

58. The account of Chambers's meeting with this representative is found in his *Witness*, pp. 214–217.

59. I am grateful to Mr. Sam Tanenhaus, the biographer of Whittaker Chambers, for the information (not in *Witness*) that while he never was certain, Chambers came to think it likely that his contact at the New York Public Library may

have been an official of the Comintern named Bèla Szantil (sometimes spelled Szanto). Szantil is certainly a perfectly plausible candidate for this identification, but he is neither more nor less so than Alpari, whom he seems to have rather resembled.

60. See entry on Alpari in Lazitch and Drachkovitch, *The Biographical Dictionary of the Comintern.*

61. Lucien Vogel was a major figure in the history of magazine publishing. He was also at this time a leading fellow traveller, and he appears in the events under discussion in many capacities. References to him appear in Gross, *Münzenberg*, in Gide, *Les Cahiers de la Petite Dame*, and in the memoirs of both the Count and Countess Karolyi. I am grateful to Mr. Leo Lerman for information concerning Vogel's career in New York, following his break with the Soviets. I am especially grateful to the late Pierre Bertaux for information concerning Vogel, and his daughter, Marie-Claude Vogel.

62. See Gide, *Les Cahiers de la Petite Dame*, referring both to Vogel's role in the offer coming from Mezhropohmfilm Russ to make a film of his novel *Les Caves du Vatican*, and the suggestion that Gide make a tour of the Soviet Union in 1932.

63. Count Michael Karolyi, *Memoirs*, pp. 286–287.

64. For a description of Vaillant-Couturier's role in Stalinizing French cultural life, see Ory, *Nizan*, pp. 127–130. For Münzenberg's meeting with Marie-Claude Vogel, Vaillant-Couturier, and Kurella, see Gross, *Münzenberg*, pp. 239–241. For a photograph of Vaillant-Couturier, see Desanti, *Les Clés d'Elsa*, p. 231. For Alfred Kurella's history in the Comintern, see Lazitch and Drachkovitch, *A Biographical Dictionary of the Comintern*, pp. 207–208. For Barbusse's and Rolland's lack of standing in French cultural chic, as well as details of Vaillant's personality, see interview by the author with Pierre Bertaux, June 10, 1986.

65. Mann, *Diaries*, pp. 154–158. Also information to the author from the late Pierre Bertaux.

66. Pierre Bertaux, interview with the author, June 10, 1986.

67. For a good account of Ilya Ehrenberg's general position, see Lottman, *The Left Bank.*

68. CPA. Various documents concerning Münzenberg's use of Henri Barbusse are scattered throughout fond 495. A typical example can be found in 495.19.337., documents 1, 3, and 9.

69. Information to the author from Babette Gross.

70. On sharing the fruits of espionage between Willi and the French, see Count Karolyi, *Memoirs*, p. 283, with endnote.

71. Pierre Bertaux, interview with the author, June 10, 1986.

Chapter 3: The Lieutenant

1. I have relied upon many written sources for the life of Otto Katz. These include Gross, *Münzenberg*, Koestler, *Invisible Writing*, Regler, *The Owl of Minerva*, Kersten, "Das Ende Willi Münzenbergs," Wessel, *Münzenbergs Ende*, and Karel Kaplan, *Report on the Murder of the General Secretary*, inter alia. There is an important and quite reliable, albeit intensely hostile, footnote on him in Ruth Fischer's *Stalin and German Communism*. Voluminous information documenting his work in America is held in the National Archives of the United States, and in response to my request, a large FOIA file from the FBI has been assembled on his activities, FBI FOIA dossier #65–9266. He appears in all accounts of the Slansky Trials (Hodos, *Show Trials*, Karel Kaplan, *Dans les Archives du Comité Central*, Slanska, *Report on My Husband*, London, *The Confession*, and *The State of My Mind*, inter alia). Katz is discussed, albeit mendaciously in memoirs by Lillian Hellman, *An Unfinished Woman*, and Ella Winter, *And Not to Yield*. In addition, I am indebted for interviews concerning his activities to Mr. Paul Willert, the late Mr. Pierre Bertaux, Mr. Herman Starobin, Mrs. Margaret Regler, Mrs. Rae Bernstein, Mr. Peter Lübbe, Mr. Robert Crowley, Mr. Gus Tyler, Mr. John Hunt, Mrs. Henriette Nizan, Ms. Manuella Dobos, and Mr. Steve Nelson, among others. Many conversations with Mr. John Costello, supported by documentation from his research, have been indispensable.

2. For Katz's earliest contacts with Münzenberg, see Gross, *Münzenberg*, p. 309.

3. Pawel, *The Nightmare of Reason*, pp. 98, 142, and passim.

4. Gross, *Münzenberg*, pp. 310–311. For the intellectual ambience of the era, see passages on Kafka's connections to Kisch in ibid., and Willett, *The Theater of Erwin Piscator*, along with the passages on the Piscatorbühne in Hayman's biography of Brecht, *Bertolt Brecht*. For a memoir of the era, see also Viertel, *The Kindness of Strangers*, with references to Katz on p. 101, and passim. An amusing fictional account of the era and its people can be found in Isherwood's *Prater Violet*.

5. See Gross, *Münzenberg*, p. 311. Katz's role in the joint Comintern-NKVD assassinations in Spain is discussed in my chapter 10 on Spain. Brecht's devotion to Stalinism in its cruelest aspects is summarized in Paul Johnson, *Intellectuals* (London: Weidenfeld, 1988; New York: Harper & Row, 1988).

6. Hook, *Out of Step*, pp. 491–496.

7. FOIA dossier on Otto Katz, #65–9266.

8. Gross, *Münzenberg*, p. 311.

9. Draper, essay on Otto Katz, "The Man Who Wanted to Hang," *The Reporter*, January 6, 1953, pp. 26–30.

10. For Hollywood fellow travelling prior to 1935, see Schwartz, *The Hollywood Writers' War*, the memoirs of John Howard Lawson, Ella Winter, and many others.

11. See Meade, *Dorothy Parker*, pp. 253–254. See also Stewart, *By a Stroke of Luck*. See also Schwartz, *The Hollywood Writers' Wars*, p. 83, and passim. Katz's presence in Hollywood is mentioned by a number of other memoirists, among them Viertel, *The Kindness of Strangers*.

12. Katz's close association with Eisler is documented in the FOIA dossier on Otto Katz, Section #1; FBI memorandum of Feb. 4, 1943. Also information to the author in an interview with Mrs. Rae Bernstein, July 1991. That Lillian Hellman worked with Katz is indicated by Mrs. Bernstein's assertion to me that her husband Joseph Bernstein, who gave extensive editorial assistance to Katz in his writing, had been introduced to Katz by Lillian Hellman.

13. Information on Otto Katz and Fritz Lang, FOIA dossier on Otto Katz. Reference is also made to Katz's social life in Hollywood in the memoirs of Viertel, *The Kindness of Strangers*. Note especially pp. 101–102 and 211–220.

14. Information to the author from Mrs. Rae Bernstein.

15. See CPA fond 495.72.26. A document on the World Committee Against War and Fascism,'' addressed to Otto Katz, in which ''active'' [presumably legal] ''work in America'' is discussed. See also, CPA fond 495.19.336 and 337.

16. See Otto Katz FOIA dossier, on his expulsion from the United States in November 1940.

17. Confidential information to the author.

18. Claud Cockburn, *A Discord of Trumpets*, Willett, *The Theater of Erwin Piscator*, and Koestler *Invisible Writing*, all testify to Katz's skill as a rapid writer in several languages. I should add that Mrs. Rae Bernstein, widow of Joseph Bernstein who collaborated with ''André Simone'' on *Men of Europe*, tells me that Katz's English, while fluent, was far from perfect, and required intensive editorial help. Since many of the books by ''Simon'' or ''Simone'' appeared first in English, probably all had editorial assistance of the kind supplied by Joseph Bernstein—who was incidentally also the literary right hand, in English, of Julio Alvárez del Vayo.

19. Hellman, *An Unfinished Woman*, p. 68.

20. For Hellman's relation to Katz and his activities in New York in 1939 and 1940, I am indebted to information from Mrs. Rae Bernstein, Mrs. Ralph Bates, and Margaret Regler. No account, document, or memoir in the many hundreds I have seen mentions any imprisonment or arrest of Katz in Spain. He was in America, Paris, and the Riviera during the final phases of the Spanish Civil War. As the reader will see below, I think it highly likely (but not certain) that Katz was quietly involved in *P.M.*, in the creation of which Hellman and Hammett were intimately involved, as both William Wright and Carl Rollyson show in their biographies of Hellman.

21. Koestler, *Invisible Writing*, p. 209.

22. For Cockburn's introduction to Münzenberg, see *A Discord of Trumpets*, p. 232, and for a fairly candid account of fabricating disinformation for Katz in Spain, see pp. 306–309.

23. Cockburn, *A Discord of Trumpets*, p. 306.

24. Information to the author from Mrs. Margaret Regler.

25. Cockburn, *A Discord of Trumpets*, p. 305.

26. Information to the author, interview with Mr. Paul Willert, London, June 6, 1986.

27. Hellman, *An Unfinished Woman*, pp. 68–69.

28. Koestler, *The Invisible Writing*, p. 211. Geneviève Tabouis was a famous French political journalist; Ellen Wilkinson, a sometime fellow traveller, was a leading personality in the British Labour Party.

29. Confidential interview with the author.

30. Information to the author from the late Eugen Loebl (spelling is an anglicized version of the original Löbl).

31. For Blunt's and Burgess's claims to be "Comintern" agents, see Rees, *A Chapter of Accidents*, and Straight, *After Long Silence*, in the passages describing Burgess and Blunt attempting to recruit them. That Maly and Orlov were among the first controls of the Cambridge ring has been established by John Costello. See *The Mask of Treachery*, and the *New York Times*, June 26, 1991, p. 11.

32. On apologists for the Popular Front, see Alpern, *Freda Kirchway*, Louis Fischer, *Men and Politics*, et al.

33. The penetration of the Comintern by the NKVD and the GRU in 1935 has been explored by a number of reliable authors, chief among them Conquest, *The Great Terror*, pp. 399–408, and passim. I am grateful to Mr. Herb Romerstein for revealing to me the actual identity of "Comrade Moskfin," (or "Moskvin"). "Moskfin" was the man in charge of liquidating the Münzenberg Trust in 1935; he was in truth a founding senior officer of the NKVD, Mikhail Trilliser, who by 1935 seems to have been attached to the GRU. This information was confirmed during June 1992 by research in the Comintern archives in Moscow by Mr. Harvey Klehr, to whom I am indebted here. For "Moskfin's" role liquidating Münzenberg's enterprises, see Gross, *Münzenberg*, p. 277.

34. Information to the author from Mr. Paul Willert.

35. Radek's competence in German matters was an indispensable factor in his place within the Soviet hierarchy. See Heller and Nekrich, *Utopia in Power*, pp. 232–233. Also Lazitch and Drachkovitch, *Lenin and the Comintern*, and many other authorities.

36. See Willett, *The Theater of Erwin Piscator*.

37. A reliable sketch of Katz's relations with Piscator can be found in ibid. Babette Gross supplies much information as well. It is Cookridge who reports (without citation) the information not found elsewhere that Katz contributed to Piscator's sets, in *The Net That Covers the World.*

38. Willett, *The Theater of Erwin Piscator*, pp. 67–71.

39. Ibid.

40. Gross, *Münzenberg*, p. 311.

41. Ibid.

42. Koestler, *Invisible Writing*, p. 211.

43. Information to the author from Mr. Herbert Marshall.

44. Ibid.

45. Karel Kaplan, *Report on the Murder of the General Secretary*, p. 276.

46. Gross, *Münzenberg*, p. 311.

47. For Katz and his connection to Batista, see FOIA report.

48. Information to the author from Mr. Herman Starobin.

49. Information to the author from the late Eugen Loebl.

50. Karel Kaplan, interview with the author, Munich, Germany, July 7, 1989. See also Katz's letter to Klement Gottwald in Karel Kaplan, *Report on the Murder of the General Secretary*, pp. 272–279. That Katz was rumored to have been party to Münzenberg's death at the time of the Slansky interrogations was confirmed to me by Mr. Karel Kaplan, the principal Czech historian of the event.

51. See FO1A dossier on Otto Katz, pages relevant to June 1940.

52. Information to the author in correspondence with Mrs. Marcia Davenport.

53. Information to the author from Mr. Herman Starobin.

54. See FO1A dossier on Otto Katz, interview with Hermann Rauschnigg. In *The Mask of Treachery*, John Costello speculates on the possibility that Anthony Blunt may have attempted to mislead his British interrogators by claiming that an unknown man fitting Katz's description was his first Soviet control. Mr. Costello's subsequent study, *Deadly Illusions*, more or less divests this theory of its plausibility.

55. See Gardiner on reading Cookridge in her account of Kim Philby in *Code Name: Mary*. See also Costello on Spiro-Cookridge in *The Mask of Treachery.*

56. Guy Liddell is a figure who has repeatedly been involved in the most persistent spy story of our time, the question of the senior "mole" in British intelligence, the defender and promoter of the Cambridge spies. He was Anthony Blunt's trusted confidant, close friend, and political patron within the world of British intelligence, and his actions in the events leading up to the flight of Burgess and Maclean were all highly conducive to a successful flight and all

worked steadily against successful capture. The literary critic Goronwy Rees, who was Blunt's and Burgess's intimate friend and fellow conspirator, went to his grave vocally convinced that Liddell was himself a witting co-conspirator. Liddell's supporters in the ranks of British intelligence and among its historians are not only numerous but highly respected. Chief among these was the late Sir Dick White, the dean of the British services, who loathed Goronwy Rees and who rose to his own position in British intelligence very much under the patronage of Liddell. A number of observers for whom I have very high regard consider the case against Liddell as closed and his innocence confirmed.

I do not. I consider the case still open. I have yet to see any argument or display of evidence that, in my view, persuasively demonstrates Liddell's innocence. This does not mean I am convinced of his guilt, but as the reader will see at a number of crucial stages of the present study, the circumstantial evidence against Guy Liddell is not merely embarrassing; it is absolutely breath-taking.

Part of that evidence against Liddell comes from his having been Spiro's probable source on Katz. A possible source, in turn, of Liddell's tales about Otto is a highly placed informant named Anatoli Bakaylov, a peripatetic White Russian journalist and intellectual, very well connected in exile groups and among members of the British ruling class who concerned themselves with Soviet affairs. Not incidentally, Bakaylov was also one of MI-5's most trusted informants about Russian exiles and the interminable intelligence intrigues that perplexed and embroiled exile life. The man with whom Bakaylov worked in that capacity was the ubiquitous Guy Liddell, the man who has so often been pronounced above suspicion.

Now Bakaylov was in fact a Soviet agent—one of the more adept of his period. He was perfectly placed to feed disinformation to British intelligence, to the Foreign Office and to senior politicians, and, he did so for years, always with Liddell's imprimatur. In the happy days before the war and Otto's fall from grace, Bakaylov and Katz used to work together in all kinds of enterprises as agents together. For this information on Bakaylov, I am indebted to Costello, *The Mask of Treachery*, pp. 311–312, 602, as well as to Deacon's unpublished *The British Connection.*

57. Cookridge, *The Net That Covers the World*, p. 249.

Chapter 4: Trial, Counter-Trial, and the Dimitrov Conspiracy

1. CPA fond 495, sections 292, 248, 251, and 60 all contain extensive documentation of almost every operational (as opposed to conspiratorial) detail of the Reichstag Fire campaign. It is clear that Münzenberg kept his superiors meticulously informed on every aspect of his work. Conversations with lawyers, assessments of participants, documents of the interlocking committees, draft statements to be made by defendants, debriefings by participants, monitored correspondence between the participants and their families, summaries of press coverage, and the like fill these files.

2. Information to the author from Ms. Ruth Price.

3. For the creation of the Podlipki ''Eighth International Sports Base,'' see Gross, *Münzenberg,* pp. 264–266, 267. For the downfall of Mirov-Abramov, see Conquest, *The Great Terror,* p. 408.

4. For a useful summary of Torgler's place in German communism, see Borkenau, *European Communism.* Tobias naturally discusses Torgler's case extensively, though Torgler's tangled connection to the entire event has never been fully explored. Indispensable to that exploration would be Ruth Fischer, *Stalin and German Communism,* and especially the correspondence of Ruth Fischer with Maria Reese now on deposit in the papers of Ruth Fischer in the Houghton Library at Harvard. Many of these documents, along with other relevant documents, have been published by Peter Lübbe in his collection of the Ruth Fischer-Arkady Maslow papers, *Abtrünnig wider Willen,* in particular pp. 219, 248, and 273. Gisevius, in *To the Bitter End,* also provides some discussion of Torgler's role.

5. The leading work on the Reichstag Fire is Tobias, *The Reichstag Fire.* Tobias's bibliography is reliable and extensive.

6. For Münzenberg's planning at this stage, see Gross, *Münzenberg,* pp. 239–270.

7. Ibid., p. 249.

8. Babette Gross, interview with the author, Munich, Germany, July 6, 1989.

9. Regler, *The Owl of Minerva.*

10. Ibid., pp. 160–161.

11. *The Brown Book of the Hitler Terror and the Burning of the Reichstag,* and *The Second Brown Book of the Hitler Terror,* went through many editions and were very widely translated. Gustav Regler, Arthur Koestler, and Manès Sperber, in their memoirs, all write vividly about work in the collective that produced the books. Otto Katz himself produced a book on their composition called *Der Kampf um ein Buch.* (I have found no record of a translation.) After the war, Dimitrov himself wrote a version of the event in *Das Reichstagsbrandprozess.*

12. See Gross, *Münzenberg,* p. 251. See also Regler, *The Owl of Minerva,* and Costello, *The Mask of Treachery*, p. 298.

13. An important document for understanding this phase of Katz's career in his letter to Klement Gottwald, written on the day of his execution in Prague, and found in Karel Kaplan, *Report on the Murder of the General Secretary.* Katz's contact with Ellen Wilkinson and others is also reported in Vernon, *Ellen Wilkinson.*

14. Stewart, *By a Stroke of Luck!*

15. Because an important witness of Burgess's circle confused the name of Otto Katz with that of another member of the Soviet apparatus named Rudolph Katz,

it has often been mistakenly claimed that Otto Katz played some part in Guy Burgess's London life during the war. This is untrue: Otto Katz was in Mexico throughout the period in question; the Katz so often seen at Burgess's Bentinck Street flat was Rudolph, an agent who except in his allegiances was very unlike Otto. According to Burgess's lover Jimmy Hewett, Rudolph Katz was a compulsively lecherous homosexual and "a great fat slob." This confusion of Katzes is cleared up by John Costello, though Costello also makes clear that Burgess did have some real connection to the Münzenberg operation (*The Mask of Treachery,* p. 330). For an account of Burgess showing off among the literary communists in Paris, see Rees, *A Chapter of Accidents,* and its account of Burgess arranging for Rees and himself to dine with Theodore Dreiser.

16. See Hays, *City Lawyer.*

17. Göring's performance at the trial is reported by Tobias, *The Reichstag Fire,* pp. 221–228.

18. Information to the author from Messers. Tzvetan Todorov and Peter Semerdjiev.

19. Fischer, *Stalin and German Communism,* pp. 308–309.

20. Arthur Koestler, *The Invisible Writing,* pp. 247–249.

21. Malraux confided his general suspicions on this subject in an interview with Jean Lacouture, as they worked together preparing Lacouture's biography of Malraux. Lacouture, *André Malraux,* p. 182.

22. Preface, Popov, *Ot lajpzigskija prozes v sibirskite lageri.* I am exceedingly grateful to M. Tzvetan Todorov for having brought this important piece of evidence to my attention, and for supplying me with the literal translation of Semerdjiev's introduction, which with his kind permission I am including here.

23. Mr. Semerdjiev's claim that Pieck acted as the intermediary between the Nazi and Soviet governments is sustained by a cable found in the Central Party Archives, written by Pieck, sent to Piatnitsky, and translated from the German for Stalin's eyes only. This document conveys a proposal from the German government to Stalin suggesting that the dictator offer "Dimitrov and the Bulgarians" political asylum "in any form." Exactly as Ruth Fischer understood, Ernst Torgler was not to be included in the deal. The cable in question was received by Piatnitsky four days after the Leipzig acquittal, December 28, 1933, Christmas having intervened (CPA 495.19.248).

As for Radek's personal involvement in this entire sequence of events, Radek's probably coded telegram to "Comrade Vinogradov" in Berlin, April 20, 1933, clearly shows (1) that he was specifically ordering his agent to find information connecting the Fire to S.S. Oberführer Kurt Daluege, and thereby the SA, since Delauege was then principally involved in placing SA officials throughout the new German administration, and was thoroughly identified with SA interests; (2) that Vinogradov would be assisted in assembling this information by "discreet talks" with an official of the *Reichswehr*, Colonel Oskar von Neidermayer, a German secret agent very close to Radek, who had served as an intelligence operator and operational undercover man arranging the covert exchanges of military material and information between the Soviet government and the German army following the Treaty of Rapallo. Neidermayer was therefore an expert on the secret back channels between the two governments; (3) that the information and disinformation thus obtained would be disseminated by, among other newspapers, the *Manchester Guardian*, which was indeed, in the event, the prime English-language outlet for Münzenberg's campaign.

I regard the text of this telegram as significantly supporting my view that the common purpose of the two dictators in their collaboration at this time was to use the communist propaganda campaign over the Leipzig trial as a means of discrediting the SA in favor of the German Army, and thus preparing for the events of June 30, 1934: The Night of Long Knives. (The letter from Radek to Vinogradov is found in CPA 495.60.244a.)

24. See Karel Kaplan, *Report of the Murder of the General Secretary*. For the letter of Otto Katz to Klement Gottwald, December 3, 1952, see p. 276.

25. Both Regler, *The Owl of Minerva,* and Koestler, *Invisible Writing,* recall Dimitrov's access to *The Brown Book* while in prison.

26. Information to the author from Mr. Peter Semerdjiev: a letter dated November 6, 1992, and an extended telephone interview, November 13, 1992.

27. Babette Gross, interview with the author, July 4, 1989.

28. A useful summary of this well-known and crucial juncture in Hitler's planning can be found in Paul Johnson, *Modern Times*, pp. 296–300.

29. See also ibid.

30. Ibid.

31. Carlton, *Anthony Eden,* p. 46.

32. For Hitler's planning and behavior on the Night of Long Knives, see Gisevius, *To the Bitter End,* and Fest, *Hitler.*

33. For the Münzenberg campaign's focus on the SA, see especially the accounts of Tobias, *The Reichstag Fire,* and Sperber, *Ces Temps-là.*

34. See pp. 360–61 n. 23.

35. *The White Book on the Executions of June 30, 1934.*

36. Tobias, *The Reichstag Fire,* p. 143; also Wollenberg, *Echo der Woche,* August 12, 1949.

37. Gross, *Münzenberg,* p. 248.

38. Tobias, *The Reichstag Fire,* p. 57.

39. The intrigues with the Berlin police department are mentioned by both Koestler, *Invisible Writing,* and Regler, *The Owl of Minerva.* The most thorough

eyewitness account from within the Prinz Albrechtstrasse Police Headquarters is Gisevius, *To the Bitter End.*

40. See Gisevius, *To the Bitter End.* The von Stauffenberg plot has been widely analyzed in an extensive bibliography. I would direct the reader especially to the *Autobiography of a Spy,* by Mary Bancroft.

41. See Gisevius, *To the Bitter End.*

42. National Archives of the United States, 800.00B, dossier on Louis Gibarti, document #73. Memorandum from the Visa Division, Department of State, dated January 29, 1940, unsigned but annotated VD; AMW: MLS. For Bredow's role with the Guchkov circle, see Deacon, *The British Connection*, p. 107.

43. Toland, *Hitler*, p. 465.

44. Information citing Gibarti as the probable author of the Oberfohren Memorandum can be found in his FOIA dossier, #61-6629. A careful account of the Oberfohren Memorandum is found in Tobias, *The Reichstag Fire,* p. 104.

45. CPA fond 495.73.26.

46. See letter from Radek to Vinogradov, cited on p. 349 n. 15.

47. See Tobias, *The Reichstag Fire,* appendix C.

48. Ibid., pp. 144–146.

49. The fantasy that Hitler was merely a front man in danger of losing control of the Nazi government to the SA led the conservatives to seek covertly to assist him in resisting that threat.

It's worth noting that after the event, and once the United States was in the war, this version of early Nazi history was believed at high levels of American intelligence. In Geneva in 1942, Mary Bancroft, an OSS operative who was simultaneously intimate with Allen Dulles and Gisevius, acted as the liaison between both men in preparing the attempted assassination of Hitler in the von Stauffenberg plot—a final shot at salvation on the part of anti-Nazi German conservatives and their beloved army, this time covertly assisted by the United States. In conversations with me, Ms. Bancroft made it quite plain that Allen Dulles accepted more or less whole Gisevius's version of the early struggle within the Nazi government, and of the Reichstag Fire.

The tragedy of the conservatives' effort to ruin the SA is that it did nothing to rescue the honor of either German politics or the German army, and instead played into the hands of both Hitler and Stalin. By underestimating Hitler's own importance and (perhaps) overestimating the hated SA, they solidified Nazi power and thereby promoted the aims of both the dictators they despised.

Mary Bancroft, interview with the author, September 12, 1986.

50. See Gisevius, *To the Bitter End.*

51. Rhysselberghe, *Cahiers d'André Gide # 5. Les Cahiers de la Petite Dame.*

Notes pour l'histoire authentique d'André Gide, 1929–1937. See also Gide, *Littérature engagée,* especially the very useful chronology.

52. I have used many sources to reconstruct Gide and Malraux's trip to Berlin with their petition: The notebooks of Maria van Rhysselberghe; Gide *Littérature engagée;* Malraux, *Anti-Memoirs;* Lacouture, *André Malraux,* and others.

53. Lacouture, *André Malraux,* p. 182.

54. See the notebooks of Maria van Rhysselberghe, and the letters of André Gide to Roger Martin du Gard.

Chapter 5: The Deal

1. See Gisevius, *To the Bitter End.*

2. Walter Krivitsky, *In Stalin's Secret Service,* chapter 1.

3. For Berzin's position in Spain during the Civil War, see ibid., chapter III, "Stalin's Hand in Spain," and Conquest, *The Great Terror,* p. 209.

4. Krivitsky, *In Stalin's Secret Service,* pp. 2–3.

5. Dziak, *Chekisty,* pp. 83–84.

6. For Radek's relation to the anti-fascist campaign, see Krivitsky, *In Stalin's Secret Service,* p. 10, as well as Heller and Nekrich, *Utopia in Power,* p. 325. Gross, *Münzenberg,* pp. 179–180. See also Dziak, *Chekisty,* p. 28.

7. Heller and Nekrich, *Utopia in Power,* pp. 310–322.

8. For confirmation of Radek's view, see also Litvinov as quoted by Gustav Hilger, cited in Blackstock, *The Secret Road to World War II,* p. 262.

9. Krivitsky, *In Stalin's Secret Service,* pp. 8–15.

10. Ibid., pp. 1–25, noting especially pp. 10–11, and all references to Radek.

11. The best extant account of Krivitsky's time in the United States is found in Newton's *The Cambridge Spies,* but there are many other good accounts of the Western response to Krivitsky's defection. One of the best is Levine, *Eyewitness to History,* pp. 182–187. Krivitsky's relations to both British and American intelligence, along with his role in the unmasking of the Cambridge Conspiracy, are important and complex, and treated in a large literature. A typical example is found in *Philby: The Long Road to Moscow,* by Seale and McConville, in many references. The best and most recent account is Costello, *The Mask of Treachery.*

12. Conquest, *The Great Terror,* pp. 62–63.

13. For a thorough analysis of the movement toward the pact, see Nekrich and Heller, *Utopia in Power,* pp. 316–369. For Stalin's general strategic thinking prior to the European war, see Paul Johnson, *Modern Times,* p. 359. The reader is also directed to Dziak, *Chekisty,* chapters 4, 5, and 6.

14. Both Conquest, *The Great Terror,* and Heller and Nekrich, *Utopia in Power,* discuss Stalin's willingness to see damage done to the German communists in 1933.

15. Heller and Nekrich, *Utopia in Power,* pp. 251–258. See also Krivitsky, *In Stalin's Secret Service,* pp. 1–25.

16. Heller and Nekrich, *Utopia in Power,* pp. 309–311, citing Gnedin, *Iz istorii otnoshenii mezhdu SSSR i fashistskoi Germanii. Dokumenty i sovremennye kommentarii,* pp. 22–27.

17. Hilger and Meyer, *The Incompatible Allies,* pp. 267–268.

18. Krivitsky, *In Stalin's Secret Service*, p. 284.

19. Catherine Karolyi, *A Life Together,* p. 271.

20. Regler, *The Owl of Minerva.*

21. Lerner, *Karl Radek,* pp. 8–30.

22. Gross, *Münzenberg,* p. 179.

23. From within the Trotskyist camp, a perspective on Blumkin's demise and his relation to Trotsky is found in van Heijenoort's book, *With Trotsky in Exile.*

24. For an interesting description of the political temper in Moscow during 1934 and 1935, see Conquest, *Stalin and the Kirov Murder.*

25. Dimitrov, *The Working Classes against Fascism,* p. 47.

26. Koltsov's role in the 1935 Culture Congress is noted by Lottman, *The Left Bank.* It was confirmed to me by Babette Gross. That Katz played a leading role in the Left Book Club was first pointed out to me by Mr. Paul Willert, who noted especially that "Katz had a lot of Negrin money" (that is, money from the Stalinist Spanish government) to spend on propaganda in both Europe and England. Katz speaks of his role with Gollancz and Laski in his letter to Klement Gottwald; see above, chapter 4, note 2.

27. For Otto's role in founding the LBC; information to the author, interview with Paul Willert, June 6, 1986.

28. MacDonald, *The United States, Britain and Appeasement, 1936–1939.* Cited in Paul Johnson, *Modern Times,* p. 345.

29. Conquest, *Stalin and the Kirov Murder,* p. 104.

30. Ibid., p. 146.

31. Ibid.

32. The best account of the 1937 purge of the Red Army general staff can be found in Conquest, *The Great Terror,* chapter 7, "The Assault on the Army." Conquest's range of reference is too wide to summarize here, but he does rely, as I do, on both Orlov and Krivitsky. For a useful and incisive summary of the affair, and various positions that have been taken over it, see also Laqueur,

Stalin: The Glasnost Revelations. For an intensive reexamination of Orlov's role and information, see Costello, *Deadly Illusions.* Another book which I have found useful is Blackstock, *The Secret Road to World War II.* See also Hilger and Meyer, *The Incompatible Allies.*

33. Krivitsky, *In Stalin's Secret Service,* "Why Stalin Shot His Generals."

34. Conquest, *The Great Terror,* pp. 195–205.

35. For the Tuchachevsky affair in relation to Hitler and Germany, see ibid., pp. 195–205.

36. For Robert Conquest's thoughts on Stalin's motives for Tuchachevsky's death, see ibid., pp. 182–192.

37. Ibid.

38. Krivitsky, *In Stalin's Secret Service,* "Stalin's Hand in Spain."

39. Conquest, *Stalin and the Kirov Murder,* p. 199.

40. For Katz's links to the Miller organization and the Guchkov circle, see Costello, *The Mask of Treachery.*

41. See Conquest, *The Great Terror,* p. 199. The joke about "tele-Beneš" is cited in Blackstock, *The Secret Road to World War II.*

42. Sir Isaiah Berlin, interview with the author, January 24, 1992.

43. I should note that according to Mrs. Rae Bernstein, during the period he spent in New York in 1940, Katz made frequent reference (when speaking within reliably communist circles) to his past privileged link to President Beneš. Information to the author from Mrs. Rae Bernstein.

44. See Gross, *Münzenberg,* p. 312.

45. Silone's remark was recalled in a conversation with the author by Mr. Jorgen Schliemann.

46. Gross, *Münzenberg,* p. 312.

47. Conquest, *Stalin and the Kirov Murder,* pp. 182–183. Solzhenitsyn, *The Gulag Archipelago,* vols. 1–2, see glossary entry p. 631, and in the text, pp. 410–416.

Chapter 6: Cambridge West

1. The best study of the Washington activities of the Cambridge group is found in *The Cambridge Spies,* by Verne Newton.

2. Boyle, *The Climate of Treason,* pp. 400–410.

3. Ibid., pp. 271–273, and passim.

4. Ibid., pp. 400–405.

5. Mr. Paul Willert, phone interview with the author, June 25, 1987.

6. Costello, *The Mask of Treachery,* p. 208.

7. Arthur Martin's account of this scene is quoted and paraphrased in *Conspiracy of Silence,* by Penrose and Freeman, pp. 415–420.

8. Malraux, *Anti-Memoirs,* p. 89.

9. Maly's role is best established by Costello in *The Mask of Treachery,* especially pp. 278–285.

10. See Massing, *This Deception.* The chapter entitled ''Assignment America'' describes Massing's meetings with Maly. Hede Massing died before Maly was identified as the Cambridge recruiter and control, and she did not know his real name when she wrote her book. She did correctly identify *''der Lange''* however with ''Paul Hardt,'' without knowing that name to be one of Maly's aliases. Her description of *''der Lange''* is exactly appropriate to Maly in every detail. Indeed, Massing's precise description of him and his role is in itself persuasive evidence for the general veracity of *This Deception.*

11. Langer, *Josephine Herbst,* pp. 206–207.

12. Massing, *This Deception,* pp. 115–138, and passim.

13. Poretsky, *Our Own People,* p. 144.

14. Lewis, *Red Pawn,* p. 37.

15. For Chambers's recruitment, see Weinstein, *Perjury.* According to testimony of Louis Budenz, accepted by Flora Lewis, and confirmed by my own research in the National Archives of the United States, Noel Field was a member of the Communist party by 1927.

16. The best source of information on Noel Field is Flora Lewis's book of 1965, *Red Pawn.* Its conclusions about Field's work for the Soviets are very conservatively formulated and at no point go beyond the evidence then available. Much more has become available since that time, though it is rather scattered, especially through information released by Dr. Karel Kaplan, a member of the Dubcek government who saw much of the documentation of the period. (See Weinstein, *Perjury.*) See also Hodos, *Show Trials.* Copious information about Field's work as a secret service agent, both in Europe and in espionage with Alger Hiss in Washington, has reportedly been seen documented in the Archives of the Ministry of Information, Budapest, by Ms. Maria Schmidt, a scholar now at work on the archives of the Hungarian Secret Police.

17. The story of the Fields' time in Moscow is recounted in Lewis, *Red Pawn,* as well as in Massing, *This Deception.*

18. Massing herself reports that Krivitsky told her that Field had worked for him between 1936 and 1938. Massing, *This Deception,* p. 152.

19. Chambers, *Witness,* p. 381.

20. Massing, *This Deception,* p. 93.

21. Lewis, *Red Pawn,* p. 97.

22. Field's role in anti-fascist activity is cited by Lewis, *Red Pawn,* Hodos, *Show Trials,* and Humbert-Droz, *Dix ans dans la lutte antifasciste.* A major report from inside that experience is found in London, *The Confession.*

23. The essential outline of Noel Field's relation to Allen Dulles, beginning immediately after World War I and ending in the murderous hysteria of the Slansky Trials, has been provided by Flora Lewis in her admirable study of 1965, *Red Pawn.* Yet as the reader will see, despite the excellence of that book, I view the entire story of Noel Field, not least in his relation to Dulles and the OSS, as one that cries out for new, post–Cold War research.

24. Field's disappearance is reported in Lewis, *Red Pawn.*

25. The successive waves of mass arrests are reported in Hodos, *Show Trials.*

26. Information to the author from Ms. Maria Schmidt, Budapest, January 24, 1993.

27. The best way to be sure an intelligence secret is kept is for all parties on both sides to *want* it kept. The Soviets did not want the world to know about Noel Field. But neither, I fear, did the Americans.

In this writer's opinion, the Soviet decision to use Noel Field as the spy centerpiece for the Eastern European Terror served partly as a defensive tactic in a world-wide crisis inside the secret world precipitated by the revelations of Elizabeth Bentley, Hede Massing, and Whittaker Chambers. In Field the apparatus may have found someone to serve as a block against that American inquiry spreading east and publicizing the deceptions worked by the "anti-fascist" cadres.

The truth was that Noel Field *did* know Allen Dulles. And he *was* a double agent. Late in the war, Field had been taken on as (at least) a stringer, advising the OSS on which European anti-fascists to support. In that capacity, Field accomplished many fine things for the Soviets.

During the war, all the Western services were penetrated by the *apparat,* and this sort of "guidance" was one of its principal aims. The idea was to sabotage non-Stalinist resistance to Hitler and promote—the *apparat*: the people Stalin would install in power once Hitler was gone and the armies had retired to their barracks. The spadework for Stalinism in Eastern Europe and Germany was done by the *apparat,* and among its most effective spades were the Western secret services, the ones supplying and defining resistance to anti-Nazi struggle, through which non-Stalinist fighters could be sabotaged and the obedient promoted. For one of the most well-researched books on this aspect of wartime work, see Glees, *The Secrets of the Service.*

28. In *Show Trials,* Hodos notes this pattern in the Eastern European persecutions, but he does not very deeply explore the motivation that may have created it.

29. Beloff, *Tito's Flawed Legacy.*

30. The best study known to me of the role played by Soviet agents within the British services in subverting undesirable anti-fascist factions is Glees, *The Secrets of the Service.*

31. The relation of the Wise Men to the Washington penetrations is a large subject. The basic texts for its consideration would of course be the memoirs of Acheson, *Present at the Creation,* Bohlen, *Witness to History,* and Kennan, *Memoirs.* Acheson and Bohlen both elegantly sidestep the issue of Hiss's guilt; Kennan does not refer to it at all. They do not say Hiss was guilty; they do not say he was innocent. Bohlen merely notes that Hiss's behavior at Yalta did not strike him as compromising. The tone of the passage seems calculated more to defend the integrity of the Yalta deliberations than Hiss personally. As for Kennan in his *Memoirs,* the passage describing his decision to write the memorandum on U.S.–Soviet relations, the so-called "Long Telegram," clearly shows that he regarded the Treasury Department under Harry Dexter White as hopelessly misled by pro-Soviet opinion. In the Long Telegram itself, as in Kennan's subsequent enlargement upon it, his so called "X-article," for *Foreign Affairs* he explicitly warns of serious penetrations inside the Washington government. And, indeed, at the Treasury Department Harry Dexter White was unquestionably a witting informant for Soviet espionage.

As George Kennan later wrote in his *Memoirs*: "the penetration of the American governmental services by members or agents (conscious or otherwise) of the American communist party in the late 1930's was not a figment of the imagination . . . it really existed; and it assumed proportions which, while never overwhelming, were also not trivial" (pp. 191–192).

It is important to remember that the Wise Men owed their political position to Roosevelt's coalition and the ascendancy it gave the Democratic party, even though to a man they regarded the Soviet policy of Franklin Roosevelt and Harry Hopkins as the work of dangerously incompetent dilettantes. Like their chief, President Truman himself, they could neither endorse nor repudiate Roosevelt's approach. Meanwhile, any very public housecleaning of the Washington penetrations would have handed the populist right an all-too-useful blunt instrument for attacking Yalta, containment, and their own position in power. Richard Nixon's slogan, "Twenty Years of Treason," was directed at *them,* and it was only a few years away.

32. Hodos, *Show Trials,* p. 88.

33. Private information to the author.

34. Rees, *A Chapter of Accidents* pp. 162–164.

35. Costello, *The Mask of Treachery,* p. 548, citing Connolly, *The Missing Diplomats,* p. 33.

36. See Lamphere, *The FBI-KGB War.*

37. Philby's later career is recounted in Andrew and Gordievsky, *The KGB,* as

well as in Knightley, *The Master Spy: The Story of Kim Philby*. See also a dispatch by Richard Beetson, Washington Times Service, December 2, 1987.

38. Wright, *Spycatcher,* pp. 225–226.

39. The indispensable source on Maly's life is Poretsky, *Our Own People*. See also Costello, *The Mask of Treachery,* and very interesting references to Maly's rehabilitation with the KGB in Andrew and Gordievsky, *The KGB*.

40. Straight, *After Long Silence*. For citation of his recruitment, see pp. 100–106.

41. Ibid., p. 102.

42. The Straight family's connections to Louis Dolivet are treated in *After Long Silence*. See also Newton, *The Cambridge Spies*.

43. Straight, *After Long Silence,* p. 110.

44. Chambers, *Witness,* p. 14.

45. Orlov, *The Secret History of Stalin's Crimes*, pp. 229–232.

46. For the relation between Orlov and Maly, see Costello, *Deadly Illusions*.

47. Orlov, *The Secret History of Stalin's Crimes*.

Chapter 7: Bloomsbury and Espionage

1. Bell, *Virginia Woolf,* pp. 48, 54, 63.

2. Bell, *Virginia Woolf,* vol. 1, pp. 129–130.

3. Paul Johnson, *Modern Times*, p. 168. Reference to "the Method" is from Allen, *The Cambridge Apostles*, p. 71.

4. See Deacon, *The Cambridge Apostles*. See also Costello, *The Mask of Treachery*.

5. The story of Julian Bell's affair with Anthony Blunt is reported in Costello, *The Mask of Treachery,* pp. 151–153.

6. The death of Prince Mirsky is reported in Caute, *The Fellow Travellers*.

7. Costello, *The Mask of Treachery,* pp. 151–152.

8. I am indebted in this passage, and throughout this chapter, to John Costello's study of Blunt, *The Mask of Treachery*.

9. Holroyd, *Lytton Strachey,* vol. 1, p. 225.

10. Quoted in Paul Johnson, *Modern Times,* p. 167, citing ibid., pp. 211–212.

11. Conquest, *The Great Terror,* p. 317.

12. For a useful account of Gide's political activity at this time, see Lottman, *The Left Bank*.

13. Catherine Karolyi, *A Life Together*.

14. An excellent summary of the activities of Pascal and Dobb can be found in Costello, *The Mask of Treachery.*

15. Katz refers to this British surveillance in the letter to Klement Gottwald, written hours before he was hanged and published in Karel Kaplan, *Report on the Murder of the General Secretary.*

16. Wilkinson's visit to Katz on the Riviera is mentioned by Louis Fischer in *Men and Politics.*

17. Otto Katz's relation to Claud Cockburn figures quite prominently in Cockburn's memoir, *A Discord of Trumpets,* and in Patricia Cockburn's *Figure of Eight,* as well as Patricia Cockburn, *The Years at "The Week."*

18. Paul Johnson, *Modern Times,* p. 345, citing C. A. MacDonald, *The United States, Britain and Appeasement.*

19. Cockburn, *A Discord of Trumpets.*

20. For the proposal that the *Week* might have an American edition, see Hoopes, *Ralph Ingersoll.*

21. William Warner, *Lillian Hellman: The Image, the Woman* (New York: Simon and Schuster 1986), pp. 167–169.

22. Otto Katz's role at *Ce Soir,* and in Parisian political journalism generally, was quite well known within the apparatus during the Popular Front. *Ce Soir* was a forthrightly communist publication, and its directors were all people close to Katz, but in addition to that, Katz was directly involved in purchasing the services of journalists. (Information to the author from Mr. Paul Willert. See also Poretsky, *Our Own People.*) That *Ce Soir* was subsidized by the propaganda apparatus is plain from the discussion of it that appears in Ory, *Paul Nizan,* pp. 172–173.

23. Information to the author from Ms. Patricia Bosworth.

24. Wright, *Spycatcher,* pp. 288, 339. Wright's exact phrase is to describe Cockburn as a man "of interest to the Service as a prominent left-winger and Comintern agent" (p. 339). Cockburn was closely enough associated with the International to adopt an alias or "Party name": "Frank Pitcairn." This is however not quite the same as saying that Cockburn was a witting member of the Comintern secret service.

25. The Tetuan story appears in Claud Cockburn, *A Discord of Trumpets.*

26. Thomas, *John Strachey,* p. 149. For Strachey's appointment as Director of the World Movement Against Fascism and War, see p. 138.

27. That John Strachey was a witting member of the Soviet apparatus seems to me plainly demonstrated by his position in the Anti-War International, and Strachey's action (as described by John Lehmann in a letter to Andrew Boyle), at the time of the attempt to recruit Lehmann for work in espionage during the Viennese propaganda campaign of 1934. (See Boyle, *The Climate of Treason,*

paperback revision, pp. 105–106). But few observers would doubt Strachey's deep involvement at this late date. The case of Gollancz is perhaps more controversial. During the years of the LBC, Gollancz was at the very least a fellow traveller who was very reliably responsive to the needs of the Party, and to Strachey's direction. My guess, based on two recent studies, is that he was more than that (see Paul Johnson, *Intellectuals,* and Edwards, *Victor Gollancz.*

28. For Strachey's consultations with the leaders of the British Communist party over selections for the Left Book Club, see Thomas, *John Strachey.*

29. For Olden's relation to Münzenberg, see Gross, *Münzenberg,* pp. 229, 232.

30. Information to the author from Mr. Paul Willert.

31. I am indebted to Mr. Herbert Marshall for this observation, which he first made working in the English-language wing of Münzenberg's Mezhropohmfilm Russ in the late 1920s and 1930s.

32. Information to the author from M. François Fejtö.

33. For Hewlett Johnson's relation to Gibarti, information to the author from M. François Fejtö. For Johnson's role as a Stalinist propagandist in general, see David Caute, *The Fellow Travellers,* passim.

34. For Julian Bell's friendship with Guy Burgess, see Andrew Boyle, *The Climate of Treason,* p. 110.

35. Lehmann, *The Whispering Gallery*, p. 212. Lehmann's account of this phase of his life, especially the relation to Virginia and Leonard Woolf, can be found on pp. 184–228.

36. Costello, *Deadly Illusions*, chapter 6.

37. Dollfuss was assassinated by the Nazis in 1934.

38. See Krivitsky, *In Stalin's Secret Service.*

39. See Heller and Nekrich, *Utopia in Power.*

40. Mitchison, *You May Well Ask,* p. 195.

41. Boyle, *The Climate of Treason,* pp. 105–106.

42. Ibid., 106.

43. Maly's operation and the offices of the League Against Imperialism were side by side in the same London building. See Deacon, *The British Connection*, pp. 113–115.

44. See Rees, *A Chapter of Accidents,* pp. 117–128.

45. For the quotation and the preceding one, see ibid., p. 155.

46. Muggeridge, *The Infernal Grove,* pp. 106–107.

47. For the fascinating list of his social contacts, provided by Burgess to the NKVD, see Costello, *Deadly Illusions*. Nicolson is on the list.

48. See Costello, *The Mask of Treachery,* pp. 570–602. Mr. Costello's *Deadly Illusions* contains his best documented account to date of Goronwy Rees's service to the Soviets. See pp. 221; 245–246.

49. Glees, *The Secrets of the Service,* p. 149. See also W. J. West, *Truth Betrayed,* pp. 52–58, and passim.

50. Nicolson, *Diaries and Letters,* p. 435. Cited by Glees, *The Secrets of the Service.*

51. W. J. West, *Truth Betrayed.*

52. Milne, *Harold Nicolson,* cited in Penrose and Freeman, *Conspiracy of Silence,* p. 234.

53. Nicolson, *Diaries and Letters*, p. 349. (Entry for June 7, 1951.)

Chapter 8: In America

1. Peter Kurth, *American Cassandra: The Life of Dorothy Thompson* (New York: Little Brown, 1990).

2. See Sheean, *Dorothy and Red.* The incident is also reported in Kurth, *American Cassandra.*

3. Kurth, *American Cassandra,* p. 109.

4. Information to the author from Babette Gross.

5. That Vincent Sheean was a much-used fellow traveller at least until September 1, 1939, is proved by his signature on an open letter attacking Krivitsky, and published in major newspapers across the United States in August 1939. That he quite clearly understood Rayna Prohme's position within the apparatus is suggested in *Dorothy and Red,* and confirmed in the memoirs of John Dos Passos, *The Best of Times: An Informal Memoir.* For the role of Samson Rafaelson among the Hollywood fellow travellers, see Schwartz, *The Hollywood Writers' Wars.*

6. See Dorothy Thompson's letter to Sinclair Lewis on this event, in Sheean, *Dorothy and Red,* p. 67. Also Sheean's account of the relationship, pp. 74–77, as well as in his *Personal Memoir*, chapter 6.

7. See Sheean, *Dorothy and Red,* p. 77.

8. That Soong Chin'ling was a Münzenberg agent, see Gross, *Münzenberg,* p. 183, and the FOIA dossier of Louis Gibarti, # 61-6629, section 3. Deposition of Louis Gibarti before Special Counsel to the United States Senate, Robert Morris, Esq., and United States Senators Willis Smith and Homer Ferguson, Paris, August 28, 1951.

9. See Sheean, *Dorothy and Red.*

10. See the letters of Dorothy Thompson to Sinclair Lewis, reprinted in ibid.

11. See Thompson's book about her trip, *The New Russia* (1928).

12. Sheean, *Dorothy and Red.* Letters of Thompson to Lewis.

13. On January 29, 1940, the Visa Division of the United States Department of State filed a memorandum on Otto Katz referring to information from "an unnamed but reliable source" (National Archives of the United States, 800.00B, dossier on Louis Gibarti, document # 73). Other correspondence from this episode can be found in the National Archives, 800.00B, dossier on Katz-Breda.

14. Ibid.

15. A. A. Berle's letter of reply to correspondence was produced in an FOIA request on Katz. It is dated May 8, 1940.

16. See supra, chapter 7, note 23.

17. The documentation of Katz's troubles with emigration at this time are found both in his FOIA dossier and in his file in the National Archives.

18. Speculations about Katz's role in the murder of Münzenberg can be found in his FOIA dossier, notably in interviews with the FBI given by Herrman Rauschnigg.

19. Karel Kaplan, *Report on the Murder of the General Secretary*, p. 276.

20. Archives of the United States, Letter from R. L. Bannerman, Special Agent in Charge of the New York Division, to J. F. Fitch, Chief Special Agent, February 9, 1940, on the Ellis Island Record of Otto and Ilse Katz, 800.00B, dossier on Louis Gibarti, document # 74.

21. Katz is noted as visiting "Mrs. John Hermann [*sic*]" at 10 Fifth Avenue as of September 10, 1935, as a result of Ellis Island file # 99351/40. This information is conveyed in a report made by agent J. R. Malley to the Federal Bureau of Investigation dated February 15, 1940: New York file #65-1763. National Archives of the United States, 800.00B, dossier on Katz-Breda.

22. Virginia Spencer Carr, *Dos Passos,* p. 197.

23. See Langer, *Josephine Herbst.*

24. Hemingway, *Selected Letters,* p. 120. Also p. 114.

25. The founding of the New Playwrights' Theater, and its debt to Piscator, is discussed in the memoirs of Harold Clurman.

26. The role of Trachtenberg and Jerome is indicated in Schwartz, *The Hollywood Writers' Wars,* pp. 89–90.

27. Though much research remains to be done, the focussed and intrusive interest of the Soviet propaganda apparatus in the Los Angeles film colony has been amply documented. Lawson and Faragoh's work among the Hollywood fellow travellers and for the special unit of the Communist party USA specifically created for work in the film colony is treated, admiringly but revealingly, in Schwartz's *The Hollywood Writers' Wars.* Following the common line of such works, Schwartz seeks to promote the fantasy that the American

Communist party was in some way independent from the International and from Soviet political control generally, so that the "idealistic" enterprises of its front groups somehow were not co-ordinated to serve the Stalinist tyranny. This is a notion that present evidence uniformly contradicts: The American Communist party was always financed and ideologically controlled by the Soviet Union.

28. The dossier on Em Jo Basshe is found in the National Archives of the United States, 800.00B.

29. The sources on the life of Basshe are thin. There is a rather condescending entry on him in Kunitz and Haycroft, *Twentieth Century Authors* (1942). His plays are *Earth* (1927, New Playwrights' Theater) and *Centuries* (1928); *Portrait of a Tenement House* (1928) and *Doomsday Circus* (1938). They are not in print. He is mentioned by all memoirists of the New Playwrights' Theater, and he played a role in the Lafayette Theater of Harlem in the Negro Theater Division of the WPA, in which he worked as a director. He appears in *Most Likely to Succeed,* Dos Passos's novel, as "Eli."

30. National Archives of the United States, 800.00B, dossier on Em Jo Basshe, document #5.

31. Woolcott's review is quoted in the article on Basshe in *The Biographical Dictionary of the American Theater.*

32. Dos Passos, *Most Likely to Succeed* (1954).

33. The documents recounting this story are memoranda from the U. S. Embassy in London, based on information supplied by British intelligence. The probable source would have been Guy Liddell. They are on file in the National Archives of the United States, 800.00B, dossier on Em Jo Basshe.

34. Virginia Spencer Carr, *Dos Passos.*

35. For Dos Passos's tour of the USSR, see ibid., pp. 235–248.

36. Ibid., p. 247.

37. Ibid., p. 247.

38. Letter from John Dos Passos to Ernest Hemingway, December 24, 1928, now in the John F. Kennedy Library, Ernest Hemingway Collection, and cited in ibid., p. 248.

39. There have been numerous accounts of this episode. See Schwartz, *The Hollywood Writers' Wars,* and David Caute, *The Great Fear* (New York: Simon and Schuster, 1978).

40. V. J. Jerome and Alexander Trachtenberg's role in New Playwrights' appear in Dos Passos, *Most Likely to Succeed.* Katz's remark about Columbus and Hollywood is cited in Draper, "The Man Who Wanted to Hang."

41. National Archives of the United States, 800.00B, dossier on Katz-Breda.

42. See Viertel, *The Kindness of Strangers,* pp. 101–102.

43. An excellent albeit ''innocent'' eyewitness account of the founding of the Hollywood Anti-Nazi League can be found in Stewart, *By a Stroke of Luck.*

44. Ibid., p. 225.

45. Ibid., pp. 225–226.

46. Mann, *The Letters of Thomas Mann: 1889–1955,* pp. 330–332.

47. Schwartz, *The Hollywood Writers' Wars.* pp. 82–83 (my emphasis).

48. Wright, *Lillian Hellman,* p. 162. Wright is quoting Hellman from the *New York Times,* January 20, 1940. For an analysis of Hellman's own account of her response to the Finnish invasion, both at the time and in *An Unfinished Woman,* see Rollyson, *Lillian Hellman,* pp. 149–152. Rollyson concludes that Hellman's version of these events is ''an outrageous piece of nonsense.''

49. Lyons, *Red Decade,* p. 374.

50. A leading personage in West Coast communism who was invited to step inside the magic circle of the Hollywood Stalinists and their celebrity elite was Harry Bridges, who by 1936 was a dominating figure in the CIO, the great labor union of the era on the West Coast of the United States. The Central Party Archives now show that Bridges was a member of that apparatus, and under Soviet control. See Klehr and Haynes, *The American Spectator*, December 1992, pp. 34–36. The legal and propaganda struggle fought for decades over Bridges's presence in the United States is a saga marked by interminability. For years, the American government made every conceivable effort to expose Bridges's links to the Soviets. For years, the apparatus responded with every conceivable effort to discredit that effort and protect the more or less open secret of his subordination to Stalin and his government.

In Washington, communists within the Roosevelt administration, including almost certainly Alger Hiss's brother Donald Hiss, were in continuous maneuver to derail and discredit the government's inquiry and challenge to Bridges's power on the San Francisco docks. Meanwhile, with numbing immunity to ennui, the propaganda apparatus lionized and defended Bridges year after weary year. Among the Hollywood Stalinists, Bridges was viewed as a saintly figure. (Schwartz, *Hollywood Writers' Wars.*)

51. Lyons, *Red Decade,* p. 51.

52. Stewart, *By a Stroke of Luck.*

53. Meade, *Dorothy Parker,* p. 254.

54. See Justin Kaplan, *Lincoln Steffens.*

55. Stewart, *By a Stroke of Luck,* pp. 230–236.

56. See FOIA dossier on Louis Gibarti.

57. Justin Kaplan, *Lincoln Steffens*, p. 312. Ella Winter was a leading figure in the Committee for the Relief of the Victims of Fascist Oppression, the American branch of the World Committee for the Relief of the Victims of German Fascism, which was, of course, under Gibarti's direction.

58. Ibid., pp. 311–312.

59. Ibid., pp. 321–324.

60. Langer, *Josephine Herbst*, p. 79.

61. See ibid.

62. Though the evidence before me is vague, my impression is that Radek was probably the guiding spirit behind the Kharkov Writers' Congress. Its cultural politics seem to show his hand. Radek at this time has just (but only just) returned to Stalin's good graces, assuming the leading role in Stalinist cultural politics he would hold until he was purged.

As for the phrase, "ladies of the Kremlin," it can be found in Berberova, *Histoire,* and was used in my presence by Nina Berberova during my interview with her on January 10, 1991. The "ladies"—Russian women toiling for Stalin in European cultural life—included Baroness Budberg, Princess Koudachova, Elsa Triolet, Nunsch Eluard, and a number of others.

63. Desanti, *Les Clés d'Elsa.* Also to be recommended is an exceptionally interesting review of this book by François Fejtö, in *Encounter* (1983).

64. See Herbst, *The Starched Blue Sky of Spain,* pp. 121–122.

65. That Maxim Lieber was Katz's literary agent is mentioned in Weinstein, *Perjury,* pp. 322–324.

66. I am grateful to Ms. Elinor Langer for useful information regarding Josephine Herbst's contacts at this time.

67. See supra, note 21.

68. Weinstein, *Perjury,* pp. 134–145. For Herbst and Herrmann's link to Otto Katz, see Otto Katz, FOIA dossier #1, 65-1763. Arriving in New York on September 10, 1935, Katz cites a "friend," Mrs. John Herrmann, 10 Fifth Avenue. Katz's cover at this time, according to the report of the American authorities, was that he was researching a book on Arctic explorations. This may well be linked to Peter Smolka-Smollett's work being done at the same time on the same subject, for the apparatus. See Andrew and Gordievsky, *KGB: The Inside Story,* pp. 325–335.

69. Hemingway, *Selected Letters,* p. 548.

70. Information to the author from Mr. Robert Towers.

71. Langer, *Josephine Herbst.*

72. John Herrmann's bond to Harold Ware is discussed extensively in Langer, *Josephine Herbst.*

73. Gross, *Münzenberg,* p. 124.

74. Langer, *Josephine Herbst,* p. 171.

Chapter 9: An End to Innocence

1. A death penalty for members of the Russian Party was essential for the success of the purges, and its institution is discussed in Conquest, *The Great Terror,* pp. 23–28. The role of the death penalty in preparation for the Terror is considered as well in "Letter from an Old Bolshevik," in Nicholaevsky, *Power and the Soviet Elite.*

2. The indispensable account of the Great Terror is by Robert Conquest, *The Great Terror: A Reassessment* (revised edition of 1990).

3. Thomas Mann, *The Magic Mountain* (New York: Knopf, 1952). "Of the City of God," p. 400.

4. Stalin's attention to the details of the Röhm purge is discussed in Krivitsky, *In Stalin's Secret Service,* and in Conquest, *The Great Terror,* p. 38.

5. See Conquest, *Stalin and the Kirov Murder.*

6. Natalia Guinzberg, *Journey into the Whirlwind* (New York: 1967).

7. Ory, *Nizan,* p. 125. Also information to the author from Mme. Henriette Nizan.

8. Information to the author from Mme. Henriette Nizan.

9. Nizan's remark to Sartre is cited in Ory, *Nizan,* p. 136.

10. Ibid.

11. Simone de Beauvoir, *La Force de l'âge* (Paris: Edition Folio, 1986), p. 427.

12. The essential information on the response of the intellectual press to Nizan's defection from the Party is in Ory, *Nizan,* chapter 8. See also Lottman, *The Left Bank.*

13. The role of Otto Katz in the founding of the Hollywood Anti-Nazi League figures in many memoirs and biographies, notably Stewart's *By a Stroke of Luck,* and in Meade's *Dorothy Parker.*

14. Lottman, *The Left Bank,* chapter 12.

15. Ibid.

16. *Cahiers d'André Gide # 5. Les Cahiers de la Petite Dame. Notes pour l'histoire authentique d'André Gide. 1927–1937* (Paris: Gallimard, 1974), p. 205.

17. Ibid., p. 155.

18. Ibid.

19. Ibid., p. 152.

20. For Herbart's link to publications supervised by Vaillant, see *Cahiers d'André Gide,* and its reports of Herbart's journalistic work between 1932 and 1935, and his trip to the USSR.

21. Lottman, *The Left Bank,* p. 84.

22. Ibid. For a more detailed account, see Berberova, *Histoire de la baronne Boudberg*, pp. 259–263.

23. Regler, *The Owl of Minerva,* pp. 232–233.

24. Lottman, *The Left Bank,* pp. 92–93.

25. Ibid., p. 91.

26. Ibid., p. 93.

27. Gide, *Littérature engagée.* The text of Gide's letter is found on pp. 97–98. For the account of these events as seen from within Gide's household, see *Cahiers d'André Gide,* pp. 445–449. See also Lottman, *The Left Bank.*

28. Alix Guillain's attack on the letter is noted in *Cahiers d'André Gide,* p. 469.

29. Conquest, *The Great Terror,* p. 464.

30. For Gorky's financial ties to the pre-revolutionary Party, see Pipes, *The Russian Revolution,* pp. 369–371.

31. For Gorky's political history and his early links to revolutionary thought, see Troyat, *Maxim Gorky,* pp. 92–99. See also Pipes, *The Russian Revolution,* pp. 350–352, 369–378.

32. Pipes, *The Russian Revolution,* p. 351. This citation includes the passage from Gorky on Lenin.

33. Ibid., p. 351.

34. Troyat, *Maxim Gorky,* chapters 17 and 18.

35. Berberova, *Histoire,* pp. 250–254.

36. Ibid., p. 255.

37. Ibid., "Le Marché," pp. 223–274.

38. Ibid., p. 255.

39. The relation between Lockhart and Moura Budberg is most famously told in Lockhart's *Secret Agent.* It is also discussed and analyzed in Berberova, *Histoire.*

40. Berberova's account of the arrest of Moura Budberg and Lockhart, which closely follows Lockhart's own account, is found in her *Histoire, "Amour et Prison,"* pp. 67–106.

41. Ibid., p. 266.

42. Anthony West, *H. G. Wells,* pp. 72–76.

43. Ibid., p. 145.

44. Ibid., pp. 144–147.

45. Troyat, *Maxim Gorky,* p. 189. See also Berberova, *Histoire,* p. 279.

46. The account of Stalin and Gorky's developing mutual distrust following the Kirov murder is recounted in Orlov, *The Secret History of Stalin's Crimes.*

47. In addition to Berberova, *Histoire,* see Conquest, *The Great Terror,* p. 388.

48. See Conquest, *The Great Terror,* pp. 375–398.

49. Berberova, *Histoire,* pp. 258–259.

50. Ibid., p. 259.

51. Ibid.

52. Ibid., p. 268.

53. Accounts of Gide's Soviet trip begin of course with his own, *Retour de l'U.R.S.S.* (1936) and the next year, *Retouches à mon retour de l'U.R.S.S.* (1937). The notebooks and memoirs of the other participants are also of some value, notably Guilloux, *Carnets: 1921–1944.* Lottman's account, *The Left Bank,* is reliable and well documented. For detailed information concerning the preparations for the trip and its consequences, the *carnets* of Maria van Rhysselberghe are indispensable. I am grateful to M. Jean Malaquais, who assisted Gide in preparing for the trip, for an interview.

54. *Cahiers d'André Gide,* pp. 602–610.

55. Berberova, *Histoire,* p. 264, especially footnote.

56. Events in Spain had been moving toward crisis throughout 1936. That Alvárez del Vayo was a close associate of Otto Katz was well known during their affiliation in *Agence Espagna* during the course of the war. But in fact Alvárez del Vayo was closely associated with the Münzenberg apparatus well before that time. See Gross, *Münzenberg,* pp. 272, 311.

57. For Gide's preparations for departure, see *Cahiers d'André Gide,* pp. 539–550. I am grateful for M. Jean Malaquais, who gave me the benefit of his memories of being present in Gide's household as these events took place.

58. See *Cahiers d'André Gide,* p. 457.

59. Ibid.

60. Ibid., p. 547.

61. See Troyat, *Maxim Gorky,* p. 193.

62. See Berberova, *Histoire.* Information on this visit also appears in Desanti, *Les Clés d'Elsa.*

63. See Berberova, citing Aragon, in *Histoire,* p. 263.

64. Ibid. Also Desanti, *Les Clés d'Elsa.*

65. *Les Cahiers de la Petite Dame,* p. 542.

66. *Cahiers d'André Gide,* p. 542.

67. An account of Bukharin's visit to Gide's hotel room appears in Desanti, *Les Clés d'Elsa,* p. 253.

68. Information to the author from Mme. Nina Berberova.

Chapter 10: The Spanish Stratagem

1. The policy announced at the VIIth Congress of the Comintern is analyzed in Heller and Nekrich, *Utopia in Power,* pp. 310–311. See also Conquest, *The Great Terror,* and Gross, *Münzenberg.*

2. Dimitrov, *The Working Classes against Fascism,* p. 47.

3. Gross, *Münzenberg,* p. 276.

4. CPA, fond 495.19.337.

5. Ibid., pp. 275–282.

6. Ibid., pp. 286–288.

7. Ibid., p. 277.

8. Ibid.

9. Ibid.

10. The masked identity of Mikhail Trilliser within the Comintern at this moment in the history of the Stalinist secret services is a key and revelatory fact. I am grateful to Prof. Harvey Klehr for his assistance in identifying this imposture during his visit to the archives of the International in Moscow in June 1992; I am grateful in particular for the information, new to me, that in his guise as "Comrade Moskfin," Trilliser was under the discipline of the GRU, and not (as I had supposed) the NKVD, even though he had been a founder of the latter service. I am also most grateful to Mr. Herbert Romerstein, who first alerted me to Trilliser's clandestine role within the Comintern, and for Mr. Romerstein's original research, performed long before the archives opened, establishing that fact.

11. Gross, *Münzenberg,* pp. 282–289.

12. The reader is directed to an interesting study by M. Thierry Wolton on the work of Dolivet, Pierre Cot, Olof Aschberg, and sundry senior politicians in the Popular Front gathered around RUP: *Le Grand Recrutement.* M. Wolton's study is particularly informative about the links of RUP to the Soviet secret services, information greatly enriched by archival material newly acquired.

13. Information to the author from Mr. Michael Straight.

14. Gross, *Münzenberg,* p. 288. See also Desanti, *Les Clés d'Elsa.*

15. Lynn, *Hemingway,* p. 449.

16. Such a photograph is reproduced in Marion Meade, *Dorothy Parker: What Fresh Hell Is This?*

17. A good description of this conference, noting the oddity of its lavishness, can be found in Stephen Spender, *World within World* (New York: Simon and Schuster, 1978).

18. Gross, *Münzenberg,* p. 287.

19. CPA, fond 495.73.26, item #2: Letter from Münzenberg to Dimitrov.

20. Ibid., p. 290.

21. Ibid., pp. 290–293.

22. Ibid., p. 290.

23. Ibid., p. 291.

24. Ibid. For the military and secret service background of this decision, see also Krivitsky, *In Stalin's Secret Service,* pp. 82–90.

25. Krivitsky, *In Stalin's Secret Service,* pp. 82–84.

26. For Münzenberg's role in the earliest days of supplying Spain, see Gross, *Münzenberg,* p. 291. For a more detailed account of the role of Münzenberg's people in procuring arms for Spain in the early stages of that conflict, see Thornberry, *Malraux et l'Espagne,* chapter 1.

27. Gross, *Münzenberg,* p. 291.

28. Ibid., pp. 290–291.

29. CPA, fond 495.19.243 and especially 495.19.337.

30. Ibid.

31. Ibid. See also Buber-Neumann, *Under Two Dictators,* pp. 4–5.

32. Buber-Neumann, *Under Two Dictators,* part II, pp. 167ff.

33. Buber-Neumann's book on Milena Jasenska is a major document and has been translated into many languages. See *Milena* (New York: Schocken, 1988).

34. Buber-Neumann, *Under Two Dictators,* p. 324.

35. Gross, *Münzenberg,* pp. 291–292.

36. The historical literature on the Spanish Civil War is of course massive, and since 1975 has been undergoing considerable revision. The standard volume of 1961, Hugh Thomas's *The Spanish Civil War,* should be read in its revised edition of 1977, and supplemented by the large body of Spanish scholarship emergent since the death of Franco. The tone and direction of Thomas's first edition extended general approbation to the Popular Front and the moral credit it claimed for itself. In that spirit, he treated the accounts of both Krivitsky and Orlov with undisguised and entirely dismissive contempt. I know of no reputable authority working since the death of Franco who would adopt such an attitude. The revelations of Walter Krivitsky have been the subject of almost uninterrupted journalistic invective and pseudo-scholarly attack from the moment they appeared; their subsequent history has been one of steady confirmation in virtu-

ally all substance and most (though far from every) detail. I would direct the reader to the bibliographical note of *The Great Terror,* in its 1968 edition, p. 570, and to Conquest's comment on that note in his introduction to the 1990 *Reassessment,* p. viii. (An interesting attack on Krivitsky in matters of detail can be found in Poretsky, *Our Own People,* p. 171n, and passim.) I am especially grateful to Mr. John Costello, whose research into Orlov based on information from the Soviet archives promises to revise this entire discussion, and shows Krivitsky's account of Orlov's role in Spain is generally supported by the documents. See also Costello, *Deadly Illusions*, chapter 12.

37. See Krivitsky's *In Stalin's Secret Service,* chapter 3, "Stalin's Hand in Spain," pp. 75–116. A useful overview of the Spanish War can also be found in Johnson, *Modern Times,* chapter 9, "The High Noon of Aggression."

38. See Johnson, *Modern Times,* p. 329, and his sources, especially Salas, *Intervención extrajeras.* The question of how Stalin financed his assistance to the Spanish Republic is raised there, and a great deal of supporting material is to be found in Krivitsky, *In Stalin's Secret Service.*

39. Johnson, *Modern Times,* pp. 324–325.

40. Ibid., pp. 324–327. An interesting political account by an eyewitness can be found in Buber-Neumann's *Von Potsdam nach Moskau,* in her discussion of Heinz Neumann's Comintern work in Spain, and especially events with Alvárez del Vayo in 1936.

41. See Buber-Neumann, *Von Potsdam nach Moskau.*

42. Johnson, *Modern Times,* pp. 326, 328.

43. Krivitsky, *In Stalin's Secret Service,* p. 76.

44. Thornberry, *Malraux et l'Espagne,* pp. 33–34. Thornberry's account is by far the best and most detailed in existence. Malraux's activities were both on the level of clandestine military sales and propaganda.

45. Krivitsky, *In Stalin's Secret Service,* pp. 76–78.

46. Ibid., pp. 80–85.

47. The work of Alvárez del Vayo as a Münzenberg-man is mentioned in Gross, *Münzenberg,* pp. 272, 311. Note that Otto Katz's close link to del Vayo is mentioned in 311. It was common knowledge to all high-level witnesses, such as Louis Fischer (see *Men and Politics*). I am grateful to Mrs. Rae Bernstein for the information that del Vayo and Otto Katz remained associates in New York following the Spanish War. Alvárez del Vayo's influence over Largo Caballero figures in most standard histories of the war. As to his lifelong claim to being an "independent leftist," it should be viewed in the light of his deeds. The claim to independence would be greatly enhanced by evidence of some demonstrably independent action performed somewhere—anywhere—in his career. I have been unable to uncover one political endeavor or one public word attributable to this

man that is not unshakably rooted in the main line, seen or unseen, of Stalinist policy. The most abject functionary could not have given more reliable service. That Münzenberg or Stalin would have entrusted a real "independent leftist" with the responsibilities and level of information granted to del Vayo in Spain strikes me as improbable to the last degree. The man was almost certainly a Soviet agent under full discipline. He was certainly an obedient figure in Münzenberg's apparatus even before he began his rise as an official of the Spanish government. Whatever the history of his obedience, that obedience was always there, and so was his reward: Del Vayo was that all but unique creature, a man on whom the sun of Stalin's approval never failed to shine.

48. Johnson, *Modern Times,* p. 333. See also Krivitsky, *In Stalin's Secret Service.*

49. Krivitsky, *In Stalin's Secret Service,* pp. 83–85.

50. For the story of Tomas Harris's role in the undercover market in Spanish art, see Costello, *The Mask of Treachery,* p. 383.

51. For more on Malraux's role, see Thornberry, *Malraux et l'Espagne.* For the general gathering of cultural personalities in Spain, see Weintraub's *The Last Great Cause.*

52. Information to the author from the late Joris Ivens, Paris, July 1986. In his interview with me, Ivens was equivocal on this point. He told me that he knew Katz well, but that Katz had "nothing to do" with the film. Nonetheless, Ivens added that Contemporary Historians had been set up to avoid any suspicion about a role for Otto.

53. An excellent description of this Congress can be found in Spender, *World within World*, pp. 238–247.

54. Deacon, *The Cambridge Apostles.*

55. Krivitsky, *In Stalin's Secret Service,* p. 82.

56. Ibid., pp. 32–83.

57. Katz's presence in Valencia was widely known. See Gross, *Münzenberg,* p. 312.

58. Information to the author from Babette Gross.

59. Krivitsky, *In Stalin's Secret Service,* chapter 3.

60. Ibid., pp. 96–99. Berzin's previous history and role in Spain is also discussed in Conquest, *The Great Terror.*

61. Conquest, *The Great Terror,* p. 410.

62. Krivitsky, *In Stalin's Secret Service,* pp. 99–115.

63. Ibid., pp. 106–107.

64. Ibid.

65. Krivitsky reports the linkage between the demise of Tuchachevsky, Stashevsky, and Berzin. See also Conquest, *The Great Terror,* ''The Assault on the Army.''

66. For these events of October 1936, with *Pravda* declaring purges essential and Berzin's awareness of them, see Krivitsky, *In Stalin's Secret Service.*

67. Ibid., p. 115.

68. See Johnson, *Modern Times,* p. 333, citing Hugh Thomas, *The Spanish Civil War* (London, 1977), and also citing Salas, *Intervención extrajera.*

69. Information to the author from Mr. Paul Willert.

70. Information to the author from Mr. Herman Starobin, New York, December 1986.

71. See Gross, *Münzenberg,* pp. 311–312. See also Weintraub, *The Last Great Cause,* pp. 124, 129.

72. Del Vayo's politics and his relation to Freda Kirchway are given a highly sympathetic account in Alpern, *Freda Kirchway.*

73. During the 1930s and much of the 1940s, the *Nation* fit almost exactly the classic profile of a publication run by Stalinist agents or Stalinists close to agents of the apparatus, while using non-communists and even ''innocuous'' anti-communists (that is, writers on the arts) to provide it with the necessary air of independence. Louis Fischer played a major role in the publication between the late 1920s until the Second World War. Fischer was (at least) a thoroughly reliable Stalinist fellow traveller who was intimate with Katz and Gibarti, and fully under the influence of the Münzenberg apparatus. It is generally thought that Fischer was not under the direct discipline of the secret service of the International; Krivitsky for example viewed him as an independent fellow traveller, albeit an exceptionally obedient, witting, and highly placed one. It seems to me that Fischer can be properly described as (at least) a ''Münzenberg-man,'' that is—a Stalinist propagandist wittingly working in response to general directives from the Münzenberg organization. When Fischer broke with Stalinism over the Second World War, he was replaced at the *Nation* by Alvárez del Vayo, who was not only a Münzenberg-man but, as a major figure in Stalinist Spain, almost certainly bound to the NKVD or GRU as well. (The reader will recall that Stalin's policy was to place all Comintern activity in Spain under the direct control of the NKVD.) The *Nation*'s look of ''independence'' came from the ''back of the book,'' that is the section devoted to reviewing the arts, in which non-communists and anti-communists of the left were permitted to adopt unpolitical and even intensely anti-Stalinist positions.

74. See Martha Gellhorn, ''On Apocryphism,'' *Paris Review,* no. 79 (1981), p. 301.

75. Information to the author from Mrs. Margaret Regler.

76. Information to the author from the late Joris Ivens.

77. Lynn, *Hemingway,* pp. 465–466. See also Lash, *Eleanor and Franklin,* chapter 38, p. 567.

78. Virginia Spencer Carr, *Dos Passos,* pp. 359–363.

79. Ibid., pp. 262–263. See also the biographies of Hellman and Hemingway.

80. Virginia Spencer Carr, *Dos Passos,* pp. 366–367.

81. Ibid.

82. Ibid., p. 367.

83. See supra, note 43.

84. Virginia Spencer Carr, *Dos Passos.* It is perhaps worth mentioning that in later life Liston Oak tended to keep the story of his experiences in Spain limited to a narrow circle of his intimates. Many people very close to him were unaware that he had ever been in Spain at all, or that the pivotal event of his political life had taken place there.

85. For Oak's relation to George Mink, see Klehr, *The Heyday of American Communism,* p. 440, note 18. Oak wrote a piece about his connection to Mink in Spain in the socialist newspaper the *Call,* December 8, 1937. This relationship is discussed in Dallin, *Soviet Espionage,* p. 409. I am grateful for further details from Liston Oaks's son, Mr. Allen Oak. See also Virginia Spencer Carr, *Dos Passos.*

86. Information to the author from Mr. Allen Oak.

87. Ibid.

88. Hemingway's line about "my second war," was mentioned by the late Joris Ivens in an interview with the author.

89. A standard biographical account of Herbst's movements and action in this affair is in Langer, *Josephine Herbst,* pp. 219–233. Langer relies heavily on Herbst's essay "The Starched Blue Sky of Spain," which appeared in the *Noble Savage,* no. 1, and is reprinted in Herbst, *The Starched Blue Sky of Spain.*

90. Herbst, *The Starched Blue Sky of Spain,* p. 154.

91. Ibid.

92. I am most grateful to Mrs. Margaret Regler for the gift of a typescript of Gustav Regler's war diary during these events. The diary entries for March and April provide vivid accounts of the journalistic atmosphere in Madrid at the time, especially reports of treason by "fascist spies" among the Republican ranks. These specific provocations, and an example of the response to it by a literary man whom Herbst would regard as one of the "best men" she met in Spain, can be found in the typescript entries for April 15, 16, and 17, 1937. These are precisely the days of the events in the Hotel Florida under discussion here.

93. Fifty years later, Joris Ivens, who was present and integral to the entire event, repeated the falsehood that designated Robles as a fascist spy, and did so with the apparent confidence that the charge was true. While disclaiming unequivocal personal knowledge, Ivens even added operational details: He claimed that Robles had been sending light signals to the fascist lines by night. Ivens must have been given these details by someone, and he must have been told them during the events under discussion here. Joris Ivens, interview with the author, June 1986.

94. Herbst, *The Starched Blue Sky of Spain,* p. 154.

95. Ibid.

96. Ibid., p. 155. Note Herbst's remark about Hemingway's agreement to the deceptive course of action she had suggested: "Perhaps he agreed with too cheerful a readiness."

97. Regler's war diary speaks of the celebrations around Thaelman Day, though he himself does not seem to have been present at the castle. See also Virginia Spencer Carr, *Dos Passos,* p. 368.

98. See both ibid. and Herbst, *The Starched Blue Sky of Spain.*

99. Herbst, *The Starched Blue Sky of Spain,* pp. 156–157.

100. Otto Katz's presence at the Hotel Florida is established by Regler's war diary, entry of April 17, 1937. The specific passage reads: "In Madrid, Simon [Katz's alias] digs up some English countesses. Franco fires shells under their beds. Wilkinson also there." That Wilkinson was staying with Otto Katz in the Hotel Florida at this time is confirmed in Vernon, *Ellen Wilkinson.* The reader might also note that Claud Cockburn, whom Herbst describes as her friend, was likewise in the hotel that day, and that Cockburn was at this time deep in his political collaboration with Katz.

101. Virginia Spencer Carr, *Dos Passos,* p. 370.

102. Shipman and Hemingway's claims of Dos Passos's cowardice are summarized in ibid.

103. Ibid., p. 371. Carr relies in part on Dos Passos's *The Theme Is Freedom.*

Chapter 11: Münzenberg's End

1. The Popular Front was of course universally jettisoned with the Nazi-Soviet Pact. But it was already in decline in the apparatus by the spring of 1937. See Krivitsky, *In Stalin's Secret Service,* conversation with Slutsky reported on pp. 214–215.

2. Ibid., p. 215.

3. The assassination of Ignace Reiss has been treated in many studies. See, for example, Dewar, *Assassins at Large.* An indispensable source is Poretsky, *Our Own People.*

4. Krivitsky, *In Stalin's Secret Service,* chapter 7, ''My Break with Stalin.''

5. Münzenberg's illness is described in Gross, *Münzenberg.* Note that Gross misspells the name of the clinician: it is Dr. Le Savoureux, not Savouret.

6. See ibid.

7. Bukharin's visit to Paris is described in Cohen, *Bukharin and the Bolshevik Revolution,* pp. 365–367. See also Medvedev, *Nikolai Bukharin,* p. 122. The incident with Dr. Le Savoureux is reported in Gross, *Münzenberg.*

8. Bukharin's meetings with Nicholaevsky are extensively discussed in Nicholaevsky, *Power and the Soviet Elite.*

9. Kennan's comment is found in his introduction to *Power and the Soviet Elite.*

10. See Gross, *Münzenberg.*

11. See FOIA dossier on Otto Katz, # 65-9266, section 7, Report of the FBI, file # 100-15865, July 13, 1944.

12. Karolyi and Fischer's efforts are mentioned in Gross, *Münzenberg.*

13. Beletsky's visit to Münzenberg is mentioned in Krivitsky, *In Stalin's Secret Service,* p. 62. Gross accepts Krivitsky's account.

14. Gross, *Münzenberg.*

15. Ibid.

16. The history of *Die Zukunft* is reported in many memoirs: Gross, *Münzenberg,* Sperber, *Ces Temps-là,* Koestler, *Invisible Writing,* inter alia. It became a model for *Der Monat* and other journals.

17. Gross, *Münzenberg,* pp. 289–292.

18. See ibid. and Schliemann, ''Münzenberg.'' Also information to the author from Babette Gross.

19. See Schliemann, ''Münzenberg,'' p. 80. See also Wessel, *Münzenbergs Ende,* p. 333.

20. Schliemann, ''Münzenberg,'' p. 82.

21. Information to the author from Mr. Paul Willert.

22. The warning to Wilkinson about British intelligence is mentioned in Deacon, *The British Connection,* p. 173.

23. Philby's relation to Liddell is discussed in Costello, *The Mark of Treachery,* pp. 418, 438, 605.

24. See Gross, *Münzenberg.*

25. The presence of the apparatus in the internment camps of the period is discussed by Regler, *The Owl of Minerva,* pp. 331–354.

26. *Le Peuple,* Brussels, January 30, 1940.

27. Information to the author from Babette Gross.

28. Glees, *The Secrets of the Service,* pp. 127–132, and all other references to Sefton Delmer. Glees examines the war-time activities of Sefton Delmer—who was, if anything, closer to Münzenberg in this period than Willert—and comes to the conclusion that Delmer was under Soviet control. I find Glees's meticulously researched case interesting but too much based in inference to carry me even to moral certainty.

29. Gross, *Münzenberg.*

30. Münzenberg's hopes for help from Marcu are raised in Carew-Hunt, "Münzenberg," p. 87.

31. On Münzenberg's mood, note the small difference between Gross's account (*Münzenberg,* p. 324) and Schliemann's ("Münzenberg," p. 89).

32. A description of these penetrations of the internment camps by the apparatus can be found in Regler, *The Owl of Minerva.*

33. The story of the "Red-Headed Youth" appears in Kersten, "Das Ende Willi Münzenbergs," Gross, *Münzenberg,* Wessel, *Münzenbergs Ende,* and Schliemann, "Münzenberg."

34. See Wessel, *Münzenbergs Ende,* p. 333.

35. Ibid.

36. Schliemann, "Münzenberg," pp. 88–89.

37. Ibid., and also Gross, *Münzenberg.*

38. Gross, *Münzenberg.*

39. The departure from Chambarran is discussed in all authorities: Kersten, "Das Ende Willi Münzenbergs," Gross, *Münzenberg,* Schliemann, "Münzenberg," Carew-Hunt, "Münzenberg," Gruber, "Münzenberg," and Wessel, *Münzenbergs Ende.* Note that my information from Helen Wolff contradicts the belief common to many that Kurt Wolff was in the group moving on foot. He left Chambarran by bus.

40. Wessel, *Münzenbergs Ende,* pp. 234–235.

41. Siemsen is quoted in both Kersten "Das Ende Willi Münzenbergs" and Schliemann, *Münzenberg,*" p. 87.

42. Leo, *Frühzug nach Toulouse.*

43. See Gross, *Münzenberg.*

44. The size of the stand of woods can be estimated by maps made by the United States Corps of Engineers of the region during the Second World War, and available in the map collection of the New York Public Library.

Epilogue

1. Information to the author from Mr. Herman Starobin.

2. Otto's role in the Masaryk government is discussed in many sources. See Costello, *The Mask of Treachery,* p. 298. I am also grateful to Mr. Herman Starobin for information about his work in Czechoslovakia.

3. The death of Jan Masaryk is of course a central event in the history of the Czech coup and is discussed in all examinations of the event. The reader is directed to the personal account of Masaryk's last days provided in Marcia Davenport's memoir, *Too Strong for Fantasy.*

4. The best account to date of Field's crisis at the time of Chambers's testimony is found in Lewis, *Red Pawn.* On the other hand, it is plain that if and when the Hungarian government declassifies the documentation of Noel Field's debriefing, uncovered in 1992 by Ms. Maria Schmidt in the archives of the Hungarian Ministry of Information, a great deal in that study will be superseded by new information.

5. If the reports made to me by Ms. Maria Schmidt, the principal scholar of the archives of the Hungarian Secret Police in Budapest, are to be believed, that apparatus solved the problem of Duggan's possible indiscretion with murder. According to Maria Schmidt, because Duggan was about to be exposed, assassins threw him to his death from his sixteenth-floor law office in New York.

6. Diana Trilling, "How McCarthy Gave Anti-Communism a Bad Name," *Newsweek,* January 11, 1993, p. 33.

7. *New York Times,* December 17, 1992.

8. Massing, *This Deception.* Massing's account of the relation between Field and Hiss is found in chapter 3.

9. Information to the author from Ms. Maria Schmidt, Budapest.

10. Hellman, *An Unfinished Woman,* chapter 7, p. 69.

11. See Davenport, *Too Strong for Fantasy.* Also correspondence with the author. See also Hodos, *Show Trials.*

12. Rajk's political history, including the persecution of Mindszenty, is discussed in Hodos, *Show Trials,* pp. 36–37.

13. A tangled but elaborately researched study of this subject can be found in Glees, *The Secrets of the Service.*

14. See Nicholas Bethell, *The Great Betrayal* (New York: Time Books, 1984.)

15. The role of the Spanish volunteers in the Slansky purges is discussed in both Hodos, *Show Trials,* and London, *The Confession.*

16. Information to the author from Mr. Eugen Loebl.

17. ''There is no tree high enough to hang me from.'' This line was cited by Eugen Loebl in an interview with me. The actual words to the peroration of Katz's ''confession,'' are these: ''I have joined the U.S., British, and French anti-semites against the Soviet Union. Therein lies my crimes. I am a writer, supposedly an architect of the soul. What sort of architect have I been, I who have poisoned people's souls? Such an architect of the soul belongs to the gallows. The only service I can still render is to warn all who, by origin or character, are in danger of following the same path to hell. The sterner the punishment . . .'' But at this point Katz's voice sank to a whisper, and he could not be heard.

18. Koestler, *Invisible Writing,* pp. 493–494.

19. See Karel Kaplan, *Dans les Archives du Comité Central.* See also, Karel Kaplan, *Report on the Murder of the General Secretary,* p. 234.

Bibliography

Books

Acheson, Dean. *Present at the Creation: My Years in the State Department.* New York: Norton, 1969.

Alexander, Tania. *A Little of All These: An Estonian Childhood.* London: Cape, 1987.

Allen, Peter. *The Cambridge Apostles.* Cambridge and New York: Cambridge University Press, 1978.

Alpern, Sara. *Freda Kirchway: A Woman of the Nation.* Cambridge, Mass.: Harvard University Press, 1987.

Ambrose, Stephen E., with Richard H. Immerman. *Ike's Spies. Eisenhower and the Espionage Establishment.* New York: Doubleday, 1981.

Andrew, Christopher, and Oleg Gordievsky. *The KGB: The Inside Story of its Foreign Operations from Lenin to Gorbachev.* New York: HarperCollins, 1990.

Arendt, Hannah. *The Origins of Totalitarianism.* Third edition. New York: Harcourt, 1966.

Aron, Raymond. *Mémoires: Cinquante ans de réflexion politique.* Paris: Julliard, 1983.

Baigell, Matthew, and Julia Williams, eds. *Artists against War and Fascism: Papers of the First American Artists' Congress.* New Brunswick, N.J.: Rutgers University Press, 1986.

Baker, Leonard. *Brandeis and Frankfurter: A Dual Biography.* New York: Harper and Row, 1984.

Bancroft, Mary. *Autobiography of a Spy.* New York: Morrow, 1983.

Beauvoir, Simone de. *The Prime of Life: The Autobiography of Simone de Beauvoir.* Translated by Peter Green. New York: Paragon House, 1992.

Bell, Quentin. *Virginia Woolf: A Biography.* Vol. 1. New York: Harcourt, 1972.

Beloff, Nora. *Tito's Flawed Legacy.* London: Gollancz, 1985.

Bentley, Elizabeth. *Out of Bondage: The Story of Elizabeth Bentley*. First edition, New York: Adan Devair, 1951. Reissued, New York: Ivy, 1988. Annotated with appendices and an afterword by Haydon Peake.

Bentley, Joanne. *Hallie Flanagan: A Life in the American Theater*. New York: Knopf, 1988.

Berberova, Nina. *Histoire de la baronne Boudberg*. Biography translated from the Russian by Michel Niqueux. [N.p.] Editions Actes Suds, 1988.

Bernhard, H. et al. *Der Reichstags brandprozess und Georgi Dimitroff*. Institut für Marxismus-Leninismus beim ZK der SED, et al. Band 1, Berlin: Dietz Verlag, 1982; Band 2, Berlin, Dietz Verlag, 1989.

Blackstock, Paul W. *The Secret Road to World War II: Soviet versus Western Intelligence, 1921–1939*. Chicago: Quadruple, 1969.

Bohlen, Charles. *Witness to History*. New York: Norton, 1973.

Borkenau, Franz. *European Communism*. New York: Harper, 1953.

Boyle, Andrew. *The Climate of Treason*. Revised edition, London: Hutchinson, 1979. Paperback revision, London: Coronet, 1980.

Buber-Neumann, Margarete. *Kriegsschulplätze der Weltrevolution. Ein Bericht aus der Praxis der Komintern, 1919–1943*. Stuttgart: Seewald Verlag, 1967.

———. *Milena*, translated from the German by Ralph Manheim. New York: Seaver Books, 1978; Holt, 1988.

———. *Under Two Dictators*. Translated from the German by Edward Fitzgerald. New York: Dodd, Mead, n.d.

———. *Von Potsdam nach Moskau*. Stuttgart: Seewald Verlag, 1957.

Budenz, Louis. *Men without Faces: The Communist Conspiracy in the U.S.A.* New York: Harper, 1950.

Burke, Michael. *Outrageous Good Fortune*. Boston: Little, Brown, 1984.

Carlton, David. *Anthony Eden*. London: Allen Lane, 1981.

Carr, E. H. *Twilight of the Comintern, 1930–1935*. New York: Pantheon, 1982.

Carr, Virginia Spencer. *Dos Passos: A Life*. New York: Doubleday, 1984.

Caute, David. *The Fellow Travellers*. New York: Macmillan, 1971.

———. *The Great Fear: The Anti-Communist Purge Under Truman and Eisenhower*. New York: Simon and Schuster, 1978.

Chambers, Whittaker. *Cold Friday*. Edited and with an introduction by Duncan Norton-Taylor. New York: Random House, 1964.

———. *Witness*. New York: Random House, 1952. Reprint, Lake Bluff, Ill.: Regnery, n.d.

Cockburn, Claud. *A Discord of Trumpets*. New York: Simon and Schuster, 1956.

Cockburn, Patricia. *Figure of Eight*. London: Chatto and Windus, 1985.

———. *The Years of The Week*. London: MacDonald and Co., 1968.

Cohen, Stephen F. *Bukharin and the Bolshevik Revolution: A Political Biography, 1888–1938*. New York: Knopf, 1973. Revised edition, New York: Oxford, 1980.

Connolly, Cyril. *The Missing Diplomats*. London: Queen Anne Press, 1952.

Conquest, Robert. *The Great Terror: A Reassessment*. New York: Oxford, 1990.

———. *Harvest of Sorrow*. New York: Oxford, 1986.

———. *Inside Stalin's Secret Police. NKVD Politics, 1936–1939*. London: Macmillan, 1985.

———. *Stalin and the Kirov Murder*. New York: Oxford, 1989.

Cookridge, E. H. [Edward Spiro]. *The Net That Covers the World*. New York: Holt, 1955.

Cooper, Duff. *Old Men Forget. The Autobiography of Duff Cooper, Viscount Norwich*. New York: Dutton, 1954.

Costello, John. *Deadly Illusions*. New York: Crown, 1993.

———. *The Mask of Treachery*. New York: Morrow, 1988.

Coward, Noel. *Future Indefinite: An Autobiography*. New York: Doubleday, 1954.

———. *The Noel Coward Diaries*. Edited by Graham Payn and Sheridan Morley. Boston: Little, Brown, 1982.

Dallin, David J. *Soviet Espionage*. New Haven: Yale, 1955.

Davenport, Marcia. *Too Strong for Fantasy*. New York: Scribner's, 1967.

Deacon, F. W., and G. R. Storry. *The Case of Richard Sorge*. New York: Harper and Row, 1966.

Deacon, Richard. *The British Connection*. Unpublished, 1982.

———. *'C': A Biography of Sir Maurice Oldfield, Head of MI 6*. London and Sydney: Macdonald, 1985.

———. *The Cambridge Apostles*. New York: Farrar, Straus, 1986.

Desanti, Dominique. *Les Clés d'Elsa: Aragon-Triolet*. Paris: Ramsey, 1983.

Dewar, Hugo. *Assassins at Large*. Boston: The Beacon Press, 1952.

Dimitrov, Georgi. *Das Reichstagsbrandprozess*. Berlin: Neue Wege, 1946.

———. *The Working Classes against Fascism*. London: Gollancz, 1935.

Dos Passos, John. *The Best Times: An Informal Memoir. 1896–1970*. New York: New American Library, 1966.

———. *The Fourteenth Chronicle: Letters and Diaries of John Dos Passos.* Edited and with a biographical narrative by Townsend Luddington. Boston: Gambit, 1973.

———. *Most Likely to Succeed* (novel). New York: Prentice Hall, 1954.

———. *The Theme is Freedom.* Freeport, N.Y.: Books for Libraries Press, 1970.

Draper, Theodore. *American Communism and Soviet Russia.* New York: Viking, 1960. Reprint, New York: Vintage, 1986.

Dunlop, Richard. *Donovan: America's Master Spy.* New York: Rand, McNally. 1982.

Dziak, John. *Chekisty: A History of the KGB.* Lexington: Lexington Books, 1988.

Edwards, Ruth Dudley. *Victor Gollancz: A Biography.* London: Gollancz, 1987.

Fest, Joachim. *Hitler.* Berlin: Verlag Ullstein, 1973. English translation by Richard and Clara Winston, New York: Harcourt Brace Jovanovich, 1974.

Fischer, David James. *Romain Rolland and the Politics of Engagement.* Berkeley, Calif.: California, 1988.

Fischer, Louis. *Men and Politics: An Autobiography.* New York: Duell, Sloan, 1941.

Fischer, Ruth. *Stalin and German Communism.* Cambridge: Harvard, 1948. Reprinted with new material, New Brunswick, N.J.: Transaction Books, 1982.

Gardiner, Muriel. *Code Name: Mary.* New Haven: Yale University Press, 1983.

Gide, André. *Littérature engagée.* Texts assembled and introduced by Yvonne Davet. Paris: Librairie Gallimard, 1950.

———. *Retouches à mon retour de l'U.R.S.S.* Paris: Gallimard, 1937.

———. *Retour de l'U.R.S.S.* Paris: Gallimard, 1936.

Gisevius, Hans Bernd. *To the Bitter End.* Translated by Richard and Clara Winston. Westport, Conn.: Greenwood Press, 1947.

Glees, Anthony. *The Secrets of the Service: A Story of Soviet Subversion of Western Intelligence.* London: Cape, 1987; New York: Carroll and Graf, 1987.

Gnedin, Evgeny. *Iz istorii otnoshenii mezhdu SSSR is fashistskoi Germanii. Dukumenty i soveremennye kommentarii.* (From the History of Relations between the USSR and Fascist Germany: Documents and Contemporary Commentary.) New York: Isdtvo ''Khronika,'' 1977.

Goldberg, Anatol. *Ilya Ehrenburg; Writing, Politics and the Art of Survival.* London: Weidenfeld and Nicolson, 1984.

Gross, Babette. *Willi Münzenberg: A Political Biography.* Translated from the German by Marian Jackson. East Lansing, Mich.: University of Michigan State, 1974.

Guillbeaux, Henri. *La Fin des Soviets.* Paris: Société française d'éditions littéraires et techniques, Edgar Malfère, directeur, 1937.

Guilloux, Louis. *Carnets: 1921–1944.* Paris: Gallimard, 1978.

Hamilton, Iain. *Koestler: A Biography.* London: Secker and Warburg, 1982.

Hare, Richard. *Maxim Gorky: Romantic Realist and Conservative Revolutionary.* London and New York: Oxford, 1962.

Hayman, Ronald. *Bertolt Brecht.* New York: Oxford, 1983.

Hays, Arthur Garfield. *City Lawyer.* New York: Simon and Schuster, 1942.

Heijenhoort, Jan van. *With Trotsky in Exile: From Prinkipo to Coyoacan.* Cambridge: Harvard, 1978.

Heller, Mikhail, and Aleksandr M. Nekrich. *Utopia in Power: The History of the Soviet Union from 1917 to the Present.* Translated from the Russian by Phyllis B. Carlos. New York: Summit, 1986.

Hellman, Lillian. *An Unfinished Woman.* New York: Little, Brown, 1970.

Hemingway, Ernest. *Selected Letters: 1917–1961.* Edited by Carlos Baker. New York: Scribner's, 1981.

Herbart, Pierre. *A la recherche d'André Gide.* Paris: Gallimard, 1952.

Herbst, Josephine. *The Starched Blue Sky of Spain.* New York: HarperCollins, 1991.

Hilger, Gustav, and Alfred Meyer. *The Incompatible Allies: A Memoir History of German-Soviet Relations, 1918–1941.* New York: Macmillan, 1953.

Hingley, Ronald. *Joseph Stalin: Man and Legend.* New York: McGraw-Hill, 1974.

Hiss, Alger. *Recollections of a Life.* New York: Holt, 1988.

Hodos, George. *Show Trials: Stalinist Purges in Eastern Europe, 1948–1954.* New York and London: Praeger, 1987.

Holroyd, Michael. *Lytton Strachey.* New York: Holt, Rinehart, 1968.

Hook, Sidney. *Out of Step: An Unquiet Life in the 20th Century.* New York: Harper and Row, 1987. Reprint, New York: Carroll and Graf, 1988.

Hoopes, Roy. *Ralph Ingersoll.* New York: Atheneum, 1985.

Humbert-Droz, Jules. *Dix ans dans la lutte anti-fasciste: Les Mémoires de Jules Humbert-Droz, 1931–1941.* Vol. 3. Neuchâtel: A la Baconnière, 1972.

Isherwood, Christopher. *The Berlin Stories.* New York: New Directions, 1954.

———. *Prater Violet.* New York: Random House, 1945.

Johnson, Chalmers. *An Instance of Treason: Ozaki Hotsumi and the Sorge Spy Ring.* Stanford, Calif.: Stanford University Press, 1964. Revised edition, 1990.

Johnson, Diane. *Dashiell Hammett: A Life*. New York: Random House, 1983.

Johnson, Paul. *The Birth of the Modern: World Society 1815–1830*. New York: HarperCollins, 1991.

———. *Intellectuals*. London: Weidenfeld and Nicolson, 1988; New York: Harper and Row, 1988.

———. *Modern Times: The World from the Twenties to the Eighties*. New York: Harper and Row, 1983. Reprint, New York: Harper Colophon, 1985.

Jowitt, the Earl. *The Strange Case of Alger Hiss*. New York: Doubleday, 1953.

Kaplan, Justin. *Lincoln Steffens: A Biography*. New York: Simon and Schuster, 1974.

Kaplan, Karel. *Dans les Archives du Comité Central. Trente ans de secrets du bloc soviétique*. Paris: Albin Michel, 1978.

———. *Report on the Murder of the General Secretary*. Translated from the Czech by Karel Kovanda. Columbus, Ohio: Ohio University Press, 1990.

Karolyi, Count Michael. *The Memoirs of Michael Karolyi: Faith without Illusion*. Translated from the Hungarian by Catherine Karolyi, with an introduction by A. J. P. Taylor. London: Cape, 1956.

Karolyi, Catherine. *A Life Together: The Memoirs of Catherine Karolyi*. London: Allen and Unwin, 1966.

Katz, Otto. *Der Kampf um ein Buch*. Paris: Carrefour, 1934.

———. *The Nazi Conspiracy in Spain*. By the editor of *The Brown Book of the Hitler Terror*. Translated from the German manuscript by Emile Burns. London: Gollancz, 1937.

Katz, Otto, [ed.]. *The Brown Book of the Hitler Terror and the Burning of the Reichstag*. Paris: Carrefour, 1933.

———. *The Second Brown Book of the Hitler Terror*. Paris: Carrefour, 1934.

———. *The White Book on the Executions of June 30, 1934*. Paris: Carrefour, 1934.

Kennan, George. *Memoirs: 1925–1950*. Boston: Little, Brown, 1967.

———. *Memoirs: 1950–1963*. Boston: Little, Brown, 1972.

———. *Russia and the West under Lenin and Stalin*. Boston: Little, Brown, 1960.

Klehr, Harvey. *The Heyday of American Communism: The Depression Decade*. New York: Basic Books, 1984.

Knightley, Phillip, *The Master Spy: The Story of Kim Philby*. London: Deutsch, 1988; New York: Knopf, 1989.

Koestler, Arthur. *The Age of Longing*. New York: Macmillan, 1951.

———. *Darkness at Noon.* New York: Macmillan, 1941.

———. *The Invisible Writing: The Second Volume of an Autobiography.* New York: Macmillan, 1954; New York: "Danube Edition," Stein and Day, 1969.

Koestler, Arthur, et al. *The God That Failed: Six Studies in Communism.* With an introduction by Richard Crossman, M.P. London: Hamish Hamilton, 1950.

Krivitsky, W. G. *In Stalin's Secret Service.* New York: Harper's, 1939. Reprint, Westport, Conn.: Hyperion, 1979.

Kurtz, Peter. *American Cassandra: The Life of Dorothy Thompson.* Boston: Little, Brown, 1990.

Kuuninen, Aino. *The Rings of Destiny: Inside Soviet Russia from Lenin to Brezhnev.* Foreword by Wolfgang Leonhard. Translated from the German by Paul Stevenson. New York: Morrow, 1974.

Lacouture, Jean. *André Malraux.* Paris: Seuil, 1973. Translated from the French by Alan Sheridan, New York: Pantheon, 1975.

Lamphere, Robert J., and Schachtman, Tom. *The FBI-KGB War: A Special Agent's Story.* New York: Random House, 1986.

Langer, Elinor. *Josephine Herbst: The Story She Could Never Tell.* New York: Atlantic-Little, Brown, 1984. Paperback edition, New York: Warner Books, 1985.

Laqueur, Walter. *Stalin: The Glasnost Revelations.* London: Unwin and Heyman, 1990.

Lash, Joseph P. *Eleanor and Franklin.* New York: Norton, 1971. Paperback edition, New York: Signet Books, 1973.

Lawson, John Howard. *Film in the Battle of Ideas.* New York: Garland, 1985.

Lazitch, Branko, and Milorad M. Drachkovitch. *The Biographical Dictionary of the Comintern.* Palo Alto, Calif.: Hoover Institution Press, 1973.

———. *The Comintern: Historical Highlights: Essays, Recollections, Documents.* New York: Praeger, 1966.

———. *Lenin and the Comintern,* Vol. 1. Hoover Institution Publications no. 106. Stanford, Calif.: Hoover Institution Press, 1972.

Leggett, George. *The Cheka: Lenin's Political Police.* Oxford: Clarendon Press, 1981.

Lehmann, John. *The Whispering Gallery.* New York: Harcourt, Brace. 1955.

Leo, Gerhart. *Frühzug nach Toulouse.* Berlin: Verlag der Nation, 1985.

Leonhard, Wolfgang. *Child of the Revolution.* Translated by C. M. Woodhouse. Chicago: Regnery, 1958.

Lerner, Warren. *Karl Radek: The Last Internationalist.* Stanford, Calif.: Stanford University Press, 1970.

Levine, Isaac Don. *Eyewitness to History*. New York: Hawthorne Books, 1973.

Lewis, Flora. *Red Pawn: The Story of Noel Field*. New York: Doubleday, 1965.

Liang, Hsi-Huey. *The Berlin Police Force in the Weimar Republic*. Berkeley, U. of California Press, 1970.

Lockhart, Bruce. *Secret Agent*. New York and London: Putnam's, 1933.

London, Arthur. *The Confession*. Translated by Alistair Hamilton. New York: Morrow, 1970.

Lottman, Herbert. *The Left Bank: Writers, Artists and Politics from the Popular Front to the Cold War*. Boston: Houghton Mifflin, 1982.

Luddington, Townsend. *John Dos Passos: A Twentieth Century Odyssey*. New York: Dutton, 1980.

Lynn, Kenneth. *Hemingway*. New York: Simon and Schuster, 1987.

Lyons, Eugene. *Assignment in Utopia*. New York: Harcourt Brace, 1937; reprint, New Brunswick, N.J.: Transaction Publishers, 1991.

———. *The Red Decade: The Stalinist Penetration of America*. New York and Indianapolis: Bobbs, Merrill, 1941.

MacDonald, C. A. *The United States, Britain, and Appeasement: 1936–1939*. London: Macmillan, in association with Saint Anthony's College, 1981.

Malraux, André. *Anti-Memoirs*. Translated from the French by Terence Kilmartin. New York: Random House, Holt, 1968. *Anti-Mémoires*. Paris: Gallimard, 1967.

Mann, Thomas. *Diaries*. Translated from the German by Richard and Clara Winston. New York: Knopf, 1982.

———. *The Letters of Thomas Mann: 1889–1955*. Selected and translated from the German by Richard and Clara Winston. New York: Knopf, 1971.

Massing, Hede. *This Deception*. New York: Duell, Sloan, 1951. Reprint, New York: Ballantine, 1987.

Mayenburg, Ruth von. *Hotel Lux*. Munich: C. Bertelsman Verlag, 1978.

Meade, Marion. *Dorothy Parker: What Fresh Hell Is This?* New York: Random House, 1987.

Medvedev, Roy. *Let History Judge: The Origins and Consequences of Stalinism*. Revised and expanded edition. Edited and translated by George Shriver. New York: Columbia University Press, 1989.

———. *Nikolai Bukharin: The Last Years*. Translated by A.D.P. Biggs. New York: Norton, 1980.

Meyer, Cord. *Facing Reality: From World Federalism to the CIA*. New York: Harper and Row, 1980.

Milne, James Lee. *Harold Nicolson: A Biography*. London: Chatto and Windus, 1980–1981.

Mitchison, Naomi. *You May Well Ask: A Memoir 1920–1940*. London: Gollancz, 1979.

Morel, Jean-Pierre. *Le Roman insupportable. L'Internationale littéraire et la France (1920–1932)*. Paris: Gallimard, 1985.

Muggeridge, Malcolm. *Chronicles of Wasted Time*. Vol. 1, *The Green Stick*. London: Collins, 1972; New York: Morrow, 1973. Vol. 2, *The Infernal Grove*. London: Collins, 1973; New York: Morrow, 1974.

Münzenberg, Willi. *Propaganda als Waffe*. Paris: Carrefour, 1938.

Newton, Verne W. *The Cambridge Spies: The Untold Story of Maclean, Philby, and Burgess in America*. Lanham, Md.: Madison, 1991.

Nicholaevsky, B. I. *Power and the Soviet Elite*. Ann Arbor, Mich.: University of Michigan Press, 1975.

Nicolson, Sir Harold. *Diaries and Letters, 1930–1964*. London: Stanley Olson, ed. London: Collins, 1980.

Orlov, Alexander. *The Secret History of Stalin's Crimes*. New York: Random House, 1954.

Ory, Pascal. *Nizan: Destin d'un révolté*. Paris: Ramsey, 1980.

Pawel, Ernst. *The Nightmare of Reason: A Life of Franz Kafka*. New York: Farrar, Straus, 1984.

Payne, Robert. *The Life and Death of Lenin*. London: W. H. Allen, 1964. Reprint: London: Grafton, 1987.

Penrose, Barry, and Simon Freeman. *Conspiracy of Silence*. London: Grafton, 1986; New York: Farrar, Straus, 1987.

Persico, Joseph. *Piercing the Reich: The Penetration of Nazi Germany by American Secret Agents During World War II*. New York: Random House, 1979.

Perus, Jean. *Romain Rolland et Maxime Gorki*. Paris: Les Editeurs Français Réunis, 1968.

Philby, Kim. *My Silent War*. New York: Grove Press, 1963.

Pincher, Chapman. *Their Trade Is Treachery*. London: Sidgwick and Jackson, 1981.

Pipes, Richard. *The Russian Revolution*. New York: Random House, 1990.

Popov, Blagoj. *Ot lajpzigskija prozes v sibirskite lageri*. Edited, with a preface by Peter Semerdjiev. Second edition. Paris: Movement for the Liberation of Bulgaria, 1984.

Poretsky, Elisabeth K. *Our Own People: A Memoir of ''Ignace Reiss'' and his Friends*. London and Oxford: Oxford University Press, 1969. Ann Arbor, Mich.: University of Michigan Press, 1969.

Porter, Katherine Anne. *The Never-Ending Wrong*. Boston: Atlantic, Little, Brown, 1977.

Powers, Thomas. *The Man Who Kept the Secrets: Richard Helms and the CIA*. New York: Simon and Schuster, 1979.

Pritchard, R. John. *The Reichstag Fire: The Ashes of Democracy*. New York: Ballantine Books, 1972.

Rees, Goronwy. *A Chapter of Accidents*. New York: The Library Press, 1972.

Regler, Gustav. *The Great Crusade*. With a preface by Ernest Hemingway. Translated by Whittaker Chambers and Barrows Mussey. New York: Longman's Green, 1940.

———. *The Owl of Minerva. The Autobiography of Gustav Regler*. Translated from the German by Norman Denny. New York: Farrar, Straus and Cudahy, 1960.

Reinhardt, Guenther. *Crime without Punishment*. New York: Hermitage House, 1952.

Rhysselberghe, Maria van. *Les Cahiers de la Petite Dame. Notes pour l'histoire authentique d'André Gide, 1929–1937. Les Cahiers André Gide, #5*. Paris: Gallimard, 1974.

Richardson, R. Dan. *Comintern Army: The International Brigades and the Spanish Civil War*. Lexington, Ky.: University of Kentucky Press, 1982.

Rolland, Romain. *Inde, Journal (1915–1943)*. Paris: Albin Michel, 1960.

Rollyson, Carl. *Lillian Hellman: Her Legend and Her Legacy*. New York: St. Martin's Press, 1988.

Roosevelt, Kermit. *War Report on the O.S.S.* Prepared by the History Project, Strategic Services Unit, Office of the Assistant Secretary of War, War Department, Washington. New York: D. C. Walker, 1976.

Russell, Francis. *Sacco and Vanzetti: The Case Resolved*. New York: Harper and Row, 1986.

Salas, Jesus. *Intervención extrajera en la guerra de Espagna*. Madrid: Mostoles: Madre Tierra, 1990.

Schwartz, Nancy Lynn. *The Hollywood Writers' Wars*. (Completed by Sheila Schwartz.) New York: Knopf, 1982.

Seale, Patrick, and Maureen McConville. *Philby: The Long Road to Moscow*. New York: Simon and Schuster, 1973.

Sheean, Vincent. *Dorothy and Red*. Boston: Houghton Mifflin, 1963.

———. *A Personal Memoir.* New York: Modern Library, 1939.

Shipman, Charles. *It Had to be Revolution: Memoirs of An American Radical.* Ithaca, N.Y.: Cornell University Press, 1993.

Slanska, Josefa. *Report on My Husband.* New York: Atheneum, 1969.

Slonim, Marc. *Soviet Russian Literature: Writers and Problems.* New York: Oxford University Press, 1967.

Solzhenitsyn, Aleksandr I. *The Gulag Archipelago: 1918–1956. An Experiment in Literary Investigation.* Vols. 1–2. Translated from the Russian by Thomas P. Whitney. New York: Harper and Row, 1974.

———. *The Gulag Archipelago: 1918–1956. An Experiment in Literary Investigation.* Vols. 3–4. Translated from the Russian by Thomas P. Whitney. New York: Harper and Row, 1974.

Souvarine, Boris. *Souvenirs sur Panait Istrati, Isaac Babel, et Pierre Pascal: suivis de lettre à A. Soljenitsyne.* Paris: Editions Lebovici, 1985.

Spender, Stephen. *World within World.* New York: Simon and Schuster, 1978.

Sperber, Manès. *Ces Temps-là,* especially *Le Pont inachevé,* and *Au-delà de l'oubli: Les Porteurs d'eau.* Paris: Calmann-Levy, 1979.

Stewart, Donald Ogden. *By a Stroke of Luck!* London: Paddington Press, 1975.

Straight, Michael. *After Long Silence.* New York: Norton, 1983.

Strasser, Otto. *Hitler and I.* Translated by Gwenda David and Eric Mosbacher. Boston: Houghton Mifflin, 1940.

Tabouis, Geneviève. *They Called Me Cassandra.* New York: Scribner's, 1942.

Tchoukovskaia, Lydia. *Entretiens avec Anna Akhmatova.* Translated from the Russian by Lucille Nivat and Geneviève Liebrich. Paris: Albin Michel, 1980.

Thomas, Hugh. *John Strachey.* New York: Harper and Row, 1973.

———. *The Spanish Civil War.* Third revised edition. London: Hamish Hamilton, 1977.

Thompson, Dorothy. *The New Russia.* New York: Henry Holt, 1928.

Thornberry, Robert. *Malraux et l'Espagne.* Geneva: Librairie Droz, 1977.

Tobias, Fritz. *The Reichstag Fire.* Translated from the German by Arnold J. Pomerans. London: Secker and Warburg, 1963; New York: Putnam's, 1964.

Tolstoy, Nikolai. *Stalin's Secret War.* London: Cape, 1981.

Trepper, Leopold. *Le Grand Jeu.* Paris: Albin Michel, 1975.

Trilling, Lionel. *The Middle of the Journey.* New York: Viking, 1947.

Troyat, Henri. *Maxim Gorky: A Biography.* Translated from the French by Lowell Bair. New York: Crown, 1989.

Tuck, Jim. *Engine of Mischief: An Analytical Biography of Karl Radek*. New York: Greenwood Press, 1988.

Valtin, Jan. *Out of the Night*. New York: Alliance Book Corporation, 1941.

Vernon, Betty. *Ellen Wilkinson*. London: Croom Helm, 1982.

Viertel, Salka. *The Kindness of Strangers: A Theatrical Life*. New York: Holt, 1969.

Voros, Sander. *American Commissar*. Philadelphia: Chilton, 1961.

Weinstein, Allen. *Perjury: The Hiss-Chambers Case*. New York: Knopf, 1978.

Weintraub, Stanley. *The Last Great Cause*. New York: Weybright, 1968.

Wessel, Harald. *Münzenbergs Ende*. Berlin: Dietz Verlag, 1991.

West, Anthony. *H. G. Wells: Aspects of a Life*. New York: Random House, 1984.

West, Rebecca. *The New Meaning of Treason*. New York: Viking, 1964.

West, W. J. *Truth Betrayed*. London: Duckworth, 1987.

Willett, John. *The Theater of Erwin Piscator*. New York: Holmes & Meier, 1969.

Wilson, Edmund. *Classics and Commercials*. New York: Farrar, Straus, 1952.

Winks, Robin. *Cloak and Gown: Scholars in the Secret War, 1939–1961*. New York: Morrow, 1987.

Wolfe, Bertram. *The Bridge and the Abyss*. New York: Praeger, 1967.

Wolton, Thierry. *Le Grand Recrutement*. Paris: Grasset, 1993.

———. *Le KGB en France*. Paris: Grasset, 1986.

Wright, Peter, with Paul Greengrass. *Spycatcher: The Candid Autobiography of a Secret Intelligence Officer*. New York: Viking, 1987.

Wright, William. *Lillian Hellman: The Image, the Woman*. New York: Simon and Schuster, 1986.

Zelt, Johannes. *Proletarischer Internationalismus im Kampf um Sacco und Vanzetti*. Berlin: Dietz Verlag, 1958.

Pamphlets

Kerbs, Diethart, and Walter Uka. *Willi Münzenberg*. Zeitgenossen I. Berlin: Editions Echolot, 1988.

Perreault, Gilles, et al. *Willi Münzenberg, 1889–1940: D'Erfurt à Paris, un homme contre*. Published in conjunction with an international conference held in Avignon, March–April 1992.

Articles

Andrew, Christopher, and Harold James. "Willi Münzenberg, The Reichstag Fire, and the Conversion of Innocents." In *Deception in East West Relations,* edited by David Charters and Maurice Tugwell. London: Pergamon, Brassey, 1990.

Binder, David. Article on Alexander Orlov. *New York Times,* June 26, 1991, p. A11.

Carew-Hunt, R. N. "Willi Münzenberg." *Saint Anthony's Papers,* no. 9, (1960).

Deak, Istvan. "Hungary: The New Twist." *New York Review of Books,* August 18, 1988, p. 47.

Draper, Theodore. "The Man Who Wanted to Hang." *Reporter,* January 6, 1953.

Fejtö, François. "Letter from Paris: The Real Louis and Elsa." (A review of Dominique Desanti's *Les Clés d'Elsa.*) *Encounter,* 1983.

Gellhorn, Martha. "On Apocryphism." *Paris Review,* no. 79 (1981), p. 301.

Gruber, Helmut. "Willi Münzenberg: Propagandist for and against the Comintern. *International Review of Social History,* vol. 10 (1965), part 2, pp. 188–210.

Kersten, Kurt. "Das Ende Willi Münzenbergs." *Deutsche Rundschau* (May 1957).

Klehr, Harvey, and John Haynes. "The Comintern's Open Secrets." *The American Spectator*, December 1992, pp. 34–36.

Münzenberg, Willi. "Die Dritte Front." Berlin: 1930.

———. "Five Years of Workers' International Relief." *Inprecorr,* vol. 6, no. 61, September 9, 1926, English edition, pp. 1044–1045.

———. "Mit Lenin in der Schweiz." *Inprecorr,* August 27, 1926, German edition, p. 1838.

Oak, Liston. Report on Communist Party work in Spain. *Call,* December 18, 1937.

Schliemann, Jorgen. "The Life and Work of Willi Münzenberg." *Survey,* no. 55 (April 1965), pp. 62–91.

Wollenberg, Erich. *Echo der Woche,* August 12, 1949.

Interviews and Correspondence

Mary Bancroft
Ralph Bates
Nina Berberova
Sir Isaiah Berlin
Rae Bernstein
Pierre Bertaux
Patricia Bosworth
Michael Burke
Andrew Cockburn
John Costello
Alan Cullison
Robert Crowley
Roald Dahl
Manuella Dobos
François Fejtö
Babette Gross

Interviews and Correspondence (*continued*)

Peter Gross
Norman Hackforth
John Hunt
Joris Ivens
Kot Jelinski
Karel Kaplan
Catherine Karolyi
Harvey Klehr
Peter Kurtz
Melvin Lasky
Leo Lerman
Ruth Levine
Eugen Loebl
Peter Lübbe
Jean Malaquais
Frieda Marshall
Herbert Marshall
Mary McCarthy
Naomi Mitchison
Steve Nelson
Henriette Nizan
Allen Oak
Ruth Price
Margaret Regler
Herb Romerstein
Jorgen Schliemann
Maria Schmidt
Peter Semerdjiev
Carlotta Shipman
Janka Sperber
Herman Starobin
Michael Straight
Sam Tanenhaus
Tzvetan Todorov
Robert Towers
Diana Trilling
Gus Tyler
Ruth von Mayenburg
Sir Dick White
Paul Willert
Helen Wolff
William Wright

FOIA Dossiers

Julio Alvárez del Vayo, FOIA Dossier # 100-11688.
Louis Gibarti, FOIA Dossier # 61-6629.
Lillian Hellman, FOIA Dossier # 100-26858.
Otto Katz, FOIA Dossier # 65-9266.
Willi Münzenberg, FOIA Dossier # 105-54056.

Index